Muirhead Library of Philosophy

EDITED BY H. D. LEWIS

KANT'S METAPHYSICS
OF EXPERIENCE

KANT'S METAPHYSIC
OF
EXPERIENCE

A COMMENTARY ON THE FIRST HALF OF THE
KRITIK DER REINEN VERNUNFT

By

H. J. PATON

Emeritus Professor of Moral Philosophy in the University of Oxford.
Fellow of the British Academy

In Two Volumes

VOLUME TWO

LONDON: GEORGE ALLEN & UNWIN LTD
NEW YORK: HUMANITIES PRESS INC.

FIRST PUBLISHED IN 1936
SECOND IMPRESSION 1951
THIRD IMPRESSION 1961
FOURTH IMPRESSION 1965
FIFTH IMPRESSION 1970

SBN 04 193005 3

PRINTED IN GREAT BRITAIN BY
JOHN DICKENS AND CO LTD
NORTHAMPTON

CONTENTS

VOLUME TWO

BOOK VII

THE SCHEMATISM OF THE CATEGORIES

BOOK VIII

THE PRINCIPLES OF THE
UNDERSTANDING

BOOK IX

THE MATHEMATICAL PRINCIPLES

12

CONTENTS

PAGE

CHAPTER

CONTENTS

BOOK VII

THE SCHEMATISM
OF THE CATEGORIES

CHAPTER XXXII

CATEGORY AND SCHEMA

§ 1. *A Summary Account of Kant's Argument*

Kant believes himself to have proved generally that all objects of experience must conform to the pure categories; that is to say, the given manifold must be combined in accordance with the principles of synthesis present in judgement as such. He believes himself to have shown also, though still in the most general way, that the required combination is imposed upon the given manifold by the transcendental synthesis of imagination through the medium of the pure manifold of time. We should now expect him to show that the transcendental synthesis of imagination, if it is to hold together the given manifold in one time, must combine the manifold in certain definite ways, and that each of these ways conforms to, or is an example of, the principle of synthesis conceived in one of the pure categories. Until this is done, we have had no account of the details which alone can make his general doctrine fully intelligible.

In a sense this task is performed in the Analytic of Principles, with which we have now to deal. Kant, however, treats the whole question primarily from the side of the object, and tells us what are the characteristics which objects must have if the manifold is combined in one time: his references to the subjective machinery of cognition, and especially to the transcendental synthesis of imagination, are only incidental.[1] His complicated explanation is certainly careless in terminology, and possibly

[1] He assumes that the unity of time is imposed by the transcendental synthesis of imagination, and simply asks what characteristics objects in time must have, if time is to have unity. In the Aesthetic Kant already argued that time must be one, but the unity of time is possible only through synthesis, as is indeed implied in the Aesthetic itself, though not made explicit; compare B 160 n. I take it that apart from the unity of the time in which all objects are, the unity of apperception, and consequently experience itself, would be impossible.

confused in thought. The difficulties in following it are very
great; and it may perhaps help the reader, if I try to give
first of all, with special reference to one particular category,
a summary and very rough account of what he is doing.

We are supposed to know that every object of experience
must conform to the pure category of ground and consequent;
that is to say, the given manifold must be combined as grounds
and consequents. We manifestly do not apprehend grounds
and consequents by sense; but Kant believes we can find
something corresponding to ground and consequent in the
objects of our experience, if we consider that all objects must
be combined in one time. What he finds is 'necessary succession'; that is, invariable succession in accordance with a rule
—such that if A is given in time, B must follow.

The difficulties of this view and the question of its truth
or error do not at the moment concern us. 'Necessary succession' is supposed to be the characteristic, or way of combination,
which must be found in all objects so far as their qualities
change in one objective time. This characteristic is called the
'transcendental schema',[1] and it is imposed upon the manifold
by the transcendental synthesis of imagination.[2] In virtue
of the transcendental schema we can apply the pure category
of ground and consequent to objects of experience; for if A
must always be followed by B, we can regard A as the ground
and B as the consequent.

If this is so, we can understand how the pure category
must have objects to which it applies; for all objects must be
in one time. The pure category of ground and consequent

---

[1] It should be noted that Aristotle also spoke of τὰ σχήματα τῶν
κατηγοριῶν, and this may possibly have suggested Kant's employment
of the word; but I do not think that Aristotle's usage throws any
light on that of Kant.

[2] See A 142 = B 81: 'The transcendental schema is a transcendental
product of the imagination'. In this preliminary statement I ignore
the difficulty that Kant sometimes speaks as if a schema were a rule
of imagination rather than a characteristic imposed by imagination.
What I describe as 'characteristics' imposed by the transcendental
synthesis are characteristics belonging to the manifold as combined
in certain ways which are necessary if time is to possess unity.

is by itself empty: we cannot understand by mere examination of the category whether there are any objects given to which it must apply. Only when we consider it in the light of the fact that all objects must be in one time, can we understand that it must apply to objects so far as the qualities of these objects change in time. In so doing we find that the category as applied to objects in time has a more limited and also a more precise significance; for it then becomes the concept of a ground which always precedes its consequent in time. In other words it becomes the schematised category of cause and effect.[1]

Kant will argue in the Second Analogy that all change in objects is necessary change, or necessary succession, and so must fall under the category of cause and effect.[2] In the chapter entitled 'The Schematism of the Pure Concepts of the Understanding' he is not concerned with showing that necessary succession, or any other transcendental schema, is a necessary characteristic of objects. His aim is merely to tell us what is the transcendental schema corresponding to each pure category; and he expects us to recognise that the transcendental schema described does fall under the pure category. Such recognition is a matter of judgement.

Thus for Kant the transcendental schemata[3] are universal characteristics which, he hopes to show later, must belong to all objects *as objects in time*. These universal characteristics belong to objects, not as given to sensation, but as *combined*[4]

---

[1] I discuss later whether it is necessary to distinguish the schematised category—a phrase which Kant himself never uses—from the transcendental schema. See Chapter XXXIV § 2.

[2] If so, it must fall also under the pure category of ground and consequent—the genus of which cause and effect is a species.

[3] The schemata are transcendental (1) as imposed by the mind, and (2) as universal and necessary conditions of all objects in time. It should be understood, as always, that such a condition is not anything temporally prior to the object: it is rather an element in, or characteristic of, the object, and without it the object would not be an object for us.

[4] This combination is not only a combination of the manifold of each object: it is also a combination of different objects with one another in the system of nature.

by the transcendental synthesis of imagination in one time. What we have to do at present is to learn what these transcendental schemata are, and to see, if we can, whether each transcendental schema falls under its corresponding category.

§ 2. *Importance of the Chapter on Schematism*

In considering Kant's account of the transcendental schemata we must not allow ourselves to be put off by the obscurity of his exposition. However artificial his view may appear to be, it is an essential part of his argument.[1] If we assume provisionally that the pure categories really are derived from the form of thought, it is absolutely vital to discover whether objects, as combined by imagination under the form of time, must possess characteristics which fall under the categories. If we reject *ab initio* such derivation of the pure categories, we must still discover what plausibility there is in his view of the relation between the necessary characteristics of objects in time and the pure categories; otherwise we shall fail to understand why Kant thought as he did, not merely in this particular chapter, but throughout the *Kritik*.

Even at the worst the chapter on Schematism has more than the value of throwing light on Kant's errors. If we reject his derivation of the categories, this chapter acquires a new and special importance: it suggests the possibility of making a fresh start, and of justifying the categories from the nature of time without any reference to the forms of judgement. The Kantian doctrine might perhaps be reformed and reestablished, if we could show that the categories are implicit in our knowledge of time, and are principles of synthesis without which no object could be known to be an object in time.

Whatever be our view of the derivation of the categories,

[1] Kant himself says with justice that it is an important, and indeed absolutely indispensable, though extremely dry, investigation; and he connects it, as I do in Chapter XXXIII, with the account of Phenomena and Noumena in the *Kritik*. See *Prol.* § 34 (IV 316).

the chapter on Schematism is essential to an understanding of the Critical Philosophy.[1]

§ 3. *The Transcendental Doctrine of Judgement*

Formal Logic in dealing with concepts, judgements, and inferences considers only their form, and is concerned with the conditions of formal validity. It does not, and it cannot, give us instructions about how we can make true judgements, and still less does it tell us what true judgements we can make.[2] If by the power of judgement[3] we mean the power of deciding whether or not particular objects fall under the concepts we possess, this power is a special gift which cannot be taught, though it can be improved by exercise and helped by examples.[4]

Transcendental Logic is in a different position. The concepts or categories with which it deals are *a priori*, and therefore the objective validity, not only of the categories in general, but of each separate category, must be established *a priori*. We must be able to show not only what are the pure categories, but also what is the 'case'[5] to which each applies. This means

---

[1] As it is far from easy to follow Kant's general account of the transcendental schema, the reader who wishes to get on with the argument in detail may find it advantageous to omit the rest of this chapter on a first reading.

[2] If concepts are supposed to be given, Formal Logic can tell us how to make analytic judgements, but these are true only if there is an object corresponding to the given concepts.

[3] It is unfortunate that in English we have only one word for '*Urteil*' (judgement) and '*Urteilskraft*' (the power of judging).

[4] Kemp Smith, *Commentary*, p. 333, asserts that Kant is taking advantage of the popular meaning of judgement. However popular this meaning may be, it has a philosophical history going back, I believe, to the Aristotelian doctrine of ὅροι (ἐν τῇ αἰσθήσει ἡ κρίσις. Eth. Nic. 1109b.). It is in any case one of the most widespread and essential doctrines of the Critical Philosophy. Compare, for example, *Anthr.* §§ 40–4 (VII 196–201); *K.d.U.* III, IV, § 35, § 77, etc. (V 177, 179, 286–7, 407, etc.); *K.d.p.V.* (V 67); *Met. d. Sitten, Tugendlehre* § 13 (VI 438); *Log.* § 81 (IX 131); Letter to Prince von Belozelsky (XI 331).

[5] A 135 = B 174. The word 'case' (*Fall*) seems to imply a reference to individual objects; but since the case is to be shown *a priori*, it must be shown, not by an appeal to empirical sense-perception, but by an appeal to the conditions under which objects must be given.

that we must be able to exhibit in universal but adequate marks[1] the conditions under which objects can be given[2] in conformity with the categories.

These 'conditions' may be described as universal characteristics[3] which must belong to all objects known by means of our senses. These characteristics are supposed to be found in objects as given to sense, and for this reason they are called 'sensuous conditions'[4] or 'conditions of sensibility'.[5] Strictly speaking, these characteristics are not to be found in the manifold merely as given to sense under the form of time. They belong to the manifold as given to sense under the form of time and as *combined* in one time by the transcendental synthesis of imagination.[6] In his statement of the problem Kant insists only that certain necessary characteristics must belong to objects as sensed, if the pure categories are to apply *a priori* to sensible objects.

These universal and necessary characteristics of sensible objects are the transcendental schemata. Apart from these

---

[1] '*Kennzeichen*'; see A 136 = B 175. I do not think that the 'marks' are to be regarded as separate from the 'conditions' exhibited in the marks.

[2] A 136 = B 175. This is a relative use of the word 'given'. Objects are given absolutely under the form or condition of time. They are given relatively to the understanding so far as the given manifold is combined in one time through the transcendental synthesis of imagination. Compare Chapter XXVIII § 11.

[3] Compare A 147 = B 186 where the 'sensuous *determination* of permanence' is given as an example of such a 'sensuous *condition*'. These necessary and universal characteristics of objects are also conditions of objects, for without them there could be for us no objects at all.

[4] A 136 = B 175.

[5] A 139 = B 179; compare also A 140 = B 179 and A 146 = B 186. They are conditions of sensibility because they are necessary to the unity of time (and space), time (and space) being the more ultimate conditions of sensibility.

[6] Kant is contrasting the object as thought abstractly in the pure category with the concrete individual object which is given; and at the moment he postpones all reference to the transcendental synthesis of imagination, and concentrates on the fact that the object must be sensed.

the pure categories would be without content[1] or meaning;[2] that is to say, they would not refer to any assignable object.

Transcendental Logic must therefore be able to give us what Kant calls a Transcendental Doctrine[3] of Judgement. It must tell us what are the transcendental schemata, the necessary and universal characteristics of sensible objects in virtue of which the pure categories can be applied.[4] It must also tell us what are the synthetic *a priori* judgements which arise when we apply the pure categories to sensible objects in virtue of the transcendental schemata. These synthetic *a priori* judgements are called the 'Principles of the Pure Understanding'—and they are the conditions of all other *a priori* knowledge. In order to justify these judgements we must show that the transcendental schemata really are universal and necessary characteristics of all objects given to our senses.

---

[1] A 136 = B 175.

[2] A 147 = B 186. The content or meaning of concepts involves for Kant a reference to actual, or at least possible, objects, and in the case of *a priori* concepts a *necessary* reference to such objects. Apart from this the pure category is merely a logical form, a concept of the form of judgement or of the unity of ideas in judgement. If we regarded the pure category as *somehow* applying to objects, we could not indicate the determinations of the thing to which the category was supposed to apply. Compare A 88 = B 120, A 247 = B 304, and many other places.

[3] '*Doktrin*'; see A 136 = B 175. It might also be called a 'canon' (A 132 = B 171) or a '*Kritik*' (A 135 = B 174) of Judgement. A 'doctrine' seems to aim at the extension (*Erweiterung*) of our cognitions, a *Kritik* at their correction (*Berichtigung*); see A 12 = B 26 and A 135 = B 174. I suppose Kant uses the word 'doctrine' here because we can point out, not merely the conditions of our synthetic *a priori* judgements, but the actual synthetic *a priori* judgements which we can make: he does not mean that we can extend the use of understanding beyond the limits of possible experience. Perhaps the word is used more loosely for 'a demonstrated theory' in which everything is certain *a priori*; see *Log. Einl.* I (IX 14–15) and A 54 = B 78. In A 796 = B 824 a 'canon' is defined as 'the sum total of the *a priori* principles of the correct employment of certain powers of knowledge'; compare *Log. Einl.* I (IX 13).

[4] Kant says 'the sensuous condition' under which alone the categories can be used. The following clause shows that he has in mind all such conditions.

The whole Transcendental Doctrine of Judgement may also be called the Analytic of Principles, since the judgements with which it is primarily concerned are the Principles of the Pure Understanding. It is divided into two parts. The first part is concerned with the transcendental schemata, and is entitled 'The Schematism of the Pure Concepts of the Understanding'. The second part gives us the proof of the Principles, and is entitled 'The System[1] of all Principles of Pure Understanding'.[2]

§ 4. *Subsumption under the Categories*

The power of judgement is a power to subsume under rules, that is, to decide whether anything stands under a given rule or not.[3] All concepts, according to Kant, serve as rules,[4] and we can say that in subsumption we decide whether anything stands under a given concept or not; indeed this is the ordinary meaning of subsumption.[5] Formal Logic manifestly cannot

---

[1] The word 'system' implies an organic whole, not a mere aggregate; compare A 832 = B 860.

[2] The proof of the Principles is in the main directed to show that the transcendental schemata must be characteristics of all objects which are known to be in one time.

[3] A 132 = B 171 and A 133 = B 172. Kant's reference in brackets —'*casus datae legis*'—suggests that he has in mind the procedure of the law-courts.   [4] A 106.

[5] Kant, in his Formal Logic, extends the meaning of the word subsumption to cover the minor premise of hypothetical and disjunctive, as well as of categorical, syllogisms. The minor premise is said to subsume a cognition under the condition of the universal rule asserted in the major premise; see *Log.* § 58 (IX 120–1) and A 304 = B 360. Kemp Smith, *Commentary*, p. 336, seems to base on this the view that Kant is really concerned with subsuming under rules as opposed to concepts. I do not think this is so. In the categorical syllogism, All men are mortal, Caius is a man, therefore Caius is mortal, we subsume in the minor premise our cognition Caius under the concept of man, which is the condition of mortality. Compare A 322 = B 378, which is, however, obscure. Kemp Smith translates as if we subsumed the predicate (mortal) under its condition (man). This seems to me impossible; and I agree with Erdmann that we subsume Caius under the condition 'man' which is taken in its whole extension in the judgement 'All men are mortal'. Further remarks on the syllogism will be found below; see Chapter XXXIV § 1.

teach us how to do this, since it ignores the matter given to thought. Transcendental Logic can, however, show that objects must fall under the categories, since it takes into account the pure manifold of time and the transcendental synthesis of imagination whereby the given manifold must be combined in one time.[1]

Granted Kant's pre-suppositions, it seems to me correct to speak either of applying the categories to objects or of subsuming objects under the categories. The main objection to this usage seems to rest on the view that a category cannot be used as a predicate and cannot have instances.[2] But if the categories could not be predicates of possible judgements, and could not apply to instances,[3] they would not be concepts at all. Such a view seems to me remote from the Kantian doctrine.

I need hardly add that if Kant had used the word 'subsumption' for the activity of the transcendental imagination in combining the given manifold in accordance with the principles of synthesis conceived in the pure categories, he would indeed be guilty of misusing a technical term. I see no trace of such a usage in the chapter on Schematism. Kant is here concerned with sensible objects as described in the Transcendental Deduction, that is, as combined in one time (and space).[4]

§ 5. *The Difficulty of Subsumption under the Categories*

Whenever we subsume an object under a concept, that is, whenever we judge the object to be an instance of a universal, there must be a certain homogeneity between the object

---

[1] Compare A 55 = B 79–80 and A 76–7 = B 102.

[2] See Chapter XV § 3, and compare Kemp Smith, *Commentary*, p. 335, etc.

[3] The concepts of the forms of judgement have of course instances in the *judgements* which manifest these forms; compare A 239 = B 298. But the pure categories are concepts whose instances must be *objects* —objects whose manifold is combined in accordance with the principles of synthesis present in the forms of judgement; compare B 128.

[4] Further difficulties in regard to subsumption will be dealt with later. See Chapter XXXIV § 1.

and the concept. This is obvious enough in the case of empirical concepts, which are due to abstraction from given intuitions; in them we conceive or think common marks belonging to this and other objects given in intuition. It is also obvious even in the pure concepts of mathematics: the mathematical concept of circle, for instance, can have an example constructed in pure intuition; and since this pure intuition is homogeneous (as regards its circularity) with the empirical intuitions from which we abstract the concept of plate, there is no difficulty in saying that a plate is an imperfect instance of a mathematical circle.[1]

There may be some doubt as to the exact interpretation of this example; but Kant's main point is that whether a particular concept is empirical or pure—whether it is derived by abstraction from empirical intuition, or whether pure intuitions are constructed in accordance with it—there is always a corresponding *intuition* which entitles us to apply the concept to objects of sensuous experience. In the case of the categories there is no corresponding intuition, whether empirical or pure.[2] Hence the categories appear not to be homogeneous with the sensible objects subsumed under them, inasmuch as none of

---

[1] A 137 = B 176. I have here expanded—in the light of what follows—a statement which is too brief to be clear. Kant says that the circularity which is *thought* in the empirical concept of plate can be *intuited* in the pure concept of circle, and gives this as his reason for the homogeneity of the two concepts. His statement is obscurely expressed, and he seems to make no difference between 'an object' and 'the idea (or even the concept) of an object'; but I take his point to be that even a pure mathematical concept has a corresponding *intuition*: the category, as he goes on to show, has none. Hence the pure mathematical concept can have a certain homogeneity with objects given to empirical intuition, and with the empirical concepts of these objects; see A 138 = B 177.

Vaihinger emends Kant's statement about circularity, by transposing 'thought' and 'intuited'. This does not remove the obscurity, and it makes the distinction between the empirical concept of plate and the pure mathematical concept of circle here irrelevant; but in any case Kant's main point is that there must be homogeneity between the concept and the object (or concept of the object) which is subsumed under it.   [2] Compare Chapter XVI §§ 8–9.

the intuitions through which objects are given corresponds in
any way to the categories.[1]

In spite of the objections[2] raised to this doctrine Kant's
contention seems to me to be sound. It is obviously so, if we
remember that for him the pure categories are the forms of
judgement as applied to intuitions; but even if we ignore this,
and consider the categories only as schematised, it is hardly
less obvious, at any rate as regards the categories of relation
and modality. We can see plates in empirical intuition, and we
can construct circles *a priori* in pure intuition, but we cannot
see causes as causes,[3] nor can we construct them *a priori*.[4]

This is a real difference which it seems to me idle to deny.
Nor is the problem solved by saying that the category is the
form and the intuition the matter, and that these have no
existence apart from one another. The forms of intuition are
space and time, and the categories are forms, not of intuition,
but of thought. No doubt it is absurd to suggest that we are
first of all aware of unrelated sensations, and then subsume
them under the categories; but to interpret Kant's doctrine
as asserting such a temporal succession seems to me unjustifiable. The categories are present whenever we are aware of
an object (as opposed to a mere sensation); but this fact does
not do away with Kant's problem. Indeed it is just this fact
which raises the problem how the categories as forms of thought
can, and must, determine all objects given to sensuous intuition.

---

[1] In order to avoid misconceptions it may be said at once that
although the intuitions, considered as given intuitions, are not homogeneous with the category, yet the intuitions *as combined to form
objects in one time* are homogeneous with the category.

[2] Some of these objections rest on the view that Kant supposed
us to be aware of the pure categories and the sensuous intuitions in
separation before we are aware of them in conjunction. Supported
though this is by many even of the best commentators—for example
by Caird and even at times by Riehl—I do not believe that Kant
entertained such an idea for a moment.   [3] Compare A 137 = B 176.

[4] The difference is not so sharp in the case of the categories of
extensive and intensive quantity, where Kant himself insists we have
'intuitive evidence'; see A 160–1 = B 200, A 162 = B 201, A 180
= B 223.

If we are to understand Kant we must allow him to state his problem in his own way, and we must try to see what the problem is. We must also remember that Kant tends to state his problems sharply without giving any indication of his proposed solution.[1] In this case we already know the general lines which his solution must take; for we know, from the Transcendental Deduction, that the categories must apply to all objects because the transcendental synthesis of imagination combines the manifold in one time. This does not mean that the chapter on Schematism is superfluous. We have still to show—the argument cries out for it—that the combination of the manifold in one time imposes on all objects certain universal characteristics corresponding to the separate categories.

§ 6. *The Transcendental Schema*

Kant puts forward the suggestion that there must be a third thing to connect the category and the intuition. This mediating idea must be pure, for otherwise the connexion would be empirical; and it must be homogeneous both with the category and with the intuition. To be homogeneous with the category, it must be intellectual; that is, it must be a product of spontaneity or synthesis (which is the general characteristic of the understanding).[2] To be homogeneous with the intuition, it must be sensuous; and to be both sensuous and yet pure, it must be connected with the form of intuition. This mediating idea is the transcendental schema.[3]

In his search for the transcendental schema Kant turns, as we should expect, to time as the form of intuition.[4] The

[1] Compare Chapter XVII § 1.

[2] Kant's phrase is obscure, and the meaning seems to me uncertain. What he says in the following paragraph suggests that to be homogeneous with the category, it must be universal and must rest on an *a priori* rule. It can be this only if it is the product of the transcendental synthesis of the imagination.

[3] A 138 = B 177. This description connects it with the transcendental synthesis of imagination. Compare especially B 151 and B 162 n.

[4] The reason why Kant neglects space in this chapter is no doubt that for him space is only the form of outer intuition, while time, though it is the immediate condition (or form) of inner intuition,

pure category is a concept of the pure synthetic unity of a manifold *in general*;[1] and consequently the pure synthetic unity of the manifold of time must fall under it,[2] as the species must fall under the concept of the genus.[3] Time, however, not only contains in itself a manifold of pure intuition; it is also the form of inner sense, and so is the formal condition of the combination of all ideas whatsoever.[4] I take Kant to mean that the empirical manifold, whatever else it is, must be temporal and must have the general characteristic of being combined in such a way that it accords with the unity of time.[5]

This doctrine Kant develops with reference to what he calls a 'transcendental time-determination'.[6] Unfortunately he does not explain this phrase; it must, I think, mean, not a determination or characteristic of time itself, but a characteristic which must belong to objects so far as they are temporal and are combined in one time.

A transcendental time-determination is said to be homogeneous with the category inasmuch as it is universal and rests on an *a priori* rule. Its universality is presumably the complete universality of the categories inasmuch as it must belong to all objects; for all objects of human experience are

---

is also the mediate condition of outer intuition, and so can be described as 'the formal *a priori* condition of *all* appearances in general'; see A 34 = B 50 and compare Chapter VII § 2. But space as well as time must have its part in the schematisation of the categories, and Kant has to take space into account when he deals with the Principles.

[1] A 138 = B 177. In itself it has no reference to the manifold of *human* intuition as such, nor even to the pure manifold of space and time, but the synthetic unity of space and time must be a particular case of the synthetic unity of intuition *in general*; compare B 144-5.

[2] Kant says in A 138 = B 177 that the category 'constitutes' (*ausmacht*) the unity of time (or the unity of the transcendental time-determination—which, I take it, amounts to pretty much the same thing). In B 144 the unity is said to come into the intuition by means of the category through understanding—intuition here being intuition *in general*. See also B 160-1.

[3] Compare Chapter XIII § 6.   [4] Compare A 99.

[5] The most obvious example of this is that if time has extensive quantity the manifold in time must also have extensive quantity.

[6] '*Zeitbestimmung*'; A 138 = B 177.

in time.[1] A transcendental time-determination is also homogeneous with appearances, or empirical intuitions of objects,[2] inasmuch as every empirical intuition occurs in time and lasts through time.[3]

Hence the transcendental time-determination is the mediating idea which enables us to subsume[4] appearances (or objects) under the category. As such it is identified with the transcendental schema which we have been seeking.

All this is difficult and is hardly intelligible apart from the examples which follow; but I think we can understand that if time—and I would add space—is to be known as a unity, certain ways of combination must be found in objects the manifold of which is combined in one time (and space).[5] We can also understand that such a way of combination might be an example of a more general way of combination, or principle of synthesis, thought in the pure category. We may be able to find something homogeneous with the categories, not in intuitions themselves, but in the ways in which intuitions must be combined so as to form objects in one time (and space), or in the characteristics which objects must have if intuitions are combined in these ways.

---

[1] The sense in which it rests on an *a priori* rule is more difficult; perhaps Kant means that it is a product of the transcendental synthesis of imagination, such synthesis being governed by an *a priori* rule. The categories themselves, it should be noted, cannot be said to rest on *a priori* rules: on the contrary they may be described as the *a priori* rules in accordance with which the transcendental synthesis of imagination works.

[2] Kant, I think, has in mind, not the isolated appearance such as 'this red', but the whole appearance or intuition of, for example, a house.

[3] Kant says time is 'contained' in every empirical idea.

[4] This suggests that it is the middle term in the categorical syllogism; but see Chapter XXXIV § 1.

[5] We may put it in this way: that the empirical synthesis of apprehension must be subjected to a transcendental unity—the unity of time—and ultimately to the unity of apperception; compare A 108.

§ 7. *The Restriction of the Category through the Schema*

The transcendental schemata enable us to apply the categories to sensible objects given under the form of time, but they also restrict the application of the categories to such objects. The Transcendental Deduction has already shown us that the categories admit only of an empirical, and not of a transcendental, use;[1] that is to say, they apply only to objects of possible experience, not to things as they are in themselves. Kant reminds us[2] that concepts can have no meaning[3] unless an object is *given* for them, or at any rate for the elements of which they are composed; hence we cannot legitimately apply concepts to things as they are in themselves without considering whether such things are given to us and how they are given. For human beings things are given only as they modify or affect our sensibility and so appear to us under the forms of sensibility, that is to say, as temporal and spatial. The categories, if they are to apply to given objects, must contain within themselves more than the principles of synthesis present in the form of thought as such; for the form of thought has in itself nothing to do with the way in which objects are given. The categories must also contain in themselves formal conditions of sensibility, which Kant identifies with the formal conditions of inner sense. Only so can they contain the universal condition under which alone the categories can be applied to objects. Such is the general teaching of the Transcendental Deduction; and we have now only to indicate what are these *a priori* or formal conditions of sensibility, to which Kant has given the name of transcendental schemata.

These conditions, as I have already pointed out,[4] are ways in which the given manifold is combined in one time by the tran-

---

[1] Compare Chapter XI § 4 and Chapter LIV.

[2] A 139 = B 178.

[3] 'Meaning', as usual, may be equated with 'objective reference'. The remark about the 'elements'—compare also A 96—suggests that a fictitious concept, such as the concept of 'chimaera', may have a kind of meaning, since the elements of which it is composed have objective reference.   [4] Compare § 3 above and the end of § 6.

scendental synthesis of imagination, or characteristics which objects must have in virtue of the given manifold being so combined. The main difficulty is to know the sense in which the category 'contains' these conditions. Every pure category contains a principle of synthesis derived from the form of judgement; and the way in which the manifold is combined in one time is, on Kant's view, a species which falls under the genus conceived in the pure category. If the category contains the condition of sensibility in a more intimate sense, if it is the specific concept of this particular way of combining the manifold in one time, then Kant has in mind, not the pure category, but the schematised category.[1] The schematised category does contain in itself the transcendental schema, in the sense that it is the concept of that schema. Thus—to take the example given already[2]—the schematised category of cause and effect may be described as the concept of the *necessary succession* of grounds which precede their consequents in time.[3]

This, however, raises difficult questions as to the relation between the schematised category and the transcendental schema which can be better examined when we have studied the details of Kant's doctrine.

§ 8. *The Schema in General*

The schema, Kant goes on to say, is a product of imagination.[4] It must not, however, be confused with a picture or image, which is also a product of the imagination. A picture or image

---

[1] Compare Chapters XII § 7 and XIII § 6.   [2] See § 1 above.

[3] It is possible that Kant is referring to the way in which the category contains the schema, when he says—in A 132 = B 171—that the category contains the condition of *a priori* rules, and again—in A 135 = B 174—that the universal condition of rules is given in the category. Compare also the statement—in A 159 = B 198—that the Principles alone supply the concept (presumably the category) which contains the condition, and as it were the 'exponent', of a rule in general. I feel too doubtful of Kant's precise meaning in these passages to commit myself to any interpretation.

[4] A 140 = B 179. Kant says 'the schema in itself' in opposition, I think, to the schema as brought under the pure category by the procedure (or schematism) of the understanding.

is an individual intuition. The schema is to be distinguished from an individual intuition inasmuch as the synthesis of imagination, in producing the schema, aims only 'at unity in the determination of sensibility'.[1] This accords with the view that the schema is a way of combination or a characteristic resulting from combination.[2]

So far Kant is presumably concerned with the transcendental schema, but he proceeds to illustrate the difference between a schema and an image with reference, not to the categories, but to particular concepts. There is here a difficulty; for the transcendental schema was introduced as an idea mediating between the category and intuitions, and there was said to be no necessity for such a mediating idea between particular concepts and intuitions.[3] Nevertheless all concepts might have schemata which were necessary for other purposes than such mediation. If so, a description of what may be called the schema in general might throw additional light on the nature of the transcendental schema: it might show us what the transcendental schema has in common with other schemata.[4]

Unfortunately, Kant's account of the schema in general, while it is interesting in itself, raises difficulties rather than removes them. He deals, as usual, firstly with the pure concepts of mathematics, and secondly with ordinary empirical concepts.

If we take 'triangularity' as our example of a mathematical concept, we must, according to Kant, distinguish carefully three things: (1) the concept of triangularity itself, (2) the image of an individual triangle, and (3) the schema. The concept of triangularity is a concept of the marks common to all triangles: the schema is a rule for constructing the image

[1] Compare also A 118, A 123.

[2] One might perhaps call it a characteristic of combination. It might also be called a kind of synthetic unity.

[3] Compare K.d.U. § 59 (V 351), where examples are for empirical concepts what schemata are for categories.

[4] Unless it has something in common with these schemata, the only reason for introducing these schemata must be by way of contrast. But Kant's account hardly bears this out, though he does make a contrast later. In any case unless there really is something in common, it is unfortunate that the two things should have the same name.

a priori in intuition, or in other words a rule of imaginative synthesis. The schema, therefore, does in a way mediate between the concept and the individual image. We know what triangularity is when we know how to construct a triangle *a priori* in imagination. We know that this figure drawn on paper is an imperfect instance of triangularity, when our imagination, in apprehending the given appearances as a triangle, performs, and is known[1] to perform, the same synthesis as is necessary to construct a triangle *a priori* in imagination.[2]

In the case of simple objects like triangles, we might suppose that we recognise them merely from their common marks, that is, from their observed resemblance to one another. Even in this case we do not know that the objects seen are triangles, unless we know the principle upon which they can be constructed; but Kant's doctrine is more obvious when we consider objects of a greater complexity. We have, for example, no image of the number a thousand, but we know what a thousand is, if we know how to construct such an image. And we know that we have a thousand dots before us, if in counting the given dots we have performed the same synthesis as would be necessary to construct a thousand *a priori*.[3]

The same principle holds of empirical concepts, although in this case our power of constructing an image in imagination depends upon previous experience of the object. We know what a dog is, when we know from experience how to construct an image of dog in imagination. The schema, or rule of construction, admits of great variety in detail and so is adequate to the concept, while any individual image that we construct, or any actual dog that we see,[4] falls far short of the universality

---

[1] Such knowledge may have different degrees of 'clarity'.

[2] Compare A 224 = B 271: 'The figurative synthesis by which we construct a triangle in imagination is wholly identical with that which we exercise in the apprehension of an appearance in order to make for ourselves an empirical concept of it'. See also Chapter VI § 8.

[3] For example, we combine ten sets of ten ten times over.

[4] Kant, I believe, is here distinguishing images from objects, not as Prichard suggests, treating them as if they might be mentioned indifferently; see *Kant's Theory of Knowledge*, p. 251 n. 4.

of the concept. This is true even in the case of a simple mathematical concept. The concept of triangularity (and the rule for constructing triangles) involves the possibility of being equilateral or isosceles or scalene, but any individual image of a triangle realises only one of these possibilities.

All this is sound enough, and it is in accordance with what we have already learned about concepts.[1] But the question inevitably arises whether we can really distinguish the concept from the schema along these lines. Kant always regards a concept, not merely as a concept of the marks common to a number of objects, but as a concept of the synthesis of these marks,[2] and this means that every concept is the concept of a rule of synthesis. We might indeed regard the schema as the *rule* of synthesis unreflectively at work in imagination, and the concept as the *concept* of the rule, when the synthesis is, in Kant's phrase, brought to concepts.[3] This seems to me a possible distinction, and one which may have been at the back of Kant's mind. His language, however, prevents us from taking this as his express theory; for he says that the schema can exist only in *thought*,[4] and he speaks of it as the idea (or representation) of a method and of a universal procedure of imagination.[5] If this is to be taken literally, it destroys the distinction I have suggested.

Another interpretation is possible—that the schema, in spite of what Kant has said, is really regarded by him as a kind of schematic image. This is suggested by his statement that the schema of sensuous concepts[6] (as of figures in space) is a product, and as it were a *monogram*, of pure *a priori* imagination,

---

[1] Compare Chapters XIII § 5 and XX §§ 4–6.

[2] I pass over difficulties in regard to simple concepts like 'redness', though I imagine that Kant regards the concept of redness as involving the concept of its synthesis with possible red objects; see B 133–4 n.

[3] A 78 = B 103. The rule or schema is then what is contained or conceived in the concept.   [4] A 141 = B 180.

[5] A 140 = B 179. An 'idea' here is presumably a concept.

[6] He must mean '*pure* sensuous concepts', unless the schema of an empirical concept is confined to the mathematical properties thought in the concept. A 'sensuous concept' is one which has a corresponding intuition. If it is empirical, the concept is derived from the intuition by analysis and abstraction. If it is pure, the

through which, and in accordance with which, images themselves first become possible.[1] A monogram is now commonly regarded as a series of letters so interwoven as to constitute a whole: sometimes, though not always, it is composed of the initial letters of a name, and as such it may suggest the plan or rule of a procedure in spelling out a name. But there is an older usage in which 'monogram' meant a sketch or outline, and Kant himself seems to use it in this sense.[2] There is an interesting passage where Kant compares certain creations of the imagination to monograms in this respect—that they offer us only individual strokes,[3] determined by no assignable rule, and constitute as it were a *wavering* sketch or a shadowy outline[4] rather than a determinate picture.[5] Some of the points made here may be due to the context, but the passage suggests that if the schema is like a monogram, it is some sort of wavering and schematic image. Such a wavering image might be the imaginative embodiment of the rule in accordance with which the synthesis of imagination works.

These considerations, inconclusive as they are in themselves, throw, I fear, little light on the nature of the transcendental schemata. They tend to suggest that the transcendental schemata may share with the schema in general the common characteristic of being a rule, rather than a product, of the imagination.[6] In his detailed account of the transcendental

intuition is constructed *a priori* in accordance with the concept. A category, on the other hand, is a purely intellectual concept derived from the nature of thought.

[1] A 141–2 = B 181. Kant adds that these images are connected with the concept through the schema—which means that the schema in general, like the transcendental schema, is a mediating idea. The necessity for mediation arises here because no image can be fully congruent with the concept. [2] See A 833 = B 861.

[3] '*Züge.*' This may mean 'features', but I think it is at any rate more precise than 'qualities', which is Kemp Smith's translation.

[4] '*Schattenbild.*' This may mean a silhouette, unless it is intended to suggest something uncertain and changing. [5] A 570 = B 598.

[6] I do not deny that a rule may be regarded as a product of the imagination, if the imagination works in accordance with that rule; but it is a different kind of product from a picture on the one hand and a combination on the other.

schemata Kant speaks in places as if the transcendental schemata were rules, and even as if they were syntheses; but I
think he can be most satisfactorily interpreted if we take the
transcendental schema to be a way of combination, or a characteristic of combination, which is produced by the transcendental
synthesis of imagination.

§ 9. *Special Characteristics of the Transcendental Schema*

The transcendental schema must in any case differ in certain
respects from other schemata; and this difference Kant attempts
to make clear in one of those closely packed sentences which
he is apt to produce at the most crucial stage of an argument.

His first point is obvious. Let us suppose that a particular
schema—if this term may be used for the schema of a particular
concept (as opposed to a universal concept or category)—is a
rule of the imagination in constructing an image or an object[1]
in accordance with a particular concept. Since no intuition or
image can correspond to a category, the transcendental schema
cannot be a rule for constructing an image, or in Kant's phrase
it cannot be brought into an image.[2]

An image corresponding to the categories would have to be
constructed in pure intuition, and the nearest approach to
such an image would be time itself. Kant himself points out
that the pure image of all objects of the senses in general is
time.[3] But it would be artificial to say that time is the image
corresponding to the categories. It is better to say that there is
no corresponding image.

We now come to Kant's second point. Instead of saying—
as we might expect in view of his account of the schema in
general—that the transcendental schema is the *rule* of the
transcendental synthesis of imagination, he says that it is the

---

[1] The same process is at work whether we are constructing an
image in mere fancy, or whether we start from a given sensation or
sensations and construct an actual object of perception.

[2] A 142 = B 181.

[3] A 142 = B 182. Time and space are constructed by the transcendental synthesis of imagination. Space is the pure image of all
quantities for outer sense.

transcendental *synthesis* itself. The transcendental schema is 'simply the pure synthesis in conformity with a rule of unity in accordance with concepts in general,[1] which[2] the category expresses'.[3]

Such a use of terms seems at first sight calculated to reduce the reader to despair. We may be tempted to affirm—and perhaps this is the best way to interpret him—that if Kant means anything, he must mean that the transcendental schema is the *rule* of the pure synthesis. Certainly the schema is not to be regarded as an *act* of pure synthesis;[4] but I think Kant may conceivably mean here that the schema is that specific kind of *a priori combination* which is produced by the pure synthesis of imagination and is in conformity with the principle of synthesis (or rule of unity) conceived in the category. If this is a possible interpretation, it accords with that hitherto given.[5]

Kant's third point is also put obscurely. His statement is so complicated that it may be divided into three parts. The transcendental schema is (1) a transcendental product of the imagination; (2) it is concerned with[6] the determination of inner sense in general as regards conditions of its form (time) with respect to all ideas; (3) it is so concerned with respect to

---

[1] 'Concepts in general' must be opposed to categories. The rule of unity is a principle of synthesis involved in conception or judgement as such.

[2] The reference of 'which' is uncertain. The pure category might be said to express either the pure synthesis (compare A 78 = B 104) or the unity of the pure synthesis (compare A 79 = B 105). It might also, I think, be said to express the rule. Whichever interpretation we adopt, the general doctrine remains the same.

[3] A 142 = B 181.

[4] Nevertheless Kant (in A 143 = B 183) speaks of the schema of reality as 'the continuous and uniform *production* of reality in time', where 'production' (*Erzeugung*) certainly looks like an act.

[5] I am assuming here that the *a priori* combination may be identified by Kant with the characteristic which results from, or is manifested in, such combination.

[6] '*betrifft.*' The expression of Kant's doctrine here bears a close resemblance to his account of the transcendental synthesis of imagination in B 150 and B 152.

all ideas so far as these must be connected *a priori* in one concept in conformity with the unity of apperception.

The first part is just what we should expect. The third part is an elaborate way of saying that the ideas in question must be ideas of an object.[1] The second part, which is the most important one, I take to mean, not that the transcendental schema is itself a determination or characteristic of inner sense or of time, but that it is a determination or characteristic of all our ideas of objects—or, more simply, of all objects—so far as they are known to be combined in one time.[2]

§ 10. *Summary of Conclusions*

The obscurity of Kant's exposition places great difficulties in the way of the interpreter. The main burden of his doctrine is that the transcendental schema is a *product* of the transcendental synthesis of imagination; but the account given of the schema in general suggests that the transcendental schema might be a *rule* of the transcendental synthesis;[3] and the transcendental schema is even described in one place as if it were the transcendental *synthesis* itself.

In spite of these difficulties I have little doubt that the transcendental schema is best regarded as a *product* of the transcendental synthesis of imagination. This product is a necessary characteristic which sensible objects must have because the given manifold must be combined by the transcendental synthesis in one time.

It is not easy to state Kant's doctrine in a simple way; and yet I think that what he is trying to describe is itself compara-

---

[1] The 'concept in conformity with the unity of apperception' must be a concept of an object, and may be a category. Ideas of objects may, I think, be identified here with objects themselves so far as these are known.

[2] The references to inner sense are, as usual, a source of difficulty, and I think it unfortunate that Kant ignores space; but we must not forget that for Kant all ideas are ideas of inner sense and so fall under the form of time. 'Determination' may mean 'determining'.

[3] The rule of the transcendental synthesis may be regarded as in a sense the product of the transcendental synthesis.

tively simple, if only we can be brought to concentrate upon it rather than on the words in which it is described.

The transcendental synthesis of imagination is supposed to combine the pure manifold of time into a unity, and this unity is supposed to be necessary for, and as it were demanded by, the unity of apperception, without which knowledge is impossible. This implies that the empirical manifold must be combined in one time, and as so combined it must exhibit certain characteristic ways of combination which all objects, as temporal, must have.

Such a view is at least intelligible, but if it is to have any importance, we must make it more definite: we must show what are the characteristic ways of combination belonging to all objects as temporal. Kant believes that the unity of apperception is manifested in the forms of judgement, or of thought, considered as principles of synthesis; and he believes that the characteristic ways of combination belonging to all objects as temporal must correspond to the principles of synthesis present in the forms of judgement—or in other words they must fall under the pure categories in the sense that they must be a species of which the pure category gives the genus. He claims, as I understand him, to have proved generally in the Transcendental Deduction that this must be so; but manifestly his proof can carry little conviction unless he can show us in all temporal objects those characteristic ways of combination which he alleges must fall under the pure categories. These characteristic ways of combination are the transcendental schemata and are the product of the transcendental synthesis of imagination. They may also be described as the necessary temporal characteristics of objects, characteristics without which objects would not be sensible objects in time;[1] and they must in some sense be revealed to sense-perception, if we recognise that imagination is a necessary ingredient in sense-perception.[2]

We are not likely to get a clearer view of the transcendental

[1] Hence they are described too as 'formal conditions of sensibility.'
[2] Compare A 120 n. and B 151.

schemata until we have examined each of them in detail, but one further complication must be added. The pure category as applied and restricted to its corresponding schema becomes the schematised category: for example the pure category of *ground and consequent* as applied and restricted to the transcendental schema of *necessary succession* becomes the schematised category of *cause and effect*. This no doubt raises the question whether the schematised category is really different from the transcendental schema. Kant, although he does not use the term 'schematised category', gives to the schematised categories names[1] which differ from the names given to the transcendental schemata. Hence it is all-important that at the outset we should distinguish both the pure category and the schematised category from the transcendental schema.

[1] He generally uses what I have called the *name* of the schematised category even when he refers to the pure category, as for example in the Metaphysical Deduction, where the category derived from the hypothetical form of judgement is called by anticipation, not the category of ground and consequent, but the category of cause and effect.

CHAPTER XXXIII

THE TRANSCENDENTAL SCHEMATA

§ 1. *Category and Schema*

We must now examine the different transcendental schemata which correspond to the pure categories. I propose to state in each case (1) what is the pure category, (2) what is the schematised category, and (3) what is the transcendental schema. It will be necessary to supplement Kant's own account by information derived from other parts of the *Kritik*, and also to introduce some measure of tidiness; for his description is unfortunately incomplete and careless where we are most in need of precision.

Every pure category may be described[1] as *the concept of the synthesis*[2] *of x*, where x serves to indicate the special nature of the synthesis. The principle of the synthesis is supposed to be implicit in the form of judgement.[3] The manifold synthetised is the manifold of intuition *in general*, and the pure category has in itself no reference to space and time. Unless the given manifold is synthetised in accordance with the category, there can be no knowledge of objects. These general considerations are always applicable and need not be repeated in each case.

The schematised category may be described as *the concept*

---

[1] Kant says that the pure categories cannot be defined—see A 241 and A 245 and compare B 300—but this means that their definition is not a 'real definition'; that is, it does not show that there is any real object to which the pure categories apply.

[2] Or 'the synthetic unity'. So far as the category is the concept of an object, the synthesis must be regarded, not as the act of combining, but as the combination made by the act and supposed to be present in the object. The category might be described as the concept of an object in general so far as the manifold of the object is combined in a certain way. Nevertheless all combination is the result of an act of synthesis, and Kant tends to treat the concept of the act and the concept of the combination produced by the act as if they were the same concept.   [3] See especially for details Chapter XIV § 4.

of the synthesis[1] *of x in time.* The principle of synthesis is
the same as that of the pure category, but its application is
restricted to a manifold of intuition given under the form
of time and space.[2]

The transcendental schema is the *product* which results
from the synthesis conceived in the schematised category:[3]
as such it is a necessary characteristic of all temporal objects
and is, I think, revealed to us (at least in part)[4] through sensuous
intuition, provided that we understand intuition to involve
imagination as well as sense.

This general framework may be difficult to work out in
all details, and it may not do justice to the subtlety of Kant's
thought; but it is far better to have even an inadequate framework which may subsequently be corrected than to be faced
with a chaos of unrelated assertions.

I would again insist that we shall understand Kant only
if we interpret him as giving an analysis of what is present
in all instances of knowing an object. Every object[5] must
exhibit all the transcendental schemata, and must fall, as

[1] Or 'the synthetic unity'. The schematised category may be described as the concept of an object *in time and space* so far as the manifold of the object is combined in a certain way. When Kant deals
with the synthesis in time, his tendency to identify the concept of
the act of synthesis and the concept of the combination produced
by the act of synthesis is particularly noticeable.

[2] I think it necessary, in the light of the Principles, to bring in
space as well as time for the understanding of Kant's view. In his
account of the schematism he himself avoids references to space.

[3] If so, it is also conceived in the pure category as the 'higher
concept' under which the schematised category falls.

The transcendental schema, it should be noted, is the product of
the act of synthesis, but it may also be regarded as resulting from,
or manifested in, the combination produced by the act. In the definition
of the categories 'synthesis' is taken most naturally as 'the combination
made by the act of synthesis': in the definition of the schema 'synthesis'
is most naturally taken as 'the act which produces this combination'.
I have not thought it necessary to comment on this in the separate
definitions, and I do not think Kant makes a sharp distinction.

[4] The schemata of relation are perhaps confirmed, rather than
revealed, by sensuous intuition.

[5] We should, I think, confine our attention to physical objects—
the objects which Kant has primarily in view.

regards its different aspects, under all the categories. We must not be misled into supposing that Kant describes a whole series of syntheses which take place at different times. There is only one synthesis which combines the given manifold, whatever be its empirical character, in one time and space, although that synthesis has different aspects and imposes different characteristics on the objects combined. And similarly there is only one form of judgement, or one principle of synthesis in judgement, though this too has different aspects, which Kant treats with an excessive formalism when he finds them embodied in the different forms of judgement as described by the traditional logic.

Throughout this chapter I am trying to make Kant's position clear, rather than to criticise it. Even so, some of the details must remain obscure till we come to the further exposition in the Principles.

§ 2. *The Schema of Quantity*

Under the head of quantity the pure category is derived from the universal form of judgement 'All S is P'.[1] The name of the category is '*totality*', though it is usually referred to as 'quantity'; and it may be described as *the concept of the synthesis of the homogeneous*.[2] The ground for this description is that

[1] The order in which the categories are given in A 80 = B 106 suggests that the category of totality is derived from the singular judgement. Although the same parallelism holds in the *Prolegomena* (IV 302–3), I believe that this is a slip, and is due to the fact that in the list of the forms of judgement Kant follows the traditional order (universal, particular, singular), while in the list of the categories he follows the order by which the third can be compounded of the first two (unity, plurality, totality), because (B 111) totality is plurality considered as unity. It is only natural to derive unity from the singular judgement, as Kant himself implies that he does in A 71 = B 96, in the *Prolegomena* § 20 (IV 302 n.), and in A 245–6, where he refers to *judicium commune*. His argument would be more plausible if he derived the three categories of unity, plurality, and totality from the fact that every judgement makes use of common concepts; compare Chapter X § 5 and Chapter XIV § 8.

[2] It might be described as the concept of 'the unity of the synthesis of the manifold of a homogeneous intuition *in general*'; see A 142–3 = B 182, and compare B 162, B 203, A 242 = B 300, and A 245–6.

in the universal judgement the objects referred to by the subject-concept are considered to be homogeneous with one another.

The schematised category is *the concept of the synthesis of the homogeneous in time and space*, and may be described as the category of *extensive quantity*. The transcendental schema which is the product of this synthesis is number (*numerus*), called also quantity as a phenomenon (*quantitas phaenomenon*).[1]

The synthesis of imagination, starting from given sensations and attempting to determine an object in time and space, determines the homogeneous space which the object occupies and the homogeneous time through which it endures. This gives the object shape (which seems to include size) and duration.[2] What we are concerned with here is, however, something more general, something common to size and to duration. This something Kant describes as number.

We might have expected it to be described rather as extensive quantity, which appears to be more obviously sensuous than number.[3] Kant, however, asks himself what is the common characteristic of every synthesis which produces the different kinds of extensive quantity. His answer is that every synthesis which produces extensive quantity[4] (whether in time or space) must be a *successive* synthesis of the homogeneous.[5] In holding this he is assuming that in order to *determine* any line, however

[1] A 146 = B 186. The synthesis is here taken as an act of synthesis and is *successive*.

[2] Compare A 724 = B 752, '*Gestalt*' and '*Dauer*'.

[3] Compare A 162 = B 203 ff. Perhaps Kant's desire to connect the schema specially with successive synthesis in time is the reason why he describes the schema as number: sensuous extensive quantity is indeterminate apart from measurement.

[4] I think we must take 'extensive quantity' throughout to be *determinate* extensive quantity, that is, a quantity which is measured or specified mathematically. Kant does not deny that we can be aware of an *indeterminate* quantity or quantum without successive synthesis; see the important footnote to A 426 = B 454.

[5] A 163 = B 204 and A 242 = B 300. The successiveness of the synthesis (in the sense that we must take each unit separately one after another) is the mark of extensive quantity.

small, we must apprehend its parts one after the other, and add them together, or synthetise them into a whole;[1] and the same, he maintains, is equally true of even the smallest period of time.[2] To determine the quantity of anything is to determine how many units it contains, and these units (whatever they may be) must be successively added, if the thing is to be measured.[3]

The successive addition of homogeneous units is counting, and what it produces is number. Since space and time are homogeneous, and since all objects are in a common space and time, all objects are known (so far as they are spatial and temporal) through a transcendental synthesis of imagination which successively synthetises the homogeneous parts of space and time. Hence every object must have number, or, perhaps it would be better to say, must be numerable.

Kant's own account[4] is intelligible only in the light of his Axioms of Intuition, and it is obscured by the fact that he makes no reference to space. Thus he does not explain that intuitions must have homogeneity because they are spatial and temporal. His description of number is misleading; for he says that number is an idea which comprehends the successive addition of homogeneous units.[5] This would identify 'number' with 'counting' (unless he means that number is the idea which comprehends in a total the homogeneous units successively added). He concludes that number is therefore the unity of the synthesis of the manifold of a homogeneous intuition in general *in that*[6] I generate[7] time itself in the

---

[1] See A 162–3 = B 203. Every line is made up of parts, not of points, and mathematical measurement may choose any part it pleases as the unit of measurement; see *K.d.U.* § 26 (V 254).

[2] A 163 = B 203.   [3] A 242 = B 300.   [4] A 142–3 = B 182.

[5] Compare what he says about number in A 140 = B 179.

[6] '*dadurch dass.*' The first half of this sentence is a definition of the pure category of quantity, and it is only what is added that makes it a definition of number—unless indeed 'intuition *in general*' (as in A 724 = B 752 and perhaps in B 203) indicates only that the difference between time and space may be ignored; see Chapter XXXVII § 3.

[7] Apart from the transcendental synthesis of imagination there would be no time and no succession; compare A 99–100, A 101–2, A 107, B 154–5, and B 160 n. It must be remembered that for Kant time has reality only in relation to the human mind.

apprehension of the intuition.[1] This is so difficult as almost
to bar comment; and it remains doubtful whether Kant is
regarding number as the act of counting or not.[2] Number
may perhaps be a synthetic unity (or combined manifold)
produced by the successive addition of homogeneous units;[3]
but it cannot be either the act of counting or the unity of the
act of counting.[4]

If we reinterpret Kant's doctrine by bringing in space,
as I have done and as he himself does later, his account of
the schema appears to be sound. It may seem hardly necessary
to ask whether the schema has also a connexion with the
universal form of judgement; but there is always a possibility
that more than mere formalism lies behind Kant's seemingly
artificial expressions. The demand of all judgement, and
indeed of all conception, is that a plurality of homogeneous
units should be conceived as a totality: this is not confined
to the form 'All S is P'. Kant's doctrine may be interpreted
as asserting that because sensible objects are in space and time
and so can be measured, there must be objects which have
sufficient homogeneity to be conceived (or to be judged by
the form 'All S is P'), and that even complete homogeneity

---

[1] If this implied that the homogeneity of intuitions is derived from
the fact that the apprehension of them is successive, such an implication
would be mistaken. There is no such implication in the Axioms,
and I do not think we should impute this to Kant here. The homogeneity of objects belongs to them in virtue of the time through
which they last and the space which they occupy, not in virtue of
the time which we require to apprehend them. Nevertheless for Kant
there is neither time nor space except in so far as they are (directly
or indirectly) apprehended inasmuch as the objects in time and
space are (directly or indirectly) apprehended. And if we are to
determine any past time or any unperceived space, we can do so
only by taking up successively and combining the units by which
we measure it.

[2] Compare A 103 (and also A 78 = B 104 and A 724 = B 752).

[3] Compare Kant's own description of number in the *Dissertation*
—§ 15 *Cor.* (II 406)—as '*multitudo numerando, h.e. in tempore dato
successive unum uni addendo, distincte cognita*'.

[4] This description of number is perhaps an example of Kant's tendency to identify the concept of an object with the concept of the
synthesis by which the object is constructed.

would not render these objects indistinguishable from one another.[1] More simply, in knowing sensible objects, and indeed in knowing any individual sensible object, there must be a synthesis of the homogeneous. The pure category of quantity is therefore shown to have objective validity; and at the same time it ceases to be a mere empty form of judgement and acquires 'sense and significance' as the schematised category of extensive quantity. Even if we cannot accept Kant's derivation of the category, we need not deny that his view has more plausibility than is commonly recognised.

§ 3. *The Schema of Quality*

Every sensible object, since the synthesis through which it is known is also a synthesis of time and space, must have extensive quantity; that is, it must have homogeneous parts external to one another which can be successively counted. But every sensible object, if it is to be a real object (and not merely the form of an object), must involve more than a synthesis of time and space. Its *matter* must be synthetised with the forms of time and space, and only so can it be real. Hence the next schema is referred to as the schema of *reality*.

In spite of this it is clear from Kant's account that the pure category which has to be schematised would be better called the category of *limitation*, that is, of *reality* combined with *negation*.[2] It may be described for our present purpose as *the concept of the synthesis of being and not-being*. This category is connected by Kant with the infinite judgement 'S is non-P'. The artificiality of the form should not obscure the fact—as I

---

[1] It should be noted that, according to Kant, objects which were entirely homogeneous could nevertheless be distinguished from one another, and so could be counted, because as sensible (and not merely conceivable) they would have different positions in space. See A 263 = B 319; A 272 = B 328; A 281 = B 337-8. So far as I know Kant does not discuss this problem with reference to time.

[2] See B 111. It may also be called the category of *quality*; see A 145 = B 184.

believe it to be—that every judgement both affirms and denies,[1] and in so doing delimits, or determines, reality. It therefore demands that its object should somehow be characterised by a combination of being and not-being.

The schematised category is *the concept of the synthesis of being and not-being in time and space*, and may be described as the category of reality (or limitation) in time and space.[2] The transcendental schema which is the product of this synthesis is properly called *degree*.[3]

Kant's own account[4] of this schema is obscure and inaccurate, and it is intelligible only in the light of the Anticipations of Sense Perception.[5] He believes that the mere forms of time and space are nothing real, and that if we are to have a real object of experience, these empty forms must be filled with a given matter, which is in the first instance sensation.[6] Being in time and space is to be found only in sensation (or the sensum), and its correlate not-being is empty time and space. The synthesis of sensation with the forms of time and space, or

---

[1] It may be said that an affirmative judgement implies a negative judgement and *vice versa*, but the negative judgement is another and a different judgement. This is true of the judgement taken abstractly as a proposition, but I believe that the affirmative judgement, taken concretely, denies as well as affirms, while the negative judgement, taken concretely, affirms as well as denies; and this does not mean that there is no difference between an affirmative and a negative judgement.

[2] It may be described also as the category of quality. If we could call it the category of intensive quantity we should get a parallel with extensive quantity (compare B 202); but Kant seems to treat intensive quantity as equivalent to degree. As generally in this chapter, he ignores space.

[3] Kant calls it *sensatio* or *realitas phaenomenon* (A 146 = B 186). This is, I think, misleading. He means, not mere sensation, but *degree* of sensation, or sensation as having degree. He means also *degree of what corresponds to sensation* as well as *degree of sensation itself*.

'Degree' appears to be identified with 'intensive quantity'. Intensive quantity is given in sensation at a moment: we do not apprehend each of its parts separately and successively in order to combine them into a total (see A 168 = B 210).

[4] A 143 = B 182-3.   [5] B 207 ff.

[6] We may for the present ignore 'what corresponds to sensation'.

of being with not-being, alone gives us a determinate object.
And according to Kant this synthesis, which fills time and
space with sensation, must do so in different degrees.[1] Any
sensation that we care to take (for example, the sensation of a
red colour),[2] however faint it may be, is never the faintest
possible sensation: there is always possible a still fainter
sensation between any given sensation and complete absence
of sensation. This means that in what fills time and space
there is always a more or less which is to be distinguished
from the more or less of time and space which is filled. A
colour may be brighter than another, though it lasts for a
shorter time and covers a smaller surface. Thus every sensible
object must have a degree of its sensed qualities, and such
degree is a necessary characteristic of reality in time and
space.

This very difficult doctrine will have to be considered in
detail later.[3] Here it need only be observed that the connexion

[1] Kant seems to infer from this that when we know an object,
time and space are neither completely filled nor completely empty,
so that an object must always exhibit in itself a determinate combination of being and not-being.   [2] See A 169 = B 211.

[3] See Chapter XXXVIII. Kant's own definition of the schema is
'the continuous and uniform production of reality in time, as we
descend in time from the sensation which has a definite degree to its
complete disappearance, or gradually mount from negation to such
a degree'. Here the schema is described as if it were the synthesis itself, though we might expect it to be the product of the
synthesis.

Kant explains that 'what corresponds to a sensation' is that whose
concept indicates being (in time). He asserts that this is what is
thought in the pure concept of the understanding; but the pure
category conceives being without any relation to time, and it is the
schematised category which refers to being in time. For the schematised category being is what fills time, and not-being is empty
time.

He also says, if the reading is correct, that because time is the
form of objects *only as appearances*, what corresponds to sensation
is the transcendental matter of objects *as things-in-themselves*! This
contradicts the statement that it is 'being in time', unless he uses
the phrase 'things-in-themselves' in its physical, and not in its metaphysical, sense (see A 45 = B 63); but in that case he would hardly
call the matter 'transcendental'. There is here some looseness of

of this schema with the quality of judgements seems the most
artificial of all Kant's connexions; for it is a pure accident
that the difference of affirmation and negation is said to determine the *quality* of judgements. Nevertheless it is only fair
to Kant to recognise that this connexion does not depend
merely on the accidental use of the word 'quality' for two very
different things. Every judgement affirms or denies objective
reality. This has in itself nothing to do with time or space,
but when we translate it—in Caird's phrase[1]—into terms of
time, then what it affirms or denies is objective existence
or reality in time and space. What exists in time and space
is the sensible object, whose reality is known, in the first
instance, through sensation. Furthermore, what sensation
gives us is a quality of the object, and this quality (whereby
it fills time and space) always has degree or intensive quantity.
In this case also, if we were convinced that some schema
must correspond to the form of judgement, it would not be
unreasonable to regard the schema in question as the degree
of qualities given in sensation.[2] We know that it must be
possible to determine real objects by combined affirmation
and negation, because if there is to be experience at all, some-

expression. The matter of things-in-themselves is unknown; compare A 366. What 'corresponds' in the phenomenal object to our
sensations is the matter of the phenomenal object; this matter (whose
inner nature is unknown) we refer to a source beyond the mind;
and it is this same matter which constitutes the phenomenal object
an empirical reality (compare A 720 = B 748).

The emendation of Kant's statement by inserting the word 'not'
(which Kemp Smith accepts from Wille) is not very convincing.

[1] Compare Caird, *The Philosophy of Kant*, p. 407, and also *The
Critical Philosophy of Kant*, Vol. I, p. 441.

[2] It may be objected that extensive quantity is itself a quality of
things. Kant himself recognises extension to be a primary quality
of bodies; see *Prol.* § 13 *Anm.* II (IV 289). He also describes spatial
quanta as having the quality of shape (A 720 = B 748), and quantity
itself as having the quality of continuity (A 176 = B 218). But in
connexion with the schema he is using the word 'quality' in the
sense in which it is opposed to extensive quantity. Quality in this
sense is given in sensation, while extensive quantity is determined
by the time and space which is filled by the given quality.

thing must be given in sensation[1] and synthetised in time and space.[2] Every object must therefore exhibit in itself that combination of being and not-being which is known as degree, a combination demanded by all judgement so far as it delimits objects by affirmation and negation.

§ 4. *The Schemata of Relation*

An actual object of experience must have more than *quantity* and *quality*. It must have a definite position[3] in one common time and space, and this position is determined by its *relation* to other objects. Kant gives us three schemata of relation corresponding to the three pure categories derived from the categorical, hypothetical, and disjunctive forms of judgement; and these schemata are concerned with the necessary relation of sensible objects to one another in a common time and space.[4] Here there is no suggestion that a schema is either a synthesis or a rule of synthesis. Each schema is defined as the characteristic which is the product of the synthesis.[5]

The first pure category is the *concept of the synthesis of subject and predicate*. In the categorical form of judgement subject and predicate are for Formal Logic interchangeable; but for Transcendental Logic, since the pure category is the form of judgement as used to determine sensible objects,

---

[1] By affirmation and negation we delimit or determine time and space as well as what is in time and space. But space and time are not real things, and we determine real things only when we determine what is given in time and space. Even time and space are real only when they are filled.

It is interesting to note that Plato as well as Kant identified space with τὸ μὴ ὄν, although for Plato space was matter (ὕλη), not form.

[2] The very difficult question as to the necessity of different degrees of reality in time and space must be dealt with later; see Chapter XXXVIII.

[3] '*Dasein*', which is a *being there* (or *then*) and is equivalent to *existence*, that is, existence in space and time. An imaginary object may have quantity and quality in a sense, but only an actual object has existence in our common space and time.

[4] Kant, as usual in this chapter, ignores space, but his account is not intelligible apart from space, and must be supplemented from the doctrine of the Analogies.   [5] A 143–4 = B 183–4.

the subject is regarded as a subject which can never be a pre-dicate.[1] Apart from empirical sensation we cannot know whether anything corresponds to the thought of such a subject.[2]

The schematised category is *the concept of the synthesis of the permanent and the changing in time*, where the permanent is the unchanging subject (or substance) to which the changing predicates (or accidents) belong: the permanent is, in short, the unchanging substratum of all change, and the schematised category is the category of substance and accident (or of subsistence and inherence). The transcendental schema which is the product of the synthesis is *permanence*. Kant ignores the fact that the category, and presumably the schema, involves two correlative terms,[3] and he is content to refer to the schema indifferently as 'permanence' or 'the permanent'.[4]

The second pure category is *the concept of the synthesis of ground and consequent*. Kant habitually describes it as the category of cause and effect, but it has no reference to time. He himself says that if we leave out all reference to temporal succession, the category of cause is merely the concept of something from which we can make an inference to the existence of something else.[5] This would not enable us to distinguish

---

[1] B 129; A 147 = B 186; A 242–3 = B 300–1. I suppose Kant holds that unless this is so, there is no real distinction between subject and predicate. His argument might be more satisfactory if he merely insisted that thought demands something to think about by means of its concepts.

[2] B 149; A 243 = B 301.

[3] See B 110. Kant perhaps ignores change as a correlate of permanence, because change is dealt with in connexion with the second schema of relation, and all three schemata must be considered together.

[4] Kant is careless in his account of substance. He says (1) that it is *permanence*, the permanence of the real in time, (2) that it is the *idea of the real as a substratum* which endures while everything else changes; and (3) that it is the *permanent* or *unchanging*. The Latin name is *constans et perdurabile rerum*, or *substantia phaenomenon* (A 146 = B 186).

[5] A 243 = B 301. I think the words 'the existence of' should be omitted from this statement, but even so the definition would be unsatisfactory.

between cause and effect,[1] nor have we any right to suppose that there is any object corresponding to the concept.

The schematised category is *the concept of the synthesis of ground and consequent where the consequent succeeds the ground in time*, and it is to be described as the category of cause and effect. The transcendental schema which is the product of the synthesis is *necessary succession*, or succession in accordance with a rule.[2] This means, not that an event A must always be succeeded by *some* other event, but that it must (other conditions remaining the same) be succeeded by the event B.[3]

The third pure category is more difficult. In the disjunctive judgement we think of a whole whose parts mutually exclude, and so mutually determine, one another in the whole.[4] Hence the pure category of *communion* is *the concept of the synthesis of a whole whose parts mutually exclude and determine one another*. It has of course no reference to time.

[1] Perhaps Kant has in mind the fact that such an inference can in special cases work in both directions; for example, we can argue either from the three sides of a triangle to its three angles or *vice versa*. Or perhaps he means that inference is sometimes from effect to cause—if there is a footprint, a man has passed.

[2] Kant says also that the schema of cause is 'the real upon which, whenever posited, something else always follows.' The word 'posited' (*gesetzt*) is always puzzling. Here it seems to mean 'has a position in time', 'occurs'. The schema of effect would then presumably be 'the real which always follows upon a given event'. Causality applies, not to the succession of times, but to the succession of appearances in time.

[3] Whether rightly or wrongly, Kant always assumes that causality implies *regular* succession; and what I call 'necessary succession' is to be taken as meaning 'regular succession'. Necessary regularity, like permanence, is something whose presence can be confirmed by observation, although it cannot be established by observation.

[4] Compare A 73–4 = B 98–9 and B 112–13. We may consider this to be implied in the form of judgement 'A is either B or C or D.' In the judgement 'a triangle is either equilateral or isosceles or scalene', we divide what Kant calls the 'sphere' of triangularity into the mutually exclusive parts which constitute the whole sphere. It is irrelevant to object that this bears no analogy to simultaneity because a triangle cannot be both equilateral and isosceles at the same time; for all reference to time is excluded from the pure category.

This statement is, however, too simple for the full understanding of Kant's view. He himself gives a description of
what purports to be the pure category, but (as in the case
of causality) he does not distinguish it from the schematised
category. He says that it is 'the reciprocal causality of substances in relation to one another'.[1] It would be more exact
to say that it is 'the reciprocal causality of substances in regard
to their accidents'.[2] If we exclude all reference to time and to
terms implying time, we must say that the pure category
of communion[3] is *the concept of the synthesis of ultimate subjects
such that the predicates of the one subject have their ground
in the other, and* vice versa.[4]

The schematised category is *the concept of the synthesis
of permanent substances such that the changing accidents of
the one substance have their cause in the other, and* vice versa:[5]
it may be called the category of interaction. The transcendental
schema which is the product of the synthesis is *the necessary
simultaneity* of the accidents of one substance with those
of another, or, as Kant says, simultaneity in accordance with
a universal rule.[6]

It may be added that Kant finds permanent substances
only in space, and he believes that the different spatial parts
of a substance are themselves substances.[7]

---

[1] See A 244 = B 302.   [2] Compare A 144 = B 183.
[3] It would be well to use the term 'communion' (*Gemeinschaft* or
communio) for the pure category, and 'interaction' (*Wechselwirkung*
or *commercium*) for the schematised category. Compare A 213 = B 260
(although *communio* is there restricted to *communio spatii*) and A 214
= B 261.
[4] Compare B 257–8. This is implied in the form of judgement
'Either A is B or C is D'. This second statement does not contradict
the first, but it adds to it that the parts of the whole are themselves
subjects which determine one another in regard to their predicates.
For the significance of this see n. 7 below.
[5] Compare B 257–8.
[6] A 144 = B 183–4. I propose to use 'necessary simultaneity' as
the parallel to 'necessary succession'.
[7] *M.A.d.N.* (IV 503 and 542). Hence the parts of a whole substance
are themselves substances which determine one another in regard to
their accidents. Compare n. 4 above.

The schemata of relation are (with the exception of the schema of interaction) more plausibly connected with the corresponding form of judgement than are the schemata of quantity and quality. On the other hand it is not so clear that the characteristics imposed by the synthesis of relation must be found in all sensible objects. The transcendental synthesis of imagination manifestly imposes extensive quantity on objects, and I think we may agree that it involves a synthesis of quality also, and even that quality must necessarily have a degree. But it is certainly not obvious why the transcendental synthesis should impose necessary permanence, necessary succession, and necessary simultaneity.

This fact is explicitly recognised by Kant. In the Principles he will attempt to show that sensible objects must have all the categorial characteristics specified, but in the case of quantity and quality we are said to have intuitive certainty or evidence, while in the other cases we have only discursive certainty. Nevertheless in all cases we have certainty.[1]

§ 5. *The Schemata of Modality*

We have now seen that for Kant the one synthesis of imagination by which we construct objects in time and space has three necessary aspects: (1) it is a synthesis of time and space (the forms of intuition), and so involves extensive quantity or number; (2) it is a synthesis of appearances given to sensation (the matter of intuition) in time and space, and so involves intensive quantity or degree; (3) it is a synthesis which combines different appearances in one common time and space, and so (Kant will prove) involves permanence, necessary succession, and necessary simultaneity, or the reciprocal causality of permanent substances in regard to their changing accidents.[2]

[1] See A 161–2 = B 200–1 and A 180 = B 223; and compare Chapter XXXVI § 3, where this point will be discussed.

[2] We may speak of (1) as the synthesis of mere intuition, of (2) as the synthesis of sense-perception, and of (3) as the synthesis of experience; see A 180 = B 223. The synthesis of experience, I think, includes the first two. This should be compared with Kant's summary

These syntheses, or aspects of the one synthesis, determine different categorial features of the object of experience. The first two determine the object itself, the third determines the object in its relation to other objects. When we come to the schemata of modality, we are concerned, not with features belonging to the object, but rather with its relation to the mind which knows it.[1] Hence we have no longer to discover new aspects of the one synthesis which determines objects in time (and space): we have to observe (if we may simplify matters provisionally) that the first aspect of the synthesis which we have already described is the condition of our knowing an object to be possible;[2] the second is the condition of our knowing it to be actual; and the third is the condition of our knowing it to be necessary. Possibility, actuality, and necessity add nothing to the content of the object; but every object may be said to be known as possible, actual, and necessary, according to the different ways in which it is related to time.[3]

Kant connects the pure categories of modality with the distinction between problematic, assertoric, and apodeictic judgements. This distinction does not concern the content of the judgement, that is, does not concern the way in which different cognitions are united in the judgement. It concerns only the way in which the judgement (whatever be its content) is thought.[4] If we entertain the judgement as a logical possibility, it is problematic.[5] If we affirm its truth, it is assertoric. If

in A 145 = B 184. There we have (1) the synthesis of time itself or the production of time, (2) the synthesis of sensation or sense-perception with the idea of time, or the filling of time, (3) the synthesis of different sense-perceptions relatively to one another in the whole of time.   [1] Compare A 233–5 = B 286–7.

[2] Compare A 180 = B 223. This statement must be taken as provisional and as simplifying Kant's position unduly. The condition of the possibility of objects is agreement with the forms of space and time and also with the categories; see A 218 = B 265. See also Chapter XLIX § 2.

[3] Compare A 145 = B 184. The schema of modality is concerned with 'whether and how the object belongs to time'.

[4] A 74 = B 100. Compare Chapter X § 1.

[5] We merely conceive or suppose it.

we must think it because of the laws of thought, then it is apodeictic.[1]

The pure categories which are implicit in these forms of judgement are possibility, actuality or existence, and necessity.[2] Kant seems to hold that they, even more than the other pure categories, can be explained only by a tautology.[3] If we omit all reference to time and space, we are left only with logical possibility, which means the mere absence of contradiction in our ideas; logical actuality or truth,[4] which seems to mean no more than affirmation by the mind; and logical necessity, which would appear to be present when what we affirm is inferred from given concepts or judgements in accordance with the formal laws of thought.[5] In all this we are concerned only with the characteristics of our own thinking, and not with qualities of objects.

The pure categories of modality are therefore merely concepts of the synthesis which is present in every judgement. The pure category of *possibility* is a concept of that synthesis as self-consistent in accordance with the formal law of thought. The pure category of *actuality* is a concept of the same synthesis as professing to determine a real object.[6] The pure category

---

[1] A 75–6 = B 101. Kant finds a parallel to this in *understanding* which conceives, *judgement* which affirms an actual case falling under the conception, and *reason* which infers a logical necessity (A 130 = B 169). Logical necessity, however, would seem to cover, not only the conclusion of a syllogism, but also immediate inference, and even analytic judgements. Compare A 304 = B 361.

[2] For the sake of simplicity we may ignore their correlates impossibility, non-existence, and contingency. Kant does not appear to distinguish between existence (*Dasein* or *Existenz*) and actuality (*Wirklichkeit*). We have *Dasein* in A 80 = B 106, *Existenz* in B 111, and *Wirklichkeit* in A 145 = B 184. It might be well to use actuality for the category, and existence (as having a reference to time) for the schema.   [3] A 244 = B 302.

[4] It seems to be a claim to truth rather than truth itself. Kant himself bases the assertoric judgement in the principle of sufficient reason, while he bases the problematic judgement on the principle of non-contradiction, and the apodeictic judgement on the principle of excluded middle; see *Log. Einl.* VII (IX 52–3). I confess that I find his view here very difficult to understand.   [5] A 75–6 = B 101.

[6] This seems to be involved in its claim to truth.

of necessity is a concept of the same synthesis as following logically from other concepts or judgements in accordance with the formal laws of thought.[1] Even these pure categories must, however, as categories be supposed to determine *somehow* all objects *in their relation to the mind.*

The schematised category of possibility is *the concept of the transcendental synthesis of imagination, so far as that synthesis involves the forms of intuition.* The transcendental schema which is the product of this synthesis may be said to be *the agreement of the synthesis of different ideas with the conditions of time in general.*[2] An object,[3] as opposed to an idea, is possible, if it is compatible with the nature of time, or can be conceived as existing at some time or other.[4]

The schematised category of actuality is *the concept of the transcendental synthesis of imagination, so far as that synthesis involves the matter of intuition given at a determinate time.* The transcendental schema which is the product of this synthesis is *existence at a determinate time.*[5] An object is actual, if it is bound up with the material conditions of experience, that is with sensation.[6]

The schematised category of necessity is *the concept of*

[1] Compare A 75–6 = B 101.

[2] A 144 = B 184. We might add 'and of space in general'. We have to add also that in A 218 = B 265 Kant asserts that agreement with the formal conditions of thought is also necessary, if an object is to be possible. This completes what is said here, for the synthesis of time and space is a synthesis in accordance with the categories or the forms of thought.

[3] The example which Kant gives is the fact that an object may have contradictory characteristics in succession. The possibility that the same thing could have contradictory characteristics is unintelligible to a thought which ignores time.

[4] Kant says that the schema is 'the determination of the idea of a thing at some time or other'. This might be taken to mean that if we can imagine the thing as existing in time and space, then it is possible. But this question is complicated and difficult, for Kant holds that the sphere of the possible is not wider than that of the actual; see A 230 = B 282 ff.

[5] A 145 = B 184. Existence at a determinate time always involves a connexion with sensation.   [6] A 218 = B 266.

the transcendental synthesis of imagination as determining the given manifold with reference to the whole of time. The transcendental schema which is the product of this synthesis is *existence in relation to the whole of time.*[1] An object is necessary when the material conditions with which it is bound up are determined in accordance with the universal laws, or formal conditions, necessary for the unity of time.[2]

All this is difficult, and must be taken as a summary and provisional preparation for the Postulates by reference to which alone it can be understood.

§ 6. *Kant's Summary*

Having described the schemata in detail Kant proceeds to sum up the results which are supposed to flow from this description. Each schema is said to 'contain and to make representable'[3] certain things. I do not know what Kant means by 'make representable'.[4] I should like it to mean that the schema is a sensuous characteristic or mark in virtue of which something can be known.

The schema of the category of quantity contains and makes

[1] A 145 = B 184. The schema is said to be *aeternitas* or *necessitas phaenomenon;* see A 146 = B 186. We know the necessity of an object when we know the chain of causes which produced it.

[2] Compare A 218 = B 266.

[3] A 145 = B 184, '*enthalte und vorstellig mache.*' This phrase should be repeated each time, and I doubt whether it is satisfactory to substitute for it the word 'is', as in Kemp Smith's translation. I also doubt the propriety of adding '*nur eine Zeitbestimmung*' (only a time-determination) as is done by Adickes and accepted by Kemp Smith. The text as it stands is unsatisfactory, but I question whether it is improved by making Kant say that the schema (which *is* a transcendental time-determination) not only *contains*, but also *makes representable*, a time-determination. Kant not uncommonly equates 'is' and 'contains', but it would be strange if the schema made itself representable.

[4] This phrase is also used in A 143 = B 183; but there it is applied to a 'transition' (*Übergang*) from reality to negation which makes every reality representable as a quantum—so that the sense seems to be rather different.

representable the generation (or synthesis) of time itself in the successive apprehension of an object.[1]

The schema of the category of quality contains and makes representable the synthesis of sensation (or sense-perception) with the idea of time; that is, it contains and makes representable the filling of time.[2]

The schema of the category of relation contains and makes representable the relation of sense-perceptions to one another in the whole of time,[3] that is, according to a rule of time-determination.[4]

The schema of the category of modality contains and makes representable time itself *as the correlate of the determination of an object*;[5] that is, it indicates whether and how the object belongs to time.[6]

These statements, it must be recognised, are obscure, and they repeat rather than clarify what has already been said. Thus there is, under the heads of quantity and quality, the same tendency to connect the schema with the *synthesis*

---

[1] Number (or, perhaps better, extensive quantity) is the product of such a synthesis of homogeneous times (and spaces) in apprehending an object. It may perhaps also be a mark of this synthesis, if we do not regard the product as separable from the synthesis.

[2] Degree of sensation (or of what corresponds to sensation) is what fills time (and space). It is the product, and perhaps the mark, of the synthesis which combines sensation with time.

[3] '*zu aller Zeit.*'

[4] The permanence, succession, and simultaneity of sense-perceptions or appearances are, according to Kant, a product (and perhaps a mark) of the synthesis which combines all sense-perceptions in one time (and space). They enable us to distinguish the relations of substance and accident, cause and effect, and interaction.

[5] It may be noted that we can know times (and spaces) empirically only by knowing the objects in these times (and spaces); see A 216 = B 264.

[6] The object is possible, if it is compatible with the form of time, and so can exist at some time or other. It is actual, if its matter is given at some determinate time. It is necessary, if its existence is determined in relation to the whole of time in accordance with the Analogies. These are the ways in which the object can belong to time, or the ways in which time is the correlate of the determination of an object.

of imagination, while under the head of relation (and perhaps also under the head of modality) the schema is connected rather with the *product* of the synthesis.[1] Whatever be the difficulties of Kant's exposition, I cannot see any other way of understanding his doctrine except on the supposition already adopted—that the schemata are sensuous characteristics which must belong to all objects so far as the manifold of these objects is combined in one time (and space).

This view is, I think, borne out by Kant's conclusion.[2] The schemata are *a priori* time-determinations[3] in accordance with rules; and these time-determinations (following the order of the categories) concern (1) the time-series, (2) the time-content, (3) the time-order (or the order of what is in time), and (4) the totality of time in its relation to all possible objects. All objects must have extensive quantity so far as they extend through a series of homogeneous times. They must have intensive quantity so far as they fill time. They must be substances interacting causally with one another so far as there is an objective order of events in time. And they must be possible, actual, and necessary in virtue of their various relations to time as a whole. The first two assertions Kant regards as intuitively certain; the third requires something that may be called proof; while the fourth requires only explanation or elucidation after the first three have been established.

The last paragraphs[4] of Kant's discussion explain very clearly his view that the schemata give 'meaning' or objective reference to the categories, and at the same time restrict their application to objects of sense alone.[5] We may be tempted

---

[1] This difference may be connected with the fact that under the first two headings we have 'intuitive evidence': Kant may therefore be more inclined to lay emphasis on the synthesis, since the product is evident to all, but the synthesis is not.

[2] A 145 = B 184–5.

[3] It should now be clear that these are not determinations of time itself, but temporal determinations of objects.

[4] A 145–7 = B 185–6. The obscure sentence with which these paragraphs begin is discussed in Chapter XXXIV § 4.

[5] Compare Chapter XXXII § 7 and also Chapter LIV.

to suppose that when we abstract from the schemata which restrict the application of the categories to things *as they appear* to our senses, we shall then have pure categories which will apply to things *as they are in themselves*.[1] Kant does not deny that we must think things-in-themselves by means of the pure categories—we have indeed no other way of thinking. He does deny that such thinking can give us knowledge; for knowledge always demands intuition as well as conception. The pure categories in abstraction from the schemata have still what he calls a 'logical' meaning: they are concepts of the unity (or synthesis) of ideas which is implicit in the forms of judgement. But no object is given for them, and they have no 'meaning'—in the sense that we cannot indicate the nature of any object to which they apply; and consequently they are not a source of knowledge.[2]

§ 7. *The Number of the Schemata*

If we hold that the categories cannot be derived from the forms of judgement, it is clear that a large part of Kant's doctrine must be arbitrary or artificial, comparable in some ways to the many attempts which have been made to square the circle. Nevertheless it is unwise not to recognise the ingenuity and plausibility of his attempt, concealed though it is by the untidiness of his expressions. On the whole I must admit for myself that what surprises me most is the way in which his efforts approximate to something very like success.

It may be thought that there is one very marked failure, since we are offered only one schema for the three categories of quantity and quality, whereas for each of the categories of relation and modality there is a separate schema. Yet even here it should be observed that Kant can speak as if there were only one schema for the three categories of relation, and one for the three categories of modality.[3] He does not

---

[1] A 147 = B 186.

[2] In the text Kant says that they have no 'meaning' which might yield a *concept* of the object. He corrects 'concept' to 'knowledge' in *Nachträge* LXI.   [3] A 145 = B 184; compare § 6 above.

regard the difference between one schema and three schemata as the sharp distinction which it appears to be at first sight. How is this to be explained?

We must remember that every category is involved in knowing any object. Hence there is only one ultimate synthesis involved in all knowledge, although this synthesis is complex and has different aspects concerned with quantity, quality, relation, and modality. If we treat these aspects separately, and speak of a synthesis of quantity, a synthesis of quality, and so on, each of these syntheses in turn may be regarded as having three different aspects. Where these aspects are of greater complexity, as in the case of relation and modality, Kant gives them special treatment; where they are of less complexity, as in the case of quantity and quality, he treats them all together. His carelessness of expression[1] should not obscure the presence of three different aspects in every case.

It should, for example, be clear that in determining the *existence* of any object, we must determine it, not only as a permanent substance with changing accidents, but also as having the succession of these accidents causally determined, and as acting and reacting simultaneously with all other substances. Unless all three relations are present, Kant believes that we cannot determine the existence of any object in time and space.

So too in the case of quantity. We are given only one schema, namely number, but in numbering or measuring any object all three categories are present. Every number is a plurality of units taken as a totality, and number is said to belong to the category of totality only because totality is plurality regarded as unity.[2] The schema of quality in a similar way involves reality, negation, and limitation. Indeed it is only in this case that Kant even attempts to show the interconnexion of the

[1] For example, the suggestion that quantity is concerned only with the category of totality, and that quality is concerned only with the category of reality.

[2] B 111. A plurality, it may be added, is always a plurality of units.

categories, although this becomes a little clearer when we come to consider the Principles as a whole.

The difference between one schema and three is merely an indication of the less or greater difficulty of making clear what is involved in one aspect of synthesis; and we shall never understand the Analogies and the Postulates, unless we realise that in them we are dealing with a synthesis which is essentially one.

CHAPTER XXXIV

THE SIGNIFICANCE OF THE SCHEMA

§ 1. *Subsumption and Syllogism*

In the light of what we have learned about the schemata, we may be tempted to suppose that Kant's argument in the Analytic of Principles takes the form of a series of syllogisms in which the transcendental schema is the middle term. In the major premise we subsume the schema under its corresponding category; in the minor premise we subsume the object under the schema; and in the conclusion we subsume the object under the category.[1]

Even if this were so, the Analytic of Principles would still be properly called the Doctrine of Judgement; for it is only the two premises which Transcendental Logic has to establish, and both of these premises are for Kant matters of judgement in the technical sense.[2] The fact that the conclusion is drawn by the ordinary rules of Formal Logic does not make this chapter a treatise on the syllogism.

Nevertheless a syllogism of this kind seems an odd sort

---

[1] For example, 'All necessary succession exhibits the relation of ground and consequent.

All objective succession is necessary succession.

∴ All objective succession exhibits the relation of ground and consequent.'

The major premise is given in the chapter on Schematism, and the minor in the Second Analogy. Both premises are supposed to be matters of judgement in the technical sense.

[2] See Chapter XXXII § 3. Incidentally the view of Adickes—that Kant arbitrarily invented the whole doctrine of schematism in order to have a chapter corresponding to the chapter on judgement in Formal Logic—is the more unnecessary because Kant requires in any case such a chapter for his Principles. I have great respect for the later work of Adickes, but this suggestion, like some others made in his edition of the *Kritik*, seems to me to require no refutation. The only excuse for it is the youth of the writer at the time, and I think it unfortunate that Kemp Smith should have followed him in exaggerating the influence of Kant's so-called 'architectonic'.

of syllogism to use in the circumstances. It is a syllogism whose conclusion is known before we begin;[1] for we are supposed to have proved in the Transcendental Deduction that the categories generally must apply to objects.[2] We are not arriving at a conclusion by the elimination of a middle term; we are rather making intelligible the conclusion by discovering the precise nature of the middle term on which it rests.[3]

Kant's way of stating his doctrine lends colour to the view that he is engaged in a syllogistic argument, but I doubt whether this is the correct interpretation. For one thing the conclusion of such a syllogism is not really the conclusion at which we wish to arrive. His real aim is not to show that the object falls under the pure category, but to show that it falls under the schematised category; and we cannot do this by eliminating the middle term in the syllogism. This view is perhaps confirmed by the fact that in this chapter, as indeed elsewhere, he consistently describes the categories as if they were schematised categories.

The categories with which Kant is really concerned are the schematised categories. In the chapter on schematism he is dealing in detail with that element in the categories which has hitherto been left vague, namely the condition of sensibility which each contains. In abstraction from such a condition or schema the pure categories are without 'sense

[1] Compare the statement in A 322 = B 378.

[2] Perhaps we are even supposed to have proved generally that the schema is the middle term by which this conclusion is reached. Thus Kant says expressly (in A 139 = B 178–9) 'we have seen in the Transcendental Deduction . . . that pure *a priori* concepts contain, besides the function of understanding (that is, the form of thought) in the category, also *formal conditions of sensibility*', or in other words schemata. He also says that the categories contain the general *condition* for rules (see A 135 = B 174 and A 159 = B 198); and this condition may be the schema.

[3] We are also indicating the aspect of the object which falls under the category. It is one thing to know that an object must somehow exhibit the relation of ground and consequent, and quite another thing to know that it is the succession of changes in the object which exhibits this relation.

and significance'.[1] As restricted to their only legitimate use, that is, as applied to objects in virtue of the transcendental schemata, the categories are schematised. The schematised categories 'contain' the transcendental schemata; and the transcendental schemata are exhibited in all objects so far as the manifold of these objects is combined by imagination in one time and space.

If this is the correct interpretation, Kant's argument is wrongly viewed as a syllogism, and consists rather of two judgements. In the first judgement we recognise the schema contained in a particular category—we recognise, for example, that the category of cause and effect contains, not only grounds and consequents, but the *necessary succession* of grounds and consequents; and only so can it be regarded as the category of cause and effect. In the second judgement we recognise that all objects, so far as they are substances whose accidents succeed one another in time, fall under the category of cause and effect; or in other words that all changes happen in accordance with the law of cause and effect.[2]

There is manifestly nothing artificial in making a distinction between the concept of ground and consequent and the concept of cause and effect. It is vital to Kant's argument to specify the transcendental schema which is contained in each category and thereby distinguishes the category from the concept of an empty form of judgement supposed *somehow* to determine objects.

§ 2. *Category and Schema*

On this view the pure category is an abstraction: the only category which we can legitimately apply to objects is the schematised category. This I believe to be Kant's own doctrine,[3] and he habitually insists, especially in the second edition,

[1] Compare A 246, where they are said to have absolutely no relation to any determinate object.

[2] We shall have to consider later whether this is properly described as a judgement in the technical sense; see Chapter XXXVI § 4.

[3] Compare A 145–6 = B 185.

that the pure category is obtained when we abstract from the references to time and space contained in the schematised category.[1]

It may be suggested that if this is so, Kant's paraphernalia of pure categories, schematised categories, and transcendental schemata is unnecessarily elaborate. All we require is the schematised category, and the schematised category can be identified with the transcendental schema.[2]

This suggestion has some value as indicating a possible way of reconstructing Kant's doctrine, if we are unable to accept his derivation of the categories from the forms of judgement.[3] It has no value as an interpretation of Kant's own thought.

We may indeed say with propriety that, on Kant's view, the transcendental schema is revealed concretely to sense and imagination[4] and is conceived or 'contained' in the schematised category. There is a minor difficulty even in this; for the schematised category may be said to be a concept of the combination of the manifold in time, while the transcendental schema is rather the sensuous characteristic which results from such combination.[5] If we set this aside as an unnecessary complication, we must not forget that for Kant more is contained in the schematised category than is given in the trans-

[1] See, for example, B 162 and B 163.

[2] Compare Kemp Smith, *Commentary*, pp. 339–40. Kemp Smith even goes so far as to say that 'what Kant means when he speaks of the categories *are* the schemata'; but it should be noted that the names by which Kant alludes to the different schemata are other than the names by which he alludes to the schematised categories.

[3] See § 6 below.

[4] Kant himself sometimes speaks as if the transcendental schema were a concept; see A 146 = B 186. The transcendental schema can of course be conceived, like any other sensuous characteristic; but the concept of the transcendental schema 'contains' less than the schematised category.

[5] As, for example, beauty may be said to result from harmony or coherence in the object. I believe myself that such language is too external. Beauty is neither the logical consequence nor the practical effect of harmony or coherence; and it would be truer to say that beauty is manifested or embodied in such harmony or coherence.

cendental schema; for the category is enriched by its connexion with the form of judgement. This is true at any rate in regard to the categories of substance and cause—the two categories which we may not unreasonably conjecture to have been the starting-point of Kant's thought.

Thus, in the traditional doctrine which Kant inherited, substance is regarded (1) as the ultimate subject of all predicates and (2) as the permanent substratum of change. Both of these are conceived in the schematised category. The first Kant derives from the form of judgement. The second is given in the transcendental schema and is derived from the synthesis of the manifold in time and space. If the schematised category were a concept of the transcendental schema and nothing more, then the category of substance would for Kant be impoverished.

This consideration is more important when we consider the category of cause and effect. For Kant causality means (1) that the succeeding event has its *ground* in the preceding event, and (2) that the succeeding event follows upon the preceding event in accordance with a rule of necessary succession. Here again (1) is derived from the form of judgement, and (2) is derived from the synthesis of the manifold in time and space. The schematised category, if it contained only the transcendental schema without the principle of synthesis present in the form of judgement and conceived in the pure category, would for Kant be impoverished.

No doubt it may be thought to-day that if causality is to be admitted at all, it must be reduced to necessary, that is, invariable, succession; but the plain man, and for this purpose Kant is a plain man, believes that the effect is really *grounded* in the cause, so that such a modification of the Kantian doctrine would mean for him a definite loss.[1]

---

[1] The same considerations apply to the category of interaction. I feel more doubt in regard to the categories of quantity, quality, and modality.

§ 3. *The Transcendental Synthesis of Imagination*

So far we have considered Kant's doctrine with reference to categories and schemata. We must now consider it in relation to the active synthesis necessary for knowledge.

It is easy to see that all judgement involves the unification or synthesis of ideas,[1] and that the transcendental synthesis of imagination involves the unification of ideas in time and space. Granted that the second (or concrete) synthesis might be a species of the first (or abstract) synthesis, we have still to ask what is the relation between them. Does the synthesis present in judgement control and determine the synthesis whereby the given manifold is combined in one time and space? Kant clearly holds that the transcendental synthesis of imagination maintains the unity of time and space in response to the general demand of thought for unity in the object: the unity of apperception is 'original' and the unity of objects is 'derivative'. But there still remains the question whether the different aspects of the transcendental synthesis of imagination are determined and controlled by the different aspects of synthesis present in the form of judgement as such.

I do not find that Kant is wholly clear on this point, and perhaps we should keep open the possibility that he believed the different forms of synthesis present in judgement to follow, rather than to control, the transcendental synthesis of imagination.[2] Nevertheless it seems difficult to understand his view except on the supposition that the forms of judgement determine

[1] Compare Kant's statement that the categories, even in abstraction from all sensible conditions, have a logical meaning—they are concepts of the abstract unity (*der blossen Einheit*) of ideas; see A 147 = B 186.

[2] This is suggested chiefly by some obscure statements in Kant's casual jottings. Thus he distinguishes the *real* function of ideas from their *logical* function, and seems to suggest that the former are the ground of the latter; see *Nachlass* 4631 (XVII 615). He even says that the *sensitive* function is the ground of the *intellectual* function; see *Nachlass* 4629 (XVII 614) and compare *Nachlass* 4635 (XVII 619). His statements are, however, so puzzling that I am not sure whether they are relevant to the present question.

and control the different aspects of the transcendental synthesis of imagination.

In certain instances this is perhaps not so impossible as it might seem to be at first sight. Granted that the transcendental synthesis of imagination must impose some sort of permanence on the manifold in order to maintain the unity of time, it might be because of the demand of thought that we regard the permanent as the substratum of change and the ultimate *subject* of all predicates. Granted also that the transcendental synthesis of imagination must impose necessary or regular succession upon the given manifold, it might be because of the demand of thought for *grounds* that we regard the first event in a regular succession as the cause and the second as the effect. Even so I do not see how the demand of thought could control or determine the imposition of permanence and regular succession by the transcendental synthesis of imagination. Still less do I see how the homogeneity of the times and spaces combined by imagination could be due to the demand of thought for homogeneous objects—unless indeed Kant holds that there is in time and space as given to us by the perception of temporal and spatial objects nothing which suggests homogeneity apart from the demands of thought.[1] Above all, I can see not the slightest ground for believing that the degree of intensive quantity given to us in sensation is due to a combination made by the transcendental synthesis of imagination in *response* to the demand of thought that we should be able to affirm and deny and thereby delimit.

It is unfortunate that Kant has not given us more help on these difficult questions, but I think they should be asked even if we are unable to answer them. All we can say with confidence is that on his view each aspect of the transcendental synthesis of imagination falls under an aspect of the synthesis present in judgement as such: the former gives the species of which the latter is the genus.

[1] Time, for example, seems sometimes to race and sometimes to drag; yet we *think* that its parts are homogeneous.

§ 4. *The Schematism of the Understanding*

Kant may have thought that questions of the type I have raised are too difficult to answer. Thus he asserts that the schematism of our understanding, in its relation to appearances and their mere form, is a hidden art in the depths of the human soul: its true operations we shall hardly ever divine from nature and lay open to our gaze.[1]

This is one of the statements which have been used in support of the view that Kant believed the syntheses which are the conditions of experience to be necessarily unconscious and even noumenal. I do not believe that it can be properly interpreted in this way,[2] but here I wish to ask only what Kant meant by the phrase 'schematism of the pure understanding'.

This schematism is said to be the procedure of the pure understanding with the transcendental schemata.[3] This procedure is a kind of 'exhibition'[4]—that is, an exhibiting of the object to which the pure category applies. We are said to 'exhibit' the object of a concept, or more commonly to 'exhibit' the concept, when we supply the intuition to which the concept applies. When we exhibit an empirical concept, we provide the corresponding empirical object or intuition. When we exhibit a mathematical concept, we construct the corresponding object in pure intuition. When we exhibit a pure category, we supply the sensuous condition or schema under which alone the pure category can be employed.[5] This exhibition of the pure category is what Kant calls the schematism of the pure understanding. In this way we give objective reality, or sense and significance, to the pure categories.[6]

---

[1] A 141 = B 180-1. Compare A 78 = B 103.

[2] The fact that we have to divine the schematism *from nature* suggests that it is not noumenal.   [3] A 140 = B 179.

[4] '*Exhibitio*' or '*Darstellung*'; see *Fortschritte der Metaphysik* (*Phil. Bib.* 46c, pp. 106-7, 157, and 165). Compare A 713 = B 741 and also (for perhaps a rather different usage) A 727 = B 755.

[5] Compare A 136 = B 175.

[6] In the case of the Ideas of Reason there is no schematism, but only a symbolisation by analogy (sometimes called analogical or

I take it that by 'schematism' Kant means primarily, not the reflective exhibition of the pure category which takes place in the *Kritik* itself, but the unreflective exhibition which takes place in ordinary experience. It is this unreflective procedure which is 'a hidden art in the depths of the human soul'.

There is one other, and rather obscure, passage to be mentioned.[1] The schematism of the understanding through the transcendental synthesis of imagination is said to result in[2] the unity of all the manifold of intuition in inner sense, and so indirectly in the unity of apperception as a function which corresponds to inner sense (a receptivity).[3] Kant must mean, I think, that the schematism of the understanding supplies us, not with intuitions corresponding to the pure category,[4] but with kinds of unity (or combination) in intuitions; and that it is these kinds of unity (or combination) of the temporal and spatial manifold which correspond to the pure categories. We may regard these different kinds of unity as aspects of the one necessary synthetic unity of all the manifold in inner sense; and the one necessary synthetic unity of all the manifold in inner sense corresponds to the necessary synthetic unity of apperception. Indeed the necessary synthetic unity of apperception finds its concrete embodiment only in the necessary synthetic unity of the manifold given in time and space.[5]

symbolic schematism), an indirect (as opposed to a direct) exhibition of the concept; compare the passages in the *Fortschritte der Metaphysik* given above and also *K.d.U.* § 59 (V 351).

[1] A 145 = B 185.

[2] '*hinauslaufe.*' This word seems obscure in the present passage: it can hardly have its more common meaning of 'being equivalent to'.

[3] Compare statements about the transcendental synthesis of imagination in A 118, A 123, and B 151; also A 119. See especially Chapter XXXVI § 7.

[4] Other kinds of exhibition supply us with intuitions corresponding to the concept.

[5] Hence the schematism may be said 'to result in' the unity of apperception 'indirectly'. Compare Kant's statement that the schematism is 'the synthesis of the understanding when it determines inner sense in accordance with the unity of apperception'; see *Nachträge* LVII. Compare also the statement that the schematism concerns appearances and *their mere form*; see A 141 = B 180.

The schematism of the understanding, it appears, must work 'through the transcendental synthesis of imagination'. So far as it differs from this synthesis, it must do so in virtue of the fact that it involves a judgement (however 'obscure') that the product of the transcendental synthesis is an instance or 'case' to which the pure category applies. It must be present whenever we judge that A is the cause of B, and indeed whenever we make any judgement of experience. Needless to say, it is not made explicit in ordinary experience. What Kant is attempting to give is an analysis of elements which must be present in experience as such, not a description of experience as it appears to the unreflective mind, and still less a description of the successive stages which precede experience or are found in experience.

§ 5. *Value of Kant's Doctrine*

Kant's doctrine, if we view it as a whole, has little or nothing of that perversity commonly attributed to him by his critics. His fundamental contention that judgement as such requires a synthesis of the given manifold is perfectly sound, and it is not unreasonable to suppose that judgement as such requires certain *definite* kinds of synthesis. To accept the forms of judgement in Formal Logic as giving us an infallible clue to these definite kinds of synthesis is certainly a trifle ingenuous. Yet even here it is possible to maintain that the principles of synthesis which Kant finds by this method are really involved in all judgement as such; and I am inclined to believe that we are justified in taking this as the correct expression of his own view. The theory that the forms of judgement are forms of analytic judgements only, and are nevertheless the source of principles of synthesis, is undoubtedly perverse; but this perversity is entirely the creation of the commentators and has nothing whatever to do with Immanuel Kant. To treat the derivation of the categories from the forms of judgement as wrong-headed and inexcusable pedantry indicates, to my mind, only the failure of the critic to think himself into Kant's point of view.

In any case if we start from this derivation of the categories, an account of the transcendental schemata is absolutely essential to the consistent development of the theory. Kant would merely display incompetence as a thinker, if his account of the schemata had no relation to his derivation of the categories, however perverse that derivation might be. It is unreasonable to blame a man twice over for the same mistake; and to condemn him because his argument is consistent with his premises is wholly unjustifiable.

The doctrine of the schemata is not the result of formalism or of a so-called 'architectonic': it is a necessary part of his argument. Indeed even if we attribute his derivation of the categories to formalism in a bad sense, we ought to recognise that in his account of the schemata and of the Principles Kant is breaking away from mere formalism. He is deriving the categorial characteristics of objects from the fact that all objects must be temporal; and in this there is surely a considerable measure of truth. The connexion of the categories with the synthesis of imagination and the form of time is the most important, and the least artificial, part of the Critical Philosophy. We must not allow the difficulties of an unfamiliar and antiquated terminology to obscure the real significance of the argument.

My own complaint about this chapter is not that it follows too closely the pedantic methods of the schools, but on the contrary that it is too brief, and is lacking in clarity and precision. The schemata are obscurely described, and their connexion with the corresponding category receives no elucidation.

If we have patience with Kant's elaborate terminology, which is the terminology of his time and not of ours, and if we make allowances for a carelessness at least partly excused by the circumstances in which he wrote, I think we shall see that it is the connexion between form of judgement and category and schema which clamps together his whole argument into the firmly knit structure which it was intended to be. One part of that structure—the account of the forms of judgement given by Formal Logic—has now crumbled, and the whole

edifice may therefore seem to be in ruins, unless we admit
the possibility of reconstruction on the lines I have suggested.
But even at the worst we ought to recognise that ruin has
resulted, not because the building was so loosely put together,
but because the different parts were so closely and firmly
joined. The failure, if it be a failure, is due not so much to
the incompetence of the architect as to the use of materials,
hitherto believed to be sound, which have proved unable to
withstand the march of time.

§ 6. *The Possibility of Reconstruction*

Kant's doctrine rests upon two main foundations, firstly
the forms of judgement, and secondly the transcendental
synthesis of space and time. It is possible that the second
may stand, even if the first has been undermined. The transcendental schemata are not deduced from the forms of judgement, but from the nature of time.

If we cease to lay stress upon the different forms of judgement, and refuse to admit the possibility that these forms
may be involved in judgement as such, we shall certainly
lose something which Kant believed to be of importance,
particularly, as I have pointed out,[1] in regard to the category
of cause and effect. Yet on the other hand there might still
be much which we could retain. We might still retain the view
that judgement is necessary in order that there may be objects
for us, and that judgement presupposes the unity of apperception and demands a corresponding unity in the empirical
manifold. If we accept this, we may still hold also that the
required unity is imposed by the transcendental synthesis
of the imagination, which combines the given manifold in
one time in accordance with the demand of thought. It seems
to me obvious that this implies the necessity of certain categorial
characteristics in all objects: we have only to await a further
description of these characteristics and a satisfactory proof
that without them the world as known to us would be in-

---

[1] See § 2 above.

compatible with the unity of time. Hence we can still approach Kant's Principles in the hope of discovering a proof of the necessity of certain categorial characteristics; for his proofs rest, not upon the forms of judgement, but upon the unity of time. The appeal made to the forms of judgement serves only to enrich some of the categories and to guarantee the completeness of Kant's list; and the latter point is quite certainly a mistake.

It must be added, however, that Kant is hampered throughout by his attempt to restrict the schemata to the form of time. This attempt is based on the view that space is the form of outer sense only, while time as the form of inner sense is the ultimate condition, not merely of inner, but also of outer, intuition. If we are to make a satisfactory doctrine, we shall have to work with space and time (or perhaps space-time), and it is clear that Kant's own mind was steadily working in this direction: space is not wholly neglected even in the first edition, and it becomes much more prominent in the second. Such a development of Kant's view will certainly give rise to new difficulties; for it may tempt us to regard the mind itself as spatial, and this will have consequences which Kant at least is not prepared to accept. But even in Kant's own doctrine there are many puzzles about the mind, which it is doubtful if he ever solved.[1]

[1] Professor Alexander's derivation of the categories in *Space, Time, and Deity* is, I think, partly an attempt to improve and develop Kant's doctrine along the lines suggested by the second edition of the *Kritik*. He accepts the theory that the mind is spatial as well as temporal, but I think that this leads to views of freedom and immortality which are fundamentally opposed to the views of Kant.

BOOK VIII

THE PRINCIPLES
OF THE UNDERSTANDING

CHAPTER XXXV

THE SUPREME PRINCIPLE OF SYNTHETIC JUDGEMENTS

§ 1. *The Nature of Kant's Argument*

The Principles of the Understanding set forth the main positive conclusions of Kant's metaphysic of experience; that is to say, they are the ultimate synthetic *a priori* judgements which we are entitled to make about objects of experience. To estimate their value we must understand, not only the nature of the proof by which they are established, but also their place in Kant's argument as a whole.

The Metaphysical Deduction has shown, according to Kant, that the categories are derived from the forms of judgement; and the Transcendental Deduction on its objective side has demonstrated the objective validity of categories so derived. The Transcendental Deduction on its subjective side showed generally that the transcendental synthesis of imagination imposes the principles of synthesis thought in the pure categories upon appearances given under the form of time; but no attempt was made to deal with the separate categories, or to determine the special nature of the link which connected each category with objects. This link has been treated in the chapter on Schematism, where Kant has maintained that corresponding to each category there is a sensuous condition, or schema, which entitles us to apply the category to objects in a synthetic *a priori* judgement.[1] It is now our task to establish such a synthetic *a priori* judgement for each category. Each of these synthetic *a priori* judgements is called a Principle of the Understanding.

The argument is complicated by the difference between the pure category and the schematised category. If we look at Kant's Principles we see that what they affirm of objects is the

---

[1] A 148 = B 187.

schematised category.[1] Kant himself says[2] that appearances
must be subsumed, not directly[3] under the categories, but
under their schemata;[4] and the lack of homogeneity between
appearance and category indicates that the subsumption—
that is, the direct subsumption—of appearances under the
categories is impossible.[5] The very fact that the Principles are
principles of the *empirical* use of the categories implies that
they are concerned with the schematised, and not with the
pure, categories.[6]

For reasons already given I do not think that subsumption
under the category by means of the schema involves a syllogism.[7]
Kant's exposition is not sufficiently clear, but the easiest interpretation seems to be that the chapter on Schematism shows
how the categories must be schematised, while the Principles
show how the schematised categories must apply to all objects
of experience.[8]

There is an obvious difficulty in the fact that the Principles
have to be 'proved'. The assertion of the Principles is the
work, not of reason, but of judgement; and the Principles,
although they are grounds of other judgements, are not
themselves grounded in higher, or more general, judge-

[1] This fact is obscured by Kant's use of 'substance' and 'cause
and effect' as names for the pure categories; but the pure categories
have strictly no reference to time, and the categories proved in the
Analogies, as in all the other Principles, must have a reference to time.
[2] A 181 = B 223; compare Chapter XL § 3.   [3] 'schlechthin.'
[4] This applies to all the Principles, but preeminently to the
Analogies. Kant adds that in the Principle we do indeed make use
of the category, but in its application to appearances we set the schema
in its place, or rather set the schema alongside the category as a
restricting condition (A 181 = B 224). In other words the Principles
use the category only as schematised.   [5] A 137 = B 176.
[6] Compare A 180-1 = B 223. The empirical use of the categories
is their use with regard to objects of experience; see Chapter XI § 4.
In A 161 = B 200 the Principles are said to be rules for the objective
use of the categories. The only legitimate objective use of the categories
is their empirical use.   [7] See Chapter XXXIV § 1.
[8] Hence the Analytic of Principles is not concerned with the principles laid down in the Aesthetic in regard to space and time; still
less is it concerned with the principles of mathematics. See A 149 =
B 188-9 and A 159-60 = B 198-9, and compare Chapter XXXVI § 1.

ments.[1] Hence the 'proof' of the Principles must have a very special character. A Principle cannot be inferred from something else that we know about objects: it is itself the basis of all our knowledge of objects. The proof of it depends on our seeing that without it all knowledge of objects would be impossible;[2] and Kant very properly feels himself obliged to explain the nature of his proof, and to set forth what he calls 'the supreme principle of all synthetic judgements'.

§ 2. *The Principle of Analytic Judgements*

In order to avoid misunderstanding[3] Kant first of all explains the supreme principle of analytic judgements. This is the law of non-contradiction, which he expresses in the form 'Nothing can have a predicate which contradicts it'.[4]

The purpose of this formula is to avoid reference to time, such as is found in the statement that a thing cannot both be and not be at the same time,[5] or that A cannot at the same time be both B and not-B.[6] A statement of this kind is defective; for a logical principle is not restricted to temporal relations. The reason for a formulation which refers to time is the fact of change, which means that the same thing can have contradictory predicates, not at the same time, but successively. In such a case, however, the predicates are incompatible with one another, but not with the concept of the subject to which they apply. It is only because both predicates are separated from the subject-concept that we have to say they cannot be attributed to the subject at the same time. If the first predicate is really a part of the subject-concept, the second predicate cannot be attributed to the subject at all.[7]

[1] A 148 = B 188. The German word for Principles (*Grundsätze*) is itself an indication of this.
[2] A 149 = B 188. The proof cannot be carried further 'objectively', and must be derived from 'the subjective sources of the possibility of knowledge of an object in general'. To say this is to say that it must be a transcendental proof.   [3] A 150 = B 189.
[4] A 151 = B 190.   [5] A 152 = B 191.   [6] A 152 = B 192.
[7] Thus we can say 'No *unlearned man* is learned', while we can say only 'No *man* can be both learned and unlearned at the same time'. See A 153 = B 192.

All judgements, whether analytic or synthetic, must conform to the principle of non-contradiction, which is a universal, though negative, condition of truth.[1] If a judgement is not in conformity with this principle, it is false; but if it is in conformity with this principle, it need not be true.[2]

In the special case of analytic judgements conformity of the judgement to the principle of non-contradiction is a guarantee of truth.[3] Given a subject-concept, we can make analytic judgements by the principle of non-contradiction alone. Hence the principle of non-contradiction is a *sufficient* principle of all analytic judgements. It is their highest or supreme principle, because we require no other.[4]

§ 3. *Different Kinds of Synthetic Judgement*

The primary concern of Transcendental Logic, as indeed of the whole Critical Philosophy, is with synthetic *a priori* judgements, whose origin, objective validity, extent, and limits it seeks to determine.[5] Nevertheless Kant attempts to formulate the supreme principle of *all* synthetic judgements, and we must suppose that this principle is meant to cover *a posteriori*, as well as *a priori*, synthetic judgements. He is, however, less interested in the former than in the latter, and this makes it

---

[1] A 151 = B 190. Compare A 152 = B 191 for synthetic judgements.

[2] Compare Chapter IX § 2.

[3] A 151 = B 190–1. It should be noted that Kant is assuming the subject-concept to refer to an object. Compare also A 736 = B 764.

[4] This doctrine offers not the slightest justification for supposing that the laws of thought or the forms of judgement belong for Kant only to analytic judgements. On the contrary the law of non-contradiction, as he points out in A 150 = B 189 and A 152 = B 191, applies to all judgements (including synthetic judgements); and so does his account of the forms of judgement. Kant, it should be noted, asserts in A 154 = B 193 that Formal Logic has nothing to do with the problem of explaining the possibility of synthetic judgements, and should not even know the *name* of such judgements. This implies, and I think correctly, that the distinction between analytic and synthetic judgements does not arise for Formal Logic at all. Kemp Smith takes the 'name' to be the name of the *problem*, but the general result is much the same.

[5] Compare A XII, A 10, B 23, A 57 = B 81, A 154 = B 193.

difficult to disentangle his exposition. It is not always certain whether he is speaking of all synthetic judgements or only of synthetic *a priori* judgements; and his view of synthetic *a posteriori* judgements is not made sufficiently clear.

We should naturally expect to find a common principle at work in all synthetic judgements, just because they are synthetic; but Kant regards the different kinds of synthetic judgement as connected by something more than being species of the same genus.

It will be remembered that in his first account of synthetic judgements he suggested that the problem of synthetic *a posteriori* judgements was capable of a simple solution.[1] Such judgements are dependent upon further intuition of the object referred to in the subject-concept, and so are justified by our complete *experience* of the object. I see no sign that Kant ever modified this belief, which is obviously true; but we have since learnt that such experience of objects is impossible apart from the application of the categories to given intuitions.[2] The justification of such application is to be found only in the Principles of the Understanding, which are themselves synthetic *a priori* judgements; and Kant believes that synthetic *a posteriori* judgements presuppose the Principles of the Understanding and consequently presuppose the ultimate principle which is embodied in them.

The Principles of the Understanding are not the only synthetic *a priori* judgements, and here again it is at times uncertain whether Kant is speaking of all synthetic *a priori* judgements or only of the Principles. I think we can say both that the Principles are presupposed by all other synthetic *a priori* judgements, and also that one and the same general principle is at work in the Principles and in other synthetic *a priori* judgements, such as those of mathematics.

---

[1] A 8, B 12. Compare Chapter III § 8.
[2] When we judge that this white sugar is also sweet, we are presupposing that we have before us an object which is a substance with accidents and so on.

To sum up—Kant's account deals mainly, but not entirely,[1] with the principle of synthetic *a priori* judgements; and he is concerned above all with the way in which this principle is manifested in those synthetic *a priori* judgements which he calls the Principles of the Understanding. Nevertheless his account is, I think, intended to give the supreme principle, not only of all synthetic *a priori* judgements, but of all synthetic judgements without exception.

§ 4. *The 'Third Thing'*

Kant begins his account by a general statement which does apply to synthetic judgements of every kind. In all synthetic judgements the predicate-concept falls outside the subject-concept, and we must pass beyond the subject-concept, which is supposed to be given.[2] In order so to pass we require 'something else', or a 'third thing', to justify our synthesis of subject and predicate.[3] We have consequently to ask what is the 'third thing' which is the 'medium' of *all* synthetic judgements.

The key to the problem is to be found in the Transcendental Deduction. Kant therefore begins his enquiry by a summary statement of his previous conclusions.[4] There is only one whole[5] in which all our ideas are contained. This whole is inner sense and its form, which is time. The synthesis of our ideas in time depends on imagination, and the unity of this synthesis[6]

[1] In A 155 = B 194, where he asserts that the possibility of synthetic judgements is to be found in sense, imagination, and apperception, he is manifestly referring to all synthetic judgements, and not only to synthetic *a priori* judgements; for he adds that the possibility of *pure* synthetic judgements is *also* to be found in sense, imagination, and apperception, because these are sources of *a priori* ideas. There are also other passages which refer to all synthetic judgements, but there is no attempt to deal with synthetic *a posteriori* judgements by themselves.   [2] Compare A 6 = B 10 and Chapter III § 5.

[3] A 155 = B 194. Here we have a 'third thing' which manifestly does not involve a syllogism.   [4] A 155 = B 194.

[5] '*Es ist nur ein Inbegriff.*' Mellin's emendation '*Es gibt nur einen Inbegriff*' seems to me unnecessary.

[6] The word '*derselben*' refers, I think, to 'the synthesis of ideas' rather than to 'ideas' as in Kemp Smith's translation. Compare A 158 = B 197.

(a unity which is required for judgement) depends upon the unity of apperception. Hence it is by reference to the three powers of inner sense, imagination, and apperception that we must seek to explain the possibility of all synthetic judgements. And since all three powers are the sources of *a priori* ideas,[1] it is by reference to these powers that we must seek to explain the possibility of synthetic *a priori* judgements. Indeed synthetic *a priori* judgements based on these sources[2] are not only possible, but also necessary, if we are to have a knowledge of objects which rests solely on the synthesis of ideas. Such a knowledge of objects is synthetic *a priori* knowledge :[3] it can take no account of the empirical matter of experience, but only of its form, that is, of its synthetic unity.[4]

The implication of these statements is that in order to make synthetic judgements we require, in addition to the subject-concept, a knowledge of the object[5] to which the subject-concept refers. Such knowledge, as Kant has pointed out, depends on the three powers of inner sense, imagination, and apperception. He now proceeds to examine this knowledge from the side of the object.

If any cognition is to have what Kant calls 'objective reality',[6] that is, if it is to be knowledge of an object, the object must

[1] Inner sense is the source of the pure intuition of time, imagination is the source of the transcendental schemata, and apperception is the source of the pure categories; compare A 94. All three powers are involved in every synthetic *a priori* judgement, and indeed in every synthetic judgement.

[2] Note that it is synthetic *a priori* judgements (and not the three powers, as in Kemp Smith's translation) which are necessary. The phrase '*aus diesen Gründen*' is puzzling. I incline to take '*Gründen*' not as 'reasons', but as the 'grounds' or 'sources' (*Quellen*) of *a priori* ideas. If we interpret the phrase as signifying 'for these reasons', it must mean 'because these three powers are sources of *a priori* ideas'.

[3] Knowledge which rests on the synthesis of ideas is synthetic knowledge. Knowledge which rests solely (*lediglich*) on the synthesis of ideas is synthetic *a priori* knowledge: it does not rest partly on given sensations, but contains 'nothing except what is necessary for synthetic unity of experience in general' (A 158 = B 197). Such synthetic unity involves the three powers which are said to be sources of *a priori* ideas.   [4] Compare A 156-7 = B 196.

[5] Compare A 157 = B 196.   [6] A 155 = B 194.

be capable of being *given* in some way or other. Apart from given objects our concepts are empty; and although we can *think* by means of such concepts, thinking of this kind is not knowledge but a mere play of ideas. The difficulty is to explain the exact sense in which objects are 'given'.

Kant's explanation is too compressed to be clear. To be given, an object must be immediately exhibited in intuition: it is not enough that it should be given mediately.[1] Apart from immediate intuition no object can be given; but Kant is seeking a general formula which will cover the way in which objects are given both when we make synthetic *a posteriori*, and when we make synthetic *a priori*, judgements. He therefore says that *to give an object is to relate the idea[2] of the object to experience*, either to actual or to possible experience.

We may take the 'idea' of the object to be the *concept* of the object. Where this concept is empirical, it must be related to actual experience. Where the concept is *a priori*, it must be related to possible experience. Only in this way can we show that a concept is the concept of an object which is, or can be, given.

In what sense is the concept 'related' to experience? An empirical concept is related to experience when it is borrowed or derived from experience,[3] when in short we can indicate an object of experience containing the combination of marks which is thought in the concept.[4] An *a priori* concept is related to experience when it is a concept of the conditions (or the form)

---

[1] Kant does not explain what he means by 'given mediately'. I take it that an object might be said to be given mediately in a concept: for example, the concept of chimaera refers to a describable object, but unless the object can be given immediately to intuition, the concept does not refer to a real object, and the use of the concept in mere thinking cannot give us knowledge.

[2] '*Vorstellung.*' Kant must have in mind primarily concepts, but the wider word 'idea' may be used because he is thinking also of the ideas of space and time, which are intuitions although he describes them as concepts.   [3] Compare A 220 = B 267.

[4] We need not have actually experienced the object ourselves: it is sufficient if it is connected, by means of the Analogies, with objects we have actually experienced.

of experience. In this case the concept is related to possible experience; for experience is possible only if it conforms to such conditions.[1] Although the concept of such conditions is *a priori*, it nevertheless 'belongs' to experience, because its object can be found in experience alone.[2]

Kant's main point is that *a priori* concepts can have objective reality or validity only if we can prove that they must necessarily apply to all objects of experience;[3] and we can prove this only by showing that they contain or express the necessary conditions of experience, to which all objects of experience must conform. He illustrates his point by the examples of space and time, which strictly speaking are not pure concepts but pure intuitions.[4] Even in their case his principle holds. Our ideas of space and time have objective validity, because we can show that objects must be spatial and temporal;[5] for space and time as conditions (or forms) of intuition are conditions of experience. He adds that our idea of space and time is in itself a mere schema: it is dependent on the reproductive imagination which calls up the objects of experience, and apart from them it would have no meaning.[6]

We may conclude provisionally that the 'third thing' which makes synthetic judgements possible is experience—actual experience if the judgement is empirical,[7] and possible experience if the judgement is *a priori*.

[1] Compare Chapter XLIX § 6.

[2] See A 220 = B 267. Its object is an 'object in general' so far as that object conforms to the conditions of experience.

[3] Mathematical concepts, however, apply necessarily only to *some* objects of experience; but they too express a possibility contained in the conditions of experience.

[4] A 156 = B 195.   [5] Compare B 147.

[6] This statement should be taken as qualifying the doctrine provisionally stated in A 24 = B 38–9 and A 31 = B 46. Although our intuitions of space and time are completely *a priori*, we can separate them from experience only by an act of abstraction, and apart from their relation to experience they would be mere 'phantoms of the brain'.

[7] Compare A 8 and B 12. Even this, as we shall see later, presupposes the forms or conditions under which alone is experience possible.

§ 5. *The Possibility of Experience*

Although Kant is professedly dealing with all synthetic judgements, his main interest is directed to synthetic *a priori* judgements. He sums up his position by saying that it is *the possibility of experience* which gives objective reality to all our *a priori* cognitions.[1]

The phrases 'possible experience' and 'possibility of experience' are thus treated as equivalent, but Kant indicates that it is the second phrase which best expresses his meaning.[2] The 'third thing' is not just some experience or other which we might possibly have: it is rather the form of experience itself or the necessary conditions without which no experience is possible. We should indeed get into logical puzzles if we identified the possibility of experience with the form (or the conditions) of experience;[3] but we can say that so far as experience has the form of experience it is possible, and so far as it is possible it has the form of experience.

What then is the form upon which experience depends for its possibility? The form of experience is the synthetic unity of appearances, and experience is possible only if it 'rests' on a synthesis which conforms to the categories[4] and to the unity of apperception. Without this there would be no experience or knowledge, but a mere 'rhapsody' of sense-perceptions.

Hence experience has certain principles as the *a priori* basis of its form.[5] These are the Principles of the Understanding, and they are universal rules of unity in the synthesis of appear-

[1] A 156 = B 195. For the possibility of experience see also Chapter XLIX § 6.   [2] A 157 = B 196.

[3] Compare such questions as whether beauty can, or can not, be identified with coherence (or harmony).

[4] The categories are here called 'concepts of the object of appearances in general'. This description may be intended to indicate that the categories in question are the schematised categories. Similarly the synthetic unity of appearances is a synthetic unity in space and time.

[5] A 156 = B 196. 'Form', I think, does not go with 'principles', as in Kemp Smith's translation, but rather with '*a priori zum Grunde liegen*'. These principles are the *a priori* basis of the form of experience because they express the conditions of experience and of its objects.

ances, rules which state the ways in which appearances must be combined in all experience. Inasmuch as these rules state the necessary conditions of experience, their objective reality can always be shown in ˙experience, and indeed in the very possibility of experience.[1]

The same doctrine holds, not only for the Principles of the Understanding, but for all synthetic *a priori* judgements. Unless they were related to possible experience (in the sense of describing the conditions of experience), they would be impossible; for they would have no 'third thing', that is, no object,[2] in relation to which the synthetic unity of concepts (which is affirmed in the judgement) can exhibit objective reality.[3]

Kant illustrates his point by the example of mathematical judgements.[4] We do not need experience to make synthetic *a priori* judgements about space in general[5] or about the figures which productive imagination describes in it. Nevertheless we should be occupying ourselves with a mere phantom of

[1] Kemp Smith's translation wrongly attaches 'the possibility of experience' to 'conditions'. For the idiom compare '*auf dieser ihre Möglichkeit*' a few lines further down.

[2] The conditions of experience are also conditions of the objects of experience.

[3] The German is '*an dem die synthetische Einheit ihrer Begriffe objektive Realität dartun könnte*'. Vaihinger's emendation (accepted by Kemp Smith) substitutes after *Einheit* '*die objektive Realität ihrer Begriffe*'. This misses the whole point of the argument. We are here concerned, not with the objective reality of the separate concepts employed in the judgement, but with the objective reality of their union which is affirmed in the judgement. Compare below 'the objective validity of their synthesis', that is, of the synthesis present in pure synthetic judgements.

[4] A 157 = B 196; compare A 159–60 = B 198–9.

[5] I take these to be such judgements as 'Space has three dimensions'. Kant may have in mind also the judgements in the Aesthetic, but it is unsafe to hold this in the absence of an explicit statement. The judgements in the Aesthetic are synthetic *a priori* judgements; but I am not sure whether Kant would say of them, as he does of mathematical judgements, that they relate *mediately* to experience, unless he means that they relate *immediately* to outer intuition (which is only an element in experience). If he had in mind the Aesthetic, we should expect a reference to time also.

the brain, unless we could regard space as the condition of appearances, and so of outer experience. Hence these synthetic *a priori* judgements also are related to possible experience, or rather to the possibility of experience,[1] and on this alone do they base the objective validity of their synthesis; but this relation is mediate, since the mathematician deals with space in abstraction and need not judge that it is the condition of outer intuition and so of all outer experience.[2] In the case of the Principles this relation is immediate, since they affirm directly what are the necessary conditions of experience.

The conclusion of this discussion can now be formulated. 'Experience, as empirical synthesis, is *in its possibility* the only kind of knowledge which can give reality to every other synthesis'.[3] This must mean that the possibility of empirical experience alone can give objective validity to every other synthesis. We may take 'every other synthesis' to mean 'every *a priori* synthesis';[4] but in view of what follows[5] I am inclined to think it means 'the synthesis of concepts in judgements'.[6] When this synthesis is an *a priori* cognition, that is, when it is a synthetic *a priori* judgement, it has truth[7] (or agreement with the object) only so far as it contains nothing save what is necessary for the synthetic unity of experience in general.[8]

[1] Notice Kant's preference for the latter phrase.

[2] Kant does not explain what he means here by 'mediate'. He explains later that mathematics depends primarily upon pure intuition; but its application to experience, and therefore its objective validity, depends upon pure understanding; see A 160 = B 199. If so, it depends upon the Principles of the Understanding, and not merely upon the Aesthetic. Compare also A 149 = B 189, where the possibility of mathematical judgements is said to be made intelligible by the principles of the Understanding.   [3] A 157 = B 196.

[4] This is Kemp Smith's view in his translation.

[5] The formulation of the principle of *all* synthetic judgements.

[6] Compare 'the synthetic unity of concepts' and 'the objective validity of their synthesis' above. Every synthetic judgement is a synthesis of concepts; and Kant is saying that experience *in its possibility* gives reality to all synthetic judgements.

[7] This is equivalent to 'objective reality' or 'objective validity'.

[8] Compare A 118, A 123, B 151, and A 145 = B185; also Chapter XXIX § 7. It may be objected that mathematical judgements contain more than this; for they state the conditions of a *particular* experience,

In other words synthetic *a priori* judgements have objective
validity only in so far as they express the necessary conditions
(or form) of experience and are thus related to the possibility
of experience.

If I am right in interpreting the phrase 'every other synthesis'
to cover synthetic *a posteriori* as well as synthetic *a priori*
judgements, then Kant is maintaining that for all synthetic
judgements without exception, the possibility of experience is
the 'third thing' which gives them objective validity. The actual
experience which justifies our synthetic *a posteriori* judgements
does so, not in virtue of mere sensation, but in virtue of those
conditions of synthetic unity without which no experience is
possible.[1]

It is unfortunate that Kant does not deal more explicitly
with synthetic *a posteriori* judgements. It is also unfortunate
that he does not give separate treatment to the judgements
of the Aesthetic[2] as well as to the judgements of mathematics
and the Principles of the Understanding. There too we have
synthetic *a priori* judgements which depend upon the possibility
of experience. They do so in the obvious sense that they affirm
space and time to be forms of sensibility and necessary conditions of intuition, and so of experience. But I think they do so
also in a deeper sense; for they depend upon the necessary
synthetic unity of experience which is expressed in the Principles of the Understanding.[3] This could not be made clear
in the Aesthetic,[4] because Kant was considering pure intuition
in abstraction from the rest of experience, and because a complicated system of philosophy cannot be explained in a few
pages. Nevertheless even the judgements of the Aesthetic,
since they depend upon the possibility of experience, depend

that of triangles, circles and so on. Nevertheless their objective
validity for Kant depends only on the fact that the space with whose
particular determinations they deal is a condition of experience in
general.

[1] Compare B 142.

[2] They are mentioned in A 149 = B 188, but only in order to mark
them off from the Principles of the Understanding.

[3] Compare A 149 = B 188–9.   [4] Compare B 160–1 n.

upon the Principles of the Understanding, which set forth the form, or the necessary synthetic unity, of experience in general.[1] We do well to remember that the Principles of the Understanding are formulated in the light of all that has gone before. In setting forth the necessary form of experience they are concerned, not only with the pure categories, but also with the transcendental synthesis of imagination and the forms of space and time.[2] They state the conditions of the possibility of experience. and so have themselves objective validity. And all other synthetic judgements without exception have objective validity in virtue of the possibility of experience whose conditions are adequately and explicitly expressed in the Principles alone.

§ 6. *The Principle of All Synthetic Judgements*

In the light of these considerations Kant formulates the supreme principle of *all* synthetic judgements: *Every object stands under the necessary conditions of the synthetic unity of the manifold of intuition in a possible experience.*[3]

This formula expresses Kant's supreme principle from the side of the object. It is another way of saying that synthetic judgements can have objective validity only from their relation to the possibility of experience.

It should now be clear that this formula applies to synthetic *a posteriori* judgements. These are made in virtue of actual

[1] A 156–7 = B 195–6. For this reason it is, I think, possible, but not certain, that Kant has in mind the judgements of the Aesthetic, as well as those of mathematics, when he speaks of judgements which are related *mediately* to the possibility of experience.

[2] Compare A 158 = B 197 and also A 155 = B 194.

[3] A 158 = B 197. We may be tempted to abbreviate the formula and say, more simply, that every object must stand under the necessary conditions of a possible experience. Kant, however, wishes to indicate that these conditions are all involved in the necessary synthetic unity of the manifold of intuition, a necessary synthetic unity which constitutes the essential character of all objects of experience; compare A 105, A 109, B 137, etc. The paragraph which follows in regard to synthetic *a priori* judgements shows that these conditions are not to be taken in abstraction from one another.

experience of an object, as Kant never ceases to hold; but in them we presuppose that their object stands under the necessary conditions of a possible experience as formulated in the Principles of the Understanding. Apart from such a presupposition we should have before us, at the most, a stream of momentary appearances, and we should be unable to make any synthetic judgements at all.

Kant himself makes no special reference to synthetic *a posteriori* judgements. His attention is concentrated on synthetic *a priori* judgements. Since every object must stand under the conditions of possible experience, we can see that synthetic *a priori* judgements have objective validity[1] so far as they express the necessary conditions of a possible experience.

No attempt is here made to distinguish between the synthetic *a priori* judgements of mathematics, of the Aesthetic, and of the Analytic; and I need not raise again the questions already discussed. I take Kant to refer to all synthetic *a priori* judgements without exception, though he may have in mind primarily the judgements of the Analytic. If we are to understand the objective validity of any kind of synthetic *a priori* judgement, we must 'relate the formal conditions of *a priori* intuition, the synthesis of imagination, and the necessary unity of this synthesis in a transcendental apperception to a possible experiential knowledge[2] in general'; that is to say, we must perform that analysis of the conditions of experience which has been set forth by Kant in the *Kritik* and especially in the Analytic. More simply, we must recognise that the conditions of *the possibility of experience* in general are also conditions of *the possibility of objects of experience*. This is the principle upon which the whole of the Transcendental Philosophy rests. It is the basis of the Transcendental Deduction[3] as it is

---

[1] In this passage—A 158 = B 197—when Kant says that synthetic *a priori* judgements 'are possible', he is clearly referring not to their logical, but to their real, possibility, that is, to their objective validity.

[2] '*Erfahrungserkenntnis.*'

[3] This is stated expressly in A 111 (compare also A 93 = B 125-6 and A 125-6), and it applies equally to the arguments in the first and second editions.

the basis of the separate proofs given for the Principles of the Understanding. And indeed it is the basis of all synthetic *a priori* judgements without exception; for, as we have seen, such judgements can have objective validity only so far as they express the necessary conditions of possible experience.[1]

[1] The judgements of the Analytic do so directly. The judgements of the Aesthetic perhaps do so also directly, but their full implication is made intelligible only in the Analytic; and it may be that they do so only indirectly, since (if we speak strictly) while they show space and time to be conditions of *intuition*, it is only in the Analytic that we understand space and time to be conditions of *experience* in general. The judgements of mathematics do so indirectly: they deal with determinations of space and time, but it remains for philosophy to show that space and time, and the synthesis of the given manifold in space and time, are conditions of experience.

CHAPTER XXXVI

THE PRINCIPLES OF THE UNDERSTANDING

§ 1. *Different Kinds of Principle*

The discussion of the principle of synthetic judgements is intended primarily to explain the nature of the proof which must be given for the Principles of the Understanding. The proof of these Principles is a matter of 'judgement', but Kant declines to regard them as self-evident.[1] They are proved, when they are shown to express the conditions of experience; and we can judge that they do express these conditions, only when we understand the part played by sense, imagination, and understanding as sources of knowledge.[2]

The Principles to be proved are concerned with the application of the categories, and this narrows the range of our present enquiry. Needless to say, it excludes all empirical principles. An 'empirical principle' is a contradiction in terms, for it is derived by generalisation from experience; and such generalisations, however universal they may be, are totally lacking in necessity, and particularly in that 'necessity according to concepts' which is the mark of the Principles of the Understanding.[3] The principles of the Aesthetic are also excluded, for they are concerned, not with the application of the categories, but with the conditions or forms of intuition.[4] And finally the principles of mathematics must be excluded, because they pass from intuitions to concepts and not from concepts to intuitions.[5] Nevertheless the possibility and objective validity

---

[1] Compare A 149 = B 188. The self-evident is commonly regarded as intelligible itself without reference to anything beyond itself, but the Principles are intelligible only in relation to experience. If we could not 'prove' the Principles by showing their relation to experience, they would incur the suspicion of being surreptitiously introduced.

[2] The proof is 'from the subjective sources of the possibility of a knowledge of the object in general'. See A 149 = B 188.

[3] A 159 = B 198. A principle, as an ἀρχή or *Grundsatz*, cannot be *derived* from anything else.   [4] A 149 = B 188.

[5] A 149 = B 188–9, A 159–60 = B 198–9, and A 712 = B 740 ff. Compare Chapter V § 8.

of the principles of mathematics depends upon the Principles
of the Understanding.[1]

In all this Kant is assuming that the categories are derived
from the forms of judgement, and so are products of pure
understanding.[2] Even if we reject this derivation, the distinction
between the different kinds of principle will still remain.
The proof of the Principles of the Understanding cannot be
intuitive like a mathematical proof,[3] but must be conceptual
or discursive, as we shall see below.[4]

§ 2. *The Principles of the Understanding*

Kant divides the Principles of the Understanding into
(1) Axioms of Intuition, (2) Anticipations of Sense-Perception,
(3) Analogies of Experience, and (4) Postulates of Empirical
Thought.[5] These correspond to the headings of quantity,
quality, relation, and modality, under which the categories
are arranged.[6]

[1] A 149 = B 189 and A 160 = B 199. The relevant Principles of
the Understanding are primarily the Axioms of Intuition and the
Anticipations of Sense-Perception.

[2] Note Kant's repetition of the distinction between understanding
as a lawgiver and understanding as a discoverer of laws. See A 126-7
and compare A 114 and B 165; also Chapter XXVII § 4. What are
ordinarily called the laws of nature are all subject to the Principles
of the Understanding, and this is why they convey a suggestion of
necessity.

[3] See especially A 719-20 = B 747-8. The difficulty that some of
the Principles have immediate or intuitive certainty (or 'evidence')
—see A 160 = B 199-200 and A 180 = B 223—is discussed in § 3 below.

[4] In § 3; compare also Chapter XXXII § 5. At present it is sufficient
to say that we cannot construct an object in *a priori* intuition for the
categories, as we can for mathematical concepts.

[5] These titles must not be thought to describe the Principles. We
have a Principle of Axioms, a Principle of Anticipations, and a
Principle of Analogies, but this does not mean that one Principle is
an axiom, another an anticipation, and another an analogy; compare
Chapter XXXVII § 7.

[6] A 161 = B 200. There is, it need hardly be said, nothing artificial
in the correspondence between the categories and the Principles. If
there were not such a correspondence, the whole of Kant's argument
would be absurd. The fact that the Axioms and Anticipations have
only one Principle each, while there are three Principles both for the

The categories of quantity and quality are concerned with the *objects* of intuition (both pure and empirical), while those of relation and modality are concerned with the *existence* of these objects in relation either to one another or to the understanding.[1] The categories of quantity and quality are called mathematical categories, and the corresponding Principles (the Axioms and Anticipations) are called the Mathematical Principles. The categories of relation and modality are called dynamical categories, and the corresponding Principles (the Analogies and Postulates) are called the Dynamical Principles.[2]

It must not be thought that the Mathematical Principles are principles of mathematics, or that the Dynamical Principles are principles of dynamics. All the Principles of the Understanding are supposed to be general, and are not restricted, as are the principles of geometry and dynamics, to objects of outer sense.[3] They are called Mathematical and Dynamical, because they account respectively for the possibility of mathematics and (physical) dynamics.[4]

Analogies and for the Postulates, is due to the fact that the Principles are concerned primarily with the schematised categories. The reason why there is only one schematised category of quantity and one of quality I have already explained in Chapter XXXIII § 7.

[1] B 110. In A 160 = B 199 Kant asserts that the mathematical principles concern mere *intuition*, and the dynamical principles concern the *existence* of an appearance in general. For reasons to be stated later, I think this way of expressing the distinction to be less satisfactory. See Chapter XXXVII § 5.

[2] See B 110 and A 162 = B 201.

[3] This is what Kant means when he says in A 162 = B 202 that the Principles are those of pure understanding in relation to inner sense (*without regard to the difference in the ideas given in inner sense*). The Principles do not exclude objects of outer sense, for all our ideas, even those of physical objects, belong as modifications of the mind to inner sense; see, for example, A 98–9. Time and inner sense are in the first edition stressed unduly at the expense of space and outer sense, but even in the first edition the Principles are concerned primarily with objects in space.

[4] A 162 = B 202. They are the presuppositions, rather than the principles, of mathematics and dynamics, and they find their chief application in these sciences. In the *Nachträge* LXIV–LXV, as given

In the second edition[1] Kant added a footnote, which is important as a statement of his technical terms. The Mathematical Principles deal with the synthesis of the homogeneous, a synthesis of homogeneous elements which do not necessarily belong to one another. Such a synthesis is divided into aggregation (the synthesis of extensive quantity) and coalition (the synthesis of intensive quantity). The Dynamical Principles deal with the synthesis of the heterogeneous, a synthesis of different elements which necessarily belong to one another, such as substance and accident, or cause and effect.

All this will become clearer when we study the Principles themselves.

§ 3. *Intuitive and Discursive Certainty*

Kant asserts that the Mathematical Principles possess intuitive certainty, while the Dynamical Principles possess only discursive certainty.[2]

by Benno Erdmann, Kant seems to express dissatisfaction with this division. The Mathematical Principles are divided into formal (the Axioms) and real (the Anticipations). The formal Principles are connected with pure and applied mathematics, and also according to Erdmann with dynamics; but it seems to me that this must be a misunderstanding of Kant's note, and that Kant must have intended to connect the real Principles (the Anticipations) with dynamics, as he does in *Nachträge* LXV and in the *Metaphysische Anfangsgründe der Naturwissenschaft*. The Analogies and Postulates are called *physiological*, and are divided into physical (the Analogies) and metaphysical (the Postulates), as in the footnote added in the second edition of the *Kritik* (B 201–2 n.). Rational 'physiology' is the philosophical science of *nature* (whether corporeal or spiritual); see A 846 = B 874, and *Metaphysik*, p. 12.

[1] B 201–2 n. Kant's Latin terms often throw light on the ordinary German expression.

[2] A 162 = B 201; compare A 160 = B 199–200 and A 180 = B 223. Intuitive or mathematical certainty (*intuitive Gewissheit* or *anschauende Gewissheit*) is called 'evidence' (*Evidenz*). See *Log. Einl.* IX (IX 70) and A 734 = B 762. '*Evidenz*' seems to be used in a more general sense in A 180 = B 223, but '*evident*' is used in the technical sense in A 733 = B 761. 'Certainty' is here 'objective certainty' (certainty for everyone): that is to say, the ground (*Erkenntnisgrund*) of these Principles is objectively (and not merely subjectively) adequate. See A 822 = B 850, A 820 = B 848, and *Log. Einl.* IX (IX 70).

In spite of this assertion intuitive certainty is usually said by Kant to belong to mathematics only, while philosophical certainty is always discursive.[1] *Philosophical* knowledge is *rational knowledge from concepts; mathematical* knowledge is *rational knowledge from the construction of concepts.*[2] A philosophical proof is always a proof by means of concepts, and so is discursive; a mathematical proof is by the construction of concepts and is intuitive.[3] Kant even says that axioms are synthetic *a priori* principles which possess immediate certainty, and that philosophy has no principles which deserve the name of axioms.[4] In other words, the synthetic *a priori* principles of philosophy never possess intuitive or immediate certainty.[5]

Unless I have overlooked one of Kant's subtle distinctions, we have here a contradiction, at least in words. At the same time there is a real difference between the proof of the Mathematical, and the proof of the Dynamical, Principles, and it is this real difference which Kant is trying to express. Perhaps the contradiction can be at least partly explained, if we

[1] *Log. Einl.* III and IX (IX 23 and 70–1). Compare A 734–5 = B 762–3.

[2] A 713 = B 741. Compare *Log. Einl.* III (IX 23). Rational knowledge is opposed to empirical knowledge: it is grounded not on experience, but on reason. To 'construct a concept' is to exhibit *a priori* the intuition which corresponds to the concept. We cannot construct an object for the categories in pure intuition: we can only show that, although they are not derived from experience, they express the necessary conditions of a possible experience.

[3] A 734–5 = B 762–3. Compare *Log. Einl.* III and IX (IX 23 and 70–1). A philosophical proof is also said to be 'acroamatic' because it uses words, not intuitions. Only a mathematical proof can be called a 'demonstration'; for 'demonstration' implies the use of intuition. This doctrine has a close affinity with Plato's account of the mathematical sciences and dialectic in the *Republic*.
Compare also A 714 = B 742: 'Philosophical knowledge considers the particular only in the universal; mathematical knowledge considers the universal in the particular, or rather in the individual, yet always *a priori* and by means of reason'. The whole passage should be consulted. [4] A 732 = B 760.

[5] Kant says expressly in A 733 = B 761 that even the principle of the Axioms of Intuition is not itself an axiom, but a principle derived from concepts.

remember the difference between the category and the schema.
The schema of extensive quantity (i.e. number[1]), and perhaps
even the schema of intensive quantity (i.e. degree[2]), can be
constructed in intuition *a priori*, and this may be the reason
why Kant says that the Mathematical Principles have intuitive
certainty.[3] I presume that the categories of quantity and
quality cannot be so constructed, and so far as these are
involved in the Mathematical Principles, the Mathematical
Principles, like all other Principles of the Understanding, have
only discursive certainty. In the case of the Dynamical Principles
there is no possibility of constructing even the transcendental
schemata, let alone the categories.

Kant himself implies that we are not yet in a position to
understand his doctrine in regard to this point.[4] He bases
this contention on the view that the Dynamical Principles
exhibit an *a priori* necessity only under the condition of empirical *thinking* in an experience: the Mathematical Principles are
unconditionally necessary.[5] The emphasis in this statement
appears to rest on the word 'thinking' (which I have italicized);
but the difficulty remains that even the Mathematical Principles
must be necessary only in relation to experience. Kant appears
to recognise this, and to suggest that a necessity in relation to
experience can be absolute or unconditioned; for he asserts
that the *a priori* conditions of *intuition* (with which the Mathematical Principles deal, and from which they derive their
character) are absolutely (*durchaus*) necessary *in relation to a
possible experience*. The Dynamical Principles have their
conditional necessity (in relation to empirical thinking), because
they deal with the conditions of the *existence* of objects of a
possible empirical intuition, and these conditions are in themselves contingent.[6] This is obscure, and I am uncertain of its

---

[1] For the construction of number, see A 724 = B 752.

[2] Such at least is Kant's own view in A 179 = B 221.

[3] As I have pointed out in Chapter X § 7, this does *not* mean that
there is no discursive or conceptual element present.

[4] A 161 = B 200.   [5] A 160 = B 199.

[6] 'Contingent' does not mean 'due to mere chance,' but 'necessary
under a condition'. See also A 766 = B 794.

precise meaning; but we can perhaps say at present that the unconditional necessity of the Mathematical Principles is due to the fact that these are concerned with objects primarily as appearances given to *intuition*, while the conditional necessity of the Dynamical Principles is due to the fact that they are concerned with objects primarily as *judged* to exist in time and space. The factor of intuition is dominant in the first case, the factor of thought in the second; but in both cases the necessity is derived from the relation of the Principles to a possible experience, which is always a combination of intuition and thought.[1]

§ 4. *The Proof of the Principles*

What then are we to say of the proof of the Principles? Whatever be the intuitive element involved in some cases, the proof is always a discursive proof, a proof from concepts, like all other proofs in philosophy;[2] but it is not for this reason either illegitimate or uncertain.

The Principles of the Understanding are synthetic *a priori* judgements and cannot be derived from mere analysis of concepts.[3] They cannot be proved by mathematical methods of construction, nor can they be proved *directly* from concepts, for in that case they would be mere dogmas.[4] If they can be proved at all, they must be proved *indirectly* from concepts.

[1] For the subsequent development of this doctrine, see A 178 = B 220 ff., and also A 216–17 = B 263–4. It may be added that the schemata of number and degree can be constructed because of their close connexion with intuition. Number and perhaps degree seem to be necessary for knowledge of time and space: the categories of relation have no meaning apart from change, which is simply an empirical fact; compare B 3. This is why the proposition 'Every change has its cause', although it is *a priori*, is not a *pure a priori* proposition.

[2] Compare especially A 719–20 = B 747–8 and A 722 = B 750.

[3] I have shown in Chapter X § 7 that discursive judgements are not necessarily analytic. Compare A 733 = B 761.

[4] A 736 = B 764. The philosophy which Kant condemns as *dogmatic* offers us synthetic *a priori* judgements which are supposed to arise directly from concepts and to apply to things-in-themselves. The only judgements which we can be justified in proving directly from concepts are, I take it, analytic judgements.

An indirect proof depends upon the relation of concepts to something wholly contingent, namely possible experience. The Principles of the Understanding can be apodeictically certain only if possible experience (or 'something' as an object of possible experience) is presupposed.[1] They are nevertheless properly called 'principles' (*Grundsätze*), because they have the peculiar property that they make possible the very experience which is their own ground of proof, and in experience itself they are always presupposed.[2]

This is the clearest expression in Kant of the doctrine which has already been set forth. Such a doctrine must always raise the question whether Kant's method of proof is, or is not, circular. To take the most important case, the case of causation, it would be (as I have already pointed out[3]) a vicious circle, if Kant argued that because we commonly assume causation in ordinary experience, therefore causation is a necessary condition of experience; and that because causation is a necessary condition of experience, therefore we are justified in our common assumption.

Kant's argument, whether it be right or wrong, does not merely accept our common-sense assumptions, and then argue that because these are present in experience, they must be the conditions of experience. What he assumes in his proof of the Principles is that for experience of objects (1) there must be sensuous intuitions given under the forms of time and space;

[1] A 736-7 = B 764-5. To say this is only to repeat what has already been said. We establish the Principles, not directly from the concepts which they employ, but by showing that these concepts express the conditions of possible experience, and consequently must apply to all objects of experience.

It may be observed that when Kant says that a proposition is apodeictically certain, he means that it is universally and *objectively* necessary (valid for all). It can be this only if its ground (*Erkenntnisgrund*) is objectively adequate. Apodeictic certainty is connected with rational certainty, the certainty of mathematics or of philosophy. But certainty can be rational and empirical at the same time, when, that is to say, we know an empirically certain proposition from *a priori* principles. There may therefore be apodeictic certainty even in connexion with an empirical truth. See *Log. Einl.* IX (IX 66 and 71).

[2] A 737 = B 765.   [3] Chapter XXX § 5.

(2) there must be an imaginative synthesis of such sensuous intuitions in one time and space; (3) there must be judgement.[1]
These assumptions, I suggest, are all sound, as is also the
assumption that if different objects are judged to belong to
one and the same objective world, they must be judged by
one and the same self.[2] The one doubtful assumption which he
makes is that all the forms of judgement, including the hypothetical, are essential to judgement as such; but this assumption
—although it undoubtedly increases his confidence in the
argument of the second Analogy and, as I have suggested above,[3]
is probably regarded as enriching his conclusion—does not play
any part in that portion of his argument which seeks to show
that all objective succession is necessary or regular succession.

If the principle of causality (in the sense of necessary succession) could be established on the basis of the assumptions
which I have asserted to be sound, I do not think that the
argument could be described correctly as a vicious circle.[4]
Whether his more doubtful assumption can be so interpreted as
to justify us in regarding causality as more than necessary
succession can, for the present, be left an open question.

Kant has given us his general analysis of what must be
involved in every human experience, and has explained what
the categories are and how they are schematised. He now
asks us to *judge* whether the Principles, which affirm the
necessary application of the schematised categories to objects,
state the conditions necessary for any experience of the kind
he has analysed. His 'proof' is, as he says, a judgement made in

---

[1] Compare A 158 = B 197. Hence our proof is said in A 149 =
B 188 to be a proof from the subjective sources of a knowledge
of the object in general.

[2] This is the simplest way of asserting the necessity of the unity
of apperception, and has to be understood in the light of Kant's
doctrine of the self.

[3] See Chapter XXXIV § 2.

[4] The argument for the assumptions themselves might still be a
vicious circle, but I do not think that it is so. We must always remember
that for Kant the conditions of experience are not merely necessary
in relation to experience, but have an intelligible necessity in themselves when considered in isolation; see Chapters VII § 4 and XXX § 5.

the light of his previous analysis, and not a syllogistic inference from the truths which he claims to have established.

§ 5. *Modern Science and the Principles of the Understanding*

It should be clearly understood that Kant's main, although not his sole, object in the Analytic of Principles is to establish the ultimate philosophical basis of mathematics and the physical sciences.[1] He is attempting to justify the application of *a priori* mathematical thinking to the actual world of physical objects and to establish the principle of the uniformity of nature. The problems which he attempts to solve are, I believe, no less important now than they were in the eighteenth century, but his solutions must be judged in the light of the science of his time.[2]

In recent years we have been informed that science has no need for the category of substance nor even—what is much more remarkable—for the category of cause and effect. If this is true, *cadit quaestio*: Kant's proof of substance and causality—and these are in some ways the most important of his categories—can be no more than a squaring of the circle. I must confess, however, to some sympathy with the view that these categories, and especially the category of cause and effect, are not to be lightly set aside. Some of the distinguished exponents of the philosophy of modern physics seem to take a delight, a delight which is certainly human and probably also useful, in stressing the paradoxes of modern theory rather than in showing the continuity of its development. The plain man, and even, if I may use the phrase, the plain philosopher, is merely foolish when he attempts to criticise the physicist in his own domain; but physics cannot be identified with the whole of human experience, nor can the practical devices which it uses at a particular moment claim to be accepted without further exami-

---

[1] The more special principles of these sciences he seeks to establish in the *Metaphysische Anfangsgründe der Naturwissenschaft*.

[2] I must confess that I feel myself handicapped in this matter, since my acquaintance alike with past and present science is that of an outsider.

nation as eternal philosophical truths. It seems to me probable that when the historian looks back upon the present age, he will see our modern theories developing continuously out of the old, and will perhaps be surprised that they appeared so paradoxical and so revolutionary. It is clear enough to-day—was it ever really doubtful?—that the traditional theories of space and time are in need of modification; and if Kant were right in holding that experience of a world in space and time is impossible apart from substance and causation, we should expect that the traditional theories of substance and causation would also require to be modified. Nevertheless modification is very different from mere blank rejection,[1] and I doubt whether we are at present obliged to say that the category of substance, and still more the category of causality, must be abolished for ever from the sphere of human thought.

It would be futile upon my part to discuss the ways in which Kant's doctrine of the categories must be modified. He assumed Euclidean space, and if we are to understand his argument, we must do the same. It is our task to estimate the value of his argument as it stands; and if we conclude that it is sound on the basis of his assumptions, I see no reason to suppose that it is now wholly without value, or that the method of his proof (as opposed to the details) could not be of use for the modern theory of science.

[1] Professor Alexander, who has done so much to modify Kant's doctrine, says (*Space, Time, and Deity*, Vol. I, p. 191): 'I cannot think that this part of Kant's doctrine is so innocently inadequate as is often believed'.

BOOK IX

THE MATHEMATICAL PRINCIPLES

THE AXIOMS OF INTUITION

§ 1. *The Principle of the Axioms*

The Principle of the Axioms of Intuition is: *All intuitions are extensive quantities.*

This is the formula of the second edition.[1] Both here and in the Anticipations and Analogies Kant seems to have been dissatisfied with his original formulation of the Principle. In each case he offers us a new formula in the second edition, and the reason for the change is not always easy to see. In each case he offers us also a new proof in the second edition, which he places immediately in front of the first proof. The obscurity of the original proof, obscurity complained of from the publication of the *Kritik* to the present time, is the reason why he attempts what he believes to be a better version.[2]

In the first edition Kant very properly began his proof by defining his terms. In the second edition these definitions are retained in their original position; and the placing of the second proof before the first has the unfortunate result that if we are reading the second edition, we have to face Kant's most important argument before we have learned the exact meaning of the terms employed.[3]

---

[1] B 202. In A 162 the Principle is: *All appearances are, as regards their intuition, extensive quantities.* It is difficult to say why in the second edition Kant should have altered this formula, especially as the conclusion of the argument in the second edition conforms more closely to the formula of A than to that of B. Mellin believed that in the formula of B Kant really intended to assert that all *appearances* (not all *intuitions*) are extensive quantities. This is supported by the conclusion of the argument in B, and Kant is not speaking of intuition *quâ* intuition, but of intuition *quâ* appearance of an object.

[2] Compare B XXXVIII.

[3] For this reason the reader, or at any rate the beginner, is well advised to consider the A proof with its definitions before he examines the B proof.

§ 2. The Proof in the First Edition

In the Principle of the Axioms the argument turns on the nature of extensive quantity. Extensive quantity is defined as that in which the representation of the parts makes possible (and therefore necessarily precedes) the representation of the whole.[1] This definition is by no means clear, and Kant does not give us any further elucidation of its details except such as may be extracted by inference from his argument. His main point appears to be that an extensive quantity—and by this, I think, he must mean a determinate extensive quantity[2]—is one which can be known only by a *successive* synthesis of the parts.[3]

[1] A 162 = B 203. I use the word 'representation' here for '*Vorstellung*' (rather than the word 'idea') because Kant may mean 'the representing' or—since the word 'represent' is full of ambiguities—'the knowing'. Here, as always, we are handicapped in English, because we have no satisfactory word which covers indifferently 'sensing' and 'conceiving' or 'thinking'. The word 'precedes' must, I think, be used in a temporal sense; for Kant's point appears to be that the synthesis of the parts must be successive.

[2] We can intuit an *indeterminate* quantum as a whole, if it is enclosed within limits, without requiring to construct its totality through measurement, that is, through the successive synthesis of its parts; see A 426 n. = B 454 n. Furthermore we can recognise that something is a quantum—here, I take it, an *indeterminate* quantum—from the thing itself without any comparison with others (as units of measurement), namely when a multiplicity of the homogeneous constitutes one whole. To decide *how great* it is, we always require something else (which is also a quantum) as its measure; see *K.d.U.* § 25 (IV 248). When we measure, we must have a successive synthesis, and only thus can we have a *determinate* extensive quantum.

[3] Compare A 163 = B 204 and A 167 = B 209. It might be objected that this statement (if true) is rather a consequence than a definition of the nature of extensive quantity—the synthesis must be successive because the parts of an extensive quantity are external to one another; but Kant, I imagine, holds that the proper definition of an extensive quantity is a statement of the way in which it can be constructed, and that a *determinate* extensive quantity can be known (and so can be an object) only through successive synthesis.

The argument of the second edition suggests that an extensive quantity is one which can be known only by a (successive) synthesis of *homogeneous* parts; and this is implied in the category of quantity itself. Nevertheless homogeneity is not the distinguishing mark of extensive quantity; for according to B 201 n. it belongs to intensive quantity as well.

Since space and time are extensive quantities, Kant's definition makes explicit a presupposition which runs through the
whole of his argument[1]—the presupposition that the parts of
space, like those of time, can be known only one after another.
He concerns himself first of all with pure space and time, the
space and time which we study in mathematics in abstraction
from sensible objects;[2] and he maintains that any space and
time about which we think must be constructed by an act
which is a successive synthesis of parts. In geometrical thinking
we must construct in pure intuition a figure corresponding to
our concept, and the construction must be a successive synthesis.
The same principle applies when we think of any determinate[3]
stretch of time.

From this general principle Kant proceeds to draw conclusions as to the necessary character of all objects as appearances.
Empirical appearances are commonly regarded by him as
intuitions, but here[4] he distinguishes within appearances what
he calls 'mere intuition',[5] that is, intuition in abstraction
from sensation. Such 'mere intuition' is intuition of the space
or time occupied by the appearance, the form of the appearance as opposed to its matter.[6] Since every appearance contains
this element of mere intuition, it must be known in apprehension through the successive synthesis of parts;[7] that is

---

[1] It is present throughout the Transcendental Deduction.

[2] This is true also of B 154 where it is said that we must *think*
a line, a circle, and even time itself, by means of a successive spatial
construction or synthesis.

[3] The word 'determinate' is important, I believe, in the argument
of both editions.

[4] A 163 = B 203; compare A 167 = B 208–9.

[5] '*blosse Anschauung.*'

[6] The 'mere intuition' is presumably the empirical form of the
appearance, namely, that determination of space or time (or both)
which belongs to the appearance: the matter of the appearance is
what is given in sensation. Compare A 128, B 207, and also Chapter
VI § 8.

[7] Compare A 224 = B 271: 'The figurative synthesis by which
we construct a triangle in imagination is wholly identical with
that which we exercise in the apprehension of an appearance in
order to make for ourselves an empirical concept of it'.

to say, it must be an extensive quantity. In other words every appearance is intuited as an *aggregate*, that is, a plurality of previously given parts. As we shall see in the following chapter, there is another kind of quantity to which such a description does not apply.

It should be noted that we must synthetise the spatial, as well as the temporal, element in appearances, and so far space is as important as time.[1] The special importance of time arises from the fact that the synthesis must be a *successive* synthesis. This necessary successiveness of the synthesis is the special mark of extensive (as opposed to intensive) quantity. It also enables us to find by abstraction a common element, namely number, which is present whether extensive quantity be spatial or temporal; for number is produced by a successive synthesis (or addition) of homogeneous units, whatever these units may be.[2]

The proof given in the first edition is in some ways defective. In spite of the fact that number was said to be the schema of quantity, there is no explicit reference to number, or even to the successive synthesis of the *homogeneous* with which number has been connected.[3] Kant's proof in the second edition is more elaborate; and although it does not refer to number, it does refer to the synthesis of the homogeneous.[4]

§ 3. *The Proof in the Second Edition*

In the second edition Kant again regards appearances as 'containing' form and matter, the form being an intuition of space and time, the matter being given in sensation. Hence[5]

---

[1] Like time it may be the source of the homogeneity of the parts.

[2] The internal character of the units synthetised is for arithmetic a matter of indifference; compare A 720 = B 748 and A 724 = B 752.

[3] A 142 = B 182.

[4] Curiously enough, he does not in the second edition assert this synthesis to be successive, but the omission seems to be a mere oversight.

[5] B 202; compare B 207. Kant says that 'all appearances contain, as regards their form, an intuition in space and time'. I take this to be an intuition of the determinate space or time referred to immediately

if we are to apprehend appearances,[1] there must be a synthesis of the manifold[2] whereby the idea of a determinate space or time (namely, of the determinate space or time occupied by the appearance) is produced.[3] This means that there is a combination of the *homogeneous* manifold of space or time, and consciousness (clear or obscure) of the synthetic unity of the homogeneous manifold.

Now consciousness of the synthetic unity of the homogeneous manifold of intuition *in general* is consciousness of the pure category of quantity (or totality). Consciousness of the synthetic unity of the homogeneous manifold of space or time is consciousness of the schematised category of extensive quantity.[4]

thereafter, the space or time which the appearance occupies. If so, it is identical with the 'mere intuition' of the first argument.

An appearance can hardly be said to contain the intuition of all space and time; and the fact that the intuition is said to be *in* space and time suggests that it is an intuition of a part of space and time. The phrase 'space *and* time' may imply that Kant is thinking primarily of physical objects; but it may perhaps be due to the greater importance attached to space in the second edition—we always require outer intuition to show the objective reality of the categories (B 291).

Kant adds that an intuition in space and time is the *a priori* condition of all appearances. This need not, I think, imply that he is immediately concerned with intuitions of space and time as infinite wholes; but it must imply that in knowing the determinate space and time of an object we are knowing these as parts of the one infinite space and time.

[1] 'Apprehension' is used, as generally by Kant, to mean 'the taking up into empirical consciousness'; compare A 99 ff. and A 120. Here, as usual, it is a successive synthesis (in which reproduction plays a necessary part).

[2] This manifold I take to be the pure homogeneous manifold of space or time; the synthesis of this manifold conditions the concurrent synthesis of the empirical manifold in space or time.

[3] This is the doctrine of all the versions of the Transcendental Deduction, whatever their differences in terminology. Note that Kant speaks here of 'space *or* time', not 'space *and* time', presumably because the synthesis need not be concerned with spatial appearances.

[4] See Chapter XXXIII § 2. Kant himself says that the consciousness *is* the category. The name he gives to the category—the concept of a quantum—suggests that he has in mind the schematised category, as we should anticipate; but the reference to intuition *in general* may suggest that he has in mind the pure category. Perhaps 'intuition *in general*' is not intended to have the usual technical sense (which

It is not wholly clear whether Kant is concerned primarily with the pure category or the schematised category. If we take him to be concerned with the schematised category,[1] the argument is relatively simple. We can have sense-perception of an *object* as an appearance only by synthetising the pure and homogeneous manifold of the determinate space or time which it occupies. Hence one condition of the sense-perception of an object is the synthetic unity of the pure and homogeneous manifold of a determinate space or time.[2] But synthetic unity of the pure and homogeneous manifold of space or time is precisely what is thought in the category of extensive quantity. Therefore all objects as appearances must fall under this category, or in other words they must be extensive quantities.[3]

associates it with the pure category): it may indicate only that the difference between space and time can be ignored. Such a usage seems to be found in A 724 = B 752 (and perhaps in A 142–3 = B 182) in speaking of number; but there it indicates that we are concerned with a *quantitas* (see § 8 below), not with a *quantum*. Furthermore the category is identified with consciousness of the synthetic unity of the homogeneous manifold of intuition in general only *so far as thereby the idea of an object first becomes possible;* and this perhaps suggests that the category in question is schematised.

Kant, it should be noted, does not in this passage use the phrase 'the synthetic unity of', which has been introduced by Vaihinger (and is accepted by Kemp Smith). The insertion of the phrase makes for clarity, but I am not sure that it is necessary.

[1] If we take him to be concerned with the pure category, there is no real difficulty; but in that case the reference to the schematised category is introduced only when he comes to deal with extensive quantity at the end.

[2] Kant himself speaks of 'the synthetic unity of the manifold of the given sensuous intuition'. For the sake of simplicity I take the 'given sensuous intuition' to be 'mere intuition' as opposed to sensation. If we take 'intuition' to be used in the ordinary sense, we must add that its synthetic unity is, as we have shown, also the synthetic unity of a pure and homogeneous manifold.

[3] Note that appearances or intuitions in space or time 'must be represented through the same synthesis as that whereby space and time *in general* are determined'. This suggests, I think, that in determining the space or time of an object we are determining a part of a wider whole which must be determined in the same way.

§ 4. *Successiveness of Synthesis*

There are many minor difficulties in following Kant's argument. These arise mainly from his failure to make clear whether he means 'intuition' to be taken as 'pure intuition', and whether he means 'the concept of a quantum' to be the pure category or the schematised category. Such difficulties are more in the expression than in the thought; and I do not believe we need take seriously his omission to state, in the argument of the second edition, that the synthesis of extensive quantity is necessarily a successive synthesis.

The more philosophical difficulties centre in the successiveness of the transcendental synthesis. If we accept this successiveness as necessary to mathematical construction, its presence in all empirical apprehension requires a more detailed defence than Kant has given us. When we know how to construct a triangle or a circle, we can recognise at sight that a figure drawn on paper is an example of what we are thinking about; and although such a recognition takes time, it seems impossible to believe that (for example) we construct each side of the seen triangle by running successively through its parts. Nevertheless it may fairly be said that if there were any doubt on the subject, we should test the figure by considering whether it could be constructed in this way; and that a successive synthesis is the basis on which our recognition rests. Indeed, if Kant is right, to recognise this figure as a triangle is to recognise, however 'obscurely', that it is the product of such a construction.

If Kant were going further than this, and were maintaining that when we see a triangle, we always do construct what we see by running our eye successively along the three sides,[1] then I think we should have to say that he is mistaken. When I look at the rafters on the ceiling I see a series of parallel lines, and I have no reason to believe that I must follow successively the contour of each line before I can see such a series.

---

[1] To maintain this is like maintaining that when we judge three people to be approaching, we must count them in succession. For a further discussion of this point see Chapter XLII § 1.

Kant's language may in places suggest that he took the more extreme view, though I find it hard to believe that he could have advanced, without any attempt at argument, a doctrine which on the face of it finds no corroboration in experience. The psychological question whether we can, in the case of familiar figures, recognise wholes at a glance is in any case irrelevant. Kant is maintaining that we must think of any space and time, however small, as a whole to be constructed by the successive synthesis of parts. He is also maintaining that in the case of any spatial or temporal intuition we must traverse the parts successively, if we are to make the intuition determinate.[1] If we take him to be concerned only with *determinate* extensive quantities, his contention seems to me to be true —it is certainly true when we are concerned with determination by measurement—and it is sufficient for his argument.

If we grant the necessity of construction in all mathematical thinking, Kant's insistence on the successiveness of the synthesis is not to be dismissed as manifestly irrelevant. There is a successiveness also in our thinking and in our sensing; but such successiveness does not constitute the essential nature of thought as such or sensation as such.[2] From the Critical standpoint, which refuses to accept the view that the phenomenal world exists in its own right independently of thought, successiveness of synthesis is essential to the presence of determinate (though not of indeterminate) extensive quantity; and it is the successiveness of the synthesis of apprehension (so far as this is concerned with space and time) which guarantees the applicability of the mathematics of extension to the phenomenal world. I do not wish to dogmatise on these difficult matters, but Kant's view is not to be refuted merely by assuming the transcendental realism which he denies. It is also to be

[1] I find some difficulty in understanding how far Kant regards shape or figure as kind of quantity. Broadly speaking, he is concerned in this chapter with determinate quantity, quantity determined by measurement, and for this we do require a successive synthesis.

[2] Compare A 143 = B 183, B 208, A 168 = B 210, for the gradual changes in degree of sensation. This will be considered in the following chapter.

noted that the intuitionist school of mathematicians, who have rejected the Kantian view of space, attempt to base the whole structure of mathematics on a doctrine which, so far as I understand it, appears to follow Kant's view pretty closely in this respect.[1]

The successive synthesis of extensive quantity, so far as it is concerned with the pure manifold of time or space, is a continuous synthesis[2]. The fact that we must run through all the parts in order to know the whole does not mean that the whole has a finite number of parts. In measuring we choose a unit (such as a foot) arbitrarily, and interrupt our synthesis whenever we have traversed the length of the unit.[3] The possibility of such interruption in a continuous synthesis does not make the object measured a discrete quantity; and Kant would have been very much surprised to learn that his view was incompatible with the continuity of space and time.[4]

§ 5. *Intuition and Object*

It may be thought that the Principle of which Kant has offered a proof applies to intuitions as intuitions, and not to intuitions only so far as they are intuitions of an object. Kant's own language supports this view when he says that the Mathematical Principles are concerned only with *intuition*.[5]

---

[1] See Black, *The Nature of Mathematics*, especially pp. 186 ff. I must, however, add that Mr. Black's account of Kant's doctrine is so astonishingly inaccurate as to disturb my confidence in him when he deals with other matters on which he is doubtless better informed.

[2] A 169–70 = B 211–2.

[3] For Kant's view of measurement see *K.d.U.* § 26 (V 251 ff.). The unit must be taken as the product of a continuous synthesis. I think Kant means to assert this in A 171 = B 212, when he says that appearance as a unity (or unit) is a quantum and so a continuum.

[4] See Sidgwick, *The Philosophy of Kant*, p. 92. It is of course true that by means of number we can represent any quantum as discrete, but we must distinguish a quantum which is discrete in itself from a quantum which is continuous in itself, but represented by us as discrete. See *Metaphysik*, p. 31.

[5] A 160 = B 199. In B 110 he says, more correctly, that the mathematical categories are concerned with *objects of intuition* (as opposed to the *existence* of these objects). Even in A 160 = B 199 he adds

If these words were to be taken literally, the Principle of the Axioms would be out of place here—as many commentators have held—and ought to be relegated to the Aesthetic.

This view, it seems to me, in spite of the support given by some of Kant's looser expressions, is incompatible with the argument of the second edition; and it fails to recognise the interconnexion of the different Principles of the Understanding, all of which without exception are directed towards establishing the necessary characteristics of every *object* of experience. In the Mathematical Principles we consider the object in abstraction from its relation to other objects, and we find that the object in such abstraction must have extensive and intensive quantity; but these categorial characteristics are products of the one transcendental synthesis which also imposes upon objects the categories of relation and modality. We must not imagine that because we can consider in abstraction aspects of what is essentially one synthesis, we are therefore concerned with something other than an object of experience.

It is true that every intuition, and even that every image of our fancy and our dreams, is spatial and temporal, and may therefore be described in a loose sense as an extensive quantity; but if it is to be an extensive quantity in the strict sense, it must occupy a *determinate*[1] space and time. Kant means, I think, that it must be determined by measurement, and so must be a determinate part of the one space and time in which all objects are. When we perceive an object, the appearance given in intuition occupies such a determinate space and time, and can be measured exactly. The images or

that the *a priori* conditions of intuition are absolutely necessary in relation to a possible *experience*. In the Analytic we are concerned, not with conditions of intuition in abstraction, but with conditions of intuition as conditions of a possible experience and its objects; and one of these conditions is the successive synthesis of the pure and homogeneous manifold of our common time and space.

[1] B 202; compare 'a determinate quantity of time' in A 163 = B 203. The infinity of time is said to mean that every determinate quantity of time is possible only through limitation of the one individual whole of time; see A 32 = B 47-8.

pseudo-objects of our imagination and our dreams cannot be so measured,[1] because they do not occupy such a determinate space and time. What Kant is trying to show is that all objects of sense must be exactly measurable or numerable—and this means (although the momentary abstraction fails to bring this out) measurable in relation to all other objects of experience. It is only as intuitions (or appearances) of *objects* that our intuitions are measurable as extensive quantities; and it is only as appearances of *objects* that they must be represented by the same synthesis which determines time and space *in general*,[2], and must be subject to the category of quantity without which no object can be thought.[3]

§ 6. *The Doctrine of the Aesthetic*

For these reasons I regard it as an error to maintain that Kant is repeating unnecessarily the doctrine of the Aesthetic, and that he does so through the influence of an artificial plan described by some commentators as 'architectonic'. The doc-

[1] They are indeterminate quanta.

[2] B 203. Time and space *in general* are the one time and space in which all objects are.

[3] I cannot here enter into the more elaborate aspects of this contention. To determine the size of anything we always require thought as well as sense, and we always presuppose that it occupies a determinate part of our common space. This is obvious when we determine the size of the heavenly bodies, but it is equally true, although less obvious, when we determine the size of a table. An image has no measurable size, unless we assign to it, however arbitrarily, a position in space at a definite distance from ourselves; and to do this is to make it a sort of pseudo-object. When we imagine castles in Spain or dream of marble halls, these edifices have no exact dimensions; and if we find that dream-measurements are assigned to them, we may equally find that they are dream-substances and the product of dream-causes. There is no difference in this respect between the Mathematical Principles and the Analogies. Both are concerned with *objects* in a common time and space, and both find a sort of imitation of themselves in the world of dreams and fancy.

We can of course measure the time through which an image or a dream lasts, but to do this is to measure the time of our apprehension, and to make our apprehension itself an object. Similarly we can explain the causes of our dreams, but then we are no longer dreaming; we are making our acts of dreaming into objects of thought.

trine of the Aesthetic is in manifest need of the additions here
supplied, and it is all-important to recognise that when we
determine an object, there must be present the same synthesis
of a homogeneous space and time as is necessary for the determination of space and time *in general*. This is a matter, not of
mere intuition, but of thought by means of the categories.

There is a greater show of plausibility in the criticism that
Kant, so far from repeating the doctrine of the Aesthetic, is
actually contradicting it. The charge of contradiction can
be repelled only when we realise that in the Aesthetic Kant is,
as he says, abstracting from the element of thought; and that
consequently the doctrine of the Aesthetic is provisional, and
must be supplemented and corrected by what comes later.[1]

In the Aesthetic it was argued that times and spaces are
known only as limitations of one infinite time and space; and
consequently the 'original' idea of infinite space and time must
be a pure intuition, from which the concepts of temporality
and spatiality are derived. Kant even went so far as to say of
space that it is represented as an infinite *given* quantity.[2] The
Aesthetic, in short, regards the idea of the whole as making
possible the idea of the parts; whereas we have now been told
that it is of the essence of extensive quantity for the idea of
the parts to make possible the idea of the whole.[3]

The contradiction is due partly to the fact that in the
Aesthetic, since Kant abstracts from the element of thought,
he is bound to ignore the presence of synthesis.[4] Hence he
has to speak as if the unity of space and time were dependent
merely upon intuition, and as if the pure intuitions of space and
time were given as one and even as infinite (or at least were
'represented' as an infinite given quantity). He has now

---

[1] Compare Chapter V, especially § 8.

[2] B 39. Compare A 24 and see Chapter V § 8.

[3] A 162 = B 203. It should, however, be noted that if the whole
precedes the parts logically (or objectively) and the parts precede
the whole temporally (or subjectively) there is no contradiction. The
whole makes possible the parts in a sense different from that in which
the parts make possible the whole.

[4] Except in so far as it is presupposed by synthetic judgements.

explained that although the ideas of space and of time must be intuitions, since they are ideas of one infinite whole, the unity of these intuitions, like the unity of every intuition of an object, depends on a synthesis of imagination in conformity with categories and the unity of apperception.[1] When we are told that space is represented as an infinite *given* quantity, we must add that it can be so represented only because the manifold is combined or synthetised by the understanding,[2] although Kant makes no reference to synthesis in the Aesthetic.[3]

In this way at least some part of the contradiction can be explained, but there remains an element of truth in the Aesthetic which Kant fails to express in the Analytic. The synthesis which constructs space and time by the addition of part to part is itself dominated by an idea of the whole, and this fact is here ignored by Kant, except in so far as he implies that the synthesis of quantity, like every other, must accord with the unity of apperception. To understand fully his view of space and time we must supplement the doctrine of the Aesthetic and the Analytic by the doctrine of the Dialectic.[4]

[1] Compare B 160–1 n. and A 107.

[2] See B 130, B 134, B 161, and compare A 105.

[3] In A 24 space was said to be represented as an infinite given quantity because of the absence of limits in the advance of intuition. This advance manifestly requires synthesis, but Kant makes no attempt to emphasise this. He omits the passage in the second edition. Compare Chapter V § 7.

[4] Especially in the Antinomies. Kant's doctrine is elaborated further in the *Metaphysische Anfangsgründe der Naturwissenschaft* (IV 481–2). There he recognises a relative or material space which is movable and is capable of being perceived or sensed, that is, can be symbolised (*bezeichnet*) through that which can be sensed. Such a relative or movable space, if its movement is to be perceived, presupposes a wider relative space in which it moves, and so on *ad infinitum*. Absolute space on the other hand is not material and cannot be perceived; it means only a wider space which is relative to every other, a space which I can always think as outside others and extend indefinitely. Such a wider space is still in a sense material, but as I know nothing of the matter which symbolises it, I abstract from the matter and represent it as a pure and absolute space, an immovable space in which other spaces move. To regard it as an actual thing is a mistake, and a misunderstanding of reason in its Idea. For Kant's doctrine of *Bezeichnung* (*signatio*) see *Anthr.* § 38 (VII 191).

Such an investigation is beyond the scope of the present book, but I believe that his theory is more coherent than many of his critics are prepared to admit.

§ 7. *The Axioms of Geometry*

Although Kant's primary aim is to establish the applicability of the categories to objects of experience, he regards the Principle of the Axioms as the basis of the objective validity of pure mathematics, that is, of its application to physical objects. He discusses briefly (1) geometry, (2) arithmetic, and (3) the application of these, but especially of geometry, to objects of experience. The discussion does not profess to be other than elementary, and on that level it must be judged.[1]

The mathematics of extension (that is, geometry) rests on the successive synthesis of the productive imagination in the construction of figures. This is true in particular of the axioms of geometry, and consequently the Principle is called the Principle of the Axioms.[2] Axioms, we must remember, are *a priori* synthetic principles which are immediately certain, and this immediate certainty is due to the possibility of 'constructing' concepts, that is, of 'exhibiting' *a priori* in intuition an object corresponding to the concept.[3] As principles, the axioms of geometry express or formulate the conditions of *a priori* intuitions of space and of spatial figures, the conditions, that is to say, of our rules for constructing geometrical figures.[4]

[1] For further remarks on this point, see Chapter VII §§ 5–8. In the present chapter I ignore the many difficulties raised by the developments of modern mathematics.

[2] Compare A 733 = B 761. As distinguished critics have objected that this Principle is not an axiom, it is necessary to point out that although Kant in A 161 = B 200 speaks loosely of the Principle as if it were an axiom, when he comes to formulate it, he describes it, not as an Axiom, but as a Principle of Axioms.

[3] See A 732 = B 760 and *Log. Einl.* III (IX 23).

[4] A 163 = B 204. Kant says they formulate the conditions under which alone the schema of a pure concept of outer appearance can arise. The schema would seem to be the rule for constructing a triangle, square, and so on; see A 141 = B 180. It may possibly be space itself (see A 156 = B 195), though space is also referred to as the pure image (*Bild*) of the quanta of outer sense (see A 142 = B 182).

Such axioms are that between two points there can be only one straight line, and that two straight lines cannot enclose a space.

In the Aesthetic Kant had already presumed such axioms to be intuitively certain.[1] He now adds that this intuitive certainty depends on an imaginative construction which, in conforming to the particular concept involved, conforms also to the category of quantity. He makes no reference to the axioms concerned with time which he mentioned in the Aesthetic, but the same considerations would apply in this case also.[2] All these axioms are concerned with extensive quantities which Kant calls quanta, which we may here take to be figures in space and durations in time.[3]

§ 8. *Quantitas and Quantum*

At this point[4] Kant makes a distinction between '*quanta*' and '*quantitas*'. This distinction raises problems of Kantian terminology through which it is not easy to thread one's way. In English we can distinguish between 'quantum' and 'quantity', although the words are often used ambiguously and without precision. The ambiguity in German is increased by the fact that the same word[5] has to do duty for both.

The pure category of quantity (or totality[6])—which I

---

[1] See B 41. The example there given is that space can have only three dimensions. The presence of intuitive certainty does not imply the absence of thought; compare Chapters X § 7 and XXXVI § 3.

[2] See A 31 = B 47. The axioms are that time has only one dimension, and that different times are not simultaneous but successive.

[3] Time, it may be noted, is sometimes described as 'protensive' instead of 'extensive' (see *Metaphysik*, p. 37), and Kant has here confined the mathematics of extension to geometry.

[4] A 163 = B 204.

[5] '*Grösse.*' Strictly speaking, *quantitas* is '*die blosse Grösse*' or '*Grösse überhaupt*'; compare A 717 = B 745 and A 242 = B 300.

[6] Totality includes in itself the moments of plurality and unity, and is definitely said to be the category to which number belongs (as a schema); see B 111. Curiously enough in the *Prolegomena* § 21 (IV 303), when Kant gives the three moments of quantity (*Quantität*), he speaks of unity as the measure or unit (*das Mass*), plurality as quantity (*die Grösse*), and totality as the whole (*das Ganze*). Similarly in *Metaphysik*, pp. 31–2, he connects 'quantum' primarily with plurality

have defined as the concept of the synthesis of the homogeneous[1]
—may be called '*quantitas*'.[2] The schematised category I have
called the category of extensive quantity, and defined as the
concept of the synthesis of the homogeneous in time and
space.[3] Though Kant, so far as I know, does not employ the
phrase, the schematised category might be called '*quantitas
extensiva*'.[4]

The concrete instances in which *quantitas* is manifested
are naturally called *quanta*, and the word 'quantum' is applied
by Kant both to space and time (the only original quanta[5])
and to empirical objects so far as these are extended in space
and time. We might indeed express the Principle of the Axioms
itself by saying that all appearances are extensive quanta.[6]

As I have already pointed out,[7] Kant habitually uses concrete
words for the purpose of expressing concepts; and the category
may be referred to indifferently as the concept of *quantitas*
or the concept of *quanta* in general or even as the concept of a
quantum.[8]

So far there is no real difficulty. But *quantitas* may also be
used for a special kind of instance in which *quantitas* (the

(*multitudo*). Perhaps this is part of his doctrine that the infinite is
a quantum without being a whole; see Chapter XV § 2. Perhaps
(like the use of 'reality' for the category of quality) it has no special
significance.

[1] See Chapter XXXIII § 2.

[2] See A 142 = B 182. The same usage is implied in A 146 = B 186.

[3] Kant does not distinguish the schematised category from the pure
category with sufficient precision, but it is manifestly the schematised
category with which he is concerned in the present passage. The
'homogeneous in time and space' is here the pure homogeneous
manifold of time and space.

[4] In *Metaphysik*, p. 32, he speaks of *quantitates* as extensive and
intensive, but there the usage is concrete, not abstract.

[5] A 725 = B 753.

[6] The word is sometimes translated as 'magnitude'. This tends
to obscure its connexion with the category of quantity, and Kant
uses '*magnitudo*' in a different sense; see *K.d.U.* § 25 (V 248).

[7] Chapter IX § 4.

[8] The last usage is the one employed in B 203. We can add the
word 'extensive' to make clear that we are dealing with the schematised
category.

category) is present, and we can speak of *quantitates* in the plural. We must distinguish between such *quantitates* and *quanta*,[1] although they have the common characteristic that they can be constructed *a priori* in mathematics. Examples of *quanta* are the spatial figures of geometry[2] and also durations.[3] These have a quality as well as mere quantity—in the case of spatial figures that quality is shape or figure.[4] When we abstract entirely from the quality,[5] then we have *quantitates*, which Kant identifies with numbers.[6] These I take to include the constants and variables of algebra as well as the numbers of arithmetic.[7]

The only source of difficulty here is the use of the word '*quantitas*' both for the universal and for certain special instances of the universal, namely numbers; but there is, I fear, still a further complication. I will put it in my own way by saying, although Kant does not use the phrase, that we can treat any *quantum* (even an empirical object) as itself a *quantitas*. We do so by abstracting from all its qualities, and this happens when we measure it, that is, when we ask how big it is.[8] This question can be answered only by saying how many units it contains, and the answer must be by means of numbers.[9] Such a *quantitas*, although not a number, always involves

---

[1] We may ignore the cases where these words are used without being distinguished. E.g. in *Metaphysik*, p. 32, *quantitates* clearly covers *quanta*.

[2] A 717 = B 745.　　　　　　　[3] A 720 = B 748, A 724 = B 752.

[4] '*Gestalt*'; see A 720 = B 748. Kant does not say what the corresponding quality is for durations, in which he is less interested; but I suppose that every duration has the quality of being one-dimensional.

[5] '*Qualität*' or '*Beschaffenheit*'; see A 720 = B 748 and A 717 = B 745.

[6] A 717 = B 745 and A 720 = B 748. Compare Chapter VII § 6.

[7] In *K.d.U.* § 26 (V 251) Kant speaks of the estimation of quantity as mathematical if it is by means of number-concepts *or their signs in algebra*. In A 146 = B 186 number is *quantitas phaenomenon*.

[8] A 163 = B 204. In *Metaphysik*, p. 32, Kant speaks of *things* as *quantitates*.

[9] We may of course have to be satisfied only with approximations obtained by means of number-series which progress *ad infinitum*; see *K.d.U.* § 26 (V 251).

number and comparison with a standard or unit of measurement: I think it is better called a *determinate* quantum. A quantum can be recognised at sight and need not be compared with anything,[1] but it is then, I think, an *indeterminate* quantum.

Every determinate quantum, since it is the product of a continuous and successive synthesis, can (as I have already pointed out[2]), be measured by interrupting the synthesis whenever we have traversed the length of the unit chosen as our standard of measurement.[3] We may ignore for the present the difference between continuous and discrete quanta,[4] and we may also ignore the fact that there are some quanta which are not extensive.[5] Granting Kant's presuppositions, we may take him to have proved that every object must (in one aspect of it) be a determinate continuous extensive quantum; we can always determine its objective quantity by numbers or measurement.

This seems to me to be the essence of Kant's doctrine. If we take the schematised category to be concerned only with *determinate* extensive quantity,[6] we can understand why he insists on the successiveness of the synthesis and on the presence of number. It is only by counting or measuring—a procedure which is necessarily successive—that we can determine the extensive quantity of any object. In this as in all other cases (though Kant does not make his view too clear)

[1] *K.d.U.* §§ 25 and 26 (V 248 and 251) and compare again A 426 n. = B 454 n. All estimate of *quantitas* is relative to the unit we take, and in the last resort this is a *quantum* which is not itself estimated mathematically as a *quantitas*, but only aesthetically in mere intuition by the eye (or I suppose by touch). Compare also A 240 = B 299.

[2] See § 4 above.

[3] The *quantitas* of anything may be described as the *quantitas* of my progression in space and time; see *Metaphysik*, p. 39.

[4] See A 526–7 = B 554–5.

[5] See A 143 = B 183 and A 170 = B 212.

[6] I think Kant is entitled to define his technical terms as he pleases; and it does not seem to me to be too paradoxical to say that we have extensive quantity only so far as we have exact measurement. I confess that I discovered this only at the last moment—partly from reading the Master of Balliol's book on Kant—but it seems to me to solve many difficulties.

the schema has to be established if we are to justify our application of the pure category. The schematised category combines in itself the pure category and the schema: it is not only a concept of the synthesis of the homogeneous, but a concept of that *successive* synthesis of the homogeneous manifold of time and space whereby alone an object can be quantitatively determined in regard to its extent.[1]

Needless to say, we do not require to measure an object before we can regard it as an object; but in regarding it as an object we presuppose that it can be measured. We know *a priori* that an object must have extensive quantity, but we do not know *a priori* what extensive quantity an object must have. Its actual measurements are to be determined by empirical methods alone.[2]

§ 9. *The Formulae of Arithmetic*

Arithmetic (under which we may include algebra) is a more abstract science than geometry and is concerned, not with *quanta*, but with *quantitates*, which may be described generally as numbers.[3]

Arithmetical propositions have intuitive certainty,[4] and depend upon a construction; they are synthetic and not analytic. In the judgement $7 + 5 = 12$ the left-hand side of the equation gives us the idea of 7, the idea of 5, and the idea of an operation (namely adding); but we have to perform that operation by means of a construction before we can get the

[1] I still have difficulties as to the distinction between the schematised category and the schema, but I do not wish to waste time on subtleties.

[2] These general considerations are true as regards all the categories. It is interesting to note that in the *Nachträge* LXX Kant explains that the homogeneous manifold must be taken together in accordance with concepts of quantity, because we cannot intuit space and time for themselves. The fact that we cannot intuit empty or absolute space and time is a reason which he repeatedly gives for the necessity of employing all the categories.

[3] See A 163 = B 204, A 717 = B 745, A 724 = B 752, and compare *K.d.U.* §§ 25–6 (V 248 ff.). Compare also A 146 = B 186.

[4] A 164 = B 205. They are 'evident' in the technical sense. See Chapter XXXVI § 3.

right-hand side of the equation.[1] Such a construction Kant calls symbolic, and believes to be impossible apart from intuition.[2]

According to Kant there can be no axioms in arithmetic, only formulae.[3] Arithmetic, like geometry, does presuppose certain general principles—if we may call them so[4]—of a purely analytic character, for example that if equals be added to, or subtracted from, equals, the results are equal;[5] but axioms, strictly speaking, are synthetic. On the other hand the propositions of arithmetic—such as $7 + 5 = 12$—although they are synthetic, are not universal, and an axiom must be universal. Such propositions are therefore called by Kant 'number-formulae'.[6]

The proposition $7 + 5 = 12$ Kant regards as a singular synthetic *a priori* proposition. He must mean that the proposition is concerned originally with this 7 and this 5, although he admits that the use of these numbers afterwards is universal. I take his view to be that when we have seen this 7 and this 5 to be equal to 12, we can affirm that the sum of any 7 and any 5 is equal to 12:[7] we do not require to repeat the operation of adding the separate units in every case.

---

[1] Here again, as in the case of recognising a triangle, we need not go through the process of adding $7 + 1 + 1 + 1 + 1 + 1$, but our addition of $7 + 5$ rests ultimately upon such a process. In the *Nachträge* LXXI Kant proposed to omit this insistence on the synthetic character of the judgement in view of the discussion introduced in B 16.

[2] Compare Chapter VII §§ 6 and 7.   [3] A 164 = B 204-5.

[4] Kant himself calls them principles (*Grundsätze*) in B 16, but immediately denies that they serve as principles (*Prinzipien*).

[5] The examples given in B 17 for geometry are: the whole is equal to itself or $a = a$; and the whole is greater than the part or $(a + b) > a$. These 'principles' are said to be valid even in mere conception (*nach blossen Begriffen*); they are admitted in mathematics because they can be 'exhibited' in intuition. This is another case where analytic judgements are not 'about' concepts—as is maintained by Kinkel and Hermann Cohen—but 'about' objects.

[6] '*Zahlformeln*.' Schulz (*Prüfung der Kantischen Kritik*, Vol. I, p. 219) argued in 1789 that there are two axioms in arithmetic, namely $a + b = b + a$ and $c + (a + b) = (c + a) + b$.

[7] It may be objected that there is only one 7 (*the* number 7) although there are many groups of 7 things. This seems to me to be an error which is refuted every time we say that $7 + 7 = 14$. There is only

On the other hand we have to remember that the axioms of geometry, although they are stated as universal propositions, also rest according to Kant's theory on the construction of individual instances, as do all mathematical propositions without exception. Mathematics as such deals with the universal in the particular, or rather in the individual;[1] and the difference between geometry and arithmetic on which Kant is here insisting seems to be little more than a difference in expression.[2] On his view both sciences deal with individual instances; both sciences construct these instances *a priori* in accordance with a principle; and both sciences extend their conclusions to all other individual instances constructed on the same principle. This is possible because we can see in the individual instance that the conclusion follows only because of the principle of construction employed.[3]

§ 10. *The Application of Mathematics to Objects of Experience*

The Principle of the Axioms is intended to show the objective validity of pure mathematics: it is our justification for applying pure mathematics to objects of experience. Kant's contention is general, but his argument is confined to geometry.[4] He states his case first of all in terms of the Aesthetic: empirical

one seven-ness, but it has many instances. Such is the doctrine which I believe to have been held by Plato in the *Republic*. It is certainly attributed to him by Aristotle; see *Metaphysics*, A 6, 987b, 14 ff. But these matters are highly controversial, and I have no wish to speak dogmatically on a matter where I have no claim to expert knowledge.

[1] See A 714 = B 742 and also A 734 = B 762.

[2] The fact that we can construct a triangle in different ways and a number in only one way has surely no direct connexion with the difference between an axiom and a number-formula (or between a universal and a singular proposition). The variation in triangles rests on the fact that they are figures of two dimensions; and it may be true that we require axioms in geometry because space is a continuum of more than one dimension.

Kant's further objection—that if we call number-formulae axioms, there will be an infinite number of axioms in arithmetic—is valid only if we assume that there cannot be an infinite number of axioms.

[3] Compare A 715-16 = B 743-4 and Chapter VII § 7.

[4] His failure to deal with arithmetic is very remarkable, since the schema of quantity is number.

intuition is possible only through the pure intuition of time and space, and what geometry asserts of pure intuition must undoubtedly apply to empirical intuition.[1] For the full understanding of his doctrine it must be added that the synthesis which is necessary for knowledge of empirical objects must involve a synthesis of time and space, and this point he duly proceeds to make. The synthesis of spaces and times, which are the essential forms of all intuition, is what makes apprehension, and therefore outer experience, and therefore all knowledge of physical objects, possible; and what pure mathematics proves about space (by means of its *a priori* constructions) must be valid of objects in space.[2] It is mere sophistry, he maintains, to suggest that though mathematical lines are infinitely divisible, the actual lines in nature might be made of simple parts or physical points.[3]

All such sophistical doctrines rest on the supposition that physical objects are things-in-themselves, and consequently cannot be known *a priori* to conform to theories which have been proved independently of experience. Granted this supposition, Kant believes the doctrine to be true, and adds that on this supposition geometry itself would be impossible[4] —presumably upon the ground that it would deal only with the creations of our own fancy.[5]

Such an argument would manifestly have no weight with those who hold that mathematics does deal only with a world of fancy, and that there is no known reason why it should sometimes apply to actual things. For those who hold such a view Kant's argument is a *petitio principii*,[6] and in any case it

[1] A 165 = B 206.   [2] A 165–6 = B 206.

[3] Compare *Prol.* § 13 *Anmerk.* I (IV 288).

[4] A 166 = B 207. Yet Kant admits that mathematics is possible on the Newtonian view.

[5] *Prol.* § 13 *Anmerk.* I (IV 287). In A 165 = B 206 Kant says we should deny objective validity to space and consequently to all mathematics, and should not know why or how far mathematics could be applied to appearances.

[6] He assumes that we can construct only Euclidean space, and consequently that the space of the actual world and of physics must be Euclidean.

is too elementary to meet the difficult problems of the present day. Nevertheless I cannot believe it to be a mere accident that geometry—whether Euclidean or any other—should be developed *a priori*, and yet should be found to apply to the actual world. There must be an intelligible connexion between the development of pure mathematics and its application to the physical world, and the reasons for that connexion ought to be found in an analysis of experience such as Kant has offered. We cannot afford to ignore the fact that our experience depends essentially upon an imaginative construction based upon sensation and controlled by thought, and that this imaginative construction is always a synthesis of space and time or of space-time. However much Kant's doctrine may be in need of modification, it is by no means merely to be set aside.

CHAPTER XXXVIII

THE ANTICIPATIONS OF SENSE-PERCEPTION

§ 1. *The Principle of the Anticipations*

The Principle of the Anticipations is: *In all appearances the real, which is an object of sensation, has intensive quantity, that is, a degree.*

This is the formulation of the Principle in the second edition.[1] In the first edition the Principle is formulated thus: *In all appearances sensation, and the* real *which corresponds to it in the object* (realitas phaenomenon), *has* intensive quantity, *that is, a degree.*[2] Since the argument added in the second edition conforms to the formulation of the Principle in the first edition, the change in expression would seem to imply no change in the thought, and I can see no reason for it other than a desire for brevity.[3]

There is some uncertainty as to the meaning of the terms employed by Kant, and these must be considered before we can estimate his proof.

The word 'Anticipation' might be applied to all the Principles[4] (and indeed to all synthetic *a priori* judgements): they all anticipate experience and inform us, before any particular experience, what necessary characteristics an object of that experience must have. The word is, however, peculiarly appropriate to the Principle we are about to consider. It is most remarkable that we should be able to anticipate experience on its empirical side and to have *a priori* knowledge of its matter, a matter which must be given through empirical sensation.[5]

---

[1] B 207.   [2] A 166.

[3] The brevity both here and in the Axioms is secured at the expense of details which do not cease to be parts of Kant's doctrine.

[4] A 166–7 = B 208. For a similar statement about the word 'Analogy', see A 180–1 = B 223.

[5] A 167 = B 208–9. The Principle of the Axioms dealt only with the form, as opposed to the matter, of *appearances*. The Principle

Since all the Principles are concerned with the application of the categories (or the schematised categories) to objects, I think we may take 'appearances' to mean appearances as determinate objects. In the Anticipations[1] we consider one characteristic which must belong to every determinate object— Kant is thinking primarily about physical objects—and although we consider this in abstraction from the other characteristics which every object must have, we must understand this Principle in the light of the others, and we are certainly not examining the nature of sensation in itself without regard to the fact that it is sensation of an object.[2]

'Intensive quantity' is identified by Kant with 'degree'.[3]

of the Anticipations may be said to deal with the form of *the matter of appearances*, an essential characteristic which belongs to the matter as such (and to sensation as such) apart from the time and space which it fills; compare A 176 = B 218. Every Principle must be formal, and the present Principle is no exception. In A 161 = B 201 Kant himself indicates that the Anticipations are concerned only with the *form* of quality.

[1] I use this as a shorter way of saying 'the Principle of the Anticipations'.

[2] Compare Chapter XXXVII § 5 for further development of this general view.

[3] See A 168 = B 210. Degree is degree (or intensive quantity) of a quality, and by quality—which is not here defined—Kant means such things as colour, taste, heat, weight, and resistance. See A 176 = B 218 and (for the particular qualities) A 168 = B 210, A 169 = B 211, A 174 = B 216, and also *Prol.* § 24 (IV 306). In A 173 = B 215 impenetrability seems also to be regarded as a quality comparable with weight; this is presumably the same quality as resistance. It is not made clear whether all these qualities are on the same level. Colour and taste are said to be qualities of *sensation* in A 175 = B 217, and are *contrasted* with the real which corresponds to sensation; in A 176 = B 218 quality is *identified* with 'the real of appearances' (*realitas phaenomenon*); and in A 173 = B 215 impenetrability and weight (the result of the forces of repulsion and attraction) are implied to be *identical* with the real in space. For the purposes of dynamics Kant identifies the 'real' or the 'matter' of objects of outer sense with 'moving forces' (*bewegende Kräfte*), that is, with a combination of the forces of repulsion and attraction. See *M.A.d.N.* 2. *Hauptstück* (IV 523) and compare A 265 = B 320–1. We must remember that for Kant the primary qualities are in a special sense objective, and to these impenetrability—see *Prol.* § 13 *Anmerk.* II (IV 289)—and presumably weight belong. Compare Chapter II § 1.

It is defined as 'that quantity which is apprehended only as unity, and in which plurality can be represented only through approximation to negation = 0'.[1] An extensive quantity is made up of parts (quantities) outside one another in space or time, while an intensive quantity is given as a whole and all at once. A foot is made up of so many inches and an hour of so many minutes, and it is because we have separate ideas of the parts that we can have an idea of the whole;[2] but when we experience a degree of heat we have an idea of the whole without having separate ideas of its parts.[3]

The chief difficulty of Kant's account is to be found in the words 'real' and 'sensation'. Are these meant to be the same or are they meant to be different? The formula in the first edition[4] distinguishes them explicitly, and so does the argument in

[1] A 168 = B 210. This, I think, explains what Kant says in A 99 —that every idea, *as contained in one moment* (that is, in abstraction from the synthesis of spaces and times), can be nothing but absolute unity. Compare Chapter XIX § 1. Extensive quantity is also a unity, but its plurality is represented by parts outside one another. The plurality of intensive quantity is not represented by parts outside one another, but every degree contains a plurality, because it contains all lesser degrees down to zero. This is what Kant means by saying that its plurality is represented through approximation to negation.

[2] See A 162 = B 203.

[3] Kant believes that in experiencing a degree of heat we pass successively and continuously from our starting-point through the intermediate degrees to the final degree; but at every stage we have before us a degree which is one and indivisible.

Prichard (*Kant's Theory of Knowledge*, p. 262) points out that this is true of velocity. 'A mile can be said to be made up of two half-miles, but a velocity of one foot per second, though comparable with a velocity of half a foot per second, cannot be said to be made up of two such velocities; it is essentially one and indivisible.' Kant does not use velocity as an illustration—I think because it is not directly sensible—but he recognises it elsewhere as an intensive quantity, pointing out that its parts are not outside one another as are the parts of space. See *M.A.d.N.* 1. *Hauptstück* (IV 493–4).

[4] The formula in B says only that the real, which is an object of sensation, has intensive quantity, and does not say that sensation has intensive quantity; yet even here the real seems to be distinct from the sensation, if it is the object of sensation. Sensation is essentially subjective, although we use it for knowledge of objects—see *K.d.U. Einl.* VII (V 189).

both editions.[1] The real is what corresponds to sensation, and what corresponds to sensation must be different from sensation itself. Nevertheless the carelessness of Kant's language, together with the fact that he is keeping in the background some of his doctrines as unsuited to Transcendental Philosophy,[2] makes it difficult to determine the precise meaning of 'sensation' and 'real' and the precise sense in which the real 'corresponds to' sensation.

There would seem to be three possibilities: (1) that sensation is our sensing and the real is the sensum;[3] (2) that sensation is the sensum considered as a modification of the mind, while the real is the quality of the object revealed or given in the sensum;[4] and (3) that sensation is the sensum considered as revealing a quality of the object, while the real is the moving forces (*bewegende Kräfte*) of repulsion and attraction which fill space and constitute the solid bodies of common sense and the substances of physical science.[5]

[1] In the argument of the second edition Kant does not speak of the real corresponding to sensation; but he does speak of 'the real of sensation'; and he says that corresponding to the degree of sensation we must ascribe a degree to objects of sense-perception, so far as sense-perception contains sensation. The distinction is also supported by his ascribing to objects a degree of influence upon sense.

[2] In opposition to 'Rational Physiology' (the *a priori* science of corporeal and spiritual nature). Compare A 171 = B 213; A 846–7 = B 874–5; and also § 7 below.

[3] This receives some support from A 172 = B 214. There every *reality* in sense-perception has a degree, and every sense (*Sinn*) has also a determinate degree of the receptivity of sensations.

[4] When we are actually perceiving an object, the sensum and the quality would seem to be the same thing regarded from different points of view; but the sensum is thought to be only at the moment of sensing, while the quality has a semi-independent existence (in space and time) which we determine by thought. When we see white sugar, we think that it is sweet, even although we are not tasting it. Such is the simple statement of Kant's view. It has to be modified by the further doctrine that secondary qualities exist only in relation to the individual, while primary qualities are the same for all men. All these statements anticipate the doctrine of the Analogies.

[5] Compare A 265 = B 320–1, A 273 = B 329, A 277 = B 333, A 284 = B 340. Note particularly that *realitas phaenomenon* is identified with moving forces in A 265 = B 320–1, and in A 273 = B 329 with the obstacles and reactions in nature (*Hindernisse* and *Gegenwirkungen*) which are due to such forces.

Of these possibilities the first is unimportant and may be neglected; the third is a statement of Kant's dynamical theory of matter and has strictly no place in a *Kritik of Pure Reason*; the second alone must be adopted for the interpretation of Kant's argument.[1] The Anticipations can tell us only that the quality of objects must have a degree corresponding to the degree of our sensations.[2] This is the universal principle of which the dynamical theory of matter is a particular application.[3]

The Principle of the Anticipations is concerned with the matter as opposed to the form of objects, and here also there is an ambiguity. Sensation is itself spoken of as the matter, but usually as the matter of *intuition* (or sense-perception or experience);[4] the matter of the *object* is what corresponds to sensation.[5] Kant has in mind, at least partly, matter—or the qualities of matter—as it is known to physical science;[6] but

[1] If we take this interpretation, we can understand why Kant does not maintain a sharp distinction between 'sensation' and 'the real': to say that there are degrees in sensation is also to say that there are degrees in the qualities of the objects revealed in sensation.

[2] This is in accordance with the second possibility suggested above; but we must add that while some qualities are revealed directly in sensation, others are known indirectly by inference from sensation.

[3] In *M.A.d.N.* (IV 523) the following is said to be the universal principle of dynamics—that all the *real* of objects of outer sense, which is not merely determination of space (place, extension, and shape), can be regarded only as *moving force*. This abolishes the notion of the solid, or absolute impenetrability, and sets in its place the forces of repulsion and attraction which are necessary for the idea of matter.

[4] In A 42 = B 60 and A 167 = B 209 sensation is the matter of sense-perception; in A 50 = B 74 the matter of sensuous knowledge; in A 267 = B 323 the matter of intuition; and again in A 167 = B 209 the matter of experience. It will be remembered that in A 146 = B 186 *realitas phaenomenon* is itself identified with *sensatio*.

[5] A 20 = B 34, A 143 = B 182. I concern myself here only with the matter of the phenomenal object. The inner nature of that matter as it is in the thing-in-itself is to us unknown.

[6] Matter is identified by Kant with *substance*, and perhaps the *real* should be regarded as the qualities of matter. In A 176 = B 218 quality is identified with the real of appearances (*realitas phaenomenon*), and it is quality which has a degree. In A 186–7 = B 229–30 Kant

on the whole the matter of an object as treated in the Anticipations is its sensed qualities, which are distinguished from its
extensive quantity, that is, from its size and duration and
perhaps its shape.[1]

Broadly speaking, Kant is about to argue that an object is
more than the space which it occupies and the time through
which it lasts. It is real as filling a determinate space and time,
and what fills space and time must have intensive quantity
or degree.

§ 2. *The Proof in the First Edition*

We have seen that 'apprehension' involves a successive
synthesis of what is given in sensation, and therefore a synthesis
of the times and spaces occupied by what is given; and that
consequently every object must have extensive quantity.
But apprehension is more than a successive synthesis of times
and spaces; and we can abstract from the successive synthesis
and consider apprehension as a mere momentary 'taking up'
of the given. We can therefore say that in the appearance, or
object, there is something the apprehension of which is not a
successive synthesis producing a whole by the addition of part
to part. What is apprehended in this way can have no extensive
quantity.

So far at least Kant would seem to be right. He does not
mean that we can sense something in a mere point of time and
space without reference to anything else;[2] that is utterly

points out that the determinations or accidents (and so presumably
the qualities) of a substance are always *real*; but he warns us against
the danger of separating the accident from the substance, and reminds
us that the accident is only the way in which the substance exists.

[1] Shape is not an extensive quantity, but (like extension and also
position) it is a determination of space rather than of the real considered in abstraction from the space which it fills; see *M.A.d.N.*
(IV 523).

[2] I do not think Kant holds that we cannot be aware of the colour
red as extended without running successively through its parts: he
does hold that we cannot determine its extent except by running
successively through its parts; see A 426 n. = B 454 n.

opposed to the doctrine of the Second Analogy. He does mean
that when we are aware of anything in space and time, it must
have a quality distinct from being spatial and temporal. We
are aware of colour, taste, or resistance; and whether we regard
these as sensa (that is, modifications of our mind) or as qualities
of objects, they fill time and space, and their complete absence
would mean that time and space were empty.[1] When time
(and space) is filled, we have reality (*realitas phaenomenon*);
when it is empty we have negation = o.

Now, Kant asserts, every sensation is capable of diminution
so that it can decrease and gradually vanish. Therefore between
reality (*realitas phaenomenon*)[2] and negation, or between any
given sensation and complete absence of sensation, there is a
continuous sequence[3] of possible intermediate sensations.[4]
This means that the difference between any given sensation
and such an intermediate sensation is always less than the
difference between the given sensation and zero.[5] Hence
there is a more and a less of what fills time and space, and this
is distinct from the more or less of time and space which is
filled. That is to say, sensation (and the real corresponding
to sensation) has intensive quantity or degree.[6]

There is in this proof no reference to synthesis, but we

---

[1] Kant does not of course suggest that we can perceive empty
space and time; his whole argument throughout the Principles rests
on the view that we cannot. Empty time and space is a mere limit
at the most.

[2] What Kant calls 'reality in the appearance' (*Realität in der
Erscheinung*) is equivalent to '*realitas phaenomenon*'.

[3] A 168 = B 210, '*Zusammenhang*'.

[4] The continuous sequence or gradation is present both in the
sensation and in the quality of the object.

[5] If, for example, we see a red colour, there is always possible a
less red colour which is still red. See A 169 = B 211.

[6] This should be compared with the argument in A 143 = B 182–3.
There Kant points out that a sensation can fill the same length of
time more or less, until it ceases altogether. There is therefore a
sequence (*Zusammenhang*), or rather a continuous transition (*Übergang*),
from reality to negation; and this means that reality must be recognised
as a quantum quite apart from the quantum of time (or space) which
it fills.

already know that the schema of quality 'contains and makes representable' the synthesis of sensation (or sense-perception) with the idea of time.[1] This point is brought out later.[2] Needless to say, unless there were an act of synthesis involved, it would be impossible on Kantian principles to have any *a priori* knowledge in regard to sensation.

§ 3. *The Proof in the Second Edition*

Sense-perception is empirical consciousness, and must contain sensation.[3] Appearances, since they are objects of sense-perception,[4] are not merely pure intuitions like space and time, which indeed can never be perceived in the strict sense.[5] The spatial and temporal form of appearances cannot be known apart from pure intuition, but appearances themselves contain matter as well as form, the matter for some object in general.[6] This matter is described as that through which we represent something as existing in space and time,[7] and is said to be the *real* of sensation;[8] it would seem to be a

[1] A 145 = B 184.
[2] A 175–6 = B 217–8. It is also brought out in the proof added in B 207–8.
[3] B 207. Strictly speaking, empirical consciousness of an object need not contain actual sensation of the object, but sense-perception must.
[4] To be such objects, they must be known by thought as well as by sense-perception.
[5] That is, '*wahrgenommen*', which is the verb corresponding to sense-perception (*Wahrnehmung*). This point about space and time was not brought out in the first proof; it is repeated again and again throughout the Principles.
[6] Kant says 'the matters' (*Materien*). I suppose he is referring to the different qualities of the object. He is referring also to his view that every individual object is thought under the concept of an object in general.
[7] The existence or actuality of a thing depends on its connexion with the material conditions of experience, namely sensation; see A 218 = B 266.
[8] Kant here explains, though obscurely, what he means by matter as the real of sensation. He speaks of it (1) as a subjective idea which gives us only the consciousness that the subject is affected, and

quality given to us in sensation[1] and attributed by us to an object.

Now a continuous change is possible from empirical consciousness (or sense-perception) to pure consciousness (or pure intuition); the real (the sensed quality in time and space) might diminish and finally disappear from our consciousness, so that nothing would be left but a formal or *a priori* consciousness of the pure manifold of time and space. Hence there is possible a synthesis which is the production of a quantity (a more or less) of sensation, beginning from pure intuition (= o or complete absence of this sensation) and arriving at any particular quantity.[2]

Sensation has therefore a quantity peculiar to itself, and this

(2) as related by us to an object in general. *Both* these things are necessary if we are to have the real of sensation; compare Benno Erdmann, *Beiträge zur Geschichte und Revision des Textes von Kants Kritik der reinen Vernunft*, p. 56. On this view sensation, or rather the sensum, can be regarded in abstraction as a mere modification of the mind; but as related to an object and brought under the categories it is the real of sensation, a real quality of a phenomenal object. When we see a red colour, we see it as the colour of an object in space; this is not due merely to sense, but to the transcendental synthesis of imagination by which we complete the object in accordance with the categories.

[1] Qualities are given to us directly in sensation, but physical science is able to infer other qualities not given directly in sensation; compare A 226 = B 273.

[2] Kant is stating only a possibility. Time and space cannot be perceived in themselves, but only as filled, and we do not begin with empty space and time and then proceed to fill them. On the other hand I think Kant does believe that when we open our eyes and look at a red colour, we pass from complete absence of colour through various degrees up to that particular shade of red; and again that if we are looking at the colour on a dull day, and the sun suddenly shines on it, we pass continuously through different degrees from the dull to the bright colour.

It should be noted that there can be a transition from reality to negation as well as a transition from negation to reality, but the transition from negation to reality is the one which is described by Kant as a synthesis. If this is a synthesis, the transition from reality to negation looks more like omitting elements from a synthesis, but there is still a synthesis of the elements retained.

quantity is not extensive, since[1] in sensation *quâ* sensation[2] there is no intuition of time or space, and so no parts outside one another. It is therefore an intensive quantity, and it arises because in apprehension empirical consciousness can[3] pass in a certain time[4] from absence of the sensation to the given amount of sensation. Since sense-perception of objects always involves sensation (in addition to intuitions of time and space), we must ascribe a corresponding intensive quantity to such objects.[5]

We should expect Kant to mean by this that the sensed qualities of objects—colour, sound, taste, etc., and especially resistance and weight, if these can be said to be sensed qualities —must have intensive quantity. I believe this is what he does mean, but he suddenly asserts[6] that this intensive quantity is a degree of influence[7] on sense. Such a statement may suggest that Kant has at the back of his mind a doctrine of physical matter as the cause of sensation[8]. But this doctrine is here

---

[1] Kant gives as another reason that 'sensation *quâ* sensation is not an objective idea.' I do not see why the subjectivity of sensation should be a ground for saying either that it involves no intuition of space or time or that it must be an intensive quantity—unless indeed Kant means that sensation as subjective can be nothing more than a consciousness of being 'affected'; compare B 207.

[2] B 208, '*an sich*'. Here again we are dealing with sensation in abstraction.   [3] Kant again is speaking of a possibility.

[4] The fact that it takes time, however brief, to pass from absence of sensation to a given degree shows it is only by abstraction that we separate intensive from extensive quantity. At every moment during the period of transition we have a different degree before us.

[5] 'Such objects' seems to be an abbreviation for 'the qualities of such objects', but it is a legitimate abbreviation which it would be pedantic to avoid.

[6] This may be compared with his equally sudden assertion in B 225 that the quantum of substance in nature can neither be increased nor diminished.

[7] 'Influence' (*Einfluss, influxus* or *actio transiens*) is the technical term for the action of one substance on another, and so indicates a particular kind of causality. Compare Baumgarten, *Metaphysica* § 211 (XVII 71).

[8] The same doctrine is present in the first proof, if we regard that proof as continuing to the end of the first paragraph of B 211. It is,

irrelevant, and on the whole it seems better to suppose that these words are used without any very precise or definite significance.[1]

§ 4. *Intensive Quantity*

Let us set aside for the moment the view that our sensations are caused by physical objects. Even so, Kant's Principle requires working out in detail,[2] and the exact bearing of his argument is not always certain. Nevertheless we may say that he is directing attention to an important element in experience, and to one which has at least some appearance of being known *a priori*.[3]

Needless to say we cannot tell *a priori* that any particular shade of colour must be found in nature. The most we can say *a priori* is that in passing from a paler to a darker shade, we must pass through all the intermediate shades. If a psychologist informs us that there is no such transition and that our sensations are discontinuous, I certainly do not feel myself

however, there touched upon only in passing, because (as Kant points out correctly in A 169 = B 210) this Principle has nothing to do with causality.

[1] If we consider the quality of the object to be directly given in sensation, it is not unnatural to say loosely that the quality is the cause of the sensation, and that objects have different degrees of influence on sense.

[2] Thus sound, for example, has loudness, pitch, and timbre. Do all of these have degrees or only the first? A similar distinction can be made in colour, and possibly in other sensible qualities. It seems best to suppose that Kant is here concerned only with degrees of loudness in sound and of depth in colour; but there are other continuous gradations—such as higher and lower in pitch—the relation of which to gradations of intensive quantity ought to be considered.

[3] Curiously enough, this was partially admitted by Hume, who asserted—contrary to the central principle of his philosophy—that if there were a man who had never seen a particular shade of blue, and if all other shades were put before him, 'descending gradually from the deepest to the lightest', he would be able to have an 'idea' of the missing shade, even although it had never been conveyed to him by his senses. See *Treatise*, Book I, Part I, Section 1.

in a position to contradict him.[1] Yet I find it hard to think my belief in degrees of sensible qualities due merely to generalisation from experience. No doubt I could not have such a belief apart from experience; but just as I know, when I see a line, that a shorter line is possible, so I seem to know, when I see a shade of colour, that a paler shade is possible,[2] and that the paler shade could fill the same area and last for the same time. And it seems as reasonable to say that there is an infinity of possible paler shades between any given shade and zero, as it is to say that there is an infinity of possible shorter lines between any given line and zero. We may well hesitate nowadays to assert that we know anything *a priori*, but is there any ground for saying that one of these statements is known *a priori* and the other not? And can we really maintain that either of these statements rests on precisely the same basis as the statement that forget-me-nots are blue?

Kant believes that the Principle of the Anticipations, like that of the Axioms, has immediate or intuitive certainty,[3] and we must, I think, agree that if it has certainty at all, the certainty must be intuitive. But for Kant such intuitive certainty implies the possibility of constructing in intuition an object corresponding to a concept, and this at once raises difficulties. His own doctrine is that qualities cannot be constructed *a priori*,[4] and yet he asserts that I can determine

---

[1] The physical stimulus can be gradually increased for some time before we recognise any change in the sensible quality, but I doubt whether that proves change cf sensation to be discontinuous. The sensation may vary continuously with the stimulus even when the variation is not perceptible. The fact that we can watch a moving body for some time—for example, the sun or the hands of a watch—without recognising that there is a change of position does not prove that motion is discontinuous; and the same principle may, I think, hold also of change in the perceived qualities of objects.

[2] This seems to be all that is necessary to justify Kant's contention, even if he himself thought he could go further. He believes that the continuity of all change—including change of degree—can be proved; but the fact that he excludes such a proof from Transcendental Philosophy (see A 171 = B 213) suggests that continuity of change may not be necessary to his present argument.   [3] A 160-2 = B 199-201.

[4] See A 714-5 = B 742-3, and compare *Log. Einl.* III (IX 23).

a priori, that is, construct, the degree of the sensation of sunlight by combining some 200,000 illuminations of the moon.[1]

We may perhaps admit, with Hume, that we could in imagination fill up a gap in the shades of one colour; but if we were acquainted only with the degree of brightness produced by one moon, we manifestly could not create in imagination the brightness which would be produced by 200,000 moons, nor could we know *a priori* that such a degree of brightness would not be blinding. Such considerations are, however, irrelevant. Kant is not concerned with the extent to which we can create images in imagination, a question to be settled only by empirical psychology. He is concerned, as he says, with the rules of a *mathematical* synthesis.[2] If we are given a foot, we know how to construct a line 200,000 feet long, but we do not know what such a line would look like without actual experience.[3] Similarly it may be maintained, not that we could construct *a priori* the actual appearance of the sun, but that we know the principle (or schema) of such a construction.[4] Kant must mean only that we can construct the degree in abstraction, giving it a place in the scale of degrees and so making it numerable—not that we can imagine every possible degree of a given quality.[5]

---

[1] A 179 = B 221. This seems to imply that, given a particular quality, I can construct its different degrees *a priori*.

[2] A 178 = B 221; compare the difference between the mathematical and the aesthetic estimate of quantity in *K.d.U.* § 26 (V 251 ff.).

[3] Compare A 140 = B 179.

[4] This is supported by Kant's assertion in A 175–6 = B 217 that the real means merely the *synthesis* in an empirical consciousness in general; and again in A 723 = B 751 that we can have *a priori* only indeterminate concepts of the *synthesis* of possible sensations (so far as they belong to the unity of apperception). Compare A 143 = B 183 where the schema of reality, as the quantity of something so far as it fills time, is the continuous and uniform *production* of reality in time; and see also A 720 = B 748.

[5] Compare again Kant's statement in A 161 = B 201 that in the *a priori* determination of appearances we are concerned only with the *form* of a quality (or a quantity). In A 176 = B 218 he says that about the qualities of appearances we know *a priori* only that they have a degree—all else is left to experience.

A fuller account of the intuitive certainty claimed for the proof of this Principle, and also a more elaborate treatment of the details, would have been welcome. In particular we require to know a great deal more about the relation between the concrete constructions of imagination and the abstract constructions of mathematics.[1] Nevertheless if we know that there is possible a continuous transition from any given degree of intensity to zero (just as there is possible a continuous transition from any given line or area or volume to zero), we know that there is a possibility of measuring such a degree (just as there is a possibility of measuring a line or area or volume), and that such measurements can be expressed in numbers. It is this point alone—the applicability of mathematics to appearances—which Kant is attempting to establish.[2] He has not adequately brought out the differences of the two cases,[3] but, so far as I can see, his doctrine is sound.[4]

§ 5. *The Synthesis of Quality*

It may be thought that Kant has no right to use the word 'synthesis' for our apprehension of degree, and that he has failed to connect this kind of synthesis with the nature of time and space.

The first objection seems to me one of terminology, and if synthesis means the holding together of a plurality in unity, there certainly is a synthesis of degrees as well as of extensions; every degree is a plurality in unity, since although it is an indivisible whole, it contains all the lesser degrees between it and zero.

---

[1] We could not know how to construct a line 200,000 feet long unless we could actually construct short lines in imagination, and the same principle must, I think, hold in regard to degree.

[2] See A 178 = B 221.

[3] One of the most important differences is that in measuring a degree of intensity, for example of heat or weight, we translate it into terms of extensive quantity; we use a thermometer in the one case and a pair of scales in the other.

[4] For a defence of this doctrine see Cassirer, *Kants Leben und Lehre*, pp. 191–4.

The second objection is more weighty. We can say at the most that time and space must be filled with the real which is given to sense, if we are to be aware of real objects, or even to be aware of an actual determinate part of space or time.[1] We can hardly assert *a priori* that this reality must have degrees if it is to fill space and time.[2]

The transcendental synthesis of imagination by which we construct our phenomenal world in space and time is not merely a synthesis of empty times and spaces, but a filling of time and space with what is given to us in sensation, or a synthesis of sensation with time and space. The actual intensity of the object's qualities, like its actual size or duration, is known to us through experience alone.[3] Nevertheless since experience always involves a transcendental synthesis, every object must have both extensive and intensive quantity of some sort, and our knowledge that it must do so is no generalisation from experience, liable at any moment to be contradicted, but is rather a synthetic *a priori* judgement affirming the necessary conditions apart from which human experience would be impossible. Such is the Kantian doctrine, and I do not think it can be dismissed as obviously untenable.

As regards the connexion between degree and the categories of reality, negation and limitation,[4] I have already offered such defence as is possible—see Chapter XXXIII § 3. There are, however, one or two further points to be noticed. Reality

---

[1] This is why Kant can speak of the schema of quality as a time-determination. We determine actual spaces and times only through the synthesis of sensation (or reality) in time. Nevertheless the character of this synthesis (as imposing degrees upon reality) seems to be proved independently of the nature of time (or space).

[2] The theory of atoms and the void (which Kant never claims to disprove on *a priori* grounds) seems to offer an alternative view—unless we hold that, inasmuch as it presupposes that parts of space are empty, it is not a theory of how space is filled.

[3] Compare A 176 = B 218. Like the actual size or duration of objects, it depends on the thing-in-itself. The character of our minds determines only that the thing-in-itself must appear to us to have some size and duration and to have qualities of some degree.

[4] It is noteworthy that the proof of the Anticipations is directed primarily to the schema, not to the schematised category.

(when schematised) is the given quality which fills time (and space), while negation is the empty time (and space) which is filled. For a determinate object we require the combination of the two. I think Kant holds that the object both fills and does not fill time (and space), so far as its qualities have a degree and have not a greater degree; so that there are different degrees in which we combine reality and negation (or quality and time) in order to have a determinate object under the category of limitation.

The full meaning of his doctrine is, however, apparent only when we understand his dynamical theory of matter. He believes that there is a real opposition of moving forces which is, as it were, logical opposition translated into terms of time and space, just as the relation of cause and effect is the logical relation of ground and consequent translated into these terms. What fills space is matter, which Kant identifies with the movable;[1] and matter fills space through a combination of the moving forces of repulsion and attraction.[2] It is the real opposition of these opposing forces which explains how space can be filled, and yet filled in different degrees. This is an empirical illustration—it is, of course, not a deduction possible in pure philosophy—of Kant's principle that a real object must be thought under the category of limitation, which involves a combination of reality and negation.[3]

---

[1] '*das Bewegliche.*'

[2] For this reason Kant attaches special importance to the quality which he calls resistance or impenetrability, and also to the quality which he calls weight. The former reveals the power of repulsion in bodies, while the latter reveals the power of attraction. It is primarily through the resistance of bodies (both to our own body and to other bodies) that we became aware of what is assumed by common sense to be solidity.

[3] The whole doctrine can be understood only by an examination of Kant's *Metaphysische Anfangsgründe der Naturwissenschaft*, but a sort of summary is to be found in the chapter on Dynamics—the 'general appendix' (IV 523 ff.). There the *real* in space (commonly called the solid) fills space through the force of repulsion; the force of attraction is *negative* in relation to the real (the proper object of outer sense), for it penetrates space and thereby cancels or negates the solid (or the impenetrable); the *limitation* of the first force by

§ 6. *The Causality of the Object*

When Kant maintains that because our sensations must have a degree, the qualities of objects must have a degree, he is to some extent anticipating his doctrine of substance and accident; but this is at least partly justified by his analysis of the concept of an object, when he argued that our ideas (including sensa) refer to an object, or are appearances of an object, inasmuch as they are synthetised or united in accordance with the necessary unity of apperception. To say that our sensa reveal the qualities or accidents of substances is only an elaboration of this doctrine and a translation of it into terms of time; and Kant is perhaps entitled in his present argument to keep the doctrine of the First Analogy in the background.[1]

On the other hand the doctrine that physical substances are the causes of our sensations is as irrelevant to the Anticipations as is the doctrine that physical substances are the causes of changes in each other.[2] We completely misunderstand Kant, if we imagine him to be arguing that we first of all have a sensation, and then infer that the sensation must be caused by some quality in an object.[3] He is not maintaining that the cause of that which has degree (namely, sensation) must itself also have degree.[4] He is maintaining that the qualities of objects

the second determines the degree in which space is filled. Kant believes that either of these forces by itself would result in the emptying of space. The modern theories in regard to positive and negative electricity would be equally welcome to him as an illustration.

[1] This shows again how all the Principles are bound up together and must not be considered in isolation, although they have to be expounded in succession.

[2] A 169 = B 210. The first kind of causality is called by Professor Price 'vertical causality' and the second 'horizontal causality'; see *Perception*, p. 86.

[3] Here as always any attempt to interpret Kant as trying to explain the temporal development of experience results in error.

[4] The statement about 'the degree of influence on sense' in B 208 ought not to be interpreted in this sense. Kant does maintain—see A 168 = B 210—that reality in time and space may be regarded as a cause, and says that the degree of *reality* as a cause is called a 'moment' as being apprehended, not successively, but instantaneously, for example, in the 'moment 'of gravity. To say this is not to say that

as given or revealed to us in sensation must have degree. Whether scientific thought is able to infer other qualities which are not revealed directly in sensation we need not here discuss.[1]

Nevertheless Kant does believe that human sensations are caused by a physical stimulus,[2] although in his view this cannot be known *a priori*: we know *a priori* only that every event must have a cause. The cause of any particular event can be discovered by experience alone; and it is by experience alone that we discover certain physical stimuli to be the causes of our sensations.

The exact method of this discovery it is not Kant's business to explain, nor does he attempt to do so; but granted that we possess the concept of causality and are aware of a world of physical objects, the fact that when we fall we invariably hurt ourselves, and when we approach the fire we invariably feel warm, is itself enough to suggest a causal connexion between physical bodies and inner states. There is no reason why Kant should not accept any empirical account (such as is offered by physiology or by psychology) that explains the nature of the stimuli causing our sensations or the method of determining the character of these stimuli.[3]

the extensive quantity of an object is irrelevant to causation, or even to the causation of degrees of sensation. One brilliantly illuminated surface may cause the same degree of sensation as many less brilliantly illuminated surfaces of the same extent; see A 176 = B 217 and compare A 179 = B 221. In this illustration we are of course not supposed to be looking at the direct source of the light, but, for example, at a wall illuminated alternately by one lamp or six candles.

[1] Compare his view that there is a magnetic matter pervading all bodies, and that this could be perceived, if our senses were finer (A 226 = B 273).

[2] Compare, for example, A 213 = B 260. The ultimate cause or ground is the thing-in-itself; see Chapter II §§ 2–3.

[3] A valuable discussion of this problem is to be found in Price, *Perception*, Chapter X. We must not imagine that accounts of the kind indicated explain how we come to know physical bodies: they presuppose that we already have this knowledge.

§ 7. *The Doctrine of Continuity*

The rest of Kant's exposition[1] elaborates the details, and indicates the applications, of his general theory. It offers little difficulty in the way of interpretation.

Quantities are said to be continuous, if no part of them is the smallest possible part, that is, if no part is simple.[2] However small the quantity may be, there is always a smaller quantity between it and zero. Kant believes he has shown that intensive quantity is characterised by such continuity, because there is a continuous gradation between any given intensive quantity (or degree) and zero. He now maintains that since no part of time or space is the smallest possible part, space and time are continuous (extensive) quantities. It follows that points and moments are not parts of space and time, but only limits or boundaries. Every part of space is itself a space, and every part of time is itself a time, so that space and time are made up of spaces and times, not of points or instants.[3] We cannot say, for example, that any two points on a line are next to one another; either they are the same point, or else there is a line between them in which an intermediate point can be taken.

Continuous quantities as so described, whether extensive or intensive, are the product of a continuous and uninterrupted synthesis, for which reason they can be called 'flowing'.[4] When the synthesis is interrupted, that is, stopped and then repeated, what is produced is an aggregate. Thus if 'thirteen dollars' means a particular measure (a mark) of fine silver, it constitutes a continuous quantity, or quantum[5], for no part of it is the smallest possible.[6] If it means thirteen silver coins, it is an aggregate, or a number, of coins; for it is composed of so many discrete units, each of which is the smallest possible part of the sum of thirteen dollars.[7]

---

[1] A 169–176 = B 211–218.   [2] A 169 = B 211.

[3] I believe that even this doctrine, like so much else, is questioned by modern mathematics.   [4] A 170 = B 211–12, '*fliessend*.'

[5] Kant seems to imply here—as also in A 171 = B 212—that a quantum is necessarily a continuous quantity, but in A 526–7=B 554–5 he speaks of *quanta continua* and *quanta discreta*.

[6] Kant believes that matter, like space, must be infinitely divisible.

[7] Kant adds that each unit is a quantum, since unity is at the basis

Kant maintains that all appearances or objects are necessarily continuous quantities, both as regards their extensive quantity (determined by the synthesis of the space or time which they occupy), and also as regards their intensive quantity (the degree of the qualities determined, directly or indirectly, by the synthesis of sensation).[1] He maintains also—what is a much more difficult proposition—that it is easy to prove, with mathematical evidence, the necessary continuity of all change (all transition of a thing from one state to another).[2] Such a proof he does not here offer—on the ground that it presupposes empirical principles, and so lies outside the limits of Transcendental Philosophy, and belongs to what he calls 'the universal science of nature'.[3] Nevertheless in the Second Analogy he does set forth what professes to be such a proof.[4]

of every number. He means, I presume, that in counting objects we ignore their internal differences, and treat them as homogeneous or continuous. The identification of number with an aggregate seems to treat number as discrete, and looks like treating numbers as if they were only integers.

[1] A 170 = B 212 ; A 171 = B 212.   [2] A 171 = B 212–3.

[3] A 171 = B 213. The science referred to, since it is opposed to Transcendental Philosophy, is presumably Rational Physiology (*physiologia rationalis*), so far as that is immanent and not transcendent. Both sciences are part of speculative metaphysics; but Transcendental Philosophy (which covers the *Kritik of Pure Reason*) deals only with concepts and principles which apply to *objects in general*, while Rational Physiology deals with *nature*; and since nature is divided into corporeal and spiritual nature, the science is divided into Rational Physics and Rational Psychology (*physica rationalis* and *psychologia rationalis*). Rational Physics is so much more important than Rational Psychology that it is at times regarded as the only metaphysical science of nature—although Kant believes that there is an immanent Rational Psychology as well as the transcendent Rational Psychology repudiated in the Paralogisms. Rational Physics is said to realise, that is, to give 'sense and significance' to Transcendental Philosophy. See A 845–6 = B 873–4; B 17–18; B 20 n.; and compare *M.A.d.N. Vor.* (IV 467) and the final remark to the third main part which deals with mechanics (IV 552–3).

The difficulty of all this is that Rational Physics and Rational Psychology are particular, and not universal, sciences, and the discussion of change *in general* cannot be confined to either. For this reason Kant refuses it a place in his discussion of Rational Physics; see *M.A.d.N.* (IV 553).   [4] A 206 = B 252 ff. See also *Metaphysik*, pp. 54 ff.

§ 8. *Empty Space and Time*

If it be granted that there is an infinity of degrees alike in our sensa and in the qualities of objects which our sensa reveal, sense-perception, and consequently experience (which is knowledge through combined sense-perceptions[1]), can offer no proof of empty space or time. We cannot perceive empty space or empty time, since sense-perception always involves sensation; and Kant believes we cannot infer empty space or time either from the objects we perceive or from the fact that the qualities of perceived objects have different degrees—he even goes so far as to say that we ought not to assume empty space or time for the purpose of explaining phenomena. By this he means only that we ought not to assume empty space and time to be *necessary* for the purpose of explaining phenomena.

We find by experience that when two bodies have the same volume, one may be, for example, heavier than the other. We argue from this that one contains more matter than the other, and we are tempted to assume that the lighter body must therefore contain more empty space. This was the doctrine of the atomists, who maintained that everything was composed of atoms and the void. Such a doctrine was supposed to rest upon experience, but it really rests on an unexamined metaphysical assumption—the assumption that what fills space can differ only in extensive quantity, so that if a body is lighter, it must contain fewer atoms, and therefore more empty space. Once we admit that the same reality can fill space in greater or less *degree*, a smaller degree of reality may completely fill the same volume as is filled by a greater degree. Hence the inference which argued to empty space from differences in the qualities of bodies of the same volume was illegitimate.

Kant's contention is, as he says, to be taken only as an illustration of his more general doctrine that the real which fills determinate times and spaces differs, not only in extension, but in degree. When we discuss the nature of weight or resistance or heat, we are passing beyond pure philosophy, and dealing

[1] B 161. Compare B 219.

with problems which must be settled by experience. The theory of the atomists was a mechanical theory of matter, which Leibniz and Kant opposed with a dynamical theory. Kant is not arguing that pure philosophy can decide between these two theories, but only that the dynamical theory ought not to be excluded on the basis of what is really a metaphysical assumption. In this he is undoubtedly right.

§ 9. *Kant's Conclusion*

As usual, Kant finishes with a short summary of his argument. He stresses once more the surprising fact that we can anticipate sensation, which is the empirical element of sense-perception, although we can do so only in regard to its degree. He points out—what with his usual carelessness he failed to make explicit in the argument of the first edition—that degree involves a synthesis of the given, a synthesis which we can consider in abstraction from the synthesis of extensive quantity and regard as complete in every moment.[1] Finally he remarks about quantities in general that we know *a priori* only one quality which they must possess, namely continuity;[2] about quality we know *a priori* only that it must have intensive quantity or a degree.

---

[1] This is consistent with the view that we pass gradually in time from a lesser degree to a greater or *vice versa*; see B 208. All the lesser degrees previously experienced are held together, or synthetised, at any moment in an indivisible unity.

[2] I do not see how Kant reconciles this with his recognition of aggregates, which are discrete quantities, although the units of which they are composed are continuous quantities; see A 170–1 = B 212.

BOOK X

THE ANALOGIES OF EXPERIENCE

THE ANALOGIES OF EXPERIENCE

CHAPTER XXXIX

THE PRINCIPLE OF THE ANALOGIES

§ 1. *The Formulation of the Principle*

Just as there is one Principle of the Axioms and one Principle of the Anticipations, so there is one Principle of the Analogies; but because the synthesis described in the Principle of the Analogies is more complicated than the synthesis described in the other two Principles, Kant finds it necessary first to state the *general* [1] Principle of the Analogies, and then to deal in detail with the three separate rules or laws or Principles in which the general Principle is manifested. It must not be forgotten that in this case, as in the others, there is only one synthesis (or one aspect of the universal synthesis), and that this one synthesis involves three categories.[2]

In the second edition the Principle is formulated as follows: *Experience is possible only through the representation*[3] *of a necessary connexion of sense-perceptions.*[4]

This necessary connexion,[5] or *nexus*, is imposed upon the given manifold by the transcendental synthesis of imagination, and is a connexion of correlated, but heterogeneous, elements; the relations involved are those of substance and accident, of cause and effect, and of reciprocal causality (or interaction) between substances.[6] The Analogies are therefore concerned

---

[1] *'allgemeine'*; see A 176 and A 177 = B 220.

[2] Compare Chapter XXXIII § 7.

[3] *'Vorstellung.'* This means the 'representing' or 'conceiving' or 'thinking'.

[4] B 218. 'Sense-perceptions' (*Wahrnehmungen*) are here equivalent to 'appearances' (*Erscheinungen*). Compare B 160.

[5] *'Verknüpfung.'* This is identified with *nexus* in B 201 n. It is a special case of combination (*Verbindung*), combination of the manifold *as regards i's time-relations*. The necessity of 'connexion' should not be confused with the general necessity of 'combination' proved in the Transcendental Deduction. Compare Baumgarten, *Metaphysica* § 14 (XII 27).

[6] The first two are the examples given by Kant in B 201 n. The relation of interaction (reciprocal causality or influence) combines both. Compare B 111.

with relations of heterogeneous elements which necessarily belong to one another, while the Axioms and Anticipations were concerned with homogeneous elements which do not necessarily belong to one another.[1]

The Principles of the Understanding are proved by showing that they express the conditions of experience, through which alone experience is possible.[2] The general Principle of the Analogies as formulated in the second edition professes to state such a condition, but it omits to state—perhaps in the interests of brevity—that the 'necessary connexion' which is the condition of experience is a necessary connexion *in time*, and is concerned with the existence[3] of appearances in time. This point is emphasised in the formula of the first edition, which is as follows: *All appearances are subject, as regards their existence, to* a priori *rules in accordance with which their relation to one another in time is determined.*[4]

The main point of these formulae is a simple one. Kant believes that every object of experience must have a definite or determinate position in a common objective time;[5] and that it can have such a definite position only if it is subject to the rules of necessary connexion in time laid down in the three

[1] See B 201 n. Two extensive quantities or two degrees are homogeneous, and we cannot say that where one is, the other must be. Accident is not homogeneous with substance nor effect with cause, and we can say that where one is, the other must be.

[2] Compare Chapter XXXV §§ 5–6. Necessary 'connexion' is a special element in, or condition of, that synthetic unity of appearances through which alone experience is possible; see especially A 156 = B 195 and A 158 = B 197.

[3] '*Dasein.*' See A 178 = B 221; alsc A 179 = B 221–2, A 160 = B 199 and B 201–2 n. To exist is 'to be there', to have a definite position in time or in time and space.

[4] A 176–7. Kant says '*a priori* rules of the determination of their relation to one another in one time'. These 'rules' are the Analogies.

[5] The theory of Relativity demands a reinterpretation of the word 'definite'; for the time of an event may be measured differently by different observers. Nevertheless if the measurements can all be translated into terms of one another, and if, knowing one measurement, we can say *a priori* what the others must be, we are, I think, still entitled to say that every event has a definite position in a common time (or a common space-time).

Analogies. As usual, his formula ignores space, although his main concern in the Analogies is with physical objects. The combination of a theoretical insistence on time (at the expense of space) and a practical concern with objects in space (to the neglect of mental events in time) is a source of difficulty in his argument.

§ 2. *The Argument in the First Edition*

The argument of the first edition is obscurely expressed. There is, first of all, a short introduction [1] explaining why there must be three rules to determine all the relations of appearances in time. These rules are the three Analogies; and the general principle of the Analogies, like that of all other Principles, rests on the necessary unity of apperception in one of its different manifestations or aspects. It rests on the fact that the unity of apperception, in respect of all possible empirical consciousness or sense-perception, is necessary *at every time*.[2] Hence it rests on the necessary synthetic unity of all appearances *as regards their relation in time*.[3] Unless all appearances (or objects) were related in one common objective time, the unity of apperception, and so experience, would be impossible.

If we grant its presuppositions—that the unity of apperception is the condition of the thought necessary for experience, and time is the condition of the intuitions necessary for experi-

---

[1] A 177 = B 219. This is dealt with at the end of the present subsection.

[2] A 177 = B 220. The unity of apperception is not limited to a particular time, but applies to all times. Compare Chapter XXI § 5.

[3] The main difficulty of this inference is the reason obscurely added by Kant: 'because the unity of apperception is the *a priori* condition of all possible empirical consciousness' (*da jene a priori zum Grunde liegt*). What rests on something as a condition need not rest on what that something conditions. The unity of apperception and the unity of appearances, however, may be said to condition one another mutually; and indeed Kant often speaks as if they were the same thing; compare, for example, B 134 and A 108. If '*jene*' could refer forward to the synthetic unity of appearances, the argument would be easier, but I doubt whether this is possible.

ence—there seems to be little difficulty in this contention; but Kant supports it by a brief defence. Original apperception is related to inner sense (the totality of all ideas), and indeed is related *a priori* to its form. We should expect this form to be time, but Kant describes it as 'the *relation* of the manifold empirical consciousness *in time*'. Time as the form of inner sense is made up of relations[1] and seems to be identified here with the temporal relations of our ideas, though usually it is regarded as the condition of these relations.[2] In any case the fact that original apperception is related to time, as the form of inner sense, implies that all our ideas must be united, *as regards their time-relations*, in original apperception.[3] I think we may add that Kant means '*as regards their objective time-relations*'; for he makes his contention depend on the fact that everything must be subject to the transcendental unity of apperception, if it is to belong to my knowledge and to be an object for me.[4]

There must, then, be synthetic unity in the time-relations of all appearances or sense-perceptions,[5] a synthetic unity which is determined *a priori* and is a necessary condition of experience. This synthetic unity is expressed in[6] the law

[1] Compare B 67, where time is said to 'contain' the relations of succession and simultaneity and (curiously enough) of the permanent, and to 'contain' nothing but relations.

[2] See A 30 = B 46. It should, however, be remembered that Kant has considered (in the Axioms and Anticipations) the time-series and the time-content; and he is now expressly concerned only with time-order or time-relations; see A 145 = B 184.

[3] Compare A 99, B 150-1, B 152, and B 160-1, all of which prepare us for the present argument. Compare also A 142 = B 181.

[4] This is the general argument of the Transcendental Deduction applied to the special case of temporal relations; compare B 139-40. Such difficulties as it has are the difficulties of the general argument.

[5] 'Synthetic unity in the time-relations of appearances' is for Kant the same thing as 'synthetic unity of appearances as regards their time-relations'. The simplest statement is that appearances must be related to one another in one common objective time.

[6] Kant says it *is* the law. This law is more general and ultimate than the *a priori* rules which are its embodiments—namely the Analogies.

that all empirical time-determinations must stand under the
a priori rules of time-determination in general, these rules
being the three Analogies.[1]

The reason why there are three Analogies is stated in the
introduction.[2] There are only three modes of time—permanence, succession, and simultaneity. Hence we require three
rules for all the time-relations of appearances; and in accordance with them we can determine the *existence* of every appearance in regard to the unity of all time.[3] These rules are prior
to experience and state the necessary conditions under which
alone experience is possible.

The three modes of time, it should be noted, appear to be
identical with the three transcendental schemata of the categories of relation :[4] they are *a priori* time-determinations which
concern the time-order, that is, the order of appearances
in time.[5]

§ 3. *The Modes of Time*

The word 'mode' as used in modern philosophy has no very
precise meaning and is frequently a source of confusion.
In the time of Kant a mode of anything was sharply distinguished from its essence, its attributes, and its relations. The
essence consists of certain primitive and constitutive marks
called strictly *essentialia*. The attributes are not part of the
essence, but they have their sufficient ground in the essence

---

[1] A 177–8 = B 220; compare A 217 = B 264. Compare also the
formula of the first edition in A 176–7; this is the formula which he
here professes to prove. If we are to determine the time at which
any particular appearance exists, we must do so in conformity with
those *a priori* rules apart from which, according to Kant, there could
be no unity in time or in temporal relations.   [2] A 177 = B 219.

[3] I should prefer to say 'in one common objective time'. Kant seems
on the whole to avoid such a usage, perhaps because it suggests that
time is a thing in itself and is something complete and whole.

[4] See A 143–4 = B 183–4 and also Chapter XXXIII § 7. Kemp
Smith translates '*Beharrlichkeit*' as 'permanence' in A 143 = B 183
and as 'duration' in A 177 = B 219. This fails to bring out the identification of the mode of time and the schema.

[5] See A 145 = B 184–5.

and are derivative from it. The modes are inner determinations which have not their sufficient ground in the essence and are not derivative from it.[1] Relations, which are regarded as external, have likewise no sufficient ground in the essence and are not derivative from it. Thus a man may be rational (an essential) without being either learned (a mode) or a master (a relation).[2]

According to this usage a mode is clearly a characteristic or determination of that of which it is the mode. There is an older usage in which a mode is not such a characteristic or determination, but is dependent on that of which it is the mode.[3] Thus Descartes speaks of rest and motion as modes of space.

We have already seen[4] that Kant, when he speaks of the transcendental schemata as time-determinations, does not mean that they are determinations or characteristics of time itself,[5] but rather that they are determinations or characteristics which must belong to objects so far as these are temporal and are combined in one time. The same considerations must apply when he speaks of permanence, succession, and simultaneity as modes of time. He could not possibly mean by this that it is of the essence of time to be permanent, successive, and simultaneous; and equally he could not mean that time may be, but need not be, permanent, successive, and simultaneous. He must mean on the contrary that only in time can

---

[1] Hence the German for 'mode' is '*zufällige Beschaffenheit*' (a contingent characteristic). A mode is 'contingent', because we can have the essence without the mode, although we cannot have the mode without the essence.

[2] Compare also Chapter III § 6.

[3] Compare Spinoza's definition of a mode: *Per modum intelligo substantiae affectiones, sive id, quod in alio est, per quod etiam concipitur.* Time is not a substance, but the temporal characteristics of every object are dependent on time: they can be, or be conceived, only through that of which they are the modes, namely, time, and yet they are not characteristics of time itself.

[4] See Chapter XXXII § 6.

[5] The definitions of the transcendental schemata are in any case sufficient proof of this contention.

appearances be conceived as permanent, successive, and simultaneous.[1]

Thus he can say that change (or succession) does not affect time itself,[2] but only appearances in time;[3] and even that simultaneity is not a mode of time itself,[4] because the parts of time are not simultaneous but successive.[5] At the very moment when succession and simultaneity are said to be modes of time, they are also said to be ways in which the permanent exists.[6]

It is confusing to be told both that certain characteristics are modes of time, and that they are not modes of time itself. Kant ought to have explained clearly what he meant by 'a mode of time' and 'a mode of time itself'; but I can see no real inconsistency in his thought and no very great difficulty in understanding what he means.[7]

From the first mention of modes of time[8] Kant seems to regard them as equivalent to 'time-relations of appear-

[1] This usage approximates to the usage of Descartes. Compare A 30 = B 46 where the idea of time is spoken of as the condition of simultaneity and succession.

[2] Time itself (*Zeit selbst, Zeit für sich, Zeit an sich selbst*) is habitually treated as equivalent to absolute or empty time, particularly in the statement that it cannot be perceived. Compare B 207, A 172 = B 214, B 219, B 225, A 183 = B 226, A 188 = B 231, B 233, A 192 = B 237, A 200 = B 245, B 257, A 215 = B 262.   [3] A 183 = B 226.

[4] Kant is either using 'mode' here loosely for a 'characteristic', or else he means (what would be more consistent) that the modes of time are not modes of empty or absolute time, but of time as filled.

[5] A 183 = B 226. Kant, it should be observed, immediately adds to this that there can be no succession in time itself; so we must not take this to mean that succession *is* a mode of time itself. Nevertheless succession has a particularly close connexion with time, since the parts of time are themselves successive.

[6] A 182 = B 226. This is apparently equivalent to being modes of the existence of the permanent (A 183 = B 227).

[7] Adickes (followed by Kemp Smith) finds here a flat contradiction to be explained only on the view that Kant tacked together notes written at different times without observing their inconsistency.

[8] It should, however, be noted that in A 81 = B 107 *quando, ubi, situs*, and also *prius* and *simul*, are said to be modes of pure sensibility, by which Kant means modes of time and space. Here again he seems to use 'mode' in a sense approximating to that of Descartes.

ances'.[1] He says expressly of succession and simultaneity, just after mentioning them as modes of time, that they are the only relations in time.[2] Later on he again equates the three modes of time with time-relations: (1) the relation to time itself as a quantity (the quantity of existence, i.e. *duration*);[3] (2) the relation in time as a series (*succession*); and (3) the relation in time as a sum or totality[4] of existence (*simultaneity*).[5] These statements show that the modes of time are not modes of time itself.

From all this we may, I think, conclude that when Kant affirms permanence, succession, and simultaneity to be modes of time, he does not mean that time itself, speaking strictly, is permanent or successive or simultaneous—and this he expresses by saying that permanence, succession, and simultaneity are not modes of time itself. He does mean that the permanence, succession, and simultaneity of objects is possible only in time, and is inconceivable apart from time. Permanence, succession, and simultaneity are the three fundamental temporal relations which, Kant believes, must be found in all objects (so far as they are objects in time).

Permanence is not quite on the same footing as succession and simultaneity, since succession and simultaneity may be described as modes of the existence of the permanent or ways in which the permanent exists.[6] But this doctrine must be

---

[1] A 177 = B 219.

[2] A 182 = B 226. Compare also A 179 = B 222 where 'time-relation' and 'mode of time' appear to be equated.

[3] Duration seems here equivalent to permanence.   [4] '*Inbegriff*.'

[5] A 215 = B 262. This passage explains why Kant says that succession and simultaneity are the only relations *in time*, since permanence is a relation *to time*. The words in the last two brackets are '*nacheinander*' and '*zugleich*', which I have translated as 'succession' and 'simultaneity' respectively. Kemp Smith eliminates the brackets.

[6] A 183 = B 227; A 182 = B 226. Again, as we have seen above, permanence is described as a relation to time, rather than a relation in time. If this were taken strictly, permanence would be a relation and not a mode; but obviously permanence is not merely a relation between time and something non-temporal, for the permanent must endure in, or through, time. Further, the category of substance is said to stand under the head of relation, more as a condition of relation

reserved till we consider Kant's account of substance. Here we are concerned only with the general character of Kant's argument in the three Analogies. What he proposes to maintain is roughly this—that since all objects of experience must exist in time, they must be characterised by permanence, succession, and simultaneity; and that these temporal characteristics of objects, if they are objective characteristics, must be necessary, or must be determined in accordance with an *a priori* rule. Whether we accept or reject his view, we must at least recognise that he is attempting to apply the general principle of the Transcendental Deduction: that what distinguishes an object from a succession of subjective appearances is just the necessary combination of these appearances imposed by the nature of our thought and by the transcendental synthesis of imagination working through the medium of time. The application of that general principle in the Analogies is by far the most important part of his doctrine; and although Kant regards his argument as strengthened and enriched by the connexion between the categories of relation and the categorical, hypothetical, and disjunctive forms of judgement, the argument itself rests upon the three modes of time and the general principle that objectivity involves necessary combination,[1] or necessary synthetic unity, in accordance with the transcendental unity of apperception.

§4. *The Argument in the Second Edition*

In the first edition Kant, as we have seen, lays most stress on the unity of apperception, although he makes it clear enough that the necessary synthetic unity of the time-relations of appearances, in accordance with the unity of apperception, is the condition of all *objects* of experience.[2] In the proof added in the second edition he concentrates his attention on the

than as itself containing a relation (A 187 = B 230). Even apart from these statements, it is in itself obvious that permanence differs from succession and simultaneity.

[1] Necessary 'connexion' is, as I have said, a special case of such necessary 'combination'.   [2] A 177 = B 220.

necessary synthetic unity which is the condition of *objects*, and leaves it to us to remember that all synthetic unity is grounded on the unity of apperception.[1] Furthermore he treats the argument generally, without repeating the details about the different modes of time.

Experience is empirical knowledge: it determines an object through empirical sense-perceptions. Since, however, it determines an *object*, there must be more in experience than empirical sense-perception; there must be a synthesis of sense-perceptions. As we know from the Transcendental Deduction, what is essential to experience as *knowledge of objects* (and not mere intuition or sensation) is the synthetic unity of the given manifold in one consciousness.[2] This synthetic unity is the necessary synthetic unity which is grounded on the unity of apperception and is the condition of there being an object.

Synthesis, Kant insists, is not to be found in sense-perceptions, and still less can we find in sense-perceptions necessary synthetic unity. This is the general principle in which Kant agrees with Hume; but here he is thinking primarily (if not exclusively) of the necessary synthetic unity which is to be found in the connexion, or *nexus*, of heterogeneous elements which necessarily belong to one another, as for example cause and effect. Sense-perceptions, considered in themselves, come to us in an order in which we can descry no necessity. Apprehension—here as always closely connected, if not identified, with sense-perception—is a mere taking up and putting together the given manifold; it contains in itself no idea that the given appearances are necessarily connected in space and time.[3]

---

[1] B 218–19. It would be absurd to regard this change of emphasis as an inconsistency. In the changes added in the second edition Kant generally lays more stress upon the object, I presume because the unity of apperception was liable to be misunderstood as merely subjective. Compare B 139–40 and B 142.

[2] This is a clear reference to the unity of apperception.

[3] Apprehension—if we may judge by Kant's general view of it— involves more than a taking up and holding together of appearances in the order in which they are given. It arranges the given appearances

So far Kant is merely summing up the doctrine of the Transcendental Deduction. He now proceeds to develop his theory in two sentences, the first of which exhibits that curious compression and complexity usually to be found at the crux of his arguments.

First of all he applies his general principle to what he calls 'relation in the existence of the manifold'. By existence[1] he means being in time, and for simplicity's sake we may say that 'relations in existence' are the relations of succession and simultaneity.[2] An object exists either before or after or along with another. Since experience is experience of objects, experience of the temporal relations of objects is an experience of objective temporal relations. *In experience we know the objective order of objects or events*, not merely the order in which we come to know these objects or events, or the order in which we can arrange them by the exercise of uncontrolled imagination.[3]

in space and time, so that we can apprehend, not merely a succession of given appearances, but an empirical object such as a house. What apprehension cannot give us is the necessity of these arrangements or combinations, and apart from necessity there is, according to Kant, no difference between an objective, and a merely subjective or imaginary, combination. Furthermore this necessary connexion (which is the mark of objectivity or existence in space and time) is not merely necessary connexion within the object apprehended, but necessary connexion with other objects to which it is related in space and time.

[1] '*Dasein*' or 'there-being'.

[2] Permanence, as I have said, is on a slightly different footing.

[3] Kant says that in experience we have to know 'the relation in the existence of the manifold, not as it is put together in time, but as it is objectively in time'. The word 'it' presumably refers grammatically to the manifold; and the words 'put together' (*zusammengestellt*) suggest a connexion with 'apprehension', which was said above to be a 'putting together' (*Zusammenstellung*) of the manifold. The general sense is, I think, that though in apprehension we 'put together' the given manifold in certain temporal relations—whether in the order in which the manifold is given to us or in an order which we create in imagination—in experience we know that the manifold is in these relations, and not merely that we have put it together in these relations; compare A 191 = B 236.

Kemp Smith translates '*Zusammenstellung*' as 'placing together' and '*zusammengestellt*' as 'constructed'.

In view of the doctrine of the Transcendental Deduction—
that objectivity implies necessity, and that objective unity (or
combination) is necessary unity (or combination)—we might
expect Kant to assert straight away that an objective temporal
order is a necessary temporal order (or a temporal order
in accordance with a rule). He prefers to take a longer way
round to arrive at this conclusion, and indicates that if we
could perceive time itself—that is, empty or absolute time
apart from the events in it—this conclusion would not follow.
There is, however, no possibility of determining the objective
order of events through the direct perception of a time which
is objective and absolute, *for time itself cannot be perceived
by sense*.[1]

Kant thus makes two assumptions: (1) that in experience
we are aware of the objective order of events; and (2) that
we cannot perceive time itself. He argues that therefore we
can determine the existence, or the temporal position of
objects, only through their combination in time in general,
and therefore only through concepts that connect them *a priori*.
Since such concepts always involve necessity, experience
is possible only through representation of the necessary connexion,[2] or *nexus*, of sense-perceptions or appearances.[3]

§ 5. *The Assumptions of the Argument*

Kant's exposition is a summary statement of the general
principles which are at work in the detailed proofs of sub-

---

[1] There is indeed an empirical or relative space which is an object
of experience, and can be called sensible, inasmuch as it is symbolised
(*bezeichnet*) by what can be sensed; and presumably the same must be
true of time. But in that case we are considering individual spaces and
times as filled (and, I think, as indeterminate), not the one absolute
and infinite space and time which we construct in thought and treat
as a whole in which all relative spaces and times have a determinate
position. See *M.A.d.N.* 1 *Hauptstück* (IV 481–2).

[2] The different forms of that necessary connexion are (1) the connexion of permanent substance and changing accident, (2) the connexion of cause and effect, and (3) the connexion of substances acting
causally upon one another.

[3] I take sense-perceptions to be here equivalent to appearances.

stance, causality, and interaction. It can hardly be judged till we have followed the arguments of the Analogies; but since it professes to be a proof, it deserves to be examined as if it were relatively self-sufficient.

Firstly as to its assumptions—are we entitled to assume (1) that we are aware of the objective order of events in time, and (2) that time itself cannot be perceived?

The second assumption, which is repeated again and again throughout Kant's argument,[1] is surely sound. What we perceive is not time itself, but changes in time, and we measure time, not in itself, but by the changes which take place in it. Are we entitled also to assume that we are aware of an objective order of events in time?

I think it will hardly be denied that we at least seem to distinguish the order of events from the order in which we come to know them; and Kant's statement is true as an analysis of our experience, even if it is nothing more. For myself, I cannot even see how we could be aware—as Hume admits we are aware—of a succession of appearances in time, unless we distinguished the time of our knowing from the time of what we know. To be aware of any succession is to be aware now of what is past.

Even in the simplest kind of experience which we can imagine—an experience in which the object is only a succession of appearances in time—we can distinguish the objective order of the appearances from the subjective order of our knowings. The order of the appearances is in such a case the same as the order of our perceivings, but it is not the same as the order of our rememberings; for we can remember a later event and then remember an earlier event. Memory is not merely the *recalling* of a past event, but the *recollecting*

---

[1] B 225, A 183 = B 226, A 188 = B 231, B 233, A 192 = B 237, A 200 = B 245, B 257, A 215 = B 263. The same assumption is found in the Anticipations, see B 207 and compare A 172 = B 214. It is not found in the Axioms, but Kant's marginal jottings suggest that it might be used there also; see Erdmann, *Nachträge* LXX. We must use the category of quantity because we cannot intuit space and time in themselves.

of it as past, that is, as having a position more or less definite in past time, and therefore (since we cannot perceive time itself) as coming before some events and after others. To have memory is to be able, as it were, to move backwards and forwards in the past.

It may be objected that the order of our rememberings or knowings is just as much an objective order as the order of given appearances. This is true, but it means merely that we can make our own knowings an object to ourselves; and this truth Kant (in spite of some careless statements suggesting the contrary) can, and does, hold as part of his doctrine. It remains none the less necessary to distinguish the order of our knowings from the order of what we know, and there is no impropriety in using the words 'subjective' and 'objective' for the purposes of this distinction.

Kant may have in mind also the fact that we can imagine,[1] and even think, events to be in an order different from that in which they actually occurred. Here too we have a subjective order opposed to an objective order, and to deny this distinction is to make nonsense of human experience. In the main, however, the subjective order is for Kant the order of events occurring in the subject, while the objective order is the order of events occurring in the object.

I suggest then that the assumption which Kant makes is legitimate and necessary, since apart from it there could be no experience, even of the most elementary kind.[2] Consideration of the details which Kant takes to be implied in the assumption must be reserved till later.

---

[1] Compare B 233 and also B 140. I take it that this second distinction, the distinction between the real and the imaginary, might be made with reference either to the order of events occurring in the subject or to the order of events occurring in the object. We can construct an imaginary account of our own mental history as well as of the history of objects.

[2] The same assumption is made in the Transcendental Deduction (see especially B 139–40 and B 141–2).

§ 6. *The Conclusion of the Argument*

Kant's conclusion is asserted in three stages. Of these the first is not likely to be denied. Granted that we are aware of an objective order in time, and granted that we cannot perceive time itself, the position of objects in time[1] can be determined only through 'their combination in time in general'. The time at which objects exist is determined only by their relation to other objects which they precede, succeed, or accompany in a time which is one and the same for all objects.

Kant's second contention is this—that to determine the position of objects in time 'through their combination in time in general' is to determine it through concepts connecting[2] objects *a priori*.

This is the Critical solution of the problem, and Kant believes it is the only possibility that remains; for we have rejected the view that sense-perception can by itself determine the temporal position of objects,[3] and we have also rejected the view that we have a direct perception of absolute time itself. Neither empirical nor pure intuition can account for our experience of objective relations in time, and we must seek for an explanation elsewhere. If we are to determine objective temporal position through the combination of objects in time in general, we can do so only through concepts which are not derived either from empirical or from pure intuition; and these concepts must connect objects *a priori*, that is, independently of experience.

The sense in which these concepts connect objects (or the

---

[1] B 219. Kant says the 'existence of objects', but existence is position in time.

[2] Note the transition from the more general term 'combination' (*Verbindung*) to the more specific term 'connexion', or *'nexus'* (*Verknüpfung*). I take it that Kant is thinking of 'connexion' in both cases, in spite of the variation in terminology. The 'connexion' is a connexion in time, and might be described equally as an objective connexion of the *manifold* in time; compare 'the relation in the existence of the manifold' in B 219 a little earlier.

[3] Apart altogether from Kant's special views about synthesis, it should be obvious that the order of our sense-perceptions is *not* the order of what we ordinarily take to be objective events in time.

manifold of objects) *a priori* is not here explained. I take it that not only do we think (rather than intuit)[1] the connexion of objects in accordance with these concepts: the connexion is actually imposed on the manifold by the thinking mind.

Kant's view is that objective temporal connexions (which we all claim to experience) are found in experience only because they are imposed by the understanding. More precisely, these connexions are imposed by the transcendental synthesis of imagination which combines given appearances in one time and space in accordance with the categories of the understanding.[2] For example, in all experience we synthetise given sensible qualities[3] as accidents of permanent substances in time and space. We do so in accordance with the demands of thought, not in accordance with the deliverances of sense; and if we did not do so, there could be no such thing as experience, nor could 'objective temporal position' have any meaning for us.

We do not make explicit to ourselves the nature of such concepts as 'substance' and 'accident' till experience is highly developed; and still less do we ascribe their origin to the demands of thought. These facts (which are neither ignored nor denied by Kant) have no relevance as criticisms of his doctrine. Even when I make so simple a judgement as 'This apple, which was green, is now red', I have not only combined the given manifold in accordance with the category of substance and accident by a transcendental synthesis of the imagination: I have also presupposed the category in my judgement itself.

---

[1] Compare Chapter XXXII § 5; and also (for the relation of concepts and intuitions) Chapters V § 8 and IX § 5.

[2] It is not difficult to see that the unity of apperception involves the unity of time and of all objects in time, and that this unity might be impossible unless objects were combined in certain ways by the transcendental synthesis of imagination. The main difficulty is to see how these different ways of combination can be imposed in response to the demands of thought. For these demands of thought under the head of relation see Chapter XIV § 8 and also Chapter XXXIV § 3.

[3] Or at any rate sensible qualities given to outer sense.

Kant's third contention is that concepts which thus connect objects (or the manifold of objects) *a priori* involve necessity; and therefore experience (as experience of an objective order in time) is possible only through representation of the necessary connexion, or *nexus*, of appearances.[1]

This third contention is little more than an expansion of what has already been said. An *a priori* connexion must be universal and necessary: the very concept of such a connexion involves necessity.[2] Kant does not consider the possibility that the connexion might be purely arbitrary. If it were, there could be no objective connexion in time, and so no experience. And indeed Kant already claims to have shown generally in the Transcendental Deduction that objectivity involves necessity. In the sequel he will argue that the different forms of objective connexion in time must involve necessity.[3]

It may be observed that in this case the argument of the second edition, as of a more general character, is rightly placed before the argument of the first edition. It maintains only that the necessary connexion of appearances in time is a condition of experience. The fact that there are three forms of such necessary connexion, and different rules for each of these forms, is a further development of the general argument.

§ 7. *The General Character of the Proof*

It must never be forgotten that the proof of the Analogies, like that of the other Principles, rests upon the possibility of experience, experience being regarded as 'knowledge in which *all* objects must in the last resort[4] be capable of being given, if the idea of them is to have objective reality for us'.[5] Kant says expressly that the Analogies could never be proved

---

[1] B 219. 'Representation' (*Vorstellung*) is here conception.

[2] Compare A 2 and B 3–4.

[3] See especially B 233–4, where we find a parallel to the present argument.

[4] '*zuletzt.*' Does this qualification refer to the fact that some objects, e.g. electrons, are too small to be given directly to our senses? See A 226 = B 273 and compare Price, *Perception*, p. 297.

[5] A 217 = B 264.

in regard to objects which were things-in-themselves.[1] He says also that it would be utterly useless to attempt a dogmatic proof of the Analogies, that is, a direct proof from concepts.[2] We may analyse our concepts of objects as we will, but we can never pass by mere concepts from an object and its existence to the existence, or mode of existence, of anything else;[3] we could never prove, for example, by an analysis of the concept of 'event', that every event must have a cause. In Kant's opinion the proof of the Analogies is incompatible with both realism and rationalism; and indeed realism and rationalism can, he believes, offer no proof either of substance or of causality or of interaction.

Just because Kant's proof rests upon the possibility of experience, it is to him a matter of indifference whether he argues from the unity of apperception or from the unity of objective time-relations; for the synthetic unity which is necessary for any kind of objectivity is grounded on the unity of apperception, and the unity of apperception is manifested only in the synthetic unity of objects, and preeminently in the synthetic unity of their time-relations. He appeals to experience and its possibility as the 'third thing' which alone can justify synthetic *a priori* judgements;[4] and because the essential form of experience consists in the synthetic unity of the apperception of all appearances,[5] he can discover the *a priori* conditions of the necessary time-determination of all existence in the phenomenal world, conditions apart from which all empirical time-determination would be impossible.[6] These conditions are expressed in rules of synthetic unity *a priori*,[7] rules through which alone the existence of

---

[1] A 181 = B 223.

[2] A 216–7 = B 263–4. Compare A 736 = B 764.

[3] A 217 = B 264.

[4] Ibid. Compare A 155 = B 194 and A 259 = B 315.

[5] I think he ought to add here a reference to the fact that time is the ultimate form of all our intuitions. Time and the unity of apperception are the ultimate conditions through which alone experience is possible.   [6] A 217 = B 264. Compare also A 177–8 = B 220.

[7] A 217 = B 264.

appearances can acquire synthetic unity as regards their time-relations.[1]

The Analogies in short are rules which must govern all appearances, if they are to be appearances of objects in one and the same objective time. The unity of the time in which all objects exist is grounded on the unity of apperception, which is manifested only in synthesis according to rules.[2] The particular character of the rules of synthesis in regard to existence in time seems, however, to be determined, partly at least, by the fact that absolute time cannot be perceived. If it could be so perceived, we could apparently determine the temporal position of objects immediately,[3] and 'as it were empirically',[4] by reference to absolute time. As absolute time cannot be perceived, we determine the temporal position of objects only by their relations to one another in time, and the rules in accordance with which we do this are *a priori* rules which are valid for any and every time.[5]

We shall be in a better position to estimate the value of this doctrine when we have considered the proofs in detail. Here I would only say that Kant has at least a genuine and important problem; for even if we reject the concepts of substance and causality, we ought to give some account of what we mean by an objective order of events which is distinct both from the order of our knowing and from the order created by mere imagination.

---

[1] A 215 = B 262. This means, for example, that there can be no objective succession apart from the law of cause and effect. I take 'rule' in all these passages to refer to the Analogies, and not to the empirical laws of nature, which we discover in conformity with the Analogies.

[2] Compare A 216 = B 263.   [3] A 215 = B 262.

[4] B 233. I presume this means in a way analogous to empirical observation.

[5] A 216 = B 263. I take 'rules' throughout this paragraph also to mean the Analogies.

CHAPTER XL

THE SPECIAL CHARACTER OF THE ANALOGIES

§ 1. *The Analogies are Regulative*

Kant's further account[1] of the special character of the Analogies is little more than an elaboration of what we already know.[2]

The Mathematical Principles were concerned with appearances, or more precisely with the synthesis of time and space and the synthesis of sensation necessary for knowledge of appearances as appearances of objects.[3] The Analogies are concerned with the *existence* of appearances as objects, that is, with their relation to one another in respect of their existence.[4] Kant asserts that we can construct *a priori* not only the extensive quantity, but also the degree of appearances.[5] We cannot construct the *existence* of appearances not given to us, although we can infer some kind of existence from what

---

[1] A 178 = B 220 ff.

[2] See A 160 = B 199 ff. and Chapter XXXVI § 2.

[3] For the reference to objects, see B 111 and Chapters XXXVI § 2 and XXXVII § 5.

[4] A 178 = B 220. This seems to be the same as their position relative to one another in time.

[5] A 178–9 = B 220–1; compare Chapter XXXVIII § 4. Kant's statement in A 178 = B 220–1 is particularly obscure. 'The way in which something is apprehended in appearance can be so determined that the rule of synthesis can at once, in every empirical example that comes before us, give this intuition *a priori*, that is, can bring it into existence from the example.' The words *a priori* must, I think, go with 'give' and not (as Kemp Smith takes them) with 'intuition'. The word '*daraus*' I translate as 'from the example': it is omitted in Kemp Smith's translation.

Kant is here concerned with the possibility of constructing *a priori* both the extensive, and the intensive, quantity of an empirical intuition. I do not understand his references to the empirical example; but I think he must intend to say, not that we can construct the empirical intuition *a priori*, but that we can so construct the quantity and the degree (and consequently the number) involved in the intuition. Compare A 714–15 = B 742–3.

is given; for example, we can know that a given event must have some cause, but apart from experience we cannot say what that cause must be.[1]

For this reason the Mathematical Principles are said to be 'constitutive'; to be constitutive always implies for Kant the possibility of construction.[2] The Analogies are merely 'regulative'; they tell us what we must look for in experience, but they do not enable us to construct it *a priori*.

§ 2. *The First Meaning of 'Analogy'*

Hence there is a difference between a mathematical analogy (or proportion) and Kant's Analogies of Experience, although both are concerned with what he elsewhere calls an agreement in relation.[3] Mathematical analogies are formulae which express the equality of two *quantitative* relations (or ratios); and just because we can construct quantities, we can determine the fourth term in a proportion when three are given.[4] The Analogies of Experience are concerned with two *qualitative* relations; and since quality cannot be constructed, we are unable to construct the fourth term, when the other three are given.[5] All we have is a rule for seeking the fourth term in

---

[1] This statement is elaborated in A 766 = B 794. We cannot know *a priori* that sunlight will melt wax and harden clay; but we can know *a priori* that if wax melts, *something* must have preceded upon which the melting has followed in accordance with a fixed law—the law, I take it, that every event must have a cause.

[2] Construction again implies the possibility of immediate certainty or 'evidence'. See Chapter XXXVI § 3.

[3] '*Analogia*' is equated with '*eine Übereinstimmung des Verhältnisses*'; see *Metaphysik*, p. 90.

[4] If $2 : 4 = 3 : x$, we can say what x must be.

[5] The Analogies are no doubt concerned with qualitative relations, but the factor of quantity cannot be ignored, as is shown by Kant's insistence that the quantum of substance can neither be increased nor diminished (B 224). It is curious that he does not discuss the quantitative equivalence of cause and effect: perhaps he thinks this is sufficiently indicated in his account of substance. References to quantity (both extensive and intensive) in connexion with causation are to be found in A 168–9 = B 210, A 176 = B 217, and A 179 = B 222. In the last of these passages he appears to imply that, for

experience, and a mark[1] whereby it can be detected. We know, for example, that effect is to cause as the melting of wax is to x:[2] we cannot say *a priori* what x must be, but we know that it must have the mark of invariably preceding such melting.

§ 3. *The Second Meaning of 'Analogy'*

There is a further sense in which the term 'Analogy' is applicable to the Principles with which we are at present concerned. Kant leads us up to this sense by a remark which, he declares, applies to all the Principles, but preeminently

example, if we are given an effect, we can say that it must have a preceding cause, but we can tell *a priori* neither what that cause is nor what its quantity is. I do not know how he would deal with the objection that we can know the cause to be quantitatively equivalent to the effect. It might almost be said that we are capable of constructing both the existence of the cause and its quantity, but not its empirical quality. Kant is of course right in holding that although we might be able to infer some existent or other *a priori*, we could not know it determinately; that is, we could not anticipate the difference between it and other existents, this difference being revealed to empirical intuition alone. See A 178 = B 221.

[1] I presume that the 'marks' are permanence, regular succession, and regular simultaneity—the three transcendental schemata. Compare A 136 = B 175. Kant suggests later—in A 203 = B 249—that sequence in time is the sole empirical criterion by which we distinguish cause from effect. In that case he is concerned with two events known to be causally connected, and the only question there is which is the cause and which is the effect. We may nevertheless take the mark of a cause to be that it invariably precedes the effect. Needless to say, this by itself is not sufficient to determine the cause of anything; night, for example, is not the cause of day. If Kant were writing a treatise on induction, he would be obliged to discuss in detail the conditions under which we are entitled to say that A is the cause of B. He is, however, concerned with something much more general, with the justification for believing the world to be governed by causality. To treat the Analogies as an essay in inductive logic can lead to nothing but misunderstanding.

[2] The fact that the melting of wax is taken to be an instance of 'effect', and x to be an instance of 'cause', means that the relation between them is an instance of the causal relation. Perhaps it might be better to say that the melting of wax is to x as other events are to their causes.

to the Analogies.[1] The Analogies have meaning and validity only in their empirical, and not in their transcendental, use; that is to say, they have meaning and validity only as applied to objects of a possible experience, not as applied to things-in-themselves.[2] Hence our proof of them can have reference only to their empirical use, and appearances must be subsumed, not directly[3] under the categories, but under their schemata.

This doctrine is already familiar to us from the discussion of the transcendental schemata,[4] but Kant deals with it here in an extremely elaborate and complicated way.[5] His main point is, however, comparatively clear. When we, for example, say that effect is to cause as the melting of wax is to x, we do so only in virtue of the schema of necessary succession; and in so doing we treat the relation of the necessarily succeeding

---

[1] A 180 = B 223. Kant makes a similar statement about the term 'Anticipations' in A 166-7 = B 208-9.

[2] See A 139 = B 178 and A 146 = B 185; and compare Chapter XI § 4 for a fuller statement and also Chapter LIV § 3.

[3] '*schlechthin*' (A 181 = B 223); compare A 138-9 = B 177-8.

[4] Compare especially Chapter XXXIV §§ 1-2 and also Chapter XXXV § 1.

[5] See A 181 = B 223-4. Kant's statement is unusually full of relative pronouns which may refer to many different nouns. The commentators take different views of these references, and even feel compelled (perhaps not without reason) to make emendations. It is perhaps impossible to determine the precise meaning of Kant's words, but Kemp Smith's translation—apart from two sentences—gives what seems to me an adequate statement of Kant's thought. Of the two sentences beginning 'But such unity can be thought . . .' the first seems to me doubtful, and the second seems to me impossible. Of the correct translation I am uncertain, but Kant, I think, means something like this: The synthesis of appearances can be thought only in the schema; the pure category contains the form (function of unity) of this synthesis in abstraction from all restricting sensuous conditions; that is, it contains the form of this synthesis as a synthesis of the manifold *in general* (not as a synthesis of *appearances* in time). Compare Chapter XXXII §§ 6-7. I take 'synthesis *in general*' to be equivalent to 'synthesis of the manifold *in general*'; compare B 129-30, B 144-5, and B 150-1. For what the pure category contains, see A 138 = B 177: for what the schematised category contains, see A 139-40 = B 178-9.

to the necessarily preceding as analogous to the relation of consequent and ground which is thought in the pure category.[1] The ways in which we combine appearances in time in accordance with the Analogies of Experience is analogous to the ways in which the manifold in general is combined in the categorical, hypothetical, and disjunctive forms of judgement, and so in the pure categories of relation.[2]

To say this is, I think, to say that the schemata are analogues of the pure categories: the synthetic unity of the manifold of *appearances in time* (which is thought in the schema) is analogous to the synthetic unity of the manifold of *intuition in general* (which is thought in the pure category).[3] In this doctrine there is nothing really novel, but only a new way of expressing what Kant has taught all along.[4] Since the Principles can be proved only in their empirical use, and since appearances can be subsumed directly only under the schemata, we must, in applying the Principles to appearances, substitute the schema for the category as the key to its use, or rather we must set the schema alongside the category as its restricting condition.[5]

I take it that this doctrine holds of all the Principles, although

[1] We may expand our previous 'analogy' into the form 'The melting of wax : x = the necessarily succeeding : the necessarily preceding = consequent : ground'.

[2] 'By these Principles we are justified in combining appearances only according to an analogy with the logical and universal unity of concepts'; A 181 = B 224. Compare also A 147 = B 186 and A 142 = B 181.

[3] For example, the (ultimate) subject is to its predicates as the unchanging or permanent is to the changing in time; the consequent is to the ground as the necessarily preceding is to the necessarily succeeding in time; and so on.

[4] Kemp Smith's statement (*Commentary*, p. 358) that 'it implies that it is only in the noumenal, and not also in the phenomenal, sphere that substantial existences and genuinely dynamical activities are to be found' seems to me due to misunderstanding. It is sufficiently refuted by Kant in A 146–7 = B 186.

[5] A 181 = B 224. There are difficulties here in Kant's text into which I need not enter, but he is manifestly saying that only schematised categories can be applied to objects.

it is preeminently true of the Analogies.[1] Whether it is a particularly valuable way of expressing Kant's general doctrine
is another question. It is perhaps not unreasonable to suppose
that the title 'Analogies of Experience' was chosen by Kant
primarily because of the first sense which he ascribes to the
word 'analogy' in this connexion.

---

[1] Compare Kant's statement at the beginning of the paragraph
(A 180 = B 223). This statement need not cover the whole of the
paragraph, but there is nothing in the argument to suggest restriction
to the Analogies. Kant's doctrine would not apply to the Mathematical
Principles, if the categories must in themselves possess correlates—
see B 110—in order to enter into an Analogy; but I see no indication
of this in the argument. I presume that the analogy between category
and schema is more obvious in the categories of relation, partly
because both categories and schemata have correlates, and partly
because there is less likelihood of our identifying the category and the
schema.

CHAPTER XLI

THE FIRST ANALOGY

§ 1. *The Principle of Permanence*

'In all change of appearances substance is permanent, and its quantum in nature is neither increased nor diminished.'

This is Kant's formula in the second edition. The reference to the quantum of substance is commonly condemned to-day; but it at least attempts to make Kant's doctrine precise, and it deserves to be considered on its own merits.

The formula of the first edition makes no reference to the quantum of substance. *'All appearances contain the permanent (substance) as the object itself, and the transitory as its mere determination, that is, as a way in which the object exists.'*

The two traditional views of substance are (1) that it is the ultimate subject of all predicates, and (2) that it is the permanent substratum of change. Kant accepts the first view as involved in the very idea of substance, and suggested by the categorical form of judgement. When we translate it into terms of time, substance becomes the permanent subject of changing predicates, or the permanent substratum of change. What Kant has now to prove is that there is a permanent substratum of change, and only so can the concept of substance have objective validity.

Kant believes that substance (as a permanent substratum) belongs only to objects of outer sense; and it is with these that his proof is really concerned, although he professes to deal with all changing appearances. Since substance is essentially spatial, and since the parts of space are outside one another, Kant holds that there must be many substances, and that every substance is made up of substances. Hence he rejects a third traditional view of substance, which defines substance as the self-sufficient.[1]

---

[1] This is explicitly stated in *Metaphysik*, p. 34. He rejects the definition of Descartes: *per substantiam nihil aliud intelligere possumus*

It must not be forgotten—Kant himself repeats it again and again—that he is concerned only with substance as appearance (*substantia phaenomenon*). We have no reason to regard ultimate reality, or the thing-in-itself, as either spatial or temporal, either permanent or changing, although it appears to human beings as a phenomenal world of permanent substances in space causally interacting with one another. The fact that in our phenomenal world we recognise, and must recognise, permanent spatial substances whose changes are not to be identified with the changes in our sensations; and even the fact that we can find the causes of our sensations in the movements of bodies, and especially of our own bodies—all this offers not the slightest ground for supposing Kant to have wavered for a moment from his belief that both the physical world and our own mental history are nothing more than an appearance to human minds. Here, as always, his empirical realism and transcendental idealism are not conflicting tendencies whose nature he fails to understand: they are on the contrary essential and interdependent parts of his philosophical system.[1] On his view we can have *a priori* knowledge of permanent spatial substances only in so far as the whole physical world is dependent on human sensibility and thought. Even if we cannot accept his view, even if we deny that it can be worked out consistently in detail, we must recognise that it has at least an initial consistency.

---

quam rem quae ita existit ut nulla alia re indigeat ad existendum (*Princ. Phil.* I, 51). He adds that Spinoza held the same view, and that this was the source of his error.

Kant himself (in B 407, B 413, and B 417 n.) speaks of substance (in connexion with the self) as meaning a self-subsistent essence (*ein für sich bestehendes Wesen*). But 'self-subsistent' for Kant is not equivalent to 'self-sufficient': it means only that which does not 'inhere' as an accident in something else, and is compatible with being 'grounded' in something else.

[1] Compare Chapter II § 2 and Chapter XXXI § 10.

§ 2. *The Argument of the First Edition*

I. *Our apprehension of the manifold of appearance is always successive, and is therefore always changing.*[1]

From this, according to Kant, it follows (1) that by mere apprehension we could never distinguish objective succession from objective simultaneity; (2) that if we are to make this distinction, and indeed if we are to determine objective relations in time at all,[2] *our experience*[3] *must have as its ground or condition something which always is, that is, something abiding and permanent*; and (3) that all objective change and simultaneity must be simply so many ways (modes of time[4]) in which this permanent exists.[5]

II. Since simultaneity and succession are the only relations in time, and since we can determine objective simultaneity and succession only as ways in which the permanent exists, we can say that *only in the permanent*[6] *are time-relations possible.*

[1] A 182 = B 225.

[2] Succession and simultaneity are the only relations in time. See A 182 = B 226.

[3] The emendation suggested by Erdmann ('*an ihm*' for '*an ihr*') means that for 'our experience' we must substitute 'the manifold as an object of experience'. I do not think the emendation is necessary, and Erdmann himself suggests it only as a doubtful possibility. 'Our experience' is equivalent to 'our experience so far as it is an experience of objective temporal relations'.

[4] For modes of time, see Chapter XXXIX § 3.

[5] Some explanation of this conclusion would have been an advantage. Even if the permanent is the ground or condition of our experiencing change (or succession) and simultaneity, and so is the ground or condition of change and simultaneity, does it follow that change and simultaneity are ways in which the permanent exists?

The clause is loosely constructed in German: '. . . something abiding and permanent, of which all change and coexistence are only so many ways (modes of time) in which the permanent exists' is Kemp Smith's translation, which follows the German very closely. The 'of which' hangs very loosely to the clause as a whole, unless Kant means 'all change and coexistence of which'; but this would merely *assume* that change and coexistence were change and coexistence of the permanent.

[6] The phrase 'in the permanent' seems to mean no more than 'in relation to the permanent'. The equivalent statement below (in A 183 = B 226) is that 'without this permanent there is no time-relation'.

So far Kant's argument is clearly—what on his principles it ought to be—an argument from the conditions of experience to the conditions of objects of experience. We could not experience any objective time-relations apart from the permanent, and therefore there can be no objective time-relations apart from the permanent.

This conclusion is then restated in other terms. The permanent is the substratum of the empirical idea of time itself,[1] and it is only by reference to this substratum that time-relations are possible.

III. Kant's conclusion so far rests, as I have said, on what he believes to be the condition of experiencing objective time-relations. He now attempts to reinforce that conclusion by an argument resting upon the nature of time.

Permanence is in a special sense an expression[2] of the nature of time, for time is the constant correlate[3] of all existence of appearances, of all change and all concomitance.[4]

The reasons for this special connexion between permanence and time would seem to be as follows:

---

[1] This clause—though it professes only to re-state what has already been said—is difficult. 'Substratum' is not defined—it seems to mean that by reference to which we distinguish objective simultaneity and succession, and consequently (according to Kant) that of whose existence succession and simultaneity are modes; compare A 183 = B 227. Kant no doubt has in mind the traditional doctrine which emanates from Aristotle. According to Aristotle change implies a succession of states in a substratum. This substratum is sometimes called οὐσία, and seems to be an element in the doctrine of substance.

'Time itself' is not empirical, and 'the empirical idea of time itself' seems to mean the empirical time-determinations of objects. This is, I think, confirmed by the clause which follows. Compare *M.A.d.N.* (IV 481) where Kant equates 'empirical space' with the totality of outer objects.

[2] A 183 = B 226, '*ausdrückt*'. In B 225 the (permanent) substratum is said to 'represent' time in general (*vorstellt*).

[3] '*das beständige Korrelatum.*' The word '*beständig*' suggests permanence. In B 224-5 time is said to be the *permanent* form of inner intuition, and it is even said that time abides and does not change.

[4] '*Begleitung.*' This is equivalent to coexistence or simultaneity.

(1) Change is not a change of time itself, but of appearances in time.

(2) Simultaneity is not a simultaneity of time itself,[1] for the parts of time are successive, not simultaneous.[2]

(3) Although the parts of time come one after another, this does not entitle us to attribute succession to time itself; for if we did so we should have to think of another time in which this succession took place.

All these arguments seem intended to suggest, if not that time itself is permanent, at any rate that permanence is more closely connected with time than are succession and simultaneity.[3] Kant adds a fourth argument connected with duration[4] in time. This argument is of a somewhat different character. It does not suggest that time itself is permanent, but rather that apart from the permanent there can be no duration in time any more than there can be succession or simultaneity.

(4) It is only through the permanent that existence in different parts of the time-series[5] acquires that kind of quantity which is called 'duration'. If we consider bare succession in itself, existence is continually ceasing and coming to be, and has absolutely no quantity at all.[6]

[1] Kant says that simultaneity is not a mode of time itself. See Chapter XXXIX § 3.

[2] He might have added for the sake of parallelism that it is not time, but appearances in time, which are simultaneous.

[3] Kant does not ask whether, if time endures or is permanent, we should require to think of another time in or through which it endures.

[4] 'Dauer.'

[5] The time-series is the series of times (or of parts of time), the time-order is the order of what is in time. See A 145 = B 184.

[6] It has—or is—mere position in an atomic 'now'. The past does not exist nor does the future. Permanence, in the strict sense, involves existence through all time, while duration is existence through some time (A 185 = B 228–9). If a duration is objective, it is in a determinate relation to all other objective durations, and so presupposes permanence. In the abstract moment there can be no duration (or quantity of *existence*), for a moment is not a part, but a limit, of time (see A 169 = B 211 and A 208 = B 253). There can, however, be a quantity or degree of *reality* in the abstract moment; see A 168 = B 210.

All four arguments are intended to reinforce Kant's original conclusion[1] from the conditions of experience—that *without the permanent no objective time-relations are possible.*

IV. *Time in itself cannot be perceived.*

V. *Therefore the permanent must be present in appearances,*[2] *and must be the substratum*[3] *of all time-determinations.*

It follows (1) that the permanent in appearances is a condition of the possibility of the synthetic unity of appearances in one objective temporal order;[4] and therefore (2) that it is a condition of experience and so demonstrably necessary.

VI. *Therefore in all appearances the permanent is the object itself,*[5] *that is,* substantia phaenomenon, *the ultimate and unchanging subject to which all changing accidents are attributed as predicates.*

Everything that changes, or can change, belongs only to the

[1] Stated in II above in the form 'only in the permanent are time-relations possible'.

[2] Note that this conclusion follows from the fact that time cannot be perceived. In the earlier stage of the argument—see I above—it was presumably still an open question whether the permanent required might not be found in time itself.

[3] This again seems to mean more than the 'condition' or 'ground'.

[4] Kant says it is *the* condition of the possibility of the synthetic unity of all sense-perceptions (where 'sense-perception' is equivalent to 'appearance'); but there are other synthetic unities and other conditions (the unity of extensive quantity, the unity of degree, and so on). The permanent in appearances is not even the only condition of an objective temporal order, for causality and interaction are so also.

The clause added—that with reference to this permanent all existence and change in time can be regarded only as a mode of the existence of what abides and is permanent—adds nothing to what has been already said, and is loosely expressed. Existence (*Dasein*) cannot be a mode of existence (*Existenz*). Perhaps Kant intended to write 'simultaneity' (or 'duration').

[5] The object was formerly regarded as the necessary synthetic unity of a group of appearances. Here it is regarded as the permanent substratum of these appearances. This doctrine is not repeated in the proof added in the second edition. Strictly speaking, the object is the substance with its accidents, not the substance in abstraction from its accidents. The synthetic unity of substance and accident is perhaps the most fundamental unity which characterises an object.

way in which this substance or these substances[1] exist; that is, it belongs to the determinations of substance.

§ 3. *The Argument of the Second Edition*

I. All appearances are in time, and it is only in time as a substratum[2] (or as a *permanent* form of inner intuition) that objective[3] succession and simultaneity of appearances can be known.[4]

II. Therefore time (in which we have to think all objective succession and simultaneity of appearances) abides and does not change; because we can know objective succession and simultaneity only as determinations of time.[5]

III. Time itself cannot be perceived.

IV. Therefore there must be found in the objects of sense-perception (that is, in appearances as appearances of an object) the permanent[6] as a substratum which represents[7] time. All

---

[1] Kant ought to have explained how there must be many substances. The reason is that substances fill space, and that every part of a substance is a substance, just as every part of space is a space. See Chapter XLII § 7.

[2] Here again we should like to know whether 'substratum' means more than 'condition' or 'ground'. Compare A 30 = B 46. To say that appearances are simultaneous is to say they are in the same time (or part of time); and to say they are successive is to say they are in different times (or parts of time).

[3] I have introduced the word 'objective'.

[4] B 224. I translate 'represented' (*vorgestellt*) as 'known'.

[5] It is typical of Kant to introduce a statement with a 'therefore' and follow it up with a 'because', confusing us with a superabundance of reasons. The 'because' would seem intended only to repeat the reason given in I above, but it adds that simultaneity and succession are determinations of time, presumably on the ground, and in the sense, that they cannot be apart from time (as their substratum or condition or ground).

The bold statement that 'time abides and does not change' seems to go even further than the first edition in ascribing permanence to time.

[6] Kant omits to say that this substratum is the permanent until two sentences later—he supposes we are intelligent enough to infer this from what has gone before.

[7] 'represents' (*vorstellt*) corresponds to 'expresses' (*ausdrückt*) in A 183 = B 226.

change and simultaneity must be capable of being perceived or apprehended[1] only through the relation of appearances to this permanent.[2]

V. The permanent substratum of appearances (or of the real[3]) is substance, and appearances (as appearances of objects) can be thought only as determinations of substance. In other words, the permanent by reference to which alone can the objective time-relations of appearances be determined is *substantia phaenomenon* (substance in the appearances). It remains always the same and is the substratum of all change.

VI. Since phenomenal substance cannot change in its existence, its quantum in nature can neither be increased nor diminished.[4]

[1] 'apprehended', as usual, is to be taken in the technical sense in which it is connected with sense-perception and involves a synthesis of the successively given.

[2] This clause corresponds roughly to I in the argument of the first edition.

[3] The real is what fills time or the time-content (*realitas phaenomenon*); see A 143 = B 183, A 145 = B 184, A 168 = B 209. It is here described as 'what belongs to existence', for to exist is to be in time or to have a determinate position in time. Its duration is the quantity of its existence, which is to be distinguished from its intensive quantity (or degree of reality). It can, I think, be identified with the changing appearances of which substance is the substratum, as is implied by the statement above, although Kant in the following sentence speaks of substance itself as the real of appearances, thereby identifying *substantia phaenomenon* and *realitas phaenomenon*. The real may cover substance as well as the accidents of substance, but it cannot be substance as opposed to its accidents.

[4] It should be noted that although there are six stages in the argument of both first and second editions, they do not exactly correspond; for I in the first argument has no corresponding stage in the second argument, and VI in the second argument has no corresponding stage in the first argument. The series II, III, IV, V, and VI of the first argument corresponds very roughly with the series I, II, III, IV, and V of the second argument. The correspondence is closer in the last three numbers of these series than in the first two.

CHAPTER XLII

SUBSTANCE

§ 1. *In what Sense is Apprehension Successive?*

The main differences in Kant's two proofs of substance are to be found in the earlier stages. The argument of the second edition starts from *the permanence of time* as the condition of determining succession and simultaneity: the argument of the first edition maintains first that *the permanent* is the condition of determining succession and simultaneity, and then connects permanence with the nature of time. Both proofs maintain that because time (with such permanence as it may possess) cannot be perceived, the permanent which is necessary in order to determine time-relations must be found in objects or appearances as their substratum or substance.

The main peculiarity[1] of the first edition is Kant's assertion that apprehension is always successive; and it is from this that he infers the necessity of a permanent (as the condition of determining objective succession and simultaneity) before he connects this permanent either with the nature of time or with the substratum of appearances.

Our apprehension—that is, the taking up and holding together of the given in sensation—is obviously successive in the sense that it takes time; but Kant has been thought to mean[2] that our apprehension is merely successive, or that

---

[1] In B XXXVII Kant says expressly that he found nothing which required alteration in his proofs; but any argument which is not used in the second edition can scarcely be regarded as essential to the proof.

[2] This view is expressed most clearly in Ewing, *Kant's Treatment of Causality*, see especially pp. 82 ff. and 105 ff. Ewing holds that 'Kant confused the true statement that our experience is always successive with the false statement that our experience is merely successive'. He takes 'merely successive' to mean that experience can in itself give us no glimpse of the coexistent.

we can never apprehend different things at the same time. I am very reluctant to accept such a view, not only because it is manifestly at variance with common sense, but also because it seems inconsistent with Kant's most central doctrines. The mere fact that apprehension is a synthesis of the manifold means that it is a holding together of different elements in one moment before the mind, and Kant himself makes it clear that all analysis presupposes such a synthesis. He does, however, hold that as contained in one moment—which is of course a mere abstraction—an idea can be nothing but absolute unity, and this means at least that it has no extension either in time or in space.[1] He maintains also that we cannot know a line, however small, without drawing it in thought, a process which he regards as definitely successive, however short be the time which it requires.[2] He might therefore believe that although we can in one moment hold together different elements before our mind, yet in so far as apprehension is reduced theoretically to a mere taking up (as opposed to a holding together) of the given, it is a taking up of what is one and indivisible; for example, that in an abstract moment of time we can 'take up' only an abstract point of space.

It is difficult to be sure of the precise meaning intended to be conveyed by such a doctrine, but Kant is quite certainly dealing with abstractions which are the product of analysis. He does not believe that any part of an appearance can be given to us in a moment of time. On the contrary, he maintains that every part of an appearance is apprehended in a *part*, and not in a *moment*, of time;[3] and he argues that every part of an appearance must be infinitely divisible, since the part of time in which it is apprehended must be infinitely divisible. Because it takes some time to apprehend any part of an appearance, therefore it must be possible to 'go through'

---

[1] A 99. Even in this case he admits that what is apprehended has a degree, in which plurality is represented by approximation to zero. See A 168 = B 210.

[2] A 162 = B 203. Compare B 154 and Chapter XXXVII § 4.

[3] A moment is not a part, but a limit, of time.

or 'expose'[1] successively any part of an appearance, however small it may be; and an appearance cannot be made up of simple parts, any more than time can be made up of moments or space of points.[2]

Kant must not be supposed to mean that in each moment of time we apprehend a simple indivisible appearance, and then join together these simple indivisible appearances into a complex appearance or sensum.[3] He is considering only ideal limits, and I see little or no ground for believing that he regarded apprehension as merely successive in this sense. Such a view fails to recognise that for Kant an *indeterminate* quantum or whole can be intuited *without* successive synthesis.[4] In the case of substance I am not sure whether Kant means more than that the different accidents of a substance must be successively apprehended;[5] and this is manifestly true. We cannot 'take up' all the accidents of a substance simultaneously.

If we take his statements to mean that apprehension is merely successive, it can hardly be denied that his doctrine is false. Even apart from the amount of space occupied by a momentary sensation, I can at the same time feel a twinge of pain, hear the barking of a dog a quarter of a mile away, and see the shining of a star which has been extinguished for a million years. No doubt all these processes take time, but they occur together; and a cross-section of them, such as is present in an atomic now, would contain elements of all three. It would be impossible to regard such a cross-section as an absolute unity, if by that is meant a unity which contains no differences.

The point I wish to emphasise, however, is that this error—

---

[1] To 'go through' (*durchgehen*) is here equivalent to 'expose' or 'set out' (*exponieren*). For the widest sense of the 'exposition' of appearances, see A 416 = B 443.

[2] For the whole argument, see *Metaphysik*, pp. 55–6.

[3] To maintain this Kant would have to maintain that time was made up of moments—a doctrine he consistently denies.

[4] See A 426 n. = B 454 n.

[5] It may be added that so far as anything is a *determinate* quantum, its parts must be successively apprehended.

even if we were justified in attributing it to Kant—does not affect his argument: firstly because there can be no doubt that many things which we apprehend successively (for example the sides of a house) are believed to be coexistent, and this admission is all that Kant requires: and secondly because we can never determine objective simultaneity merely from the simultaneity of our sensations. In the example above, although the sensations are simultaneous, the objective events are not; for the dog may have barked a little before my pain, and the star shone ages before the dog was born. Even when the events perceived are simultaneous, we cannot determine this by mere sensation apart from thought. Kant is quite right in saying that by mere sensation or mere apprehension we can determine neither objective simultaneity nor objective succession.

The special conditions or presuppositions necessary for determining objective succession are dealt with in the Second Analogy; those for determining objective simultaneity are dealt with in the Third Analogy. Kant is at present concerned with something more general, the ultimate condition of determining any kind of objective time-relation (whether of succession or of simultaneity). This general condition he asserts to be the permanent.

§ 2. *The Permanent and Time-determination*

It is obvious that the position of any appearance in time cannot be determined merely by reference to the permanent; for just because the permanent is permanent, because it is the same at all times,[1] there is nothing in it to indicate any difference in temporal position. Kant himself holds that differences in temporal position are determined by the relations of appearances to one another (before and after and along with), these relations being objective when they are necessary, that is, determined by causal law. What he is arguing at present

---

[1] We shall find later (see § 8 below) that there is a sense in which the permanent alone can change. I do not think that this affects my point; and it may be observed that Kant refers to substance as the unchanging (*das Unwandelbare im Dasein*); see A 143 = B 183.

is that apart from the permanent we could never experience such relations. The permanent is, as it were, the background against which we are aware of temporal relations.

In everyday experience we are aware of change against a background of the relatively permanent. To take the simplest (and according to Kant the most fundamental) case, that of movement, we are aware that the sun is moving in relation to objects on the earth.[1] Hence the obvious objection may be raised that for the perception of movement we require something relatively, not absolutely, permanent; and some commentators,[2] supposing Kant to be concerned with the question of measuring durations, point out that our measurements depend, not on the permanent or unchanging, but on the supposedly uniform movements of the heavenly bodies.

The question of how we measure durations seems to me irrelevant. Kant is asking how there can be any durations for us to measure, how we can be aware of changes which involve objective succession and simultaneity; and I see no reason for attributing to him the view that changes are *measured* by the unchanging and not by their relations to one another. Indeed it would surely be impossible to measure a change by its relation to the unchanging. The question is simply how we can perceive change at all.

Kant is perfectly well aware that objects on the earth are themselves moving;[3] and his statement about the movement of the sun [4] is meant only as a pictorial and popular illustration of his doctrine, from which he passes to the assertion that the permanent of which he speaks can be found only in matter. Another illustration is given in his lectures on Metaphysics,[5] where he says that a sailor could never be aware of the ship's motion, if the sea were moving along with it, unless there were something permanent, as for example an island, in relation

---

[1] See B 277–8.   [2] E.g. Paulsen, *Immanuel Kant*, p. 182.
[3] In a similar context Kant points out expressly that we can have no experience of absolute rest or absolute motion. See *M.A.d.N.* 1. *Hauptstück* (IV 487–8), where the point is worked out in detail, and compare 4. *Hauptstück*, *Allgemeine Anmerkung für Phänomenologie* (IV 559).   [4] B 277–8.   [5] p. 37.

to which the ship's motion could be observed. He there states expressly that this is to be taken only as a crude comparison.

It is, however, much easier to be sure of what he does not mean than of what he does mean. The permanent of which he speaks is the quantity of matter, and he certainly believes —as I imagine was believed generally at the time—that apart from the conservation of matter physics is impossible.[1] But it is not enough to say that the permanent in this sense is a necessary presupposition of physics. Kant is arguing that it is a necessary presupposition of our experience of change; yet no one could maintain that we are directly aware of a constant amount of matter in all our perception of change. What Kant seems to hold is that our perception of change presupposes something permanent, although only by experience can we discover what that something permanent is.[2] The relatively permanent as against which we do perceive change is at first taken to be the absolutely permanent, but it fails to withstand scientific criticism. With the advance of knowledge we are compelled to substitute something more satisfactory, such as mass or energy. But unless we presuppose something absolutely permanent, the unity of experience would be impossible.[3]

On this point at least—whatever be his justification for it— Kant is perfectly clear. The coming into being of some substances and the passing away of others would destroy the one condition of the empirical unity of time.[4] It would mean that

[1] See *Metaphysik*, p. 34.

[2] Just as our perception of an event presupposes a cause, although only by experience can we determine what that cause is.

[3] Similarly experience always presupposes causality, though our empirical determination of actual causes may be imperfect.

[4] A 188 = B 231-2. This I take to be the unity of the time in which the world is actually experienced. The same point is made also, even more forcibly in A 186 = B 229. If new substances were to come into being—and the same principle holds if existent substances were to disappear—the unity of experience, the unity of time, and the unity of change would be gone. Kant's doctrine is fundamentally opposed to the Cartesian doctrine that all conservation is creation, that in every moment the world is created afresh.

appearances were related to two different and unconnected times in which existence flowed as it were in parallel streams [1] —which is nonsense. But there is *only one time* in which all different times must be placed, not as coexistent, but as successive.[2] This argument is the one which becomes predominant in the second edition, and we are, I think, entitled to regard it as the primary ground of Kant's theory. Indeed, since all the Principles are supposed to rest on the nature of time, the proof of permanence must find its basis in the nature of time.

On the other hand, it is important to observe, both here and throughout the Analogies, that if Kant follows his theory consistently, he cannot argue directly from the nature of time (or space) to the nature of what is in time (or space). He must on the contrary argue indirectly, that is, he must argue from the relation of time (or space) to possible experience,[3] and so must endeavour to establish the conditions of experience.[4]

We may put this point in a different way. The time with which Kant is concerned, since it is a condition of experience, is the one time in which all *objective* time-determinations are. All objective time-determinations, whether of succession or simultaneity, must be found in an object, that is, must be constituted by referring appearances to an object in which they are related; and only so can they be distinguished from merely subjective or imaginary time-relations. Since time itself cannot be perceived, experience requires a permanent object and ultimately one permanent substratum for the whole objective and phenomenal world.[5]

[1] '*neben einander*', side by side.

[2] A 188–9 = B 231–2. Kant is, I think, assuming that since absolute time cannot be perceived, there can be for us one time only if there is one permanent substance (or set of substances) in time.

[3] Compare A 184 = B 227–8, and A 736–7 = B 764–5. If he fails to do this, his proof is 'dogmatic' and to be rejected.

[4] Naturally enough, Kant does not make this point explicit in every sentence, but we must not attribute to him a direct or dogmatic argument when he leaves it to us to fill in the necessary qualifications.

[5] This argument, stated here in a summary manner, is to be distinguished from a dogmatic argument which simply asserts that change is a succession in the states of a substratum.

§ 3. *The Permanence of Time*

We get into new difficulties when we attempt to argue from the permanence of time. It is no easier to regard time as permanent than to regard it as successive—if we suppose time to endure, must there not be another time through which it endures? Nevertheless Kant is right in maintaining that the time in which events occur must be a unity. We must be able to determine the position of all events in relation to one another in one and the same time, and this means that we must be able to hold successive parts of time before us in one time. Kant's ascription of permanence to time seems to mean no more than this. Furthermore, we cannot regard existence as an indivisible point between a non-existent past and a non-existent future.[1] Existence must have quantity or duration in time, if experience is to be possible; but once we admit any duration at all, it seems difficult to deny a continuous and permanent duration.[2]

Kant, as I have pointed out, believed that permanent substances are to be found only in space.[3] No permanent object is given to us in inner sense, and for this reason he rejects all attempts to prove that the soul is a substance. It would therefore seem more satisfactory to rest the proof of substance on the nature of space. Space is permanent amid all the changes in time; and permanent substance, on Kant's view, might be regarded as necessary to 'represent' or 'express' the permanence of a space which, like time, cannot be perceived.[4] Something like this view is expressed in the *Metaphysische Anfangsgründe der Naturwissenschaft*;[5] and Kant's notes on his own

[1] Dr. Broad even goes so far as to maintain that the past is 'real'. See *Scientific Thought*, p. 66.

[2] I suppose the modern doctrine avoids this by taking events as ultimate, but I think Kant would want to carry further the analysis of an event.

[3] This view is already present in the first edition, e.g. in A 349–50.

[4] The space and time which cannot be perceived are the absolute space and time in which all things are, not the relative spaces and times which we are immediately aware of through sensation. Compare *M.A.d.N.* (IV 481).

[5] Compare e.g. (IV 503) and § 7 below.

copy of the first edition of the *Kritik* [1] show that at one time
he intended to re-write the argument in terms of space (or of
space and time). Such re-writing could not be confined to the
First Analogy—it obviously demands, for instance, a re-writing
of the chapter on the schematism of the categories. Perhaps
for this reason Kant changed his mind, and made the proof
of the second edition rest, even more than that of the first,
on the permanence of time. Nevertheless he indicates that the
proof ought to bring in space as the permanent in time; for
he takes our breath away by a later assertion that space alone
is permanently determined, while time, and therefore everything in inner sense, is in constant flux ![2]

To bring in space would make the proof of substance more
complicated, but I think also more plausible. We must be able
to hold time together as a unity, if we are to be aware of space
as permanent through time[3]—to state this is to state a necessary
condition of human experience. And Kant's argument might
be that since we can perceive neither absolute space nor absolute time, there must be a permanent in the spatial objects
of experience to 'represent' or 'express' the permanence
of space in time.

It may be thought that on idealist principles we require
no more for Kant's purpose than a permanent knowing self.
This might perhaps explain our knowledge of the succession
of our own ideas, though I doubt whether it could explain our
knowledge of the world of spatial objects enduring through
an infinite time. But for Kant the history of the individual
mind is only a succession of appearances among other known
successions, and we could not be aware even of our own mental
history except against a background of the permanent in
space.[4] There is nothing permanent in the empirical self

---

[1] See Erdmann, *Nachträge* LXXVII–LXXXIV, especially LXXX.
'Here the proof must be so expressed that it applies only to substances
as phenomena of outer sense. Hence it must be derived from space
which (with its determinations) is at every time.'

[2] B 291; contrast A 143 = B 183 and B 224–5.

[3] Or to experience objects in a space which must be the same at
all times.   [4] See B 275 ff.

as it is known through inner sense; and to suppose that we can pass from the unity of apperception to the knowledge that the soul is a permanent substance—this, according to Kant, is nothing but a paralogism of reason. The permanent which is the condition of our experience is to be found in objects of outer sense and in them alone.[1]

§ 4. *Substratum and Substance*

Kant's argument amounts to this—that since time (or space) is permanent, there must be something permanent given in experience to represent or express an unperceivable time (or space). The argument from time by itself has the disadvantage that we can decide only empirically whether the given permanent is to be found in objects of inner or outer sense. If we argued, as I have suggested, from the permanence of space in time,[2] we might perhaps reasonably infer that the permanent is to be found only in objects of outer sense, which occupy space and last through time.

Even if we admit the validity of this argument for the permanent, it may be objected that the permanent need not be the substratum of appearances: all that we require is a permanent appearance among the changing appearances. If Kant means more than this—and surely he does mean more than this—what is his justification for saying that the permanent must be in objects or appearances *as their substratum*?

This seems to me the most difficult point in the whole of Kant's argument. In the first edition he asserts straight away that if we can determine objective succession and simultaneity only by relation to the permanent, succession and simultaneity must be ways in which the permanent exists, and that the permanent must be the substratum of the empirical

---

[1] See the Paralogisms of Pure Reason, A 341 = B 399 ff., and also the Refutation of Idealism.

[2] This seems to me the correct presupposition of Kant's argument. By appealing to the permanence of space we do not do away with the reference to time, nor do we eliminate the necessity for holding successive times together in the unity of one time.

idea of time.[1] In the second edition he takes time as the substratum of succession and simultaneity,[2] and he seems to imply that the permanent, as representing or expressing time, must therefore be the substratum of successive and simultaneous appearances.[3] It is for this reason that he calls it substance, and asserts that the real (that is, the given appearances) can be thought only as its determinations.

In all this one thing at least is clear. Kant is not arguing from the pure category (or the form of categorical judgement) that the permanent must be the subject of all predicates and therefore the substratum of all change. He is arguing, on the contrary, that because the permanent is the substratum of all change, therefore it is (in the world of phenomena) the ultimate subject of all predicates.[4] If this interpretation is sound, his argument for a permanent substratum of change is independent of the derivation of the categories from the forms of judgement, although he doubtless thinks that when substance is described as the ultimate subject of predicates, something is added to the view that it is the permanent substratum of change.

About this problem it is very easy to talk nonsense, but Kant seems to believe that in order to represent the unity of time (or the permanence of space in time) we require more than the continuous ceasing to be and coming into existence of a qualitatively identical appearance. We require something which neither comes into existence nor ceases to be. Coming into existence and ceasing to be, or in one word change, is nothing other than a way in which the permanent exists, and the permanent is not merely one among many appearances, but is the substratum of all appearances.

[1] A 182–3 = B 225–6.

[2] B 224. Substratum in this sense is equated with the permanent *form* (or *condition*) of inner intuition; compare also A 30 = B 46.

[3] It should, however, be observed that simultaneity and succession are not related to time as accidents are to a substance; for they are not 'modes of time itself'.

[4] That is to say, he is arguing, as we should expect, from the schema to the category.

This view is confirmed by the general account given of substance. Kant distinguishes sharply between a substance and its accidents. The latter are only ways in which substance exists,[1] or ways in which the existence of a substance is positively determined.[2] We do indeed distinguish the existence of the accidents as *inherence* from the existence of the substance (which is *subsistence*);[3] but this is only a method—and a rather misleading method—of asserting that the accidents are the ways in which substance exists. Kant says it is inevitable that if we distinguish inherence and subsistence, we shall come to think of the substance as existing apart from its accidents, and the accidents as existing apart from the substance. The whole history of the doctrine of substance bears out the truth of this assertion, and he rightly rejects such a view as turning a logical distinction into a real separation.[4] He is always clear that we know a substance only through its accidents, just as it is the condition of human knowledge that we know a subject only through its predicates.[5]

If a substance is known only through its accidents, it cannot be merely one appearance among others and distinguished from them solely by the fact that it is unchanging or permanent. Such permanence, I take it, would in any case be for Kant

---

[1] A 186 = B 229.

[2] A 187 = B 230. Even negations are determinations of substance—they express the not-being of something in substance, not the not-being of substance itself. See A 186 = B 229.   [3] A 186 = B 230.

[4] He seems even to deny that we can rightly speak of a relation between substance and accident; and for this reason he maintains that the category of substance and accident is placed under the head of relation, not because it itself is a concept of relation, but because it is the condition of relations—that is, of time-relations, namely succession and simultaneity.

[5] See *Metaphysik*, p. 33. In this place he approves the view, which he attributes to Locke, that substance is a support (*Träger*) of accidents, and asserts that when we think of a substance as existing apart from its accidents, we think of something quite unknown. He calls this 'the substantial' (*das Substanziale*) and identifies it with 'something in general' (*etwas überhaupt*) or, in other words, with the transcendental object (when that is regarded as other than the unity of its appearances). The same view is present in A 414 = B 441.

only the continuous ceasing to be and coming into existence
of a qualitatively identical appearance; and this would not
be sufficient for his theory. Whatever be the precise meaning
of 'substratum', and whatever be the adequacy of the Critical
proof, the view that substance is the permanent substratum
of all appearances must be regarded as an essential part of
his doctrine.

§ 5. *Can Substance be Perceived?*

If substance is the permanent substratum of appearances
and is known only through its accidents, we are faced with
a further difficulty. How can we know that substance possesses
a permanence which its accidents do not? Is the permanence
of substance something which cannot be perceived, although
it has to be presupposed as a condition of our experience
of objective change? Such a doctrine would be very peculiar;
for the reason why the permanent had to be presupposed
as the substratum of appearances was that time itself cannot
be perceived. If the permanent equally cannot be perceived,
what are we to make of Kant's argument?

It seems clear enough that on Kant's view we must be able
in some sense to perceive, not only substance, but also the
permanence of substance; the problem is to determine exactly
what that sense is. The permanence of substance is presupposed
by experience, and so is known *a priori*; but we must be able
to find the permanent in actual experience and to discover
examples of it by ordinary observation.[1]

That permanence can in some sense be observed is stated
or implied by Kant in several passages. For example, he
asserts explicitly that the permanence of matter as appearance
can be observed.[2] We can apparently seek for permanence

---

[1] The same doctrine holds of causality.

[2] A 366. This is implied also in A 350. Kant also implies that we can
find by outer sense a permanent appearance (or intuition) in space:
see A 364 and B 412. We must not, however, take this to mean that
substance is only one (permanent) appearance among many other
(changing) appearances.

by a comparison of sense-perceptions, though this is not the usual method for determining the presence of substance, nor could it be carried out with sufficient completeness: no amount of observation can establish the strict universality which belongs to an *a priori* concept.[1]

We are given little help for the detailed working out of this problem, but manifestly it has to be considered from the point of view of common sense and of science as well as from the point of view of philosophy.

It is always difficult to describe the point of view of common sense or ordinary experience; for the plain man does not make his presuppositions explicit to himself, but simply takes certain things for granted. We all observe the motion of the sun in relation to the unmoving earth, the motion of the ship in relation to the unmoving island, and so on. More fundamentally, we all take it for granted that a thing remains the same while its qualities change, and even that the physical world is abiding or permanent amid its changes.

What is taken to be permanent may vary at different times and for different purposes, although permanence is always assumed and also to some extent observed. But it seems not unreasonable to assert that what is taken to be permanent is in general what fills space,[2] and above all what may be described as the solid.[3] Observed qualities are taken to be qualities of a solid which fills space, and even to occupy an area which is identical with the surface of the solid.[4] The permanence of the solid is partly taken for granted and partly revealed in its observed qualities. We all assume that a chair remains

---

[1] Compare A 205 = B 250–1. The example of the weight of smoke in A 185 = B 228 at least suggests that we could find empirical confirmation for our *a priori* presupposition.

[2] 'To fill space' is '*einen Raum erfüllen*'. A mathematical triangle may be thought to occupy space (*einnehmen*), but not to fill it. See *M.A.d.N. 2. Hauptstück* (IV 497).

[3] I do not of course wish to suggest that for common sense there is nothing permanent in water, fire, or air; but the solid is the most typical case.

[4] Compare Price, *Perception*, p. 143. This view cannot be maintained on reflexion.

the same when we are out of the room, and that on our return we see the same chair and not another chair with precisely identical qualities. We do so even if we find that the chair has changed; for example, if it is in a different position or has been broken.

We get into difficulties only when we begin to ask what it is that is permanent; for so many of the observed qualities manifestly are not. We discover, for example, that there is no permanence of position: our geocentric theory of astronomy must be given up in favour of one that is heliocentric, and ultimately in favour of one that is relativistic. We discover also that our solid bodies are lacking in the permanence which we at first ascribe to them: even their most fundamental qualities change, and we try to find permanence in something more ultimate, in the elements of which they are composed, in atoms, in mass or energy, and so on. This is the work of science, but the principles at work seem to be still those which were at work in our ordinary experience. Always the permanent seems to be presupposed, and its presence is at least partially confirmed by observation. Further knowledge produces fresh dissatisfaction, and our view of what is permanent has to be altered. We may even be tempted to ascribe permanence to 'a supposed I-know-not-what', which is a 'support' of accidents;[1] and this is not very far from abandoning the idea of permanent substance altogether.

On Kant's view we must necessarily employ, whether consciously or unconsciously, the concept of permanent substance in space; for otherwise we shall destroy the unity of time and the unity of experience, and we shall be incapable of making any distinction between objective change and a subjective succession of ideas. Permanent substance in space he appears to identify with mass—the matter of the time; but we must distinguish his general philosophical principle from its special application at a particular stage in the development of science. There would be nothing inconsistent with his general principle, if mass should turn out to be unsatisfactory,

[1] Compare Locke, *Essay*, Book II, Chap. XXIII, sect. 15.

and if we were compelled to put something else, for example, energy, in its place.

On this interpretation what is present alike in common sense, in science, and in the Critical Philosophy is the pre-supposition that there must be a permanent in space, and that this permanent is essentially what fills space: its presence in space is thought to be confirmed, at all the different levels, by actual empirical experience.

How do we know this permanent which fills space? We know it, as we know everything else, by the co-operation of thought and intuition. In all experience we combine or syn-thetise given appearances in time and space in accordance with certain *a priori* concepts, and we regard these appearances, thus necessarily combined, as appearances of a permanent spatial object.[1] The permanence of what fills space is always pre-supposed; but the character of what fills space is revealed, and its permanence verified, most conspicuously in our observations of impenetrability or resistance—not only impenetrability to our own bodies, but also impenetrability to other bodies. These observations give us our original unscientific conception of solidity. They also give us, especially in conjunction with observations of weight, the conception of matter (which Kant himself accepts) as that which fills space by its powers of repulsion and attraction, and is identified in a special sense with 'the real'.

§ 6. *The Quantum of Substance*

In the *Kritik of Pure Reason* Kant is not entitled to take into account empirical principles derived from observation.[2] All he can hope to prove is that in the real which fills space[3] and time there must be a permanent substratum of change. Any attempt

[1] Causality is presupposed as well as substance, but this must be considered later.

[2] Compare the opposition between 'Transcendental Philosophy and 'the universal science of nature' in A 171 = B 213.

[3] The argument as stated by Kant cannot be said to justify us in ascribing this importance to space, but I can see no other way of giving a satisfactory account of his doctrine.

to discover the empirical character of this permanent substratum, or to identify it with matter or mass or energy as known to physical science—any such attempt belongs to another enquiry, which may be called Rational Physiology.[1]

On the other hand if we eliminate all reference to physical matter, his doctrine may appear to be empty and unimportant. Is it possible for us to determine *a priori* any assignable characteristic of the permanent which is the substratum of change?

Kant appears to think that it is possible to do so, and in this way to avoid any appearance of vagueness; for in the second edition he puts forward a more precise and definite statement of his meaning.[2] He asserts that the quantum of substance in nature can neither be increased nor diminished; and he regards this as following directly from the fact that substance, as the permanent substratum of all change, cannot itself change in existence.[3]

It is far from easy to estimate the value of such a contention. We do well to exhibit caution in accepting what may appear to be facile claims to *a priori* knowledge, and such caution is fully in accordance with the spirit of Kant himself.[4] Most commentators are inclined to dismiss this more concrete assertion as an unhappy addition to Kant's general doctrine; and they may be right in so doing. Certainly his statement is much too summary, and in the absence of any further elucidation or expansion it is perhaps hazardous to offer any explanation or defence.

Nevertheless I have come to feel some doubt about the usual way of interpreting this passage, and I am no longer so sure that Kant is making a hurried and unjustifiable leap

---

[1] Compare A 845–6 = B 873–4 and A 848 = B 876.

[2] B 225. This is also expressed in the very formula of the Analogy itself in B 224.

[3] It is difficult to be sure of the significance to be attached to 'existence' in this connexion. Substance must exist at all times—see A 185 = B 228—and so presumably must have at all times a constant and abiding character, however much its accidents may change. This constant character, so far as it can be known *a priori*, can only be its quantum.   [4] Compare A 175 = B 217.

to the doctrine of the conservation of mass as accepted by the science of his time. No doubt he found in this the empirical embodiment of what he claimed to be *a priori* knowledge;[1] but his alleged *a priori* knowledge ought to be of a character so general that different embodiments might be found for it as science continues its progress by its own empirical methods.

I can see nothing in Kant's statement which justifies us in refusing to interpret it in the most general way possible so that it might apply to any empirical reality, whether mass or energy or anything else, which science may discover to be permanent in space. What he claims is that there must be a permanent which fills space, and which must be permanent in respect of its quantity. I have no wish to be dogmatic on this question; but I am inclined to think that if we can know *a priori* that the real in space is permanent, we can know this only in respect of that in the real of which alone we have *a priori* knowledge, and there is nothing whatever in the real of which we have *a priori* knowledge except its quantity.[2] If such be the presupposition of Kant's argument, I do not say that his argument is sound; for there are far too many pitfalls in the way. But I think we can affirm that his argument is not to be summarily dismissed, and even that without some addition of this kind his general doctrine would be so vague as to be almost useless.

§ 7. *Material Substance*

If we are to understand Kant's theory we must look at it in its concrete form, even although this involves an empirical side which, strictly speaking, has no place in the *Kritik of Pure Reason*. He identifies substance with matter as known to the science of his time, and finds in the contemporary doctrine of the conservation of matter the empirical confirmation of his more general principle that the quantum of substance in nature can neither be increased nor diminished.

[1] This is evident even in the first edition; see A 185 = B 228.
[2] Compare A 176 = B 218. The quantity of the real as such is intensive.

This is shown by his account of the philosopher who was asked the weight of smoke.[1] The answer given was that the weight of smoke could be determined by subtracting the weight of the ashes from the original weight of the fuel which had been burned.[2] If, however, we wish to follow Kant's theory in detail we must go to the *Metaphysiche Anfangsgründe der Naturwissenschaft*, a work which attempts to combine the principles of the Critical Philosophy with a bare minimum of material derived from empirical observation.[3] It is concerned only with objects of outer sense and in particular with the matter of which they are composed.

In this work material substance is described as that in space which is movable *in itself*—that is, in separation from everything else which exists outside it in space.[4]

It must be remembered that Kant's account of matter presupposes the truth of all the Principles of the Understanding and especially of the three Analogies. When he proves matter to be substance, he starts from substance, not as meaning the permanent,[5] but as meaning the ultimate subject of existence—the addition of the words 'of existence'

---

[1] A 185 = B 228. For the origin of this story see Lucian $Δημ ώνακτος$ $βίος$ (Vol. II, p. 203, of Teubner edition).

[2] On the margin of his copy of the *Kritik* Kant added 'How did he know this? Not from experience'. See *Nachträge* LXXXV.

[3] This work was published in 1786 just before the publication of the second edition of the *Kritik*. There Kant deals with matter under the heads of quantity, quality, relation, and modality—these four heads giving us respectively (1) phoronomy (the pure theory of motion), (2) dynamics, (3) mechanics, and (4) phenomenology. He starts from the empirical fact that the fundamental determination of any object of outer sense must be motion; for it is by motion alone that outer sense can be affected (IV 476). Matter is described under the four heads as follows: (1) matter is the movable in space; (2) matter is the movable so far as it fills space; (3) matter is the movable so far as, *quâ* movable, it possesses moving force; and (4) matter is the movable so far as, *quâ* movable, it can be an object of experience. See *M.A.d.N.* (IV 480, 496, 536, 554).

[4] *M.A.d.N.* (IV 502).

[5] Perhaps the reason for this is that the doctrine of the conservation of matter is to be proved later.

is unusual[1]—which is never a predicate. 'Matter is the subject of everything which can be reckoned to the existence of things in space; for apart from matter no subject could be thought except space itself. The concept of space, however, is not the concept of any existent, but is merely the concept of the necessary conditions of the external relations of possible objects of outer sense. Therefore matter, as the movable in space, is substance in space'.[2]

Kant then argues that all the parts of material substance, so far as they are themselves subjects, and not merely predicates of other matters, must themselves be substances. The parts are, however, subjects, if they are themselves movable[3] and are consequently something existing in space independently of their combination with other adjacent parts of material substance.[4] Therefore the movability of matter, or of any part of it, is a proof that the movable, and every movable part of it, is substance.[5]

To speak more generally—Kant's view is that since material substance is spread out in space, its parts must be outside one another. These parts, since they can be moved, or separated from the whole of which they are parts, must themselves be substances.[6]

Kant clearly regards the scientific idea of matter as developing from the commonsense idea of solidity or impenetrability which is revealed to us by the sense of touch.[7] Matter is the movable which fills space, and it does so, not in the sense in which a mathematical triangle may be thought to occupy[8]

---

[1] Kant wishes to refer to a real, and not merely a logical, subject. See B 129.

[2] *M.A.d.N.* 2. *Hauptstück* (IV 503). Compare the argument I have suggested in § 3 above.

[3] '*wenn sie für sich beweglich . . . sind.*'

[4] '*ausser ihrer Verbindung mit anderen Nebenteilen.*'

[5] *M.A.d.N.* 2. *Hauptstück* (IV 503).

[6] *M.A.d.N.* 3. *Hauptstück* (IV 542). This explains how Kant can pass from 'substance' to 'substances' in A 184 = B 227.

[7] *M.A.d.N.* 2. *Hauptstück* (IV 510).

[8] '*einnehmen.*' To fill space is '*einen Raum erfüllen*'. See *M.A.d.N.* 2. *Hauptstück* (IV 497).

space, but by resisting the penetration of other movables.[1] To penetrate into space is a motion—in the initial moment it may be called a tendency to penetrate—and to resist this motion is to cause its diminution or reduction to rest. Resistance—for reasons into which I need not enter—is therefore to be regarded as itself a cause of motion, and a cause of motion is called a moving force.[2] Hence matter fills space through moving force,[3] and the fundamental moving forces by which it does so are those of repulsion and attraction.[4]

The quantity of matter is the aggregate[5] of the movable in a determinate space. So far as all its parts are considered as working (moving) together in the same direction, it is called 'mass'. A mass of determinate shape is called a 'body' (in the mechanical sense).[6] The quantity of matter is measured through the quantity of motion at a given velocity.[7] The quantity of motion of a body (that of a point consists only in a degree of velocity) at the same velocity is measured through the quantity of the matter moved. These two statements do not constitute a vicious circle; one explains the meaning of a concept, the other its application to experience. The quantity of the movable in space is the quantity of matter; but *the quantity of matter* (the aggregate of the movable) *shows itself in experience only through the quantity of motion at an equal velocity* (for example, through equilibrium).[8]

I mention these details—which I do not profess to understand, and which are perhaps themselves not wholly intelligible apart from the whole argument from which they have been extracted—in order to show the background for Kant's view

[1] *M.A.d.N.* 2. *Hauptstück, Erkl.* 1 (IV 496).

[2] '*bewegende Kraft.*'

[3] This presupposes the doctrine of the Second Analogy.

[4] *M.A.d.N.* 2. *Hauptstück* (IV 497 ff.). This is simply an empirical fact.

[5] '*die Menge*'. This is a whole whose parts are outside one another. See A 163 = B 204 and compare *M.A.d.N.* 3. *Hauptstück* (IV 539).

[6] *M.A.d.N.* 3. *Hauptstück, Erkl.* 2 (IV 537).

[7] *M.A.d.N.* 3. *Hauptstück, Lehrsatz* 1 (IV 537). I omit the proof of this.   [8] *M.A.d.N.* 3. *Hauptstück* (IV 540).

that the necessary permanence of substance is realised in the conservation of matter. The quantity of matter is, according to Kant, the quantity of substance in the movable, and is not the quantity (or degree) of a quality of substance (such as repulsion or attraction).[1] The quantity of substance is the mere aggregate of the movable, the movable being what constitutes matter; for it is only this aggregate of the moved which, with the same velocity, can give a difference in the quantity of motion. For reasons into which again I do not enter, the quantity of substance in matter can be estimated only mechanically (that is, through the quantity of the motion belonging to the matter), and not dynamically (that is, through the quantity of the originally moving forces.)[2]

§ 8. *The Conservation of Matter*

From this Kant goes on to establish the three laws of mechanics, the first of which is especially germane to the First Analogy.[3] '*In all changes of corporeal nature the quantity of matter in the whole remains the same, unincreased and undiminished.*'[4]

Kant's proof presupposes it to have been proved in the *Kritik* that amid all the changes of phenomenal nature substance is permanent, which he here takes to mean that no substance can come into being or pass away. Here, as he says,

---

[1] *M.A.d.N.* 3. *Hauptstück* (IV 540). This shows clearly that the permanent is not for Kant one appearance among others, although it 'shows itself in experience'.

[2] *M.A.d.N.* 3. *Hauptstück* (IV 541). The quantity of the originally moving forces is a degree.

[3] The second law is that all change of matter has an outer cause—every body endures in its state of rest or motion, in the same direction and with the same velocity, if it is not compelled through an outer cause to abandon this state. See *M.A.d.N.* (IV 543).

The third law is that in all imparting of motion action and reaction are always equal. See *M.A.d.N.* (IV 544).

The second and third laws are intended to stand to the Second and Third Analogies as the first law stands to the First Analogy.

[4] *M.A.d.N.* 3. *Hauptstück, Lehrsatz* 2 (IV 541).

he has to show only what substance in matter is. The proof
runs as follows.

In all matter the movable in space is the ultimate subject[1]
of all the accidents which inhere in matter; and the aggregate
of this movable, whose parts are outside one another, is the
quantity of substance. Therefore the quantity of matter, as
regards its substance, is simply the aggregate of the substances
of which it consists. Therefore the quantity of matter cannot
be increased or diminished, unless a new substance comes
into being or passes out of being. But amid all change of matter
substance never comes into being or passes out of being.
Therefore the quantity of matter can neither be increased nor
diminished, but remains always the same in the whole; that
is, it endures somewhere in the world in the same quantity,
although this or that matter can be increased or diminished
through addition or subtraction of its parts.[2]

This proof (which concerns substance only as an object of
outer sense) rests upon the view that the quantity of an object
in space must consist of *parts outside one another*; that these
parts, so far as they are real (that is, movable), must necessarily
be substances; and that consequently the quantity of spatial
substance cannot be increased or diminished without the creation
or extinction of substance, which is impossible.[3]

---

[1] He ought, I think, to say 'substance'.

[2] *M.A.d.N.* 2. *Hauptstück, Lehrsatz* 2, *Beweis* (IV 541–2). Prichard
(*Kant's Theory of Knowledge*, p. 273) maintains, following Cook Wilson,
that Kant's doctrine implies that there may be creation and extinction
of substances. I cannot see the justification for this view, if a substance
is made up of substances, and its parts can move independently. For
Kant constant quantity is a consequence of the permanence of substances, not an equivalent expression for it.

[3] This argument, Kant believes, would not hold if we supposed
the soul, an object of inner sense, to be a substance; for such a substance could have a quantity (that is, an intensive quantity) *which did
not consist of parts outside one another*, and since its parts would not
therefore be substances, it could increase or diminish without trans-
gressing the principle of the permanence of substance. Kant uses this
doctrine in order to refute attempts to prove the immortality of the
soul on the ground that the soul is a simple substance. Compare
B 413 ff.

§ 9. *The Empirical Criterion of Substance*

I set forth this proof, not in order to defend its validity, but to show where Kant finds in experience the permanent whose necessity he believes he has proved. The doctrine of substance, like that of causality, is confirmed by empirical observation, and receives concrete meaning only in experience. Its necessity can never be proved by experience, but must be proved, if at all, by reference to the conditions of possible experience (particularly the unity of time and space).

Kant himself points out that to establish the permanence of any substance by comparing our different sense-perceptions would be a very inadequate method.[1] We do not use observed permanence as our empirical criterion of substance. A better and easier empirical criterion of substance is action.[2] This is mentioned by Kant, not in the First Analogy, but in the Second, because it presupposes the truth of causality.

Causality leads to the concept of action, and action to the concept of force, and thereby to the concept of substance.[3] Kant excuses himself from working this out in detail as inappropriate to a mere *Kritik* of pure reason, but he asks himself how we can make an inference from action to the permanence of what acts.[4]

This question can, Kant believes, be easily answered by his

[1] A 205 = B 251.

[2] '*Handlung.*' A 204 = B 249; A 205 = B 250.

[3] A 204 = B 249. Causality is the quality of a substance, in so far as substance is regarded as the cause of accidents. Action (which can be ascribed only to substances) is the determination of the force of a substance as a cause of a certain accident, and it must have a real effect (unlike power or *Vermögen*, by which we represent the possibility of force). 'Force' (*Kraft*) is used for the relation (*respectus*) of substance to the existence of accidents, in so far as substance contains the ground of these accidents. We know forces only through our observation of changes, and it is the duty of science to reduce forces to as few fundamental forces (*Grundkräfte*) as possible.

I take these definitions from *Metaphysik*, pp. 34–5, but it must be remembered that these lectures are printed from students' notes, and their accuracy (from internal evidence) is not always to be relied upon.

[4] A 205 = B 250.

Critical method. Action means[1] the relation[2] of the subject
of causality to its effect. Every effect consists in an event, and
therefore in the transitory;[3] hence the ultimate subject of the
event or the effect is the permanent which is the substratum
of everything that changes. The reason alleged for this is that
—according to the principle of causality—actions are always
the first grounds of all change[4] (or exchange) of appearances, and
cannot therefore lie in a subject which itself changes[5] in the
sense in which appearances change; for then it would be necessary to have other actions and another subject which determined
this change.[6]

This argument is not clear without an explanation of what
is meant by the 'subject of causality' and its relation to the
permanent substratum of change. Kant, however, affirms as
his conclusion that the first subject of the causality of all
coming into being and passing away (in the field of appearances) cannot itself come into being or pass away.[7] Hence the
presence of action gives a sure ground for asserting the presence
of empirical necessity[8] and permanence in existence, and there-

---

[1] '*bedeutet*.'

[2] If this relation is identified (*Metaphysik*, p. 34) with force, action
(as a determination of force) ought to be a determination of that
relation, not that relation itself.

[3] The transitory 'signifies' (*bezeichnet*) time considered as successive,
just as the permanent in appearances 'expresses' or 'represents' time
considered as permanent.

[4] The word here is '*Wechsel*', which implies an exchange of states of
a substance. See § 10 below.   [5] '*wechselt*.'

[6] '*Wechsel*.' Kant's argument in certain respects bears a resemblance
to the argument that motion presupposes a prime mover which is not
itself moved. This argument was used by St. Thomas as a proof of
the existence of God (see *Sum. Theol.* I, II, 3, and compare *Sum. c. Gen.*
XIII), and appears to be of the type rejected by Kant in the Antinomies. No doubt there are differences in the two cases, but I
feel so uncertain of the present argument that I prefer to make no
comment.

[7] A 205 = B 251. This statement is equivalent to the statement
that the first subject of causality does not admit of change in the sense
of exchange (*Wechsel*).

[8] 'Empirical necessity' would seem to be the necessity which is to
be found in the phenomenal world of experience.

fore the presence of substance as an appearance (*substantia phaenomenon*).[1]

§ 10. *The Concept of Change*

The concept of change has to be interpreted[2] in the light of the doctrine that succession can be determined only in relation to the permanent.[3] Coming into being and passing away are not to be taken as changes of what comes into being and passes away. A change is a way of existing[4] which follows upon another way of the same thing's existing. That is to say there is an exchange, or substitution,[5] of one state[6] of a thing for another state of that thing, but the thing itself must remain the same thing. We cannot say that a thing has changed, unless it remains the same thing; and we can put this paradoxically by saying that it is only the permanent, or substance, which changes, while the transitory, or the accidents, do not change, but rather are exchanged, for one ceases to be and another takes its place.[7]

---

[1] A 206 = B 251.

[2] A 187 = B 230. The correction or interpretation (*Berichtigung*)—not the 'justification' (*Berechtigung*) as Prichard translates it—of the concept of change rests upon this doctrine of permanence. Prichard maintains (*Kant's Theory of Knowledge*, p. 274) that Kant's method here is a dogmatic argument which proves the necessity of a permanent substratum by an analysis of the nature of change. I do not see how the passage can be so interpreted in view of its context, for Kant is here explaining how change is to be understood in the light of the doctrine that has been established. His previous argument does not rest on a definition of change, but on the contention that there can be no experience of *objective* succession unless objective succession is taken to be a change in or of the permanent. If the argument rested on a definition of change, it would be open to Lord Balfour's objection that we may very well be content with 'alternation' in place of 'change'; see *A Defence of Philosophic Doubt*, p. 114.

[3] The permanent is only one of the conditions of determining succession, but it is a necessary condition.

[4] '*eine Art zu existieren*.'　　　　　　　　　　[5] '*Wechsel*.'

[6] '*Zustand*.' This word has a temporal significance. See *Metaphysik*, pp. 34–5. A timeless object has no states.

[7] This point is difficult to put clearly owing to the ambiguity of words. Kemp Smith uses the word 'alteration' for what I call 'change',

In the light of this[1] we can say that when we perceive a change, we perceive a change in a permanent substance, and never an absolute coming into being or passing away. In our empirical knowledge it is always the permanent which makes possible the idea of a transition from one state to another, or from not-being to being; and these states are always recognised as being exchanged for one another in the permanent. This is, I think, empirically true; what we perceive—or seem to perceive—is a thing changing colour, not one colour and then another. Kant reinforces this statement by insisting that since we cannot perceive an empty time, we cannot see a coming to be except by reference to what was before; and he argues that if we attach what comes to be to what was before—as we must—we are obliged to regard what was before as enduring up to the coming to be, and what comes to be can be regarded only as a determination of what was before, that is, of the permanent. The same is equally true as regards passing away, for we cannot perceive an empty time after such a passing away.[2]

§ 11. *Science and Experience*

Kant believes—if I may attempt to summarise the results of this difficult discussion—that his doctrine of permanent substance is a necessary presupposition, not only of Newtonian physics, but of ordinary everyday experience. At first sight this seems difficult to accept, but perhaps the scientific notion of substance, like the scientific notion of causality, is the result of clarifying a concept which is assumed without question by common sense. The world which is revealed to us in experience

and 'change' for what I call 'exchange'. The German words are '*Veränderung*' and '*Wechsel*'. Watson translates them as 'change' and 'alternation', which seems to me better than Kemp Smith's terminology.

[1] A 188 = B 231.

[2] All this confirms the view that Kant is not arguing from a definition of change, or from an analysis of the concept of change, but from the conditions of our experiencing an objective temporal order or succession.

certainly seems very different from the succession of unrelated impressions and ideas to which it is reduced by the analysis of Hume. What we seem to perceive is not a colour, but a coloured surface or a coloured body; and when we are aware of a change of colour, we seem to be aware not merely of one colour and then another colour, but of a permanent body which changes in colour.[1]

No doubt such bodies are regarded by common sense as only relatively permanent, and the common-sense concept of body is extremely crude in comparison with that of science. Nevertheless the solid bodies which for common sense possess the changing qualities revealed to our senses are essentially what fills space;[2] and science in determining more precisely, the character of what fills space, not only refines—and perhaps even refines away—the concept of body, but gives a new and precise meaning to the permanence which bodies are supposed to possess.

If Kant could be said to have proved that the permanence of what fills space is a necessary condition of our experience of succession in time, he would have given an answer to Hume; and the importance of his principle would be enormously increased if he were justified in deducing as a consequence that the quantum of substance in nature can neither be increased nor diminished. Further than this, as Kant recognises, it is impossible to go without calling in the aid of empirical facts; it belongs to science alone to determine the accidents of substance, as it belongs to science alone to determine the cause of any given effect.

---

[1] Most changes in the spatial world we regard as changes of bodies, and perhaps this might be extended to all changes, although there is clearly need of a separate discussion for such changes as are observed in a flash of lightning or in a bird's song.

[2] In all experience, as we combine the given appearances in one space and time by means of the transcendental synthesis of imagination, we combine our given sensa as accidents or qualities of what is supposed to fill space; and there is much to be said for the view that such acts of combination are *a priori*, that is, they do not depend on the particular character of the given sensa.

Kant's science is now superseded, and we need attach no importance to the detailed theories which he accepted. What we have to consider is his central doctrine—that if science is to be science, and if experience is to be experience, it must necessarily employ the concept of substance and accident as well as the concept of cause and effect.[1] I confess that in the present condition of science it is difficult for one who is not a scientist—and perhaps impossible for one who is—to share Kant's belief; but I think it not unreasonable to ask whether these concepts are being definitely abandoned in favour of others, or whether they are being modified and corrected with the advance of knowledge. That Kant's conclusions are not yet wholly superseded is shown by a statement of Emile Meyerson, himself not the least distinguished among modern exponents of the philosophy of science, in which he asserts of the attitude of the most advanced physicists that it '*confirme nettement la supposition que la science, la raison scientifique, aspire profondément à concevoir un réel de substances en tant que substrat et explication des phénomènes changeants. Tout pas accompli dans la direction opposée apparaît au savant comme un sacrifice, un renoncement*'.[2] If language so Kantian can be used of the fundamental concepts of modern science, it is still worth enquiring into the reasons by which the Critical Philosophy attempted to establish the necessity of these concepts.

[1] I think we must take this to imply, not only the permanence of substance, but its permanence in regard to quantity; and this means that the quantum of the real which fills space cannot be increased or diminished. If we reject this addition, Kant's doctrine loses much of its importance.

[2] Quoted in *Mind*, N.S. Vol. XLI, No. 163, July 1932, p. 382.

CHAPTER XLIII

THE SECOND ANALOGY

§ 1. *The Principle of Causality*

In the second edition the Principle established by the Second Analogy is called 'the principle of temporal succession in accordance with the law of causality'. In the first edition it is called 'the principle of production',[1] where production seems to be equivalent to 'causation'.

The formula of the second edition is as follows: *All changes*[2] *take place in conformity with the law of the connexion*[3] *of cause and effect.*[4]

The law of cause and effect has for long appeared to be one of the most fundamental, if not indeed the most fundamental, of all the presuppositions accepted alike by science and by ordinary experience; and although its universality even in the physical world appears to be questioned to-day by physicists, as it has in the past been questioned by theologians, nevertheless to set it aside altogether, without putting something in its place,[5] would deprive us of the main clue by which we have

---

[1] '*Erzeugung.*' This word, I think, like the English word 'production', implies force or activity in the cause.

[2] '*Veränderungen.*' This has been explained in A 187 = B 230 as involving the exchange (or succession) of the determinations of a permanent substance.

[3] '*Verknüpfung.*' Connexion, or *nexus*, involves a synthesis of heterogeneous elements which necessarily belong to one another. See B 201 n.

[4] B 232. In the first edition the formula is: *Everything that happens* (*that is, begins to be*) *presupposes something upon which it follows in accordance with a rule.* See A 189. 'To happen' is to be an objective event.

[5] It is not always easy to draw a sharp distinction between interpreting an old concept in a more satisfactory way and putting a new one in its place. We must in any case hold to-day that the concept of causality requires reinterpretation, or at the very least that the meaning of the concept cannot be taken as obvious and in need of no further analysis.

sought to understand the nature of the world. Hence it would be difficult to exaggerate the importance of a valid proof of causality, which quite certainly can never be given us by ordinary inductive methods, since in such methods causality (or something akin to causality) is already presupposed. It would also be difficult to exaggerate the importance which Kant's proof has in the system of the Critical Philosophy; for it is here, more than anywhere else, that we must find the answer to Hume, and it is here that the doctrine of the Transcendental Deduction attains its most characteristic and most fundamental application.[1]

In such a case we are entitled to demand that the argument offered us should be water-tight. There ought to be no doubt about its interpretation, and it ought to be capable of withstanding a cool and sceptical scrutiny such as Hume brought to bear on everything which claimed to be *a priori* knowledge. Unfortunately there is a real difficulty in understanding some of Kant's statements, and a still greater difficulty in understanding the relation of his statements to one another. To unsympathetic critics it may easily seem that he is one of those philosophers who conceal the weakness of their argument under a cloud of words. I believe, on the contrary, that his obscurity is due to the fact that he is struggling with new and difficult thoughts. I believe also that, even if he is in error, there is much in his view which is worthy of serious consideration.

One point is perfectly clear. Kant is arguing that if we are to distinguish the objective succession of events in the phenomenal world from the subjective succession of our ideas, we must regard the former succession as necessarily determined, that is to say, as governed by the law of cause and effect. This contention he does not claim to be self-evident. It depends on

---

[1] This claim may be made also for the Third Analogy (as combining in itself the First and Second Analogies), but the Third Analogy seems in some ways little more than an application or extension of the principles already established, and the number of arguments brought forward in the Second Analogy shows that for Kant the real crux of his doctrine is to be found here.

Critical doctrines which have already been established; and what we want to know is the precise nature of the Critical doctrines presupposed and their precise relation to the contention which we have now to consider.

It might be thought that objectivity has already been shown to involve necessity, and that consequently objective succession must be necessary succession. But in that case Kant's elaborate proof would be superfluous. All that Kant claims to have shown is that appearances, to be appearances of an object, must be united in the synthetic unity of apperception, or must have that necessary synthetic unity without which they cannot be thought by one mind.[1] This necessary synthetic unity must indeed for Kant be such that it can be thought in all the forms of judgement; for the forms of judgement are the forms of synthesis without which thought is impossible, and there are no objects apart from thought. But Kant is not arguing that because we must be able to judge any object under the form 'if A, then B', therefore every object must be governed by the law of cause and effect.[2] On the contrary, the hypothetical form of judgement is for him an empty form awaiting an object; and what we now have to prove is that all objects given to us under the forms of space and time must have a characteristic which enables them to be judged by the hypothetical form of judgement. That characteristic is necessary succession, and the proof of necessary succession must be a proof independent of the form of judgement.

Kant is certainly presupposing that space and time are forms of sensibility, and that appearances given under the forms of space and time are therefore not things-in-themselves, but appearances of things-in-themselves to human minds. There can be no reasonable doubt that he regards this presupposition as essential to his argument. He also believes all objective com-

---

[1] I have already pointed out in Chapter XXX § 3 that this contention remains extremely vague unless we can describe this synthetic unity in detail.

[2] Such an argument would be manifestly invalid, since the hypothetical form of judgement involves no reference to time.

bination and connexion of appearances to be determined by a
transcendental synthesis of imagination working through
the medium of time.[1] What he has to show is that if we are to
experience objective changes in one common homogeneous time
whose parts succeed one another, there must be a succession
of appearances which is necessary, and so is governed by the
law of cause and effect.

§ 2. *The Six Proofs of Causality*

Kant shows his sense of the importance of the present
argument by a multiplication of proofs which recalls the method
of the Transcendental Deduction. We have, as usual, a proof
added in the second edition, while in the first edition we have
what are commonly regarded as five successive proofs.[2] Thus
we have:

Proof I   B 232–4 (two paragraphs).
Proof II   A 189–94 = B 234–39 (four paragraphs).
Proof III   A 194–5 = B 239–40 (two paragraphs). This is
followed by a third paragraph of a more general character
(A 195–6 = B 240–1), which cannot be considered as belonging
specially to Proof III.
Proof IV   A 196–9 = B 241–4 (three paragraphs).
Proof V   A 199–201 = B 244–6 (three paragraphs).
Proof VI   A 201–2 = B 246–7 (one paragraph).

This multiplicity of proofs has given rise to the theory that
they were composed at different times and represent different
levels of Kant's thought. As such theories of origin are, in my
opinion, of no help for the understanding of the argument, I

[1] No doubt he believes also that this transcendental synthesis of the
imagination is itself determined by the pure categories, and in particular by the pure category of ground and consequent; but I do not
think this is one of the premises of his argument. On the contrary,
this doctrine is fully established in regard to ground and consequent
only when it has been proved that all objective succession is necessary
succession.

[2] This division I take from Adickes in his edition of the *Kritik*. It is
accepted by Kemp Smith.

propose to ignore them. It should, however, be noted that these proofs are not to be regarded merely as different versions of the same proof added arbitrarily to one another. If we consider the first edition by itself we have at least some appearance of development. Proof II (the first in the first edition) develops the argument as a whole; Proof III is an indirect proof stating the impossible consequences which follow if the principle of causality is denied; Proof IV at least professes—if it does not altogether carry out its professions—to appeal to actual experience for confirmation; Proof V brings out and elaborates the dependence of the argument on the nature of time; while Proof VI is intended to be a summary, and a much-needed summary, of the main points or 'moments' of the argument. I can see no reason why Kant—whose method of writing is very different from that of Professor Moore or Professor Prichard—should not have composed this series of arguments in the order in which they are printed, and Proof IV is the only one which in my opinion can reasonably be regarded as superfluous.[1]

§ 3. *The First Proof*

The proof added in the second edition[2] begins with an introduction which is clearly intended to suggest that the Second Analogy rests on the First Analogy as a necessary presupposition. This is not made explicit in the proofs themselves; but Kant presumably held that only a belief in permanent substances filling space entitled him to assume, as he does, a contrast between the simultaneous characteristics of a house and the successive characteristics of a moving ship.

The introduction is a 'reminder'[3] of what we have already

[1] It may be observed that this multiplication of proofs is not only known to have been a feature of Kant's teaching: it is also explicitly present, though not to the same extent, in such an early work as the *Nova Dilucidatio*; see *Sectio* III (I 410–11).

[2] B 232–4. In the case of the Second Analogy I deal first with the proof given in the second edition because its importance might fail to be appreciated, if it were considered as the last of six proofs. As the terms employed have been already defined, this course does not suffer from the usual disadvantages. Compare Chapter XXXVII § 1.

[3] B 233, '*Vorerinnerung*'.

learnt[1]—that succession (or exchange) of appearances is only a 'change' of permanent substances, that is, a successive being and not-being of the determinations of a substance which does not itself either come into being or pass away, but whose existence is positively determined in different ways at different times.[2]

Kant's proof runs as follows:

I. I *perceive* that appearances follow one another; and this means that at different times I perceive different states of the same thing or things.[3] Hence in sense-perception of this kind I am connecting[4] two different sense-perceptions or appearances[5] in time.

II. Connexion (or *nexus*) is a species of combination or synthesis necessary for knowledge of objects. It is never the work of mere sense or intuition, but is the product of a synthetic power of *imagination*,[6] which determines inner sense in regard to its time-relations.[7]

---

[1] In A 187–8 = B 230–1. See Chapter XLII § 10.

[2] Kant's argument may seem 'dogmatic' in this passage, because he says that the concept of change presupposes one and the same subject as existing with two opposite determinations, and therefore as enduring. I think, however, that this analysis of the concept of change is for Kant a consequence of establishing the necessity of permanent substance, and not a premise from which such a necessity is proved.

[3] B 233. The reference to 'things' shows that Kant considers himself now entitled to assume more than Hume admitted. Hume admitted only consciousness of a succession of appearances. Kant believes himself to have proved that we are justified in ascribing successive states to a permanent substance or substances.

The 'opposition' attributed to states of the same thing I take to be manifested in difference.

[4] '*verknüpfe.*' This is used in the technical sense to indicate 'connexion' or '*nexus*'. See B 201 n.

[5] I take 'sense-perceptions' to be here equivalent to 'appearances'.

[6] Here as so often sense-perception is connected (if not identified) with the synthesis of apprehension, which is the work of imagination.

[7] This last clause might seem to imply that the connexion so far is subjective. Inner sense is determined so far as imagination successively brings different appearances before the mind. Kant may, however, have in mind an objective connexion. In that case he goes on to explain that it involves more than imagination.

III. Imagination uncontrolled by *thought* can combine appearances in different ways, either B after A or A after B. As far as mere imagination is concerned, although we are aware that we are imaginatively putting appearances in a particular temporal order, we cannot be aware that the appearances are states of an *object* and occur in that order independently of our imagination. Hence sense-perception, so far as it is a synthesis of the given by means of mere imagination, does not determine the *objective* temporal relation of successive appearances.[1]

Whatever be the difficulties in this assertion, Kant is clearly right, if he is saying that neither by mere sense nor by mere imagination, nor by any combination of the two, can we determine the objective order of events.

Kant's reason for this assertion is the doctrine which lies at the root of all the Analogies—that *time itself cannot be perceived*. If time itself could be perceived, we could, he believes, determine in relation to it the order of appearances in the object itself, and this process of determining would be

---

[1] There is a whole series of subjective orders distinct from the order which we believe to be objective. Thus the subjective order of our *sensings* is different from the objective order; for what we sense successively we may believe to be simultaneous. The subjective order of our *imaginings* may also be different from the objective order, when what we imagine is real events—I can imagine the death of Caesar after imagining the battle of Actium. Again I can imagine *an order of fictitious events*, and even this order (while still a subjective order dependent on my imagination alone) may be different from the order of my imaginings; for I may choose to imagine first a fictitious event and then the fictitious events which led up to it. Even in *imagining real events* I can imagine them to take place *in an order different from their actual order*, and I can do this without asserting that imaginary order to be real. For example I can imagine America to have declared war on Germany when the *Lusitania* was sunk, and can try to estimate the probable consequences. Of course if I imagine that America actually did declare war on Germany when the *Lusitania* was sunk, that is not mere imagination but erroneous thinking. Even in the case when I imagine real events, there is an element of thought present in the recognition that the events are real; and there is also an element of thought present, if I recognise that the order in which they are imagined to be is not their actual or objective order.

akin to empirical perception. The death of Julius Caesar would, I suppose, be actually given to perception with the mark upon it of a particular moment on the Ides of March, B.C.44, and all subsequent efforts to recall his death in imagination would necessarily recall that particular mark as an inseparable part of the whole event recalled.[1] Because this is not so, we are compelled in experience to determine the objective temporal order of events by their necessary connexion with one another.

IV. This last point is the point which Kant duly proceeds to make. If we are to know the objective relation[2] of appearances to one another in time, we must not only imagine, but *think*, the temporal relation of the appearances (that is, of the successive states of substance), and we must do so in a particular way—our thought of it must be such that '*thereby*[3] it is determined as necessary which of the appearances must be placed (or posited[4]) before and which after'.[5]

---

[1] We should, I suppose, know that the successive appearances of a house were objectively simultaneous, because each appearance would have the mark of the whole time through which it endured. But perhaps it is a mistake to render too precise an alternative which is admittedly impossible.

[2] B 234. Kant says 'If we are to know the objective relation of appearances *as determined*', but this seems to be equivalent to knowing it, or knowing it as objective. For sense-perception without thought this objective relation is undetermined or unknown (as objective); for thought it is known (as objective). 'Determined' here cannot *mean* 'necessarily determined'. In *Metaphysik*, p. 23, Kant says that 'to determine' is of two opposites to posit (*setzen*) one, and this may be relevant, since by 'positing' we must understand the absolute positing of thought, not the arbitrary and subjective positing of imagination.   [3] '*dadurch*.'

[4] '*gesetzt*', 'placed' or 'posited'. This word is especially prominent in the second edition. Actuality is absolute position, so that the object is posited (*gesetzt*) in itself, and not relatively to my understanding (*Metaphysik*, pp. 27–8; compare A 598 = B 626 and also B 142). Existence is also said to be *positio absoluta* (*Metaphysik*, p. 25).

[5] More simply—if we are to know that AB is an objective succession, we must not only sense A and then B and combine them in that order in imagination: we must also think that B *necessarily* follows A. Such thinking may of course be 'obscure': perhaps we should say that we (consciously or unconsciously) 'assume' or 'presuppose' that B *necessarily* follows A.

It is on this statement that the whole of Kant's argument turns. What comes before it is, I suggest, clearly sound. What follows merely renders explicit the consequences of this assertion; for a temporal succession which is determined as necessary is a succession determined in accordance with the law of cause and effect.

V. The thought or concept involved is therefore a concept of *necessary synthetic unity*,[1] and consequently a pure concept of the understanding,[2] not a concept derived from sense-perception by the ordinary method of abstraction. The pure concept in question is called, with unusual elaborateness, the concept *of the relation of cause and effect*[3], which relation is such that the cause determines the effect *as its consequence or sequel in time*.[4] This means that the later event could not precede the earlier event,[5] as it can for imagination uncontrolled by thought. It means also that if the earlier event occurs, it must be possible to *perceive* the later immediately thereafter; whereas if two events are merely imagined as successive, the perception of the first event does not imply that the later event can also be perceived immediately thereafter—or indeed at all.[6]

[1] It is a concept of a particular kind of necessary synthetic unity, the necessary unity (or causal *nexus*) of appearances whose succession is an objective succession.

[2] It will be remembered—see Chapter XXXIX § 6—that in B 219 Kant argued from the *a priori* connexion imposed by the concept to necessity. Here he argues from the necessity of the connexion to the *a priori* character of the concept.

[3] Kant believes that all necessary, and indeed all objective, succession is causally determined, but not that the earlier event is necessarily the cause of the later. Night, for example, is not the cause of day.

[4] The reference to temporal sequence distinguishes the schematised category of cause and effect from the pure category of ground and consequent.

[5] This is naturally subject to the proviso that B1 (the effect of A1) can precede A2 (the cause of B2).

[6] I think that this is Kant's meaning—not that if two events are merely imagined as successive, the second event may be something which need not be perceivable at all (as when I imagine that a particular incantation of Circe might cause men to turn into swine). But the statement is obscure.

VI. Hence it is only because we subject[1] the succession of appearances (and so all 'change'[2]) to the law of causality that experience (as empirical knowledge of appearances and their objective succession) is possible. Since the conditions of the possibility of experience are necessarily the condition of the possibility of phenomenal objects,[3] phenomenal objects, or objects of experience,[4] are necessarily subject to the laws of cause and effect.

§ 4. *The Object and its Temporal Relations*

The first proof in the first edition[5] also begins with an introduction. This introduction reaffirms Kant's general account of the nature of an object and prepares the way for the special case of objective succession.[6]

One great difficulty in following Kant's argument is the ambiguity of his terms. Thus in the argument of the second edition 'appearance' was used primarily for the different states of a substance, states which succeed one another in the object.[7] In the present argument 'appearance' is used for a whole

---

[1] '*unterwerfen.*' I do not think Kant means that we first have a subjective succession of appearances, and then make it objective by bringing it under the law of cause and effect. Rather in being aware of an objective succession we are necessarily considering it as determined by the law of cause and effect. Kant may, however, be arguing from the necessity in the order of apprehension to necessity in the order of events in the object. See § 5 IV below.

[2] It must be remembered that 'change' is succession (or exchange) of the states of a substance. Kant is here talking of objective change or succession.

[3] If the objects we know were things-in-themselves, we could never know, according to Kant, that they were governed by causal law.

[4] Kant says 'appearances themselves as objects of experience'. He may mean 'appearances so far as we know them to be successive states of objects'.   [5] A 189–94 = B 234–9.

[6] For the general account see A 104 ff. and B 137, and compare also A 197 = B 242 ff. Kant uses the phrase 'transcendental object' in A 191 = B 236, a phrase not used in the additions made in the second edition, but I believe the general doctrine of the object to be the same in both editions. See Chapters XX § 2, XXII §§ 1–2, and LV § 3.

[7] B 233.

object, such as a house.[1] It is not easy to be sure whether this usage is maintained consistently throughout: in some places it may seem more natural to take 'appearance' to be a part or state of the object. Let us, however, say broadly that the appearance is the whole object, and that its parts or states are 'the manifold of the appearance'. We can then say that the apprehension of the manifold of the appearance is always successive; and this is equivalent to saying that our ideas of the parts follow one another.[2]

I need not consider again the precise sense in which Kant regards apprehension as always successive.[3] If Kant's view were that we never directly apprehend even the subjectively coexistent or simultaneous, he would be wrong, and his argument would so far be weakened. There can, however, be no doubt that we commonly regard as coexistent what has been successively apprehended, for example, the different parts of a house; and this is a sufficient basis for the argument. We must remember that the whole appearance and its parts may alike be described as 'ideas': they are not things-in-themselves. The whole appearance, it may be said, is made up of parts which are successively apprehended; and it is thus a sum or aggregate of ideas,[4] which, so far as our apprehension is concerned, may be described as following one another.

The question then arises whether these ideas (or parts) follow one another in the object (or the total appearance). In order to answer it we must consider what we mean by 'object'.

Every idea, so far as we are aware of it, may be called an object; but this clearly is not the sense required here. We want to know the meaning of 'object', when we speak of our ideas,

---

[1] A 190 = B 236. In A 192 = B 237 it is used for a moving ship.

[2] A 189 = B 234.

[3] See Chapter XLII § 1. If by the manifold of (or in) the appearance Kant means the parts of such an object as a house—and this is the example he himself gives in A 190 = B 235 and A 192 = B 237-8—his statement is true in the sense that we could never perceive all the parts of a house simultaneously.

[4] Compare A 191 = B 236.

not as objects, but as 'designating' or 'symbolising'[1] an object.[2]

If we take our ideas to be objects merely in the sense that we are aware of them, then, Kant says, they do not differ from apprehension (which is the 'taking up' of the given into the synthesis of imagination).[3] I believe he means by this that they do not differ *as regards their time-relations*.[4] The time of an idea *quâ* idea present to consciousness is the time of its apprehension; and since our apprehendings are successive, we can say that our ideas are always produced successively in the mind. This means that the manifold of appearances[5] is always produced successively in the mind as it is taken up by our acts of apprehension.

Kant asserts that if appearances were things-in-themselves, we could never decide from the succession of our ideas how the manifold (that is, the parts) of these appearances is combined in the object. The reason he gives is that we have to deal only with our ideas and the character of things-in-themselves is quite outside our sphere of knowledge.[6] But obviously if appearances were things-in-themselves—and such is the hypothesis he is considering—this would not be the case.

The argument is badly expressed; but I take Kant to mean

---

[1] '*bezeichnen*'; A 190 = B 235. Kant here seems to mean that our idea (for example, a seen colour) is taken as characterising the total object (for example, a house).

[2] In this passage (A 189–190 = B 234–5) Kant seems to use 'appearances', not for the total object, but for the parts or ideas of which it is made up. This might perhaps be questioned; for in A 190–1 = B 236 the whole appearance is described as an idea whose transcendental object is unknown. For the sake of clearness I have avoided the use of the word 'appearance' here.

[3] This is the usual technical sense of 'apprehension'.

[4] Compare A 194 = B 239. I cannot believe that Kant means to identify the manifold apprehended with the *act* of apprehending it; and the 'differences' of which he speaks in the Second Analogy are to be understood as differences in temporal position.

[5] I take Kant to mean that, for example, the parts of a house are produced successively in the mind.

[6] A 190 = B 235.

that if we regarded an appearance,[1] for example, a house, as a thing-in-itself, then we could never pass from the succession of our ideas (in which the parts of the house are given one after another) to knowledge of the way in which these parts were combined in the house itself.[2] All we have given us is the succession of our ideas. If by means of imagination we combined these ideas (or what is given in them) in one and the same time and regarded them as coexistent, we could never know that this combination represented anything in the thing-in-itself. For we know nothing of things-in-themselves except that they are supposed to 'affect' us through our ideas.[3]

If we grant this, we are brought face to face with the Critical problem. We are assuming that appearances, such as houses,[4] are not things-in-themselves. We are also assuming that nothing is given to us except our ideas: the whole house is a given idea in the sense that it is given to us in parts (or ideas) which are always successive.[5] Can we then explain how the parts (or the manifold) of the appearance have a temporal combination—for example, as coexisting—in the appearance itself? On Critical

---

[1] If we take 'appearance' here to mean the parts of the whole object, the argument runs on the same lines. We could never know from these successively given parts how they were really combined in the object.

[2] Strictly speaking, we should not know that there was anything which could be called a 'house': we should only know that certain given ideas succeeded one another.

[3] If we take this as the proper interpretation of Kant's argument, we may doubt whether it is intended to stand on its own feet: the language used seems to imply that Critical principles are already presupposed. If time is a form of our sensibility, we can never be justified in ascribing temporal relations to things as they are in themselves. Kant hopes to show later that objective succession and coexistence could never be known except as necessary succession and coexistence, and he believes that if objects were things-in-themselves we could have no knowledge of necessity.

[4] A 190 = B 235. Here again it is quite easy to restate the problem, if we take appearances to be the successively given parts of a whole object, and not the whole object itself; but I prefer to suppose that Kant is using 'appearance' in the latter sense, as he does in what immediately follows.

[5] Note that in A 191 = B 236 the whole appearance (of a house) is said to be given and to be an aggregate of ideas.

principles a house is an appearance, or object, which is neither a thing-in-itself not a succession of ideas in us. How on such a basis can we justify our belief that although the parts of the house are apprehended successively they are nevertheless coexistent in the object? As Kant says, 'How can the manifold be combined in the appearance itself, when the appearance is nothing *in itself*?'[1]

Kant himself emphasises the difficulty of this question for the Critical Philosophy.[2] From the point of view of ordinary experience or of science a house is quite properly regarded as a thing-in-itself.[3] From the Transcendental point of view it is only an appearance, that is, an idea whose transcendental object (here clearly equal to the thing-in-itself) is unknown.[4] Yet we are trying to make a distinction between the succession of ideas (in which the parts of the object are given) and the given appearance as a whole. We are regarding the whole given appearance as the object—the phenomenal object—of these ideas in spite of the fact that it is only a sum or aggregate of these ideas. And we are supposing that our concept of 'house', which is presumably extracted by analysis from the successive ideas of our apprehension,[5] must be in agreement with this object, if we are to have truth. How can this be possible?

At this stage Kant offers us his *general* solution of the problem. He stresses the fact that the agreement of our concept with the object is empirical truth;[6] and he implies that if we can state the conditions under which alone a concept can agree with its object, that is, if we can state the formal conditions of empirical

[1] A 191 = B 236. That is, when the appearance is not a thing-in-itself at all.

[2] Prichard (*Kant's Theory of Knowledge*, pp. 280 ff.) argues that this difficulty is insuperable.

[3] Compare A 45–6 = B 63.　　　　　　[4] A 190–1 = B 236.

[5] It can be so extracted only because our ideas have been combined in accordance with the categories; in particular because they are regarded as states of a substance, states whose relative position in time is determined by causal law.

[6] Compare A 58 = B 82 ff., A 157–8 = B 196–7, A 237 = B 296, A 451 = B 479, and *Log. Einl.* VII (IX 50–1).

truth,[1] then we can answer the question, 'How can the manifold be combined in the appearance itself?'

The formal conditions of empirical truth must be formal conditions of experience (and so of objects).[2] Kant, however, has in mind, not the Mathematical Principles (which are concerned with *intuition* as such), but the Dynamical Principles, and in particular the Analogies; for these are concerned with the *existence* of objects, and are necessary only under the conditions of empirical *thinking* in an experience.[3] When we speak of 'the manifold as it is combined in the appearance (or in the object) itself,' we mean the manifold as it is combined in accordance with the Analogies, and not as it is combined arbitrarily in imagination or as it is given to us successively in apprehension. The object can be distinguished from the ideas successively given in apprehension, because (although it is itself only an appearance, and indeed a complex of ideas) 'it stands under a rule which distinguishes it from every other apprehension and makes a particular kind of combination in the manifold necessary.'[4] The 'rule' under which the object stands is most naturally taken to mean one of the Analogies.[5] Kant adds 'That in the appearance which contains the condition of this necessary rule of apprehension is the object'.

In this passage there are many difficulties of interpretation. Kant's argument is quite general; and if he means the 'rule' to be 'a formal condition of empirical truth' (as I think he must), then the rule cannot be confined to the Second Analogy.[6]

---

[1] We are not asking, 'Under what conditions does this concept of house agree with this house?'—that depends on the details thought in the concept and given in sensation. We are asking 'Under what conditions is it possible for any concept to agree with any object?' —or perhaps better 'How on Critical presuppositions is it possible that there can be any object with which our concept may agree?'

[2] Compare A 202 = B 247 and A 62–3 = B 87.

[3] A 160 = B 199.   [4] A 191 = B 236.

[5] The fact that Kant speaks of a 'rule', and not of a 'law' or 'principle', does not exclude the Analogies; see for example A 177–8 = B 220 and A 180 = B 222.

[6] Still less could it be a particular causal law except in the sense that to stand under the general law of causality is always to stand under a particular law.

The 'rule' might equally well be the Third Analogy: indeed
the only case which Kant has so far considered is the case of
objective coexistence, which is governed by the Third Analogy.[1]
Nevertheless for the sake of simplicity we need consider only
the case of objective succession, in which case the rule would be
the Second Analogy.[2]

The Second Analogy may certainly be described as a rule
which makes a particular kind of combination in the manifold
necessary. But can we say that 'it distinguishes an appearance
from every other apprehension'?[3] Above all can we describe
it as 'a rule of apprehension'? We shall find similar puzzles
in what follows.[4] At present I think we need only say that
whatever we may make of Kant's terminology, the applicability
of the law of cause and effect does, on his view, mark out an
objective succession from a merely subjective succession,
and does render it necessary that our apprehension should
follow a certain order.[5]

There are special difficulties in the final statement: 'That in
the appearance which contains the condition of this necessary
rule of apprehension is the object.'[6] We may compare with
this the statement that the object is regarded as 'that which

---

[1] It is true that the proof of the Third Analogy does not make use
of the term 'rule', but we must remember that the schema of communion is the coexistence of the determinations of different substances
'in accordance with a universal rule'; see A 144 = B 183–4. Compare
also A 217 = B 264.

[2] Compare the parallel passage in A 202 = B 247. The schema of
causality, it may also be recalled, is the succession of the manifold so
far as that succession is subjected to a rule; see A 144 = B 183.

[3] We should expect him to say either (1) that it distinguishes an
appearance as object from every other *idea* apprehended or (2) that it
distinguishes the *apprehension* of an appearance as object from every
other kind of *apprehension*. It is hard to be sure whether Kant's
language, when he thus seems to equate apprehension and its object
(or content), is due to carelessness or not; there seems to be a kind of
method in it, but without further justification or explanation it is a
source of confusion. Compare the difficult assertion already noted
(A 190 = B 235) that our ideas as objects of consciousness are not
different from apprehension.   [4] See especially A 193–4 = B 238–9.

[5] So far it might be called loosely 'a rule of apprehension'.

[6] A 191 = B 236.

prevents our cognitions from being haphazard or arbitrary;'[1] and again that 'all appearances, in so far as through them objects are to be given to us, must stand under *a priori* rules of synthetic unity'.[2] I have already argued[3] that Kant in these passages does not suggest that necessary synthetic unity (which is the essential characteristic of a phenomenal object) is due to the transcendental object regarded as a thing-in-itself. Similarly here there is no ground for thinking that he is speaking of the transcendental object.[4] I take it that in this passage, as elsewhere, he is identifying the object with the necessary synthetic unity of the manifold.[5] This necessary synthetic unity contains in particular a necessary synthetic unity of time-determinations[6] or, more simply, a necessary time-order[7]; and it is this necessary time-order in the appearance which is the condition of a necessary rule of apprehension,[8] notably in the case of objective succession.[9]

---

[1] See A 104.

[2] See A 110. Compare B 137, 'Object is that in the concept of which the manifold of a given intuition is united'; and also A 158 = B 197.

[3] See Chapter XXII § 2.

[4] It would be strange indeed to speak of the transcendental object as 'in the appearance', if by the transcendental object is meant the thing-in-itself.

[5] Strictly speaking, the object is the manifold *so far as that manifold possesses necessary synthetic unity*.

[6] Compare A 177–8 = B 220, where the necessary synthetic unity in time-relations (or time-determinations) is clearly the unity of the time-order.

[7] In A 145 = B 184–5 the schemata of relation are concerned with the time-order in regard to all possible objects.

[8] Here Kant is concerned with the rule as a rule of apprehension, and he finds its condition in the object, although he spoke previously of the appearance as an object in so far as it (and not the apprehension) stood under the rule. Difficulty again arises from the fact that the rule governing the *appearance* and the rule of *apprehension* seem to be both distinguished and identified.

[9] The case of objective coexistence is more complicated. If we consider only objective succession, Kant's doctrine is expressed more clearly in A 193 = B 238, where he says that objective succession consists in the *order* of the manifold of appearance, an order in accordance with which one apprehension follows another *in conformity with a rule*.

If we take the 'rules' of which Kant speaks to be the Analogies, he appears to regard them both as rules governing objects and also as necessitating thereby the order of our apprehensions.[1] The phrase 'condition of a rule' is puzzling wherever it occurs, but on this interpretation it may not unreasonably be taken to mean a transcendental schema.[2] It is natural enough to speak of an object as 'containing' the transcendental schemata;[3] and the schemata of relation as a whole are concerned with the necessary time-order,[4] which I have assumed to be what Kant describes here as the condition of a rule.[5] It is in any case the transcendental schemata of relation which Kant must show to be present in objects, if he is to prove the truth of the Analogies.[6] Indeed he has to show that an object exists as an object only so far as there are present in it the transcendental schemata of relation. His immediate task is to show that succession in the object must be necessary succession.

§ 5. *The Second Proof*

I. We are now in a position to get on with our task and to consider the special case of objective succession.[7] Kant insists that we could not perceive an objective event or change without

[1] In the latter sense he appears to describe them as rules of apprehension.

[2] It should be noted that Kant speaks of the categories as containing the condition or conditions of *a priori* rules; see A 132 = B 171, A 135 = B 174, and also A 140 = B 179. In these contexts the 'conditions of a rule' seem to be the transcendental schemata; and this suggests that we should at least ask ourselves whether the phrase can have the same meaning here.

[3] This seems to be implied in A 139 = B 178, where Kant says that time is contained in every empirical representation of the manifold. The whole passage should be consulted.

[4] See A 145 = B 184. The 'time-order' is the objective and necessary order of the manifold in time. Where the Second Analogy is the rule, the condition is the schema of 'necessary succession'; and necessary succession in the object is the condition of necessary succession in our apprehension.

[5] The phrase occurs also in A 193 = B 238–9, where it is a source of new difficulties.

[6] Compare A 181 = B 223–4.

[7] A 191–4 = B 236–9.

perceiving something else immediately before it; for we can no more perceive something happening after an empty time than we can perceive empty time itself. But in perceiving the front and back of a house our apprehension is just as successive as it is when we perceive an objective change, so that the mere successiveness of our apprehension does not prove the successiveness of what is apprehended.[1]

II. There is, however, another point to be noted. Suppose that we are aware of an objective succession, that is, of an event α followed by an event β. Let our sense-perception of α be called *a* and our sense-perception of β be called *b*. *Then if the succession is objective, that is, if α is followed by β in the objective world, a must precede and cannot follow b, and b must succeed and cannot precede a.* If a ship is moving down stream,[2] we cannot first see it lower down and then see it higher up, whereas in the case of a house (where there is no such objective succession) we can see first the front and then the back or *vice versa*.[3]

It is absolutely vital not to misunderstand this crucial statement. Kant is not arguing from the observed irreversibility of my sense-perceptions to an objective succession. He is on the contrary arguing from an assumed objective succession to the irreversibility of my sense-perceptions. He is not saying that I find I cannot reverse the order of my sense-perceptions,

---

[1] In this passage Kant speaks of distinguishing one synthesis of apprehension (or sense-perception) from others, as I think he ought to have done above, instead of speaking about distinguishing an *object* from other *apprehensions*.

[2] It should be noted that the earlier position of the ship is not the cause of the later. Kant's doctrine is that every objective succession must be causally determined, not that it must be a sequence of cause and effect.

[3] No doubt the order of the appearances of the house to me is determined by the movements of my body, but it is not determined by any change in the object, that is, in the house. If I make my mental history an object to myself, the successive appearances of the house are actual objective events, and as such they are as much determined as any other objective events.

and then conclude I must be dealing with an objective succession. Such a statement, even if it were true—and I think it is false[1]—could never justify us in affirming any kind of necessity; we could only say that we had hitherto found our sense-perceptions to occur in a particular order and no other. Kant starts with the assumption that we are aware of an objective succession, and asserts that, if so, our sense-perceptions *must* occur in a particular order. The order in the succession of sense-perceptions is in this case *determined* by the order of events.[2] There is a rule governing our apprehension, a rule which is always to be found when we are perceiving objective events, and it makes the order of our successive sense-perceptions (in the apprehension of these successive events) a *necessary* order.[3]

III. In this case[4] therefore—that is, in the case where we are *ex hypothesi* perceiving an objective succession—*we must derive the subjective succession in our apprehension from the*

[1] Unless we already assume that we are perceiving objects, and indeed that the objects perceived are substances. I think Professor Prichard is right (*Kant's Theory of Knowledge*, p. 294) in saying that we do not begin by knowing a subjective succession and then pass to a knowledge of objective succession either by finding that the subjective succession is irreversible or in any other way. Indeed is there any meaning in talking about the irreversibility (or for that matter the reversibility) of a subjective succession, unless we are already presupposing the existence of an objective world in time? In a subjective succession considered solely by itself we could say only that our ideas had occurred in the order in which they had occurred.

[2] Compare A 192 = B 237: 'The order in which the sense-perceptions succeed one another in apprehension is in this instance determined, and to this order apprehension is bound.'

[3] A 193 = B 238. In the above paragraph I am not denying that on Kant's view the irreversibility of our sense-perceptions may entitle us to assert objective succession, if we already assume that we are perceiving objects whose states must be either successive or coexistent: I deny only that such an *observed* irreversibility can by itself give us necessity. The necessity which Kant attributes to the subjective order of our sense-perceptions is not known by observation, but is a consequence of its 'derivation' from an objective order. And indeed for Kant necessity can never be known by mere observation.

[4] '*in unserem Fall.*'

objective succession of appearances.[1] If the subjective succession is not derived from an objective succession,[2] it is arbitrary and undetermined,[3] and does not enable us to distinguish one appearance from another as regards the time of its occurrence in the objective world. In short it proves nothing about the temporal connexion of the manifold in the object.[4]

IV. The objective succession of appearances is then said —and this seems to be a mere expansion of what has been said before—to consist in that order of the manifold of the appearance according to which[5] the apprehension of the preceding

[1] The appearances in question are events or changes in the phenomenal world. In this much-quoted sentence Kant, as so often, confuses his readers by beginning with a 'therefore' and following it up with a 'because'.

[2] Kant's own expressions are very abbreviated, but I take *'jene sonst'* to mean 'the subjective succession when it is not derived from an objective succession' and *'jene allein'* to mean practically the same.

[3] Kant may be here repeating what he has already said about the house, that where there is not a series of objective events or changes, there is nothing to make our apprehension begin at one point rather than at another in its synthesis of the manifold. His statement that in such a case the subjective order is 'wholly arbitrary' and 'wholly undetermined' seems to be exaggerated. It is perhaps possible for him to mean that when we set aside all considerations about objective succession (or coexistence), when in short we consider the subjective order of our sense-perceptions in complete abstraction from any kind of objective order, the subjective order is undetermined and arbitrary in the sense that it is a given order for which we can see no reason and in which we can find no necessity. Such a statement I believe to be true.

[4] The difficulty of this is that it is an indication, if not a proof, of the coexistence of the manifold. Hence there is something to be said for the alternative interpretation suggested in note 3 above, since the subjective order, considered in abstraction from the objective, is always (according to Kant) successive and does prove nothing about the temporal connexion of the manifold in the object.

[5] 'according to which' surely implies that the subjective succession is derived from, or determined by, the objective succession. The passage may be compared with that in A 191 = B 236, where Kant speaks of 'that in the appearance which contains the condition of the necessary rule of apprehension'. Kant seems to me to regard the subjective and objective successions as, so far, distinct, not, as Professor Prichard suggests (*Kant's Theory of Knowledge*, p. 289), as identical. The identification, I think, comes later.

event follows the apprehension of the succeeding event *in accordance with a rule*.[1] Here the rule is clearly what Kant calls a rule of apprehension—a rule that (in virtue of the objective succession αβ) sense-perception *a* must be followed by sense-perception *b*. And Kant goes on to say that *it is only because of this rule*[2] *that I am entitled to say of the appearance, or object, itself* (and not merely of my apprehension) *that there is in it a succession*. He even adds that to assert a succession in the object *is the same thing* as to say[3] that I cannot arrange my apprehension otherwise than in just this succession.

The interpretation of this is a matter of the greatest difficulty. Kant is not, I think, merely repeating what he has already said—that when I am aware of an event α followed by an event β, the sense-perception *a* must be followed by the sense-perception *b*, and that such a necessary succession of sense-perceptions must always be present whenever there is awareness of an objective succession. He is passing beyond what is, on the face of it, an affirmation of common sense to its interpretation on Critical principles. If the event α and the event β were things-in-themselves, it is manifest that we could never pass from the common-sense assertion that, in perceiving the objective succession αβ, sense-perception *a* must be followed by sense-perception *b* to the quite different assertion that the objective succession αβ is itself causally determined. Kant appears to be arguing that since the event α and the event β are, on Critical principles, only the content of sense-perceptions *a* and *b*, the attribution of necessary succession to *a* and *b* (on the ground of the objectivity of the succession αβ) is *ipso facto* an attribution of necessary succession to α and β;

[1] This, for Kant, is the same as 'necessarily follows'.

[2] '*dadurch*.' The following sentence, I think, supports this interpretation, but it is possible that '*dadurch*' should be translated more loosely as equivalent to 'in this way', that is, 'where there is an order in the manifold which necessitates a succession of apprehensions in accordance with a rule'.

[3] '*so viel bedeutet als*.' It is in this sentence, I think, that we get the identification of the objective order with the *necessary* subjective order, an identification which Professor Prichard maintains has already been made. See note 5 on previous page.

and the necessary succession is in both cases identified with succession *in accordance with a rule*.

This contention seems to me to be the crux of Kant's argument.

V. My interpretation seems to be confirmed by what follows. *In accordance with such a rule* (which hitherto has been spoken of as a rule of apprehension) *there must therefore* be present in what precedes an event the condition of a rule[1] *in accordance with which*[2] *this event always and necessarily follows*, so that, the first event having been given, I must always be able to go on and apprehend or perceive the second event.[3] This process cannot be reversed, for when the second event is given I cannot go back and apprehend the first event.[4]

---

[1] Kant seems to mean here that in the total state of affairs which precedes the event there must be present something upon which the event must follow. He does not mean that the cause of the lower position of the ship is its previous position higher up the stream. The presence of this 'something' is 'the condition of a rule'.

In A 191 = B 236 'the condition of a rule' seemed to be the transcendental schema, and it may appear that the present use of the phrase is entirely different; but it should be noted that the transcendental schema of causality is described, not only as succession in accordance with a rule, but also as 'the real upon which, whenever posited, something else always follows' (A 144 = B 183). This is the condition of the applicability of the category or law or rule of cause and effect. It is thereby of course also the condition of the applicability of a particular causal law—the general law is manifested only in particular applications.

[2] 'Which', I take it, refers to 'rule'.

[3] I have introduced this last clause, because its introduction seems to be assumed by the following sentence, which says that I cannot 'conversely' go back from the event and determine (by apprehension) what precedes it.

[4] This statement seems obvious enough, but Kant thinks it necessary to support it with a reason. 'For no appearance goes back from the succeeding point of time to the preceding, although it must be related to *some preceding point of time*; on the other hand, the advance (of appearances presumably) from a given time to the determinate succeeding time is necessary'. This contrast of the *determinate* succeeding time with the *indeterminate* preceding time seems to rest on the fact that the succeeding time is given with its content in perception, whereas the preceding time can (unless we remember what happened

Hence because an event is essentially something which follows upon something else,[1] I must necessarily relate it, when perceived, to something else in general[2] which precedes it and upon which it follows in accordance with a rule, that is, necessarily. In this way the event, as the conditioned in time, gives a sure indication that there is *some* preceding condition or cause. The preceding condition or cause does not merely indicate that there is *some* event which must follow as effect; it actually *determines*[3] the event (in the sense, I take it, that it must necessarily be followed by an effect which, if we knew what to look for, we could actually perceive).[4]

Kant's insistence that we cannot go on to *perceive* the cause which we presuppose whenever we are aware of an objective event—a point which seems almost too obvious to state—is presumably due to the fact that for him all events are in the last resort ideas or appearances to human minds. He has to insist that nevertheless we can and do place or 'posit' unperceived (and now unperceivable) events in a time which is past.

in it) be imagined only in abstraction, for we cannot 'construct' its content by our knowledge of the general law of cause and effect.

All this bears a certain external resemblance to what I have called the Fifth Proof of causality. See below, Chapter XLIV § 4.

[1] Literally 'since there certainly is something which follows'.

[2] I do not know what its cause is, but I do know it must have some cause. Hence the phrase 'something else in general', which perhaps also indicates that what precedes is an object.

[3] For the word 'determines' (*bestimmt*) see also A 199 = B 244 and Chapter XLIV § 4.

[4] Provided our senses were adapted to it. See A 226 = B 273.

THE SECOND ANALOGY (*continued*)

§ 1. *The Third Proof*

The third proof[1] is commonly described as the indirect[2] proof, but it might be regarded as a mere appendix to the previous proof.

Kant starts with the hypothesis that what the previous argument has proved is untrue. Suppose that a perceived event is not preceded by something on which it must follow in accordance with a rule. In that case all succession of sense-perceptions would be merely subjective—through the subjective succession of sense-perceptions in apprehension it would not be 'objectively determined' which of these sense-perceptions must precede and which succeed.[3] To say this is to say that we should have a mere play of ideas[4] unrelated to any object. More precisely, our sense-perceptions could not distinguish the objective time-relations of one appearance from those of another—the time of every appearance would simply be the time of its apprehension.

The reason given for these assertions is Kant's fundamental

[1] A 194 = B 239 ff. (two paragraphs).

[2] It must be remembered that every Critical proof is in a sense indirect. The Principles of the Understanding are not established directly from concepts, but indirectly from the relation of these concepts to possible experience. See A 737 = B 765 and compare *Log. Einl.* IX (IX 71). The method of the third proof, if it is an independent proof, is *reductio ad absurdum*.

[3] A 194 = B 239. Note that it appears to be the succession of our sense-perceptions which is objectively determined only if events are governed by causal law. Compare the statement in A 193 = B 238 that the subjective succession of our apprehension is undetermined unless it is derived from the objective succession of appearances. Compare also what I take to be the statement in A 201 = B 246 that 'in apprehension there is an order of successive synthesis which an object determines'; and again (in A 191 = B 236) 'that in the appearance which contains the condition of this necessary rule of apprehension is the object'.

[4] Compare A 101, A 201 = B 247, and also § 5, below.

doctrine that whether we apprehend the successive or the coexistent, our apprehension considered in itself is always successive: in his own phrase 'the succession in apprehension is always of the same kind'.[1] I take this to imply that, so far as mere apprehension is concerned, the appearance given to us is nothing but a succession of ideas. If so, 'there is nothing in the appearance which determines the succession in apprehension[2] in such a way that thereby a certain succession as objective is rendered necessary'.[3]

This last statement appears to be expressed more clearly when Kant says that 'the mere succession in my apprehension, if it is not determined through a rule in relation to something that precedes, does not entitle us to assert any succession in the object'.[4] Whatever be the obscurity in this statement, Kant is clearly not asserting that by examining the subjective succession of our apprehensions, we can sometimes find in it irreversibility and infer therefrom an objective succession. He is, on the contrary, maintaining that from the subjective succession of our apprehensions, taken by itself, we could never pass to objective succession.

It is more difficult to be certain about the positive doctrine

[1] A 194 = B 239. This way of stating the doctrine again opens up the question whether there may not be apprehension of the coexistent over a limited area. If it were so, this might help to explain how we come to regard as coexistent what is successively apprehended: for the content of our successive apprehensions may partly overlap.

[2] The German is simply 'it' (*sie*), which I take to mean 'the succession in apprehension'. Grammatically 'it' might refer to 'the appearance'.

[3] A 194 = B 239-40. I have translated literally, but most of the commentators regard the text as corrupt. If 'as objective' could mean 'as objectively determined', it would give good sense; for the subjective succession is rendered necessary if it is objectively determined. Or again, if Kant is identifying the succession in the appearance (or object) with the succession in apprehension, a succession which is objective is a necessary succession in our apprehension. On the other hand the explanatory passage which follows suggests that Kant meant to say 'thereby a certain succession is rendered necessary and so objective'.

[4] A 195 = B 240. Note that here the rule which governs the succession of events is supposed to determine the succession in my apprehension.

asserted. Kant appears to hold that unless we believe something in the appearance to make the succession of our apprehensions a necessary succession, we cannot speak of an objective succession. This seems to me obviously true. The peculiarity of his doctrine is the view that the succession in the appearance (or in the object) must itself therefore be a necessary succession. This, I think, follows for him from the fact that the object is only an appearance, and not a thing-in-itself.[1]

Kant sums up his conclusion thus: 'When we experience an objective event,[2] we always presuppose it to be preceded by something on which it follows in accordance with a rule'.[3] Apart from this *presupposition* we could not speak of a succession in the objective world, but only of a succession in our apprehension.

Because Kant is an empirical realist, he believes that an objective succession may be directly present to my successive apprehensions. Because he is a transcendental idealist, he believes that such an objective succession, though not confined to my apprehension, is nothing apart from a possible human experience.[4] When we perceive an objective succession, the objective succession of appearances is identical with the subjective succession of my ideas; and the necessity which marks the subjective succession in such a case must mark also the objective succession. If we distinguish the two successions, the necessity in the objective succession may be said to be the source of the necessity in the subjective one. If we take it that there is only one succession, we consider that succession to be a necessary succession, and only so do we regard it as objective.[5]

The main difficulty, as throughout the Second Analogy, is that Kant speaks at times as if there were only one succession and at other times as if there were two. The succession of events

[1] Compare Chapter XLIII § 5, IV.
[2] Literally 'when we experience that something happens'.
[3] A 195 = B 240.
[4] There is something which is its ground in things-in-themselves, but that ground is beyond our knowledge.
[5] Kant says, not too happily, 'I make my subjective succession (in apprehension) objective' in virtue of the rule which governs events; see A 195 = B 240.

is a much wider series than the succession of my sense-perceptions, and there may be a succession of my sense-perceptions when there is no succession of events.[1] It is only when I perceive an objective succession that the two series so far coincide.

It may be asked why I should decide in some cases and not in others that the succession in my apprehension is necessary and consequently objective. We should never be justified in doing so if we considered the succession in my apprehension merely in itself. Kant is assuming that we are regarding the colours, shapes, sizes, and so on (which we perceive and which are consequently called our ideas or our sense-perceptions) as states of permanent substances in space.[2] Once that is assumed it is easy to discover whether our sense-perceptions are in a necessary succession or not, whether, for example, we can see the positions of a ship in the reverse order or not. Only thus can we decide whether the succession is in the ship as well as in our apprehension. Kant is not inferring objectivity in general from an observed necessity in the succession of sense-perceptions taken to be merely subjective—such a transition would be quite impossible, as he himself asserts. He is assuming objectivity, as we all must, from the start. Only on the presupposition of objectivity (or of permanent substances in space) can we find that necessity in the succession of our sense-perceptions which entitles us to assert objectivity in the succession or to attribute succession to the object.

§ 2. *Origin of the Concept of Causality*

At this stage Kant interposes a reply to those who maintain that the concept of causality is acquired by observing the repetition of similar series of events.[3] His answer is firstly that a concept so acquired could never have universality and necessity; and secondly that this view makes the common mistake of

---

[1] When I perceive successively the coexistent.   [2] Compare B 232–3.

[3] A 195–6 = B 240–1. This view contradicts Kant's theory, not only because it derives the concept of causality from experience, but primarily because it supposes we could be aware of *objective events* without having a concept of causality, however obscure. Kant is concerned here, not so much with Hume (who derives the concept

supposing that the process by which a concept becomes 'clear'[1] to our consciousness is the source (or origin) of the concept itself. The concept of causality cannot acquire logical clarity except as a result of experience, but it is at work in experience from the first.[2]

§ 3. *The Fourth Proof*

The fourth proof[3] professes to appeal for confirmation to experience. Our task is to show[4] that we never, *even in experience*, ascribe succession to an *object* except when there is a rule which compels us to observe this order of sense-perceptions—here equivalent to appearances—rather than another.[5] But although Kant makes some attempt to restrict himself to analysis of the facts, the general line of the argument can hardly be said to differ in any important way from the argument of the first proof.

He even begins by repeating his introductory account of

from awareness of a succession of *ideas* or *impressions*) as with the popular views which have 'always' been held.

When Kant speaks of an 'event' (*Begebenheit*) or of 'what happens' (*was da geschieht*), he means an objective event or happening. See especially A 198 = B 243.

[1] For 'clear' and 'obscure' ideas see Chapter XIX § 8.

[2] Similarly all thinking presupposes the law of non-contradiction from the first, but that law acquires 'logical clarity' only when we begin to think about thinking, that is, when we study logic.

[3] A 196 = B 241 ff. (three paragraphs).

[4] Kant says to show '*im Beispiele*', which Kemp Smith translates 'in the case under consideration'. I take this to mean 'the case where we experience an objective succession'; for Kant does not here offer any concrete examples of what we are considering. Compare '*in unserem Fall*' in A 193 = B 238; but the phrase seems peculiar, and perhaps suggests that an example was at one time supplied and subsequently removed.

[5] Kant adds that it is precisely this necessitation which 'first of all' makes possible the idea of a succession in the object. If we interpret this 'first of all' in a temporal sense, we must take Kant to hold that we are first of all aware of a merely subjective succession, then— Heaven knows how—we become aware of its necessity, and finally we infer an objective succession. The absurdity of this doctrine has been sufficiently exposed by Professor Prichard, but I do not believe it should be attributed to Kant if any other interpretation is possible.

In this passage I take the 'rule' to be the Second Analogy considered as determining the order of our apprehensions inasmuch as it determines the order of events apprehended.

what is meant by 'object'.[1] He insists that our ideas are only modifications or determinations of the mind occurring in a particular temporal order, and that they cannot possess reference to an object (or objective significance) merely by being related to another idea which is regarded as in a special sense an idea of the object;[2] for this idea would be just as subjective as the ideas which referred to it. He then states the Critical doctrine. The relation of ideas to an object merely imposes upon them a particular kind of necessary combination, and so subjects them to a rule or law.[3] And conversely it is only the necessity in the temporal order of our ideas which gives them a relation to an object.[4]

Kant then proceeds to deal explicitly with the case of objective succession. Since our apprehension is always successive, succession in our apprehension does not by itself establish succession in the object apprehended.[5] But as soon as[6] I perceive, or rather presuppose,[7] that in the succession of my apprehensions an idea follows in accordance with a rule from

[1] See A 189–91 = B 234–6 and Chapter XLIII § 4.

[2] The text is obscure and perhaps corrupt, but Kant seems to affirm that when we say ideas are ideas of an object, we do not mean that the object to which they refer is only a particular idea 'object' to be found among the other ideas. When we say 'the object is hard, white, and sweet', we are not referring these ideas to the idea of 'object', but to the object itself.

[3] Kant is presumably here thinking of the law of causality, although what he says is true of all the Analogies, which are concerned with the *existence* of objects and not merely with the character of the intuitions through which objects are given. Compare A 160 = B 199 and A 179 = B 222.

[4] These two statements together ought to make it clear that when Kant talks of objectivity making necessity, and necessity giving objectivity, he does not intend to imply that we have *first* necessity and *then* objectivity, or *vice versa*. This combination seems to me very important, because otherwise the second sentence, like so many others, could be taken to imply that there is a process from subjective ideas to a world of objects. This encourages me to deny the same implication when it seems to be present in similar sentences taken by themselves.   [5] A 198 = B 243.

[6] This must not be taken to imply that I am first aware of a necessary succession in what is subjective, and then infer an objective succession.

[7] The second expression would appear to be a correction of the first.

the state[1] which precedes it, I am aware of an event or objective happening; that is to say, I know[2] an object which I am compelled to place or 'posit' in a determinate position in time, a position which it must be given in view of the preceding state.[3] This is unhappily expressed, because it may seem to suggest that there is a psychological process by which we pass from awareness of the subjective to knowledge of the objective. I believe on the contrary that Kant is really trying to analyse the act of perception into its elements, as becomes clearer in what follows.

When I perceive an event, my perception contains or involves a judgement[4] that something precedes the event (for we cannot know that anything is an event unless we know that there was a preceding time in which it did not exist, and we cannot perceive a preceding time unless it is filled). This would, I think, be generally admitted; but Kant goes farther, and asserts that the event can acquire[5] a determinate or objective position in time only if we presuppose that there is in the state[6] which precedes it something upon which it always

[1] I use Kant's word 'state' (*Zustand*). This 'state' must be in some sense an idea, like the idea which follows it, but Kant believes it may also be a state of affairs. 'In accordance with a rule' always implies necessity.

[2] '*erkenne.*' Kemp Smith translates 'apprehend', but I think it is better to distinguish 'apprehension' from 'knowledge', since apprehension is only one factor in knowledge.

[3] Here again we have the same word 'state', which may be a state of mind or a state of affairs—it seems to me that Kant is leaving its character vague—but the objectivity now ascribed to what follows must belong equally to what precedes.

[4] Kant says literally 'in this idea there is *contained* that something precedes' (*so ist in dieser Vorstellung erstlich enthalten: dass etwas vorhergehe*). From this it would seem he means that the perception not only implies a *fact*, but also contains a *judgement*, though this judgement may be 'obscure' at any rate as regards the details judged. In A 201 = B 246 the perception is said to contain *knowledge* (*Erkenntnis*) of an event. But perhaps I am reading too much into the word 'idea'.

[5] The word Kant uses is 'acquire' (*bekommen*), but I do not think he means that the event first of all has no such position and subsequently acquires it.

[6] Here again 'state' is evidently used to cover the whole state of affairs of which the cause is a part.

follows in accordance with a rule.[1] Here again we have Kant's central contention that objective succession must be necessary succession, or succession in accordance with a rule.

This point is elaborated by the assertion of what Kant describes as consequences.[2] Firstly I cannot reverse the series, that is, I cannot place or 'posit' the events in the reverse order;[3] and secondly if the preceding state is posited,[4] this determinate event necessarily and inevitably follows.

Finally Kant sums up his position.[5] There is in our ideas[6] an order in which the present[7] (so far as it is an event[8]) refers to some preceding state as its *indeterminate* correlate, while the correlate stands to the event in a *determining* relation (the relation of cause to effect) and necessarily connects[9] the event with itself in the time-series.[10]

I cannot think that this proof adds anything to what has already been stated. Its language is unfortunate, so far as it suggests in places that Kant is describing a process of passing

[1] I think this already implies necessity; and when Kant says that necessary succession follows from this, he is not making an inference, but restating his contention in other terms.

[2] '*woraus sich denn ergibt.*'

[3] Note that in this case irreversibility very definitely follows from objectivity, and not objectivity from irreversibility.

[4] The word 'posited' here clearly implies existence—to exist is to have a position in time.   [5] A 198-9 = B 244.

[6] Here the causal order is expressly stated to be an order in our *ideas*, an order in which they are 'posited'.

[7] '*das Gegenwärtige.*' This must be an appearance, and so far an idea.

[8] I take this to be the meaning of '*sofern es geworden*' ('so far as it has come to be').

[9] The usual technical sense of 'connects' (*verknüpft*).

[10] This difference in the relations of effect to cause and cause to effect was elaborated in A 193-4 = B 238-9. Compare Chapter XLIII § 5, V. The cause determines the effect, but the effect does not determine the cause. This means for Kant that when we perceive the cause we can go on to perceive the effect, but not *vice versa*. I can find no evidence that this use of the word 'determines' is also intended to express the common-sense view (so hard to analyse) that the cause 'produces' the effect, and does not merely precede it. Kant's list of what he calls the 'predicables'—see A 82 = B 108—and other passages suggest that he regarded causality as more than mere necessary succession.

from awareness of the subjective to knowledge of the objective. The grounds for its central contention—that objective succession must be necessary succession—are, I think, stated less clearly than in the second proof. What appears to me to be manifest—and I regard it as an essential part of the Critical Philosophy—is that for Kant objective events are only appearances to human minds, and may even be described as ideas. The difficulty of his exposition lies in the fact that these ideas are regarded as being in a subjective succession so far as they are successively apprehended, and in an objective succession so far as they are posited, or given a position by thought, in one homogeneous time. When we are actually perceiving *events*, these two successions are asserted to coincide, and it is not always certain which of the two successions Kant has in mind.

§ 4. *The Fifth Proof.*

The fifth proof[1] is commonly regarded as totally different from all the others.[2] It is an argument from the nature of time, and it might be put in the form that there must be necessary succession in appearances in order to represent in experience the necessary succession of the parts of time[3]—just as there must be a permanent substratum of appearances in order to represent or express the unity of the one time of which all times are parts.[4] This argument closely resembles the argument for permanent substance, and it rests, as all Kant's proofs do, on the supposition that time itself cannot be perceived.

[1] A 199–201 = B 244–6 (three paragraphs).

[2] It seems to me just possible that Kant may have regarded it as an elaboration of what is obscurely hinted at in A 194 = B 239 at the end of the second proof. There he points out that the passage of appearances in time is always in one direction, and this follows upon the distinction made between the relation of effect to cause and the relation of cause to effect. The present proof follows immediately upon the same distinction, but it deals explicitly with the direction of the passage of *time* as well as with the direction of the passage of *appearances* in time.

[3] Compare A 205 = B 250 where the transitory is said to designate or symbolise (*bezeichnet*) time, *as regards its succession.*

[4] See B 225 and A 183 = B 226.

The preceding time necessarily determines the succeeding time—*in the sense that I cannot get to the succeeding time except through the preceding*.[1] This is regarded by Kant as a necessary law of our sensibility, because time is only a form of our sensibility. He holds that for this reason it is also an indispensable law of our *empirical knowledge*[2] of the time-series that appearances in past time determine all existence in succeeding time, and that subsequent appearances, as *events*,[3] take place only so far as their existence is determined[4] by previous events. The ultimate ground for this contention is that *only by reference to appearances can we know*[5] *empirically this continuity*[6] *in the sequence*[7] *of times*.[8]

Kant goes on to insist once more on the presence of under-

[1] This seems also to be the sense in which the cause 'determines' the effect. Compare Kant's definition of continuity in A 209 = B 254.

[2] The word is '*Vorstellung*' (idea), but this must here mean knowledge. The knowledge is empirical, because we distinguish different times only by the events in them.

[3] The phrase 'as events' seems to imply that we may have subjective appearances (the images of imagination) which are not events in the objective world. As events in our mental history they also are determined by past events.

[4] This determining of the existence of events is regarded as equivalent to 'fixing' it (*festsetzen*) in accordance with a rule. The word '*festsetzen*' is commonly used for fixing a time—making, in the American phrase, a 'date'—and suggests that 'to determine' is 'to posit' or 'to give a definite position' in time.

[5] Here again I think it essential to note that Kant is speaking of 'knowledge' (which involves understanding) and not of apprehension (which does not).

[6] It is important to observe that Kant uses the word 'continuity' for this 'determination' of later by earlier time. This 'continuity' is 'transferred' to appearances, for Kant speaks of the 'continuous' sequence in the series of possible sense-perceptions (A 200 = B 245). Continuity is discussed later in A 207 = B 253 ff., and at the end of the discussion (A 210-11 = B 256) Kant seems to reassert something like the fifth proof.   [7] '*Zusammenhang*.'

[8] Dr. Ewing (*Kant's Treatment of Causality*, pp. 74–6) seems to me to ignore this point, and to treat Kant's argument as if it were a dogmatic argument from the nature of time to the nature of what is in time. He also suggests that a period of time considered as pure time is as much determined by the succeeding as by the preceding period. This Kant would deny to be the case in the sense in which he uses the word 'determine'. Compare A 412 = B 439.

standing in such empirical knowledge. It is understanding which makes experience possible, for apart from understanding we cannot know objects at all; and the analysis by which it makes our ideas of objects 'distinct'[1] presupposes the transcendental synthesis—also at least partly the work of understanding—by which alone we can have such ideas to analyse.[2] In the particular case we are considering—the case of objective succession—understanding is said to transfer[3] the time-order to appearances and their existence.[4] It does so by adjudging to each a temporal position determined *a priori* in relation to previous appearances, and to do this is to judge each appearance to be an effect. Unless appearances had such a temporal position determined *a priori*, they would not accord with time itself, since all the parts of time have such a position determined *a priori*.[5] The necessity for this activity of the understanding—an activity which involves an *a priori* synthesis of appearances—is due to the fact that we cannot determine the temporal position of appearances by reference to absolute time (for absolute time cannot be perceived) but only by their relations to one another.

This argument is difficult and liable to misunderstanding.[6] If we assume—in spite of modern physics—that time must

---

[1] See Chapter XIX § 8.

[2] Compare A 103–4 and also A 77–8 = B 103.   [3] '*überträgt.*'

[4] I take it that understanding does so in the sense of ascribing to appearances, as events, a position relative to one another in one homogeneous time. This seems to be implied by the clause which follows.

[5] This looks like a dogmatic argument from the nature of time to the nature of what is in time, but in the light of the context we must take Kant to mean that under the condition stated they would not accord with time *in our experience*.

[6] The remainder of the argument (A 200–1 = B 245–6) only elaborates in difficult language what has been already said. Kant, it should be noted, explicitly says that to regard an appearance as having a determinate position in time is to regard it as an object: only so can it be said to 'exist'. He also speaks of the principle of causality as 'the principle of sufficient reason'. This seems to me mere carelessness, and I cannot believe that at the time he wrote the argument he identified the principle of causality with that of sufficient reason.

have a direction, we are entitled to say that if we are to be empirically aware of a succession of times, we must be aware of a succession of events in time; and that an event which is past in relation to another event cannot also be present or future in relation to the same event.[1] It may seem that Kant is confusing the assertion that there must be a succession of events with the quite different assertion that there must be a necessary succession of events, that is, a succession determined by causal law. Nevertheless I doubt whether he is guilty of so elementary a fallacy. He seems to be arguing, not merely from the fact that we must be empirically aware of the succession of parts of time, but from some special characteristic of that succession. This characteristic he describes by saying that we can get to a part of time only by going through the previous parts, and he identifies it with continuity. The continuity of time means that no part of it is the smallest possible part, and that in order to get from any point of time to any subsequent point we must pass through a part of time which is infinitely divisible.[2] Kant maintains that if we are to experience time as continuous, we must experience change as continuous, and he seems to regard this continuity of change as implying (if not as being identical with) causation.[3] If so, his argument cannot be considered apart from his account of the continuity of change.[4]

The whole subject is full of pitfalls, but it seems to me that we are far too apt to take time, and the continuity of time, for granted, and to ignore the question about what this must imply in regard to our perception of events.[5] If we do ignore this question, are we not assuming that we can perceive absolute

---

[1] This is all that Dr. Ewing (*Kant's Treatment of Causality*, p. 74) will allow to be a legitimate inference. It is, I think, only another way of saying that there must be a succession of events. Dr. Ewing, it should be added, recognises also the possibility of arguing from the continuity of time to the necessity of a causal connexion in objects of experience, but he does not recognise, as I think he ought, that this contention is an essential part of Kant's argument.

[2] See A 209 = B 254.

[3] Compare Alexander, *Space, Time, and Deity* (Vol. I, pp. 279 ff.).

[4] See A 207 = B 253 ff.

[5] Compare Laird, *Hume's Philosophy of Human Nature*, p. 109.

time, which, as Kant says, is impossible? The brevity of his exposition, and the uncertainty which I at least feel in regard to its precise meaning, are grounds for suspending judgement about the validity of the argument; but I am far from accepting the view that we have here an elementary fallacy, and not a serious problem which requires to be faced.

§ 5. *The Sixth Proof*

The sixth proof[1] is only a summary. It states what Kant regards as the 'moments' of an argument which is certainly in need of simplification. I will attempt to separate the 'moments' from one another, although it is not altogether easy to do so.

I. In all empirical knowledge there is a synthesis of the manifold by means of imagination, and this synthesis is always successive; that is to say, our ideas (whether their content is judged to be successive or coexistent) are always successive.

II. The succession of ideas has in imagination no determinate order—it is not necessary that one idea should precede and another follow.

We should expect Kant to be still talking about imagination as it is present in empirical knowledge generally. In that case the succession of ideas, if we consider it in its subjective aspect only, has simply the order which it has, and we can see no necessity in it.[2] But Kant goes on to say that the series of successive ideas can be taken either backwards or forwards. This is what he has hitherto asserted to occur when we are apprehending the objectively coexistent.[3] Since this seems irrelevant here, he may be talking about a free play of the imagination, which can put ideas in any order we please. If

---

[1] A 201 = B 246 (one paragraph).

[2] Compare the statement that the subjective succession by itself is arbitrary and undetermined (A 193 = B 238). For the ambiguities of this see Chapter XLIII § 5, III.

[3] See, for example, A 192–3 = B 237–8. Such reversibility is not universal, but is confined to a special case.

so, this is a new point in the first edition, though it appears
to be made in the argument added in the second edition.[1]

Fortunately the ambiguities of Kant's statement do not
here affect seriously the nature of the argument.[2] It is otherwise
when we come to the ambiguities of the following 'moment'.

III. If the synthesis is a synthesis of apprehension (that is,
a synthesis of the manifold of a given appearance), then the
order is determined in the object.

Here, although Kant does not make his meaning clear,[3]
he is considering only the case where what is apprehended
is an 'event'. When this is so, the object determines the order
in which ideas are taken up or apprehended.[4] Kant himself
puts this more precisely when he says that 'in apprehension[5]
there is an order of successive synthesis which an object determines'.[6] *In accordance with this order*, he adds, *something must
necessarily precede, and when this 'something' is posited,[7] the
other (that is, the event) must necessarily follow.*[8]

Here again I can only suppose Kant's argument to be that
when we apprehend an objective succession, the succession of
ideas in our apprehension is necessary; and since we are

---

[1] B 233. For the ambiguities of this see Chapter XLIII § 3, III.

[2] Imagination (whether considered as 'taking up' the manifold
successively or as combining the manifold in imaginary successions)
does not by itself determine the objective order of events.

[3] Unless indeed the phrase 'given appearance' is intended to indicate
that the appearance in question is an 'event' (*Begebenheit*).

[4] Compare A 193 = B 238 where the subjective succession is said
to be derived from the objective. Compare also the statement about
the object in A 191 = B 236.

[5] '*darin*. This might conceivably refer to 'object'.

[6] Grammatically the sentence may also be translated as 'which
determines an object'. Kemp Smith translates it thus, and we can
find a parallel in B 218, where experience is said to determine an object
through sense-perceptions. I think either statement would fit the
argument. Compare 'objectively determined' in A 194 = B 239 and
the corresponding footnote in § 1 of the present Chapter. It is,' as
usual, difficult to be certain whether Kant is identifying or distinguishing the subjective and objective successions.

[7] 'Posited' as usual implies position in time and so existence.

[8] Compare A 193 = B 238–9, A 195 = B 240, A 198 = B 243.

concerned not with things-in-themselves, but with appearances as possible sense-perceptions, the necessary succession of our ideas is *ipso facto* a necessary succession in the object.[1] If so, objective succession is necessary succession, and this is what Kant has to prove.

If I am right, this 'moment' contains the crux of Kant's argument. What follows is only explanatory: it brings out his view that apprehension or perception—if it is to be perception of an event or an objective succession—involves judgement.

IV. If my perception[2] is to contain knowledge of an objective event,[3] it[4] must be an empirical judgement. We must *think* that the succession[5] is determined;[6] that is, that the event presupposes another appearance in time, upon which it follows necessarily, or in accordance with a rule.

V. On the other hand, if I did posit[7] the preceding event, and the subsequent event did not follow,[8] I should be compelled to regard as a mere subjective play of my imagination what I had hitherto taken to be an event in the objective world.[9] If

[1] Compare Chapter XLIII § 5, IV.

[2] '*Wahrnehmung*' or 'sense-perception'. As we have so often seen, sense-perception and apprehension are always closely connected by Kant, and sometimes even identified.

[3] This is what Kant ought to have said above, when he said 'if the synthesis is a synthesis of apprehension'.

[4] Grammatically this must apply to 'perception'. If it could apply to 'knowledge', we should avoid the loose statement that sense-perception is judgement.

[5] '*die Folge.*' This perhaps might mean, not 'the succession', but 'the event which succeeds'. This would fit in better with Kant's grammatical construction. If we take Kant to mean 'succession', he must now mean the objective succession.

[6] Compare B 234 for a similar insistence on the necessity for thought.

[7] Here again 'posit' very clearly implies thought of the existence or occurrence of what is 'posited' at a determinate time.

[8] Kant says 'did not follow necessarily', but 'necessarily' adds nothing to the statement. In this place, as in A 193 = B 239, Kant clearly implies that if the event follows, it can be perceived.

[9] This statement should be compared with the third proof (A 194 = B 239). It suggests that the third proof is intended only as a 'moment' in the second proof.

I regarded it as somehow objective, I should call it a dream, that is, an event in my mental history.

This statement obviously requires qualification—I might for example come instead to the conclusion that I had been mistaken about the cause. Nevertheless Kant seems to me to be correct in saying that we distinguish appearances in dreams and fancy from events in the objective world by the fact that they do not accord with a world which is governed throughout by causal law.[1]

VI. The relation of cause and effect[2] is thus the condition of the objective validity of our empirical judgements[3] in relation to the series of sense-perceptions, and consequently is the condition of the empirical truth of these judgements, and therefore the condition of experience.

This may seem an unnecessarily elaborate way of saying that the principle of cause and effect is the condition of our knowledge or experience of objective succession. The reference to empirical truth shows, however, that Kant is referring us back to his general solution of the problem of objectivity (or of the existence of objects).[4]

[1] Compare A 451 = B 479, and also Laird, *Hume's Philosophy of Human Nature*, p. 115.

[2] This is elaborately described as 'the relation of appearances (as possible sense-perceptions) in accordance with which what follows (the event) has its existence determined necessarily and according to a rule by something which precedes'. It is important to observe that appearances are described explicitly as 'possible sense-perceptions'. Kant clearly regards all events as possible sense-perceptions, not as things-in-themselves, nor again as actual sense-perceptions: he is in short a transcendental idealist. Needless to add, he is not saying that in every succession known to be objective, the earlier event is the cause of the later; nor is he saying that we cannot know a succession to be objective until we know its cause. He is saying that when we know or assume any succession to be objective, we presuppose that each objective event has, in the total state of affairs which precedes it, 'something' which determines it or is its cause. As this presupposition need not be 'clear' to ourselves, we may say more simply that objective succession implies necessary succession.

[3] This looks back to 'moment' IV.

[4] See A 191 = B 236 and compare Chapter XLIII § 4. See also A 160 = B 199 at the end.

VII. All succession or change in objects of experience must therefore be governed by causal law.[1]

It is very evident that the whole argument turns on what I have marked as 'moment' III. It is also evident that Kant was careless in writing his summary; for he seems to bring in one point which has not previously been raised, and he ignores another point of importance, namely, the doctrine that absolute time cannot be perceived. There is no reference to the argument of Proof V.

---

[1] On the principle that the necessary conditions of experience are necessary conditions of objects of experience. See A 111 and A 158 = B 197.

CHAPTER XLV

THE ARGUMENT FOR CAUSALITY

§ 1. *Kant's Presuppositions*

If we are to understand Kant's argument, we must first of all be clear as to the presuppositions which he believed to be necessary. These seem to be as follows: (1) an object is a set of appearances (which may also be called ideas or possible sense-perceptions) bound together by necessity or possessing necessary synthetic unity; (2) the successiveness of our apprehensions is not by itself sufficient to justify the assertion that there is succession in the object;[1] (3) absolute time cannot be perceived; and (4) we possess knowledge of objective successions.

The first of these presuppositions is the outcome of Kant's discussion in the Aesthetic and in the Transcendental Deduction; and we must assume it for the purposes of the argument. The other three seem legitimate assumptions on any philosophical theory.[2]

Kant himself in the second edition[3] stresses a further presupposition—that all successions (and he is thinking primarily of objective successions) are a successive being and not-being of the determinations of permanent substances.[4] I believe that this presupposition is as essential to the arguments of the first edition as it is to the argument added in the second edition.

---

[1] I adopt this form of statement as sufficient for the purposes of Kant's argument.

[2] The fourth assumption may be denied by philosophers of the school of Berkeley and Hume, but even they cannot deny that we *seem* to possess knowledge of objective successions. An analysis which is compatible with what experience seems to reveal is (so far) preferable to one which is not.   [3] B 232–3.

[4] It may be objected that this is inconsistent with the first presupposition given above; but we have to remember that for Kant, if given appearances or ideas are to constitute an object, one of the ways in which they must necessarily be bound together is as states of a permanent substance in space.

Indeed it is only because we take given appearances (or ideas) to be states of permanent substances that we can speak of their order in our apprehension either as necessary or as reversible and irreversible. If we fail to recognise this as essential to the argument, we are almost bound to fall into the error of supposing that Kant is trying to explain how we can pass from knowledge of necessity in the subjective order of our apprehension to knowledge of objects. Kant's view is, on the contrary, that we can discover necessity in the subjective order only if we already assume that there are permanent objects or substances of which given appearances are states. And this view seems to me obviously correct.

In addition to these fundamental assumptions, there appear to be two minor ones: (1) when we arbitrarily imagine events in a particular order, we are not entitled to affirm that the events are in that order; and (2) when we know that a succession is objective, thought must be involved as well as sense and imagination. On these points Kant's doctrine is, I suggest, absolutely sound.

§ 2. *Kant's Argument*

Kant's main argument seems to reduce itself to the assertion that, granted these assumptions, the experience of *objective* succession must be experience of *necessary* succession; and contrariwise, if the successions we experience were not governed by necessity, there would be no experience of objective succession, nothing but a blind play of ideas which we could not consider to be experience at all.

This may seem to be mere assertion and unworthy of the name of argument. The impatient reader may be tempted to reply that if the Critical doctrine be accepted, it is indeed impossible to understand how we can have knowledge of objective succession; and that Kant, without any pretence at argument, merely asserts objective succession to be necessary because, on his presuppositions, he cannot think of anything else which could reasonably be put forward as a ground for regarding a succession as objective. The difficulty in which he finds himself, it may be said, is obvious, but we have no reason to accept his baseless assertion of necessity as the only possible way to escape from it. A simpler solution is the denial of his fundamental presupposition, namely, that an object is a set of appearances to the human mind and not a thing-in-itself.

This cavalier method would not go far to solve the real difficulty to which Kant has called attention—that when we apprehend appearances successively, we sometimes affirm objective succession and at other times we affirm objective coexistence; nor would it help us towards a proof of causality, if such a proof be possible. And although I think it is true that Kant's argument is simply an assertion, in the sense that it is an appeal to what he calls 'judgement', I do not believe that the assertion is made for no other reason than the impossibility of finding any other solution.

As I understand Kant's argument, he is offering us an analysis of what is necessarily involved in experience, and particularly in experience of objective succession. Whenever we perceive an objective succession in which event β follows event a, our perception b must follow our perception a. But since, on Critical principles, the events a and β are only appearances to us, and are in this case *identical* with the perceptions a and b, this means that where our experience is of objective succession, event β must follow event a.[1] The succession of perceptions and the succession of events are in this case not two successions, but only one. I can see no other way of interpreting the argument.

Now it seems true to say that when we perceive an objective succession, our perceptions must come in a certain order and no other. The central question is whether the recognition of this is legitimate on Kant's view of objects, or whether it rests on the supposition that objects are things-in-themselves. If we adopt the second alternative, we must regard his whole argument as an elementary fallacy—we must say that he first of all affirms necessity in the succession of our perceptions

[1] This need not mean that a is the **cause** of β, but only that β must follow upon a in accor**dance** with causal **law**.

on the ground that our perceptions are distinct from, and determined by, objective events; and that he then goes on to infer necessity in the succession of objective events on the ground that when we perceive an objective succession, there is no distinction between our perceptions and objective events. If on the other hand he is entitled to hold *both* that when we perceive events, these events are identical with our perceptions, *and* that when we perceive events, our perceptions must come in a certain order and no other, then, it seems to me, he is entitled to his conclusion.

Kant's argument here, it should be noted, bears a resemblance to the more general argument of the Transcendental Deduction: it is in fact a special application of that argument. There he asserted[1] that when we have knowledge of an object, necessity is always implied—the object is regarded as that which prevents our cognitions from being arbitrary or which imposes upon our cognitions a necessary synthetic unity. He then argued that we are concerned only with our own ideas, and that the concept of the object is simply the concept of the necessary synthetic unity of ideas, a unity which is really imposed by the nature of the mind. A study of the Transcendental Deduction will, I think, confirm my interpretation of the present argument.

§ 3. *Objective and Subjective Succession*

Such an argument is not to be lightly or easily accepted; but we ought to ask whether the distrust which, as it seems to me, it inevitably arouses is based on reason or is due to the difficulty of the human mind in adjusting itself to a revolutionary hypothesis. Even if the doctrine seems to verge on madness, there is at least a method in the madness. If the interpretation I have put forward be accepted, we can understand how the whole argument hangs together—why, for example, Kant finds it necessary to insist that an object is only a complex of ideas; why he asserts that the presence of succession in the object *means* only that I cannot arrange my apprehension otherwise than in this succession;[2] why he appears to identify what he

---

[1] See especially A 104–5. [2] A 193 = B 238.

calls 'the rule of apprehension' with the causal law of the objective succession; and why, having once made his point, he is content to assert, as if it were something quite obvious, that an objective succession must be a necessary succession.[1]

In any case it seems to me beyond question that for Kant when we perceive an objective succession, the objective succession is identical with the subjective succession of our ideas, and the same ideas or appearances are successive both as ideas in my mind and as states of the object known.[2] To some this may seem sufficient ground for rejecting his whole theory, but we must ask ourselves whether such a theory is self-contradictory or impossible.

It is clearly impossible for any believer in representative idealism; and representative idealism, though the least defensible of philosophies, seems to be the natural assumption of the human mind. But Kant is not a representative idealist, except in so far as he believes that the phenomenal world is only an appearance to us of unknown things-in-themselves. As regards the phenomenal world he is an empirical realist, and his whole philosophy is a rejection of representative idealism. If the phenomenal world is only an appearance to human minds, why should it be impossible that a succession of states in a phenomenal object[3] should also be a succession of ideas in my mind?

No doubt even in that case what is apprehended cannot be identified with my act of apprehending, but I do not think Kant maintains that it is.[4] If an idea is a content apprehended,

[1] He does so even in the argument added in the second edition, although this is placed before his more detailed exposition.

[2] In this I agree with Professor Prichard, *Kant's Theory of Knowledge*, p. 281.

[3] It must not be forgotten that Kant believes himself to have proved that a phenomenal object is a permanent substance with changing attributes, although it is only an appearance to human minds of an ultimate reality which we have no reason to regard as either permanent or changing.

[4] In A 190 = B 235 Kant does say that an idea differs not at all from my act of apprehension; but I believe from the context he means only that it does not differ from my act of apprehension *as regards its time-relations*.

it can surely be both an event in my mental history and an event in the objective world. An idea in a dream may, as a content, differ in no way from a content apprehended in waking life. We regard it as an event in a mental history, but we refuse to regard it as an event in the objective world; and our reason for so refusing is that it does not fit into the necessary succession of contents which for us constitutes the objective world. The fact that the content apprehended in waking life fits into the necessary succession which we regard as objective does not imply that such a content is not also an event in our mental history. Kant's theory may be mistaken, but I do not see that it is self-contradictory. Indeed some such theory seems to be necessary, if we hold that in waking life what we are aware of is objective reality, and not merely an idea which represents objective reality.

I do not think we can avoid this by saying that the events in my mental history are mere apprehendings. An event in my mental history is a whole in which the apprehending and the apprehended are combined. And I do not think that this doctrine means the absolute identity of the subjective and the objective. Starting from the contents successively apprehended in waking life we construct in imagination, and in accordance with the categories, a whole world of possible contents or appearances (or what Kant calls *possible* sense-perceptions), and these appearances we regard as states or determinations of permanent substances, which fill time and space. We distinguish the order of events in the world so constructed from the order of our actual perceptions and our actual thinkings; and we distinguish this world and its events from the events which appear to us in dreams or are invented arbitrarily by our fancy. The order of events and the order of perceptions are identical *only* in the case where we are directly perceiving events.

It is on the identification of the two successions in this particular case that Kant's main argument for causality rests. It would be ludicrous to suppose that events were things-in themselves, and to argue that because the succession of our perceptions is necessary when we perceive events, therefore the succession of the events is determined by causal law. And whether Kant is right or wrong, his argument is, as he says, a Critical proof which seeks to establish the conditions of our *experience* of objective succession, and it is not a dogmatic proof from an analysis of the concept of event.[1]

§ 4. *The Conditions of Experience*

An analysis of the conditions of experience is to be sharply distinguished from a treatise on the methods of induction. Kant believes that experience is essentially and always an experience of objective succession,[2] and he is arguing that it must therefore be an experience of necessary succession. His argument is of a purely general character intended to establish the principle of causality. It is no part of his business to describe in detail the methods by which we decide whether a succession is objective, and still less to describe the methods by which we determine the precise cause of a particular event.[3] The criticisms brought against him for failing to do this seem to me irrelevant. A proof of causality would in itself be an important contribution to philosophy, and it is absurd to blame anyone

[1] Prichard (*Kant's Theory of Knowledge*, p. 300) maintains that such a dogmatic proof is possible, and that there can be no other.

[2] Even where we perceive an objective coexistence (as in perceiving the different parts of a house) what we perceive is, I suggest, recognised as an object whose characteristics remain the same amid change. Kant indeed seems to hold that change is merely an empirical fact whose necessity cannot be inferred from the fact that the world is in time; but it is hard to see how apart from change of some sort we could be aware of time, and Kant himself speaks of the transitory as 'symbolising' the successiveness of time. Without such 'symbolising' I do not think we could be aware of time or of its successiveness. See A 205 = B 250 and compare A 452 n. = B 480 n.

[3] When Kant says in A 203 = B 249 that temporal succession is the only empirical criterion of the effect, he obviously means that this is the only empirical criterion by which we can distinguish effect from cause, when we already know that two phenomena are causally connected. It is most unreasonable to separate this statement from its context, and then to blame Kant for the inadequacy of his theory of induction.

because he deals with his own problem and does not deal with ours.

The modern interest in inductive methods has led to an altogether disproportionate interest in Kant's statement that when we perceive objective events the order of our sense-perceptions is irreversible.[1] It is far too commonly supposed that Kant is trying to infer objectivity, or even causality, from the irreversibility of our sense-perceptions. Yet it is surely obvious that we could not know the succession of our perceptions to be irreversible, unless we knew that we were perceiving an object and indeed a substance; we could only know that our perceptions came to us in the order in which they came. What Kant himself maintains is that *when* we perceive an objective event, our sense-perceptions must be irreversible—*not* that when we find our sense-perceptions to be irreversible, we infer that we are perceiving objective events. The word 'irreversibility' is not even used by Kant himself. It is only our shorthand method of describing that *necessity* which he finds in the succession of our perceptions when we are aware of objective events.

It should be noted that when we assume what we are perceiving to be a real object, we can by experiment[2] discover whether or not it is possible to receive sense-perceptions (or appearances) in the reverse order; and from this we can determine whether the successively given appearances are coexistent or successive in the object. If, for example, we find that we are unable to get certain sense-perceptions (or appearances) in the reverse order, we conclude that a particular succession in our apprehension is also a succession in the object. But this manifestly presupposes from the beginning that we are perceiving an object; and indeed we have no right to assert that the order of our sense-perceptions is a *necessary* order, unless we are assuming that

---

[1] A 192 = B 237. Professor Loewenberg, for example (*University of California Publications in Philosophy*, Vol. 15, p. 9) takes Kant's formula for causality to be 'irreversible succession', although he adds, very rightly, that Kant's full meaning of causality cannot be expressed by this formula.

[2] For example, in the cases of a house and of a moving ship.

what we perceive is a succession in the object.[1] We can never reach necessity by observation, and least of all by observation of the order of our own ideas as such; and even if we could, we could never be justified in inferring objectivity from a merely subjective necessity.

I cannot see why Kant should be expected to describe in detail the empirical methods by which we learn to distinguish an objective succession from an imaginary succession or from a set of coexistent appearances successively apprehended. Such a study lies presumably in the field of empirical psychology, and Kant is free to accept any reasonable account that psychology may offer. There is, for example, no reason why he should deny that in asserting the existence of real objects we depend very largely upon what Hume describes as the firmness or solidity or force or vivacity or steadiness of our ideas. All he maintains is that where objectivity is asserted, there necessity is presupposed; and that where we are convinced that appearances to us will not fit into the world as a system governed by causal laws, there we deny the objectivity of the appearances. This is obvious in the case of hallucinations, mirages, and even dreams, which may lack nothing in vivacity or force or steadiness.[2]

Again it is no real objection to Kant's doctrine to say that on his theory night must be the cause of day.[3] He has nowhere asserted that when we experience successive events, the first must be the cause of the second. He has asserted only that such a succession must be causally determined, and that in the total state of affairs preceding any event there is to be found something, 'some as yet indeterminate correlate',[4] which is the cause

---

[1] Compare Prichard, *Kant's Theory of Knowledge*, pp. 288–9.

[2] Compare A 451 = B 479.

[3] The denial of this is explained by Dr. Moritz Schlick (*University of California Publications in Philosophy*, Vol. 15, p. 102). 'Day' and 'night', he points out, are really not names for 'events' in the sense in which this word is used in science. 'And as soon as we analyse day and night into the series of natural events for which these names stand, we find that the sequence of these events must be regarded as a very good example of "causal connection".'   [4] A 199 = B 244.

of that event. Nor has he asserted that in order to know that an event is objective, we must first of all know its cause. His doctrine is, on the contrary, that when we judge an event to be objective, our judgment presupposes that the event is governed by the general law of causality, and therefore that its cause is to be found in some previous event. The determination of the cause is a matter for science alone, and the discussion of the methods by which science determines the cause is a matter for Inductive, and not for Transcendental, Logic. Kant's doctrine on all these matters seems to me to be sound. The only question is whether he has succeeded in proving that necessary succession is a condition of experience.

§ 5. *The Process to Experience*

It may be thought that some of the objections have been too lightly dismissed; for if Kant is describing the process by which we pass from awareness of a succession of ideas to knowledge of the objectively successive and objectively coexistent, he is surely obliged to give some account both of the methods by which we do so and of the reasons by which these methods can be justified.

My answer to this criticism, which raises a question of fundamental importance for the interpretation of the *Kritik*, is that Kant is not attempting to describe any process of this kind. What he is doing is to determine the necessary conditions or presuppositions of all experience; and this task is, as he himself states,[1] entirely different from the task of describing how experience develops or comes to be. I do not deny that sometimes language is used which may seem to describe a process of development, but allowance must be made for the difficulty of avoiding such language in an abstract analysis. And I refuse to believe that Kant is attempting to describe how experience develops, not only on the ground that he himself denies this whenever the question is raised, but on the more

---

[1] See especially *Prol.* § 21a (IV 304): '*Hier nicht von der Entstehen der Erfahrung die Rede sei, sondern von dem, was in ihr liegt*'. Compare also Chapters III § 3, VI § 7, and XVI § 5.

fundamental ground that such an interpretation makes Kant's argument so weak that it is hardly too much to describe it as nonsense, while my interpretation, I submit, makes it sense.[1]

It is, in the first place, impossible to believe that there is a development from awareness of the subjective to knowledge of the objective.[2] We can recognise the subjective only when we distinguish it from the objective (this is Kant's own view); for 'subjective' and 'objective' are correlative terms which mean nothing except in relation to one another. And if we started with awareness of something merely subjective, it would, so far as I can see, be impossible to pass to knowledge of the objective.

In any case—and this is my second point—Kant's argument for causality does not offer us even a plausible account of such a transition. First of all, according to this interpretation, we are aware of a subjective succession, which in some inexplicable manner we recognise to be subjective. Then we become aware in a still more inexplicable manner (for we cannot have empirical knowledge of necessity) that a particular subjective succession is necessary or irreversible. Finally we conclude—on what grounds and by what right?—that we are aware of an objective succession.[3] The harshest criticisms

---

[1] This is the central matter on which my interpretation differs consistently from Professor Prichard's penetrating analysis in *Kant's Theory of Knowledge*. He interprets Kant as explaining how experience of the objective comes to be, and I entirely accept his criticisms of the view he ascribes to Kant, but I do not believe that what he is here attacking is Kant's view.

[2] We may of course be in doubt whether a particular appearance is subjective or objective and we may resolve that doubt; but this process occurs when we have already distinguished the objective world from the subjective succession of our ideas. There must also be a process in infancy (perhaps repeated whenever we awake from sleep) whereby we pass from an awareness in which the subjective and objective are not distinguished to a knowledge in which they are. It may be possible for psychology to describe such a process, but this has nothing to do with Transcendental Logic.

[3] The further conclusion that the objective succession must therefore be a necessary succession merely adds a crowning absurdity to this absurd series.

of Kant's doctrine would be altogether too kind, if this were the proper interpretation of his argument; but such an interpretation (and I cannot see one that is more plausible, if Kant is describing a process from subjectivity to objectivity) seems to me to refute itself.

§ 6. *Causality and Time*

I have attempted to make clear what I regard as the inner core of Kant's argument—the contention that if we accept the Critical presuppositions, objective succession must be necessary succession. There is, however, a danger that in so doing we may fail to recognise the importance of the part which time plays in the argument. Kant's doctrine of time forms a strand which runs through his whole discussion, although it finds its clearest, and in some ways its most difficult, expression in the special argument which deals with the continuity and irreversibility of time.[1]

We must remember that for Kant an object may be said to *exist*, and so to be a real or actual object, only if it has a determinate position in one common homogeneous time (and space). The same doctrine applies to the special case of succession, or change, in the object, the case to be considered in the Second Analogy. If a succession is objective, then the changes which take place in objects (changes which may be called simply 'events') must have a determinate position in one common homogeneous time (and space). Kant's argument all through is that time itself (or absolute time) cannot be perceived, and therefore events can have a determinate position in time only from their relation to one another. This determinate position cannot be given to mere apprehension, since apprehension may be successive where there is no succession of events. On this he bases his doctrine that when we experience a succession of events as objective, we presume that the succession is necessary—the position of events relatively to one another can be determined in one common homogeneous time only if it is presupposed that they follow

[1] A 199 = B 244 ff. See Chapter XLIV § 4.

one another in accordance with a universal rule. Unless they do so, the whole distinction between objective succession and a succession which is merely subjective or imaginary must disappear. We are no longer in a position to make an appeal to things-in-themselves as a way of avoiding this conclusion, and it is doubtful whether they would be any help to us even if we could.

This line of argument—whether it be sound or unsound—is certainly fundamental to Kant, and it is borne out by his general account of the Analogies.[1] All three Analogies are concerned with necessary connexion in time; the Second Analogy is concerned with that rule of necessary connexion which relates to succession as one of the three modes of time.[2]

We may even say that the Analogies, and in particular the Second Analogy, express the rules of necessary connexion in time *in general*:[3] they are derived, not from given sensations, but from the nature of time as such and the necessary unity of apperception. We must not indeed imagine Kant to treat time as a thing-in-itself, a kind of receptacle which determines everything in it in certain ways. Such a view, apart from its inherent absurdity, would not help us in any way; for time itself cannot be perceived.[4] Kant's view on the contrary is that given appearances must conform to certain rules, if we are to be aware of objects in one time, and so to have empirical knowledge of time itself.

It is only a step from this doctrine to the special argument which rests on the continuity and irreversibility of time:[5] this special argument does little more than bring out details which have not been made explicit. I need not enter into its difficulties again; but it is all-important to recognise that Kant is concerned with the conditions of experiencing events in one common homogeneous time, which is here, as elsewhere, regarded as continuous and irreversible. We could not, according

[1] See B 218–19 and A 176–7 ff.   [2] A 177–8 = B 219–20.
[3] Compare B 219.   [4] Compare A 452 n. = B 480 n.
[5] A 199 = B 244 ff. Compare Chapter XLIV § 4.

to Kant, experience events in such a time,[1] we could not even have empirical knowledge of the continuity of time,[2] unless appearances conformed to causal law.

The general principle of this contention is already familiar to us from the Transcendental Deduction. The reason why the causal law prevails, and must prevail, throughout the objective world as known to us is that this world consists only of appearances, and that the human mind (for which alone this world exists) must 'posit' appearances in one common homogeneous time: to do so is to subject appearances to the universal law of causality; for without this the unity of time, and so the unity of apperception, would disappear, and there could be no experience and no objective world.[3]

However little we may like Kant's doctrine, there seems to me no reason to doubt that this is what his doctrine is.

§ 7. *Particular Causal Laws*

It cannot be too often repeated that for Kant what the mind thus imposes upon objects is the universal law of necessary succession or causation. Particular causal laws can be known only as a result of experience.[4] All such laws are only particular determinations of the one universal law which is imposed by the human mind; but they are not themselves imposed by the mind, nor can they be known *a priori*. Their particularity belongs to the matter of experience, not to its form. As such it must be due to things-in-themselves and not to the knowing mind.[5]

This doctrine taken in its widest scope—the doctrine, namely, that the universal form of all objects is imposed by the mind on a matter given by things-in-themselves—seems to be a possible hypothesis involving no internal contradiction. There may be special difficulties as regards causation,[6] but these difficulties do not affect the general principle.

---

[1] A 199–200 = B 244–5.   [2] A 199 = B 244.

[3] See especially the conclusion of the Transcendental Deduction in both editions. This type of argument is used in all the Analogies.

[4] Compare A 126, A 127–8, B 165, A 159 = B 198, and A 216 = B 263.   [5] Compare Chapter VI § 8.   [6] See § 8 below.

Although particular causal laws cannot be known *a priori*, Kant always assumes, as we all do, that it is possible for us to discover particular causal laws. He assumes, that is to say, that we can separate out particular chains of cause and effect which will be found to repeat themselves. This is seen most clearly in his continual insistence that given the cause the effect must always and necessarily follow. It is, I think, seen even in the frequent assertion that the effect must follow 'in accordance with a rule'; for a 'rule' seems to imply regularity and repetition. I believe Kant recognises the whole state of affairs which precedes any event to be the condition of the occurrence of that event; but he appears to assume that there is always one event, or series of events, which can be described as in a special sense the cause of any given effect.[1]

So far as I can see, such assumptions are not a consequence of the principle of causality, nor have they been justified by any argument.[2] It is theoretically possible that in a universe governed throughout by causal law there might be no repetitions. Kant himself recognises in another connexion that, in spite of the formal and universal laws by which nature must be governed, the given matter might be such that in nature no similarities could be found;[3] and clearly if we could find no similarities in nature, we could equally find no repetitions.[4]

This is not the place to examine Kant's solution of this problem, which concerns, not the categories, but the Ideas of Reason.[5] I doubt whether he faced its implications as regards

[1] In *Metaphysik*, p. 42, he says explicitly that an event has many *concausae*, but of many coordinate *concausae* one is the principal cause, and the others are secondary. This doctrine is clearly implied in his account of the continuity of change and of causation; see for example A 210–1 = B 256.

[2] For a different view, see Ewing, *Kant's Treatment of Causality*, p. 102. If there is any proof of the separability of particular causal series, it must, I think, lie in the fact that causal events, like substances, are spread out in space, and that the transition from cause to effect is continuous.   [3] See A 653–4 = B 681–2.

[4] I do not think Kant faced this problem sufficiently till he wrote the *Kritik of Judgement*; see especially *Erste Einleitung* V.

[5] See especially A 657–8 = B 685–6.

causality; but if we follow the general line of his thought, we may, I think, say that it is in the nature of human reason to isolate, so far as it can, relatively separate chains of causes and effects, and always to seek a further cause beyond the proximate cause which has been found. The possibility of doing so depends on the repetition of similar causal series in nature; and this repetition in turn depends, not upon the nature of the human mind, but upon the nature of things-in-themselves or, if we prefer it, on the grace of God. I imagine that in this case, as in the case of teleology, our reason bids us to examine nature *as if* it were the creation of an all-wise spirit and were adapted to the needs of human understanding.[1]

It may be said that unless there were repetitions of similar series in nature, we could never make the concept of cause and effect 'clear' to ourselves;[2] and indeed, if Kant's argument is sound, we could never become aware of objective succession, and so we could never have anything which could be described as human experience. May not such repetition be regarded as a necessary condition of experience, and is not such repetition therefore established by precisely that method of argument by which Kant seeks to establish the universal law of causality itself?

The answer to this question is most emphatically in the negative. We can indeed determine empirically certain conditions which are necessary to experience, and among these conditions is, I think, a certain amount of regularity or repetition in nature, and perhaps even the repetition of chains of causes and effects. But we cannot say *a priori* that these conditions must be fulfilled. As I understand Kant, in the case of the universal law of causality (as in the case of all Principles of the Understanding) if we grant the unity of apperception and time as a form of our sensibility, the application of the law to all events whatsoever in the phenomenal world follows as an inevitable consequence.[3] He is not saying that unless the phenomenal world conforms to the law of causality, we could

[1] Compare A 686 = B 714 ff.   [2] See A 196 = B 241.
[3] Compare A 216 = B 263 and A 217 = B 264.

have no experience of it. He is saying that there could be no phenomenal world unless it so conformed.

I would add that in this discussion Kant makes no mention of other kinds of causality, such as the possibility of free actions or final causes: these questions have to be dealt with later. But so far as I can see, the admission of such possibilities later demands no modification or qualification of his present doctrine which is concerned only with mechanical (or efficient) causation. If a succession is to be objective, it must conform to the universal law of cause and effect as here explained, although in particular cases it may conform also to further laws with which we are not here concerned.[1]

§ 8. *The Transcendental Synthesis of Imagination*

I have attempted to set forth the reasonableness of Kant's doctrine, but I must confess that I still find great difficulty in the fact that causal law is for Kant imposed upon appearances by the transcendental synthesis of imagination.

One side of this doctrine is easy enough to understand. The concept of causation, while we do not become consciously aware of it till experience has developed, seems, like the law of non-contradiction, to be presupposed at a very early stage; and in fact, if Kant is right, to be presupposed as soon as we can be said to be aware of changes in physical objects. It is in the nature of the human mind to think in terms of causes and effects long before it is consciously aware that it does so. In our everyday experience we cannot restrict ourselves, unless possibly by an effort of will, to the apprehension of given appearances, but starting from this frail basis we have before us at every moment a world which we construct in memory and in imagination controlled by thought. In this construction the concept of causality consciously or unconsciously plays a leading part, and only by its help can we know

---

[1] When we fail to find a teleological connexion and have to be satisfied with a merely mechanical, we are said only to miss an *additional* unity (*eine Einheit mehr*); see A 687-8 = B 715-16.

an objective world extending through space and time as an ordered and systematic whole.

So far Kant's doctrine offers little difficulty, and seems to me manifestly true, at least as a *prima facie* description of the facts. But there is another side to this which is very hard to believe. The orderly world which we construct on the basis of our sense-perceptions is confirmed at every moment by these continually changing sense-perceptions themselves. Our sense-perceptions must occur in an order compatible with the causal order of the objective world;[1] and Kant's doctrine is that in the last resort the causal order is imposed upon our sense-perceptions by the transcendental synthesis of imagination.

This difficulty I cannot attempt to discuss adequately here.[2] It may be that the difficulty is partly due to our tendency not to take the Copernican revolution seriously, and not to recognise that time is only a form of our sensibility which has nothing to do with things-in-themselves. I do not find it difficult to suppose that our minds are such that to them reality must appear as physical bodies in space which must conform to the laws of geometry; but for some reason I do find it difficult to suppose—and I imagine that many share this difficulty—that our minds are such that to them reality must appear, not only as a succession of changes in time, but as a succession of changes in time which must conform to causal law.

There are two ways of avoiding this difficulty.[3] One is to

[1] By this I mean that when we perceive an objective succession, our sense-perceptions, as contents, are for Kant events in the phenomenal world, and their succession is causally determined. It is much harder to believe that the transcendental synthesis determines the order of *actual* sense-perceptions (or given appearances) than that it determines the order of *possible* sense-perceptions. There is a further difficulty in the fact that our sensations are caused by physical objects, and that while primary qualities of objects are the same for all men, the secondary vary from individual to individual. The first difficulty concerns what Price (in *Perception*) calls 'horizontal' causality, while the second difficulty concerns what he calls 'vertical' causality.

[2] It is connected with the doctrine of double affection, and was one of the problems which Kant attempted to work out in the *Opus Postumum*.   [3] Compare Chapter XXXI §§ 4–5.

assert that the transcendental synthesis of which Kant speaks is a pre-conscious and noumenal synthesis which somehow constructs the whole physical world for us before we begin to know it. For this view I can find no basis in Kant, nor does it seem to me to have the least plausibility as a metaphysical theory. The other way is simply to assert that Kant's doctrine of transcendental synthesis is a mistaken kind of psychological doctrine which need not be taken seriously. I feel sure that this view is wrong; for it seems to me quite clear that there is, and must be, a transcendental synthesis by which we construct one time and one space, and that this construction does necessarily impose certain characteristics on the world which we experience. The difficulty is to understand how it can impose a causal order on the succession of my *actual* sense-perceptions.[1]

[1] I do not think Kant would claim that we have 'insight' (*Einsicht*) —that is, the insight of reason—in a matter of this kind; see A 171 = B 213.

CHAPTER XLVI

CAUSALITY AND CONTINUITY

§ 1. *Kant's Concept of Causality*

Kant offers us no detailed analysis[1] of the concept of causality such as we are familiar with in philosophical studies of science to-day. What he attempts to prove is no more than necessary succession, which he interprets as succession in accordance with a rule. If the event α occurs, then the event β, other conditions being the same, must always follow.

I think it is a mistake to infer from this that by causality Kant meant necessary succession and nothing more. His business is to prove what he calls the *schema* of necessary succession; but in so doing he believes himself to show both that phenomenal objects must conform to the pure category of ground and consequent, and that the pure category receives 'sense and significance' when it is translated into terms of time and so is transformed into cause and effect. He regards the cause as a ground of the effect, but as a ground which must precede the effect,[2] while a merely logical ground does not precede its consequence. More precisely, the cause is (or contains) the ground of the *existence* of the effect, it is a *principium fiendi*.[3]

The cause of which Kant speaks is the efficient or effective cause. He defines it as a cause through acting force.[4] The

---

[1] Some slight attempt at analysis is made in *Metaphysik*, pp. 41 ff.

[2] Compare A 91 = B 124, B 234, A 202 = B 247—and many other places.

[3] See *Metaphysik*, p. 41. The logical ground (*ratio*) is there said to be the ground of possibility or the *principium essendi*. The three straight lines in a triangle are its ground, but not its cause. The ground of knowledge, on the other hand, is the *principium cognoscendi*. Compare also de Vleeschauwer, *La déduction transcendentale*, I, p. 106.

[4] '*eine Ursache durch einwirkende Kraft.*' *Metaphysik*, p. 42. Kant regards the habit of appealing to final causes alone as 'the cushion of a lazy philosophy' (*ein Polster der faulen Philosophie*); compare A 689 = B 717.

'predicables' of causality are force, action and passion.[1] Causality leads to the concept of action or activity, the concept of action leads to the concept of force, and so to the concept of substance.[2] The relations dealt with in the Analogies are essentially *dynamical* relations.[3] Kant, so far as I can see, simply accepts the concepts of Newtonian physics in this connexion, and makes no attempt to alter or modify the concept of causality. I do not think it will be denied that for Newton the cause was supposed to 'produce' the effect.[4]

It is indeed often maintained[5] that for Kant causality can be nothing more than regular succession, because for him objects and events are only appearances or ideas, and there can be no activity or causal efficacy in ideas.[6] Such a contention seems to me unconvincing. The fact that the world is only an appearance to human minds is no reason why it should not appear to human minds as made up of substances acting causally upon one another and displaying real efficacy or dynamical causality. The only difficulty is to know what can be meant by 'real efficacy'; but this difficulty is not confined to the Critical Philosophy. Kant quite certainly believed that his doctrine was compatible with the physics of his time, and indeed was the only possible justification for the scientific concepts which were actually in use.

It may be added that for Kant causality implies the possi-

[1] A 82 = B 108.

[2] A 204 = B 249. In A 648 = B 676 force is identified with the causality of a substance.

[3] A 215 = B 262. The distinction between *communio* and *commercium* in A 213–14 = B 260–1 also serves to emphasise the same point.

[4] Compare Lenzen, *University of California Publications in Philosophy*, Vol. 15, p. 72. Kant himself uses the word 'produce' (*erzeugen*) in connexion with causality; see, for example, A 208 = B 254 and A 474 = B 502; also the heading in A 189.

[5] E.g. by Paulsen, *Immanuel Kant*, sixth edition, p. 189.

[6] Kemp Smith, *Commentary*, p. 373, also accepts this contention, but maintains that on Kant's phenomenalist (as opposed to his subjectivist) views he is able to recognise genuinely dynamical activities. He has, however, to admit that Kant's phenomenalist view of the causal relation 'receives no quite definite formulation either in this section or elsewhere in the Critique'.

bility of prediction. We can state the causal relation in the form 'if A, then B', or 'if A is posited, B must follow'. This analogy with the form of judgement does not, however, mean that the relation of cause and effect is in any concrete instance intelligible to us *a priori*. In this respect Kant agrees with Hume. We can discover the cause of a given effect, or the effect of a given cause, only by means of experience.[1] Our *a priori* knowledge is confined to the statement that every event must have a cause.

§ 2. *The Successiveness of Cause and Effect*

The three main questions in regard to causality discussed by Kant in the observations which, as usual, he appends to his proofs are (1) the successiveness of cause and effect, (2) the connexion between substance and causal activity, and (3) the continuity of change. The second of these questions has already been discussed.[2] We must now consider the other two.

Kant has expressed the Principle of causality in the first edition[3] by the formula: 'Everything that happens (that is, begins to be) presupposes something upon which it follows in accordance with a rule'. In simpler language, every event has a cause upon which it necessarily follows. Kant thinks it necessary to meet the objection that in some cases the effect does not follow the cause, but is simultaneous with it.[4] The heat of the room, for example, is simultaneous with the heated stove which is its cause. It may even be urged[5] that this is true of most causes and effects.[6] We fail to notice this because it takes some time for the cause to have its full effect, but the beginning of the effect is always simultaneous with the cause.

---

[1] A 206–7 = B 252. Compare A 171 = B 213 and also A 41 = B 58.
[2] See Chapter XLII § 9.   [3] A 189.   [4] A 202 = B 247–8.
[5] I take it that Kant is still expounding the objection with which he has to deal. Kant's reply begins later with the words 'Now we must not fail to note . . .'.
[6] If Kant were speaking in his own person I think he would have said 'all'. That he says 'most' suggests that he is still thinking of a rather crude objection. He says in the next sentence that the beginning of the effect is *always* simultaneous with the cause.

Kant's reply is obvious enough. When we say that the effect follows the cause, we do not mean that the cause comes to an end, and there is then an interval of time after which the effect begins. What we are dealing with is the *order* of cause and effect in time, and this does not mean that there is a passage or interval of time between them. On the contrary, although the time between the causality[1] of the cause and the effect is a vanishing quantity, and cause and effect are simultaneous in the sense that there is no gap between them, this does not alter the fact that cause and effect are in a temporal succession. It means only that the temporal succession is continuous.[2]

This discussion is, I think, intended to prepare the way for the doctrine of the Third Analogy.

§ 3. *The Continuity of Change*

Kant's account of the continuity of change is both more difficult and more important.[3] It is difficult in itself, and it seems to contradict the doctrine set forth in the Anticipations.[4]

---

[1] This phrase is used because a cause may in a sense be present without producing the effect, if there is some impediment which prevents it from doing so. Compare *Metaphysik*, p. 43.

[2] Kant gives two illustrations to show that in cases of seeming simultaneity we distinguish effect from cause by order in time. These are (1) the popular one that if we lay a bullet on a cushion, there follows a hollow in the cushion, but if there is a hollow in the cushion, it is not followed by the presence of a bullet; and (2) the experiment of surface-tension made first by Segner in 1751, who was led thereby to the discovery of capillary attraction. If we fill a narrow glass by dipping it into a large vessel of water, the surface of the water becomes concave in the glass.   [3] A 206 = B 252 ff.

[4] A 171-2 = B 212-13; compare Chapter XXXVIII § 7. The contradiction lies in the fact that the continuity of change was there asserted to belong to universal natural science (which I take to be Rational Physiology or Rational Physics), and not to Transcendental Philosophy; here it is discussed without any apology or explanation, whether because Kant had changed his mind on the subject or because he was unable to keep away from the problem in spite of recognising that it ought to be dealt with in another place. It is true that in the present passage he reaffirms his earlier doctrine that we have not the slightest *a priori* conception of the way in which anything can be changed; but I cannot see that there is any real difference between dealing with the form of change (which he now proceeds to do) and

It is important because of its bearing on the special proof of causality from the nature of time (Proof V), and also because of the light it throws on the doctrine of the Anticipations.

We have not the slightest conception of how change is possible, but are entirely dependent upon experience.[1] This, however, applies to change as something concrete, the succession (or exchange) of given states of a substance. We can abstract from the content of these states and consider *a priori* the form or condition of change in general, and we do so in relation to the law of causality and the conditions of time. The form or condition of change seems to be identified with the bare successiveness of change;[2] and Kant is asking 'What can be said *a priori* about change on the sole ground that it is a succession in time (in complete abstraction from the empirical character of the states of which it is a succession)?'

When a substance passes from state a to state β, t_2 (the moment at which β occurs) differs from and is subsequent to t_1 (the moment at which a occurs). Between these two moments there is always a time, however short, which may be represented by $t_2 - t_1$.

State β differs from and is subsequent to state a. The difference must be regarded as a difference only in quantity, that is, in degree,[3] since we are ignoring the qualitative differ-

dealing with the causality of change in general (which he there excluded from Transcendental Philosophy). The reference to causality does not imply any difference, for here the form of change is considered 'in accordance with the law of causality'. If the statement in the Anticipations were concerned only with motion and the present statement with change, the contradiction would disappear.

[1] It should be observed (1) that Kant identifies knowledge of moving forces with knowledge of the successive appearances which 'designate' these forces; (2) it is as motions that the appearances designate moving forces; and (3) he is concerned only with change as *change of state* (not of relative position). Thus a change of velocity is a change of state, but motion (change of place) at a uniform velocity is not a *change of state* but simply a *state* (of motion).

[2] The form or condition of change is equated with the succession (or happening) of the states.

[3] A reference to degree seems to be called for here, though it is not made explicit by Kant till A 208 = B 254. Kant gives as his reason (in A 208 = B 253) for asserting difference in quantity the fact that all

ences or empirical content of the states which are exchanged.[1] α may then be taken as zero in relation to β, and the change is a coming into existence of $\beta - \alpha$.[2]

Hence just as there is always a time between two moments, so between the two states in these moments there is always a difference of quantity.[3] The transition or passage from one state to another takes place in a time which is contained between two moments (the moment at which α occurs and the moment at which β occurs). The two moments are the limits of the time of the change, and therefore the limits of the intermediate state[4] between state α and state β. As such limits they belong to the whole change; they mark its starting-point and its finish.

Kant takes this as proving that the continuity of change, which in the Anticipations he asserted, on the ground of intuitive evidence,[5] to be possible,[6] is necessarily present in all actual change.[7]

the parts of an appearance are always quantities; but presumably he is not speaking of parts which are outside one another, and the statement seems to presuppose the doctrine of the Anticipations. This is confirmed by the fact that he refers to states as 'reality in the appearance' (*realitas phaenomenon*).

[1] This would seem to imply that when litmus paper changes from red to blue, the change can be treated as a change in degree (of colour); but perhaps Kant has in mind only primary qualities.

[2] This quantity may be either positive or negative. If the change is from 70° F. to 80° F., what has happened is the addition of 10° F. (80° F. − 70° F. = 10° F.). If the change is from 70° F. to 60° F. what has happened is the subtraction of 10° F. (60° F. − 70° F. = − 10° F.).

[3] This of course applies only when the two states are assumed to be different states.

[4] I suppose the existence of an intermediate state is assumed on the ground that time must be filled.   [5] A 162 = B 201, A 180 = B 223.

[6] B 208, A 168 = B 210. Compare A 143 = B 182-3.

[7] Kant gives two other versions of this proof in *Metaphysik*, pp. 54 and 56.

(1) Nothing passes out of one state into another immediately, that is, *per saltum*, but the transition from one state to another happens in such a way that the thing must pass through all the intermediate states. Thus one can say generally '*Omnis mutatio est continua*'.

Every state (? change) has two *termini*: *a quo* and *ad quem*. Each of these two states is distinguished as in a different moment. In every transition the thing is in two different moments. The moment in

So far Kant has dealt only with the continuity of change. He now proceeds to bring in causation. Every change has a cause which shows its causality in the whole time in which the change takes place. Hence the cause does not bring about the change suddenly, all at one moment, but in a period of time, so that just as the time increases from the initial moment t_1 to the final moment t_2, the quantity of reality (which is equal to $\beta - a$) is produced through all the intermediate grades between a and β.

Kant's answer to the question 'What can be said *a priori* about change?'—or in his own language 'How can a thing pass from state a to state β?'—is (1) that the change must be continuous, and (2) that its continuity must be due to the continuity of causal activity.[1]

which the thing is in one state is different from the moment in which it comes into the other state. But between two moments there is a time, just as between two points there is a space. Hence the transition occurs in time; for in the moments in which it passes from A to B, there is a time in which it is neither in A nor in B, but is in mutation or transition between the two.

The conclusion stated above is then said to follow.

(2) There is no state which follows immediately upon another. For if a body passes from one state into another, there must be a moment in which it goes out of the first state and a moment in which it comes into the second state. Between these two moments there is a time in which it is neither in the one state nor in the other. Therefore it is in an intermediate state, which is a ground why it passes over into the second state.

It must be remembered that the lectures on Metaphysics—the style of which differs so much, especially in the use of short sentences, from the *Kritik*—are printed from the notes of students, and are not free from the inaccuracies to be expected. I have modified the language in places. I cannot, for example, believe that Kant said '*Alle mutatio ist continua*'.

[1] He adds that a causal activity, so far as it is uniform, is called a 'moment', and that the change does not consist of 'moments' but is produced by moments as their effect. It will be remembered that in A 168–9 = B 210 he called the degree of reality as a cause a 'moment', e.g. the 'moment' of weight, and suggested that it was called a moment because the apprehension of degree was not successive but momentary. According to Adickes (*Kant als Naturforscher*, Vol. I, p. 25) Kant uses 'moment' in seven different senses, but on this I offer no opinion.

§ 4. *The Law of Continuity*

It will be observed that in the proof just given there is no attempt made to derive causation from the continuity of time as there was in Proof V, and that Kant argues directly from the continuity of time to the continuity of change. He is not arguing (or at any rate not arguing explicitly) that change must be continuous, if we are to *perceive* it in a time which is continuous.

This argument is followed up by what is generally regarded as a second argument.[1] I think it is intended rather to be a summary or explanation of what has been already set forth. Like Kant's summaries in general, it ignores points previously made (it makes no reference to causation), and it makes explicit what was previously only implicit.

The ground of the law of continuity in change is this: that neither time nor the appearance in time is composed of smallest possible parts;[2] and that in change a thing passes from one state to another through all the infinite parts (or degrees) intermediate between the two states.[3] This seems a statement of the law of continuity rather than of its ground, and can hardly be called an attempt at proof.[4]

The utility of this doctrine in science is, as Kant says, a question outside the scope of the *Kritik*. But he believes, as regards motion, that nothing can move from one place to another without passing through all the intermediate places; that nothing can pass from rest to a degree of motion, or from

---

[1] A 209 = B 254.

[2] That is, it is not composed of simple parts incapable of further division; or, as Kant says in the following sentence, no difference (in degree) of a state, and no difference in the quantity of times, is the smallest possible difference.

[3] Kant, in popular language, speaks of the state of the thing as passing through the parts to the second state, and of the second state as growing out of the first; but a state does not pass or grow at all, it is only exchanged for another state. Incidentally it may be noted that when Kant speaks of differences in degree as always smaller than the difference between *a* and zero, he is referring to absolute zero (and not to *a* as the relative zero from which the change starts).

[4] It may perhaps be intended to make explicit a principle presupposed in the previous argument.

a degree of motion to rest, without passing through the infinite intermediate degrees of motion; and that nothing can change its direction without either coming to rest and starting afresh or else moving continuously through a curved line (and not an angle).[1]

§ 5. *Continuity as the Formal Condition of Apprehension*

Kant himself warns us of the danger of accepting such proofs too easily, a danger of which we are acutely conscious in the present state of science. He seems to feel that the proof above given is especially to be distrusted, because it is a dogmatic proof, that is, as I have said, a direct proof from the nature of time to the nature of change in time. For this reason he supplements the dogmatic proof by a Critical explanation.[2] He attempts to show that the distrust of the previous argument is not really justified, because in spite of appearances we are only anticipating our own apprehension. He assumes, as always, that it must be possible for us to have an *a priori* knowledge of the conditions of our own apprehension or our own experience. His argument is interesting, because it throws light on the continually repeated doctrine that what understanding determines is inner sense.

All increase in empirical knowledge, and every advance in sense-perception, is nothing but an extension of the determination of inner sense, that is, an advance in time.[3] This is true whatever be the character of the objects known, whether we are concerned with empirical objects or with pure intuitions.

---

[1] *Metaphysik*, pp. 56–7. Changes of velocity or direction are changes of state, although uniform motion in one direction is not a change of state.

[2] A 210 = B 255. This also is commonly regarded as a separate and independent proof, and the supposed repetition of the same proof 'with unessential variations' is said to imply a composite origin for these paragraphs. See Kemp Smith, *Commentary*, p. 380. I think that an understanding of the relation between the paragraphs diminishes the force of this contention.

[3] Yet many commentators insist that for Kant knowledge is timeless, and even noumenal.

This advance in time—the advance of our experience—deter-mines everything, and is determined by nothing other than itself. It determines even the time in which it itself takes place.[1]

Hence, Kant goes on, every transition in sense-perception to something which follows in time is a determination of time through the production of this sense-perception; and since time is always and in all its parts[2] a quantity, the production of a sense-perception, considered as an intensive quantity, must pass through all the degrees (of which none is the smallest possible degree) from zero[3] up to the determinate degree of the sense-perception in question.

From this Kant concludes that it is possible to understand how we can have *a priori* knowledge of the law of change (so far as the form of change is concerned). All such knowledge does is to anticipate our own apprehension, whose formal condition, as present in us prior to, and independently of, given appearances, must be intelligible *a priori*.

It seems to me obvious that Kant intends this argument to supplement, and be supplemented by, his original contention that different states (or sense-perceptions) as occupying different moments must have a filled time between them.

[1] This, if we may judge from the following sentence, seems to be the general sense of the very obscure statement: '*die Teile desselben sind nur in der Zeit, und durch die Synthesis derselben, sie aber nicht vor ihr gegeben*'. The last six words are especially obscure, and Vaihinger emends '*sie*' to '*sind*', while Wille emends '*ihr*' to '*ihnen*'.

To discuss all the possibilities—none of which is certain—would take too much time. I should like the sentence to mean that while the parts of experience are given only in time and through the synthesis of time, nevertheless time is not given prior to (or independently of) the synthesis; compare A 452 n. = B 480 n. Although the advance of experience is an advance in time, time itself is determined, and indeed produced (see A 143 = B 182), by the advance of experience, which is essentially a synthetic act. Compare the statement about the concept of succession in B 155.

[2] This phrase seems intended to imply that no part of time is the smallest possible, for every part of time is a quantity of time and not a point of time.

[3] To judge by A 208 = B 253, zero here is the starting-point of the transition and may be represented by *a*, the sense-perception from which the transition starts.

Taken by itself it would hardly be intelligible; and if the original argument is rejected, this one is entirely without force.

This doctrine is closely connected with the Anticipations. It seems intended to show, not only that between a sensation and zero there is an infinity of different degrees of the same sensation—this is supposed to have been proved already—but also that we must necessarily pass through these degrees to arrive at the required sensation. Furthermore it is based on the nature of time, and such a basis is absolutely essential for the proof of Principles, although in the Anticipations the connexion between time and degree was by no means made sufficiently clear.

Kant's argument, so far as I understand it, takes it to be already proved that no part of time is the smallest possible part of time and no degree is the smallest possible degree; or, in other words, whatever two points of time we take there will always be another point between them, and whatever two degrees we take there will always be another degree between them. He then maintains that since any two degrees occupy two different points of time, any intermediate point of time must be occupied by an intermediate degree and so *ad infinitum*. The continuity of time implies the continuity of change.

This doctrine he regards as worthy of acceptance because the states which possess these degrees are possible or actual sense-perceptions and because time is the form of our sensibility. If time were a thing-in-itself, and if states belonged to things-in-themselves, such a proof would not be acceptable.[1] Kant rightly, I think, refuses to take time for granted, and (insisting that time is determined only through the advance in our sense-perception by means of the synthesis which is experience) he seems to argue (although his statement is not

---

[1] It would contradict Kant's central principle that we cannot have *a priori* knowledge of things-in-themselves. But the objection may be raised that Newton's time (apart from its inconceivability) would give us ground for a similar proof, and I find it difficult to be certain of Kant's answer to such an objection; compare Chapter VIII § 6. Perhaps his answer here would be that absolute time cannot be perceived.

sufficiently explicit) that this empirical determination of time as a continuous extensive quantity is impossible unless the succession of sense-perceptions by which time is filled is itself a continuous change in intensive quantity or degree.

The resemblance of this argument to the fifth proof of causality is obvious, although in the present passage it is not causality, but continuity of change, which is inferred directly from the continuity of time, and the continuity of causality (causality being taken as proved) is inferred from the continuity of change.

This latter inference is set forth in the long and intricate sentence which constitutes Kant's final paragraph. Just as time contains the *a priori* condition of the possibility of a continuous advance of the existing to what follows, so understanding (in virtue of the unity of apperception)[1] contains the *a priori* condition of the possibility of a continuous determination of all appearances (as regards their temporal position) by means of the law of cause and effect. It is only because of this possibility, only because of the inevitable sequence of causes and effects, that our empirical knowledge of time-relations is valid for all time, and is therefore universally or objectively valid.

Here again we come to Kant's central contention—that objective succession is essentially necessary succession. If we are to know, not merely that appearances have been apprehended by us in succession, but that they succeed one another in a common objective world, then their relative position in one homogeneous and continuous time must be determined by understanding in accordance with the law of cause and effect.

The whole of Kant's argument rests, I believe, on the supposition that absolute time cannot be perceived and that events in the physical world are only appearances (possible or actual) of a reality which in itself we have no reason to regard either as changing or as unchanging or as having any kind of temporal predicate. The difference between the special proof from time

[1] A 210–11 = B 256. Note that here we have one of the few passages in which an appeal appears to be made to the pure category.

(Proof V) and the others is not so great as is commonly supposed. In all his arguments Kant is maintaining that unless succession were necessary, we could not experience a world which changes in one homogeneous and continuous time, and that experience which is not experience of such a world could not be called human experience at all. Whatever be the obscurities in his exposition, and however doubtful be the validity, and even in some cases the meaning, of the different steps of his advance, I cannot help thinking that at the very least he has called attention to a problem whose very existence is too commonly ignored, and that the solution he suggests has not yet been superseded by any other.

CHAPTER XLVII

THE THIRD ANALOGY

§ 1. *The Principle of Interaction*

The Principle formulated in the Third Analogy is called in the first edition 'the principle of communion'.[1] In the second edition it is described more elaborately as 'the principle of coexistence in accordance with the law of interaction[2] or communion'.

The two formulations of the Principle are as follows:

I. First edition—*All substances, so far as they are coexistent, stand in thorough-going communion (or mutual interaction).*[3]

II. Second edition—*All substances, so far as they can be perceived in space as coexistent, are in thorough-going interaction.*[4]

The second formula has two advantages over the first. By the reference to perception it brings out the Critical character of the Principle; and by the reference to space it makes explicit Kant's view that the substances of whose interaction he speaks are spatial substances.

By 'communion' or 'interaction' Kant means *the reciprocal or mutual causality of substances in regard to their accidents.* This is explicitly stated by Kant both in the first and in the second edition.[5] The third category of relation (like the third category of other classes) springs from a combination of the

---

[1] '*Gemeinschaft.*' The Latin translation is '*communio*' or '*commercium*'. Kant is speaking of a *real* or *dynamical* communion (*commercium*). See A 213 = B 260 and A 214 = B 261.

[2] '*Wechselwirkung.*' The Latin translation is '*actio mutua*'. See *M.A.d.N.* 2. *Hauptstück* (IV 545). 'Interaction' and 'communion' are here equivalent terms, but it would be more convenient if 'communion' were used for the pure category and 'interaction' for the schematised category; compare Chapter XXXIII § 4.

[3] A 211. 'Mutual interaction' may be thought a superfluous reiteration, but Kant's words are '*Wechselwirkung untereinander*'.   [4] B 256.

[5] See B 111, B 112, A 144 = B 183, A 221 = B 269, A 244 = B 302 *et passim.* This is involved even in the description of the category given in A 80 = B 106, where communion is equated with interaction

first two categories; but it is nevertheless not a derivative concept.[1] Even if we can show that substance and causality are necessary conditions of experience, it does not follow that substances 'influence' one another. Leibniz, for example, maintained that they did not.

The empirical illustration which Kant gives of interaction is the fact that in a body the different parts (which are of course substances) mutually attract and repel one another; and the outstanding example of what he means is the law of gravitation. Kant also says expressly that the third law of mechanics— in all communication of motion action and reaction are always equal—is an application of the category of interaction to matter.[2] These illustrations all serve to confirm the view

between agent and patient. Compare also letter to Schulz in 1784 (X 344), translated by Kemp Smith, *Commentary*, p. 199.

Kemp Smith (*Commentary*, pp. 387 ff.) denies that the category of communion can be reduced to 'a dual application of the category of causality'. So far as this denial is directed against the misunderstandings of Schopenhauer, it is legitimate, but Kemp Smith appears to reject the view that communion is to be equated with the mutual or reciprocal causality of substances; for his language seems to imply that the terms 'cause' and 'causality' ought to be excluded from the description of the category. For this doctrine he offers no evidence from Kant other than the fact that in the second edition 'Kant is careful to employ the terms ground and influence in place of the terms cause and causality'.

To this it may be replied: (1) that Kant expressly describes communion as mutual causality in the second edition (B 111–12); (2) that (as Ewing has pointed out) in what is alleged to be the earliest of Kant's proofs (A 214 = B 261) the terms 'ground' and 'influence' are already used; and (3) that Kant always regards a cause as a real (but not a logical) ground, while 'influence' (*influxus*) is a technical term for transitive causal action, the action of one substance upon another outside itself. Compare B 111, and also Baumgarten, *Metaphysica* § 211 (XVII 71): '*influxus (actio transiens) est actio substantiae in substantiam extra se. Actio, quae non est influens, est immanens*'.

There may be grounds for maintaining that Kant was mistaken in regarding the interaction of substances as equivalent to their reciprocal causality, but I can see no grounds for denying that this was his doctrine; nor am I able to understand what Kemp Smith's alternative explanation of the category is.   [1] B 111.

[2] *M.A.d.N.* 2. *Hauptstück* (IV 544–5 and 551). The words used are '*Wirkung*' and '*Gegenwirkung*', which latter is equated by Kant

that for Kant communion or interaction is what he asserts it to be—namely the reciprocal causality of substances.

Professor Prichard gives another vivid illustration of Kant's meaning. 'Suppose two bodies, A, a lump of ice, and B, a fire, close together, yet at such a distance that they can be observed in succession. Suppose that A passes through changes of temperature a_1 a_2 a_3 . . . in certain times, the changes ending in states α_1 α_2 α_3 . . ., and that B passes through changes of temperature b_1 b_2 b_3 . . . in the same times, the changes ending in states β_1 β_2 β_3 . . . Suppose also, as we must, that A and B interact, i.e. that A in passing through its changes conditions[1] the changes through which B passes, and therefore also the states in which B ends, and *vice versa*, so that a_2 and α_2 will be the outcome not of a_1 and α_1 alone, but of a_1 and α_1, and b_1 and β_1, jointly. Then we can say, (1) that A and B are in the relation of influence, and also of interaction or reciprocal influence, in the sense that they *mutually* (not alternately) determine one another's states'.[2]

The general character of the doctrine which Kant seeks to establish seems to me sufficiently clear. And if he is able to prove that phenomenal reality must consist of substances in interaction, and cannot consist of substances whose states

(as also by Baumgarten, *Metaphysica* § 213) with '*reactio*'. Kant in *Metaphysik*, p. 61, distinguishes '*Rückwirkung*' as '*reactio*' from '*Gegenwirkung*' which is '*resistentia*' or '*reactio resistens*'; but this seems to be a refinement which is not applied in the present case.

Kant is particularly interested in motion; and attraction and repulsion are for him moving forces. He does not discuss, as I think he ought, the position of secondary qualities in this connexion, but they are caused by motion.

[1] I should prefer to say 'causes' or 'influences', but I suppose Prichard says 'conditions', not to deny the causality of A, but to imply that A is not the only cause.

[2] *Kant's Theory of Knowledge*, p. 303. The detailed working out of this illustration ought to be studied, but it is too long to quote here. I would only add further from the same passage '(4) that if we perceive A and B alternately, and so only in the states a_1 a_3 . . . β_2 β_4 . . . respectively, we can only fill in the blanks, i.e. discover the states a_2 a_4 . . . β_1 β_3 . . . *coexistent* with β_2 β_4 . . . and a_1 a_3 . . . respectively, if we presuppose the thought of interaction'.

succeed one another (according to causal law) in complete independence of all other substances and all other similar causal successions—then manifestly his doctrine is of importance and adds a great deal to what he has hitherto professed to prove.[1] The question is whether he is able to prove it.

§ 2. *The Meaning of Coexistence*

Interaction is the condition of our knowledge of objective coexistence—such is the thesis which Kant has to prove. But the definitions which he gives of such coexistence give rise to difficulties. In the first edition Kant's definition is as follows: 'Things are coexistent, so far as they exist in one and the same time'.[2] In this definition—since all things exist in one and the same time—Kant must mean by 'time' either an instant of time or a part of time.[3] The latter would appear to be the meaning with which he is chiefly concerned; and perhaps the word 'simultaneity' should be reserved for existence in the same instant.

There is a further difficulty about the meaning of 'thing' in this definition. A 'thing' like the earth or the moon (the examples given in the second edition) comes into being and passes away; and so it might be regarded as only a temporary determination of permanent substance (or as a substance[4] only so far as determined for a certain length of time in a particular way). In that case we could speak of things as coexisting, just as we can speak of states or determinations or accidents of substance as coexisting. Kant himself, however, seems to identify thing and substance; for he goes on to speak

---

[1] Compare Lindsay, *Kant*, pp. 128–9. Apart from the principle of interaction we should be reduced, as he says, to 'a streaky view of causation'—the world might be 'made up of a lot of quite independent chains of causation'.   [2] A 211 = B 258.

[3] I suppose that to be simultaneous is to exist at the same instant of time, while to coexist is to exist *either* at the same instant *or* through the same part (or period) of time. Coexistence is a wider term than simultaneity.

[4] Such a substance is composed of parts which are themselves substances.

of the coexistence of substances as if it were identical with
the coexistence of things.[1] But since all substances are permanent, it immediately follows that all substances coexist always,
both in every moment of time, and in every part of time,
and in all time taken as a whole. When we know that any
substance exists, we know that it coexists with all other substances, if indeed it is proper to ascribe temporal predicates
to substances at all.[2]

It is possible that a way out of this difficulty is to be found in
the technical use of 'existence'. We speak of the existence of
accidents as 'inherence', and of the existence of substances as
'subsistence'; but this distinction is misleading, for we are
apt to imagine that the substance exists in one way and the
accident in another.[3] If we refuse to make the separation, and
if we say that the accidents are the ways in which substance
exists, then by the coexistence of substances Kant may mean
coexistence *in respect of certain accidents*. And this, I think,
is what we must take him to mean.

In the second edition Kant defines coexistence as the existence
of the manifold in the same time.[4] The reference to the manifold
would seem to imply that it is the accidents of substance which
coexist,[5] and so perhaps may be taken to support our interpretation. At any rate I can see no other interpretation which
will make sense.

§ 3. *The Proof in the Second Edition*

The proof added in the second edition[6] may be considered
first. It is clearly meant to run parallel to the proof of causality
which was added in the second edition (Proof I).[7]

---

[1] B 258.
[2] Prichard (*Kant's Theory of Knowledge*, p. 306) denies that we can
properly do so.   [3] A 186–7 = B 230.   [4] B 257.
[5] Such a series of accidents of one substance (or set of substances)
as constitutes the life or history of a 'thing' may also be taken to
coexist with another series of the same kind. The earth and the moon
coexist in this sense.
[6] B 256–8.   [7] B 233–4. Compare Chapter XLIII § 3.

I. Kant starts out from the assertion that *'things' are coexistent when the sense-perception of the one can follow reciprocally on the sense-perception of the other*. By 'reciprocally' he means that we can either see A and then B, or B and then A, as we please. We can see first the moon and then the earth, or *vice versa* (just as we can see first the top and then the bottom of the house, or *vice versa*[1]). And because our sense-perceptions of these objects can thus follow one another reciprocally, we say that the objects are coexistent.

In this assertion Kant would seem to be considering 'things' whose states are taken to be constant; or at least he is ignoring the possibility that the things in question may be changing their states. He has already pointed out, in the Second Analogy, that where there is an objective succession (as in the case where the boat is moving downstream), this reciprocal succession cannot occur. We can see the boat first higher up and then lower down, but we cannot see it first lower down and then higher up.[2]

Such a doctrine seems plain and obvious enough, but there may seem to be a certain amount of obscurity on one point. Is Kant maintaining that when things are coexistent, a reciprocal succession of sense-perceptions must be possible? Or is he maintaining that when a reciprocal succession of sense-perceptions does take place, then the things must be coexistent?

I may here seem to be making too much of a very small point, but it is to be noted that in speaking of objective succession (which ought to be an exact parallel) the inference is from the objective succession to the impossibility of reciprocal succession (or reversibility) in the sense-perceptions, and not *vice versa*.[3] Furthermore, in the passage which immediately follows, 'from the fact that things are posited in the same time'

---

[1] A 190 = B 235 and A 192 = B 237–8. In Prichard's example we can see first the ice and then the fire or *vice versa*. A reciprocal succession can also be described (perhaps more clearly) as a reversible succession.   [2] A 192 = B 237.

[3] B 234. Compare also A 192 = B 237, where the inference is in the same direction.

we *conclude*[1] 'that the perceptions of them can follow one another reciprocally'. Here the inference is from objective coexistence to the reciprocal succession (or reversibility) of sense-perceptions, and not *vice versa*.

We are clearly entitled to argue from the coexistence of objects to the reversibility of our sense-perceptions of these objects. If we wish to argue in the reverse direction, we can do so only under certain assumptions; for we have no right to describe our sense-perceptions as reversible (or as irreversible), unless we assume that these sense-perceptions reveal to us (or are identical with) the states of real objects which are permanent substances.[2] Apart from this assumption we could say only that our sense-perceptions come to us in the order in which they do come: there could be no ground for saying that this order was reversible, and still less for saying that it must be reversible. The argument of the Third Analogy (like that of the Second) manifestly rests on the First Analogy as its presupposition.[3] Once we assume our sense-perceptions to be sense-perceptions of *objects* (or substances), then, as Kant asserts, we are entitled to say that because the sense-perceptions *of these objects* can follow one another reciprocally, the objects are coexistent. We can discover the reversibility of our sense-perceptions by experiment—but only on the supposition that the objects of our sense-perception are permanent substances.

If we fail to see this, we may wrongly imagine that Kant is trying to state the criterion whereby we pass from awareness of a merely *subjective* succession to knowledge of *objective* coexistence. Such a process of transition from the merely subjective to the objective does not and cannot take place: on that point I agree with Professor Prichard. I do not, however, believe that Kant is attempting to describe such a process; and if he were, his attempt would be manifestly unsuccessful.

Kant, as always, is taking experience for granted and

[1] B 257, '*abzunehmen*'. Kant says we have no perception of absolute time by which to conclude this, but he implies that we do conclude it by means of a pure concept of the understanding.

[2] Compare Chapter XLV § 4.   [3] Compare B 232–3.

attempting an analysis, not of its growth, but of its necessary presuppositions. Here he is taking for granted what he claims to have proved in the First Analogy, namely that we experience real objects as permanent substances; and this implies (what we all accept by common sense) that we can experience coexistent objects.[1] If we assume that we experience coexistent objects, then (and then alone) can we say that our sense-perceptions of these objects must be reversible. And we can also say that if by experiment we discover our sense-perceptions to be reversible (on the supposition that we are perceiving real objects), then the objects must be coexistent. The reversibility of our sense-perceptions is then a criterion by which we can distinguish objective coexistence from objective succession. It is not, and it could not be, a mark whereby we are entitled to go beyond a merely subjective succession and affirm an objective coexistence.

There is another point to be noted. Even in cases where we are perceiving an objective succession, it is possible for imagination to place the sense-perceptions in an order different from that in which they are 'taken up'.[2] Hence by a combination of imagination and sense-perception we could, although doubtless with difficulty, make a reciprocal succession of appearances such as Kant describes.[3] This possibility borders on the fantastic, and Kant does not discuss it; but it is worth mentioning, since it suggests that in ordinary circumstances we have no difficulty in distinguishing, by simple inspection, an appearance to sense-perception from an appearance to mere imagination.[4]

[1] This does not mean that we can perceive two coexistent objects in one moment of time, but that when we see first the moon and then the earth, or *vice versa*, we assume that we are experiencing two coexistent objects.

[2] B 233. Compare A 201 = B 246.

[3] We could see the ship lower down, and then imagine it higher up, and see it lower down again, and then imagine it higher up, and so on. This does not justify us in supposing that the ship occupies all these positions at the same time.

[4] This possibility is mentioned by Professor Kemp Smith (*Commentary*, p. 386). Another suggestion which he makes on the same

II. *We cannot perceive time itself, so as to conclude (from the fact that things are placed or posited in the same time) that the perceptions of them can follow one another reciprocally.*

The statement that we cannot perceive time itself (or absolute or empty time) is the usual doctrine which lies at the root of all the Analogies. It should, however, be observed that the conclusion which we cannot make *with the help of a perception of absolute time* is nevertheless the conclusion which we do make, and upon which Kant's argument rests.

It is not clear how the perception of absolute time, if that were possible, could help us to this particular conclusion, which (in the absence of such perception) we must make by means of the concept of interaction. Even if the appearances of A and B were given to us with the moment of their occurrence in absolute time as it were stamped upon them, we should still have before us only the series $a_1 \beta_2 a_3 \beta_4 a_5 \beta_6 \ldots$ (or whatever the series was), and we should not have before us what we really require, the series $a_1\beta_1 \ a_2\beta_2 \ a_3\beta_3 \ldots$ and so on. Perhaps Kant means that if we could perceive the series $a_1 a_3 a_5 \ldots$ in relation to absolute time, we could fill in the gaps in accordance with the law of continuity; and similarly in the case of the series $\beta_2 \beta_4 \beta_6 \ldots$[1]

III. Since we do not perceive empty time, *the synthesis of apprehension taken by itself enables us to say only that in the subject there is a sense-perception* a *when there is no sense-percep-*

page is less happy. He asserts that we might have 'a reversible continuous series' which did not justify an inference to coexistence. The example he gives is that of playing a series of notes, and then playing it backwards. This is, however, not a reversible series at all, but a reversed series—which is a very different thing. A reversible series is one which can be taken up or perceived in any order at any time, while the series in question can be taken up only in one order, the order in which it is played (whether it is played backwards or forwards makes no difference). It might as well be objected that a boat can reverse its engines and go upstream.

[1] It is unnecessary to discuss Kant's meaning in further detail, since the whole supposition is put forward only to be rejected.

tion b *and* vice versa.[1] By mere apprehension we could not say that the objects A and B coexist, nor could we say that they *must* coexist in order that the sense-perceptions may be able to follow one another reciprocally.[2]

This statement seems to me obviously true. Mere apprehension, apart from the element of thought, cannot give us objects, and still less can it give us coexistent objects: it can give us at the most mere ideas.[3]

There is, however, a further point. Kant appears to imply—and surely he is right—that where we have what we take to be a reversible series of sense-perceptions, we assume, not only that we are perceiving coexistent objects, but that these objects *must* coexist, if the series of our sense-perceptions is to be reversible. We cannot derive such an assumption from mere apprehension; but it is an assumption which we all make. Furthermore it is an assumption of *necessity*; and it appears to me that here, as always, Kant is endeavouring to discover the element of necessity which is involved in objectivity. He is in fact trying to determine the element of necessity which is involved in our experience of objective coexistence; and it is the presence of this element of necessity which alone entitles him to assert the presence of a pure concept of the understanding.[4]

---

[1] B 257. We could not, in my opinion and I believe in the opinion of Kant, say (on the basis of sense-perception in abstraction from thought) even that the series was reversible. We could say only that it took place in the order in which it did take place, and even this would require some element of thought.

[2] Here again this is just what we can, and must, say, if we *presuppose* that in sense-perception states of objects are given to us. This, however, is a presupposition of *thought*, to which alone is to be ascribed the concept of an object in general.

[3] When we regard given ideas as appearances of an object, we are employing the category of substance and accident, and this cannot be given in mere apprehension.

[4] This seems to be borne out by the fact that Kant begins his next sentence by saying that *consequently* a pure concept of the understanding is required; but he complicates this, as so often, by adding a further reason why it is required, namely in order to say that the reciprocal succession of sense-perceptions is grounded in the object.

If this is correct, the argument is parallel to the argument of the Second Analogy. In the Second Analogy it was easy to discover the element of necessity implied or presupposed in objectivity; for if the succession we perceive is objective, then the succession of our sense-perceptions must be necessary. Here it is not so easy; but, as Kant implies,[1] when we take ourselves to have an experience of coexistent objects, *we assume that the objects must coexist in order that the reciprocal succession of our sense-perceptions may be possible*. I take this to mean only that *we assume the reciprocal succession of our sense-perceptions to be necessarily grounded in, or conditioned by, the coexistence of objects*.[2]

Such an assumption cannot be based on mere sense-perception (which can never give us necessity); nor can it be based on a perception of absolute time (since we have no such perception).

IV. Kant then proceeds to assert that we consequently require a certain concept of the understanding *in order to say*

[1] I think this is implied; for the failure of apprehension to show that the objects *must* coexist (in order that the reciprocal succession of our sense-perceptions may be possible) seems to be his justification for affirming the presence of the category of interaction in experience.

[2] Kant cannot mean, at this stage of the argument, that the objects themselves coexist necessarily, or that the coexistence of the objects (or of their states) is determined by a necessary law.

I interpret Kant's statement in this way, both because this seems to be implied by the following sentence, and because, if interpreted as asserting more than this, the statement, taken on the level of common sense, would be manifestly false. This is clear enough, if we think of objects as things-in-themselves. Consider first the case of objective succession on that hypothesis. We can say that if we are perceiving events, or if the succession of our sense-perceptions is necessary, there must be succession in the objects; but it would be ludicrous to infer from this that we knew the actual succession in the objects to be a necessary succession, that is, one determined by causal law. All that is necessary is a matter-of-fact succession in the objects and nothing more. Similarly (on the same hypothesis) we can say that if there can be a reciprocal succession in our sense-perceptions, there must be coexistence in the objects; but it would be idle to pretend, on such grounds, that we knew this coexistence to be necessary in the sense of being determined by a necessary law.

that the reciprocal succession of sense-perceptions is grounded in the object[1] *and in this way to know that the coexistence is objective.*[2]

Let us leave over for the moment the nature of this concept, and consider only the purpose for which it is required. This purpose seems to be merely a variation of what has already been said: we have to justify our assumption (which cannot be derived from mere apprehension) that the objects must necessarily coexist if the reciprocal succession of our sense-perceptions of these objects is to be possible. We are considering the question now from the side of the reciprocal succession of our sense-perceptions; and we are asserting that where the order of our sense-perceptions is taken to be reversible, we say or assume that this reversibility must have its ground in the coexistence of the objects perceived. This seems to me to be true; according to Kant it can be justified only in virtue of a certain concept of the understanding.[3]

V. We now come to the crux of Kant's argument. If we are to justify the common-sense assumptions which we all make, *we require a pure concept of the understanding, a concept of the*

[1] We should expect him to say 'objects' (or 'coexistence of the objects'), unless he means merely 'objectively grounded'. Compare A 214 = B 261, where a subjective succession is said to rest on an objective ground, and this in turn is equated with 'being referred to appearances as substances'.

[2] '*und das Zugleichsein dadurch als objektiv vorzustellen.*'

[3] In the Second Analogy Kant maintains that if there is an objective succession perceived, the subjective succession of our sense-perceptions must be irreversible; and if the subjective succession of our sense-perceptions is irreversible, there must be an objective succession perceived. In the Third Analogy he maintains that if the objects perceived coexist, the subjective succession must be reversible; and if the subjective succession is reversible, then the objects perceived must coexist. None of these statements has any meaning except on the assumption that what we perceive is an object or permanent substance; but if we accept this assumption, together with the view that a permanent substance is not a thing-in-itself, we require the category of causality to justify our assumptions in the Second Analogy, and we require the category of interaction to justify our assumptions in the Third Analogy. Such I take to be Kant's view in brief.

reciprocal succession of the determinations of those things which coexist outside one another in space.[1]

It will be observed that whereas previously we were concerned with a reciprocal succession of *sense-perceptions*, the succession of which Kant now speaks is a reciprocal succession of 'determinations' or 'states' of the things themselves.[2] On Professor Prichard's view this transition from sense-perceptions to states of a thing is a mere confusion. I believe on the contrary that it is a deliberate identification, and that (whether the identification be possible or not) what is present in sense-perception is, on Critical principles, the state of the object. If we take the Critical Philosophy seriously and set aside all our natural prejudices, we must recognise that for it a sense-perception is not something which lies between us and the object,[3] but is a state of the object immediately present to our minds. As Kant everywhere insists, the object is composed of such possible or actual sense-perceptions bound together in a necessary synthetic unity.[4]

The method of argument is the same as that of the Second Analogy, although less clearly expressed. Kant first of all asserts a necessity which must govern our *sense-perceptions*, if our knowledge is to be objectively valid; and then he reminds us that since our sense-perceptions are identical with the states of objects, that necessity must govern these states, if our knowledge is to be objectively valid. I need not here repeat the comments which I formerly made.[5] I would, however, again insist that all this has no meaning unless we presuppose, in accordance with the First Analogy, that in genuine percep-

---

[1] B 257. I have added 'in space', which seems to be implied. Kant himself brings in space a few lines further down. The need for a pure concept—it can hardly be too often repeated—arises because we cannot know objective coexistence by means of mere apprehension or by a perception of absolute time.

[2] It is perhaps possible that Kant considers this transition to have been already made or implied in IV above, but I do not think so.

[3] That is, it is not a so-called *Zwischending*.

[4] This necessary synthetic unity implies (among other things) that the sense-perceptions are regarded as states of a permanent substance.

[5] See Chapters XLIII § 5, IV, and XLV § 2.

tion we are immediately aware of the states of permanent substances in space. Kant's problem in the Second and Third Analogies is to determine the conditions under which our experience of succession and coexistence in the states of permanent substances can be valid, it being assumed throughout that such permanent substances are not things-in-themselves.

It is more difficult in the case of interaction to state the nature of the necessity involved,[1] when we cease to regard appearances as sense-perceptions and regard them instead as states of the objects. What we have seen is that in experience of objective coexistence we assume the reciprocal succession of our sense-perceptions to be grounded on the coexistent objects, and only so can we have knowledge of such objects. We are now reminded that the sense-perceptions (whether actual or possible) are themselves states of permanent substances, and that consequently, if our common-sense assumption is to be justified, the reciprocal succession of the *states* must be grounded on the coexistent objects.

The question then arises how we are to interpret the phrase 'reciprocal succession'. I do not think that Kant can mean by this only the succession actually perceived. When we say that there *can be* a reciprocal succession of sense-perceptions, we mean that there is a possibility *both* of the succession $a_1\, b_2\, a_3\, b_4\, \ldots$ *and* of the succession $b_1\, a_2\, b_3\, a_4.\, \ldots$ [2] We can have either succession of sense-perceptions, though we cannot have both. If we now remember that, on Critical principles, actual and possible sense-perceptions are to be regarded as states of permanent objects (or substances), we can say that there is a possibility *both* of perceiving the series of states $a_1\, \beta_2\, a_3\, \beta_4\, \ldots$ *and* of perceiving the series of states $\beta_1\, a_2\, \beta_3\, a_4.\, \ldots$ We can perceive either series, but not both together.

I take it that when Kant asserts the reciprocal succession of

[1] Kant's own statement quoted above is too vague, and must be supplemented in the light of what follows.

[2] There is a possibility of taking the a's and b's in any order we please, for example, $a_1\, b_2\, b_3\, a_4\, \ldots$, but this we may ignore. It is assumed in this notation that a_1 and b_1 are simultaneous.

sense-perceptions to be grounded in the coexistent objects, he has in mind both the possible successions of sense-perceptions. Similarly when he speaks of the reciprocal succession of the states of things coexisting outside one another in space, he must have in mind both the series $a_1 \beta_2 a_3 \beta_4 \ldots$ and the series $\beta_1 a_2 \beta_3 a_4 \ldots$. These must have their ground in the things A and B.

It seems legitimate enough to infer, as Kant appears to infer, that the whole series $a_1\beta_1 a_2\beta_2 a_3\beta_3 a_4\beta_4 \ldots$ must have its ground in the things A and B.[1] There is more difficulty in the inference that the whole series is determined by A and B *together*;[2] and that the series $a_1 a_2 a_3 a_4 \ldots$ is not determined separately by A, nor the series $\beta_1 \beta_2 \beta_3 \beta_4$ determined separately by B. I presume this is supposed to follow from the fact that the reciprocal succession of sense-perceptions (and so of states) must have its ground in the *coexistent* objects (or in the coexistence of the objects).

I confess that I should have liked to see a fuller justification of this inference. Manifestly if the objects were things-in-themselves, it would (on a common-sense view) follow from their coexistence that the order of our sense-perceptions must be reversible; but it could not follow that the states of the two coexistent objects must be determined by the two objects jointly. Kant's inference, if it is legitimate, depends on the doctrine that objects are not things-in-themselves.

Whatever we may think of this inference, Kant is clearly maintaining that coexistent objects must mutually determine one another's states, and that unless this is presupposed,

---

[1] We must remember that possible, as well as actual, sense-perceptions are to be regarded as states of objects. It is, I think, a matter of indifference whether the states $a_1 a_2 a_3 a_4$ have the same degree or a different degree of the quality a, and whether the states $\beta_1 \beta_2 \beta_3 \beta_4$ have the same degree or a different degree of the quality β. When the degree is the same, we have a continuance of the objects in the same state—the case of the earth and the moon. Where the degree is different, we have a change in the states of the objects—the case of the fire and ice.

[2] The exact significance of this must be considered later; see Chapter XLVIII § 4.

we could not *know* that the order of our sense-perceptions must be reversible, and we could not *know* that the objects coexist. The doctrine stated is a necessary presupposition of our *experience* of objective coexistence, provided we accept the view that objects are possible and actual sense-perceptions (or ideas) combined together in necessary synthetic unity. If we suppose that objects are things-in-themselves, we could never infer from their coexistence that they must necessarily interact.

Such is Kant's argument. Its difficulty is obvious, but before we reject it, we must be sure that we are not rejecting it on the basis of an unconscious transcendental realism. Kant is entitled to have his argument evaluated—at least in the first instance—on the basis of his own presuppositions.

VI. The rest of the argument offers no difficulty. The concept which Kant has asserted to be necessary is a concept of the relation of substances, in which one substance[1] contains determinations or states whose ground is contained in the other. *This relation is a relation of 'influence', or of the causal action of one substance upon another. When this relation of influence is mutual or reciprocal,*[2] *as Kant has argued that it is, the concept of the relation is the concept of communion or interaction.*

VII. *The concept of interaction is therefore a necessary condition of our experience of objective coexistence.*

VIII. *It is therefore a necessary condition of all objects of experience, so far as these objects coexist.*

---

[1] The object is assumed to be a substance on the basis of the First Analogy. As we have seen, this is assumed throughout.

[2] B 258. The sentence in which this is stated seems to be corrupt, but the general sense is clear.

CHAPTER XLVIII

THE THIRD ANALOGY (*Continued*)

§ 1. *The Proof in the First Edition*

Kant's argument in the first edition[1] is of a looser texture. Curiously enough space plays a more prominent part than in the argument of the second edition. As we have seen,[2] in the interval between the two editions space was recognised by Kant to be of vital importance for the proof of substance; but apparently when the new edition was about to be published, he decided that he must rest his case primarily upon the character of time.

I. Kant asks what is the criterion or mark by which[3] one recognises the coexistence of things. His answer is 'By the fact that the order in *the synthesis of apprehension is reversible*, or (as he here says) *indifferent*'. If A, B, C, D, and E are co-existent, we can see them in any order,[4] while if they occur successively, we can see them only in the order in which they occur.[5]

Here although A, B, C, D and E may be 'things', they cannot be substances, for substances cannot come into existence or pass away.

II. At this stage Kant adopts the method used in the so-called indirect proof of the Second Analogy (Proof III)—he supposes that the conclusion which he wishes to prove is false. *The*

---

[1] A 211 = B 258 ff. (three paragraphs).

[2] See Chapter XLII § 3.

[3] '*Woran*' not '*wie*'. Compare the ordinary German idiom '*Woran erkennen Sie ihn?*' ('By what do you recognise him?').

[4] It is also true that if we can see A, B, C, D, and E in any order, they must be coexistent.

[5] Note that the inference is, in this case, from the fact that the succession is objective to necessity in the order of apprehension, and not *vice versa*. It should also be noted that what belongs to past time cannot be 'apprehended' in the technical sense of 'apprehension'.

*supposition he makes is that substances coexist without inter-
acting, and he asserts that in that case their coexistence could
not be perceived.* He still regards the substances as spatial
substances, and he suggests (without offering any reason)
that if the substances did not interact, *they would be separated
by completely empty space.*[1] If they were so separated, then—
presumably on the assumption that our apprehensions of them
must always be successive—we could recognise that the
appearances perceived existed at the time we perceived them,
but we could not decide whether the appearances[2] (considered
as appearances of objects) were themselves successive or
co-existent.[3]

Kant does not explain why on such a hypothesis we could
not distinguish objective coexistence from objective succession;
nor does he explain whether this is obvious on the basis of
ordinary experience (or contemporary science), or whether it
is obvious only on Critical presuppositions. His conclusion,
however, seems in any case to follow directly from the

---

[1] Perhaps he is assuming that they are separated in space (for if they
were combined in space they would be one substance). If the substances
so separated interact, then apparently the intervening space is filled—
one would like to be told with what (compare § 2 below). If they do
not interact, the intervening space is empty.

[2] Here Kant seems to be thinking of a series of states of substance
such as constitutes a thing or an object. It appears to be irrelevant
whether such a series is composed of states that are qualitatively
different or qualitatively alike.

[3] Kant's conclusion would follow from the fact that we cannot
perceive absolute time and that the synthesis of apprehension by itself
(as always successive) cannot give us either objective succession or
objective coexistence. Furthermore there is no possibility of knowing
that the succession of our sense-perceptions is reversible (or irreversible), unless we take these sense-perceptions to be states of
permanent substances; and permanent substances fill space by their
matter (their powers of repulsion and attraction); but the peculiarity
of the present argument is that Kant appears to rest his conclusion
solely on the assumption that apart from interaction substances would
be separated by empty space. I presume that the conclusion is supposed
to follow from this assumption because empty space cannot be perceived and the chain of our sense-perceptions would be interrupted;
compare A 213–14 = B 260–1.

general account of apprehension with which we are now familiar.

III. Since, however, we do distinguish objective coexistence from objective succession,[1] there must be more in experience than mere apprehension, which (although it does indicate the existence of what is apprehended) cannot by itself make this distinction.[2] *In addition to the bare existence of A and B* (which we know through apprehension[3]) *there must be something through which A determines B's position in time and B reciprocally determines A's position in time.*[4] Only so can we have empirical knowledge that A and B coexist.[5]

The difficulty here is to know in what sense A and B 'determine' each other's position in time. If we are to know that A and B coexist, the position of A must be determined relatively to B and the position of B relatively to A. Consequently their relative position is, I take it, on Kant's view *necessarily* determined[6]—in the sense that it is not imaginary or arbitrary: we cannot regard A and B as other than coexistent. This again implies that they necessarily coexist, since they are not things–in–themselves, but only appearances to us. Objective coexistence must, for Kant, be necessary coexistence; but it is not easy to decide whether he is saying this or something more in the present passage. We have to remember that in the case of objective succession, although the succession must be

---

[1] This is clearly the supposition on which Kant's argument rests.

[2] This depends on the supposition that apprehension is always successive. See Chapter XLII § 1.

[3] This is implied in what precedes, though strictly speaking we require more than apprehension if we are to know the existence of an object (as opposed to a mere idea).

[4] This 'something' is not absolute time, *for absolute time cannot be perceived*; compare A 200 = B 245. This important qualification is here omitted by Kant, no doubt because, after having repeated it so many times, he expects it to be understood.

[5] At this point Kant speaks of A and B as substances, but when he speaks of them as coexisting, he clearly means, not coexisting as substances (for all substances coexist), but coexisting as *substances in the possession of certain perceivable determinations*, coexisting, for example, as earth and moon.   [6] Compare B 234.

necessarily determined, it is the cause which determines the effect, not the effect which determines the cause.[1] In the case of objective coexistence does he wish to assert, not only that the coexistence is necessarily determined, but that in some further sense the coexistent objects determine each other's position in time, and that this determination is in some ways analogous to the determination of effect by cause? At this stage he can scarcely intend to *identify* such temporal determination with causation; for he goes on to explain in the next sentence that such temporal determination can take place only by means of causation. If we are to distinguish, even temporarily, between determination of position in time and causal action, I cannot see that A and B determine each other's position in time except in the sense that their coexistence is taken to be necessary.[2]

IV. *Now when one thing determines the position of another in time, it can do so only by being the cause of that thing, or of the determinations of that thing.*[3]

It is on this assertion that the whole argument of the first edition turns. It deserves—to say the least—a fuller discussion than it receives.

The principle appears to be stated quite generally: it is not restricted to the case of coexistence. The difficulty, as before, concerns the meaning to be attached to 'determining the position of another thing in time'. If we take this to *mean* 'causing' or 'acting causally upon', the statement is tautologous.

[1] B 234, A 194 = B 239, A 199 = B 244. Even as regards parts of time, it is the earlier time which determines the later (in the sense that we can get to the later only through the earlier); see A 199 = B 244.

[2] If Kant does intend to identify 'determining position in time' with 'causing', what is the ground for saying that coexistent objects must act causally on one another? No doubt if A affects and is affected by B, then A and B must be coexistent. But it is quite another thing to say that if they are coexistent, each must affect, and be affected by, the other.

[3] What Kant himself says is this: 'Now only that which is the cause of another thing or of its determinations determines the position of the other thing in time'.

If Kant means by it merely that the temporal position of one thing is determined relatively to the position of another, then the inference to causality seems to be invalid. If we consider two successive events X and Y, their position relatively to one another may be determined, and indeed necessarily determined, without X being the cause of Y. If the succession XY is objective and therefore necessary, then according to Kant it is causally determined; but the fact that it is causally determined need not mean that X is the cause of Y, for Y may be caused by something else. Similarly, one would imagine, we might hold that A and B can coexist only if their coexistence is necessary and so is causally determined; but the fact that it is causally determined need not imply that A and B must act causally on one another.

If Kant's argument rests on what he has proved in the Second Analogy, then his conclusion does not follow. Even if we could get over this, there is still a further difficulty. The Second Analogy dealt with objective succession, whereas here we are concerned with objective coexistence, and coexistence seems, at any rate at first sight, to be incompatible with causation; for the effect must succeed the cause. We may perhaps be able to avoid this difficulty by maintaining that the transition between cause and effect is continuous, and that there is no interval of time between them;[1] but at the very least the question ought to have been raised, especially as the causality with which we are here concerned is reciprocal causality.

Perhaps Kant does not mean to state his principle generally and is concerned only with things which coexist, and whose position in time must therefore be determined relatively to each other. He appears to hold that our experience of such coexistence presupposes the coexistence to be necessary,[2] or presupposes that this relative determination is necessary

---

[1] A 203 = B 248. Compare § 4 below.

[2] This is supposed to hold only on the supposition (1) that objects are not things-in-themselves, (2) that experience is more than arbitrary imagination or immediate sense-perception, and (3) that we have no direct perception of absolute time.

determination. If so, we have established the schema[1] which entitles us to apply the category of reciprocal causality or interaction. But this contention is much more complicated than the similar contention in regard to cause and effect, and a fuller discussion of its grounds and implications would have been of immense advantage.

V. One substance cannot be the cause of another substance; for no substance comes into being, but is permanent. Hence if one substance acts causally on another, it can be the cause only of the *determinations* or states of the substance on which it acts.[2]

VI. Therefore (1) if A and B are two substances known to coexist (in the sense that each of them is in a certain state, or series of states, during the same period of time), (2) if knowledge of such coexistence is possible only on the presupposition that A determines B's position in time and B determines A's position in time, and (3) if such determination must be causal determination—then *each substance must contain in itself the causality of certain determinations in the other, and also certain effects of the causality of that other*.[3]

This sums up the whole argument of the first edition. We may put the conclusion more simply by saying that *the two substances must stand in dynamic interaction (whether immediately or mediately)*[4], *if their coexistence is to be known in any possible experience*.

VII. The rest of the argument is only the common form by which all Kant's Critical arguments can be ended. The condition

---

[1] This schema is described as the coexistence of the determinations of one substance with those of the other *in accordance with a universal rule*; see A 144 = B 183–4.

[2] It is of course not the only cause of these determinations, but it may be the principal cause, as when the fire causes the ice to melt.

[3] We could, I think, say more simply that each substance must cause certain states in the other and that each substance must have certain of its own states caused by the other.

[4] Kant gives some indication later of the meaning of the clause in brackets, which by itself is obscure. Compare § 4 below.

of experience is necessarily the condition of objects of experience, and therefore substances can coexist only if they interact.

§ 2. *Interaction and Sense-Perception*

In accordance with his usual method Kant adds two further paragraphs to the proof. These are commonly regarded as two additional and independent proofs. The first paragraph[1] seems to me to be merely an appendix, which seeks to find confirmation of the theory of interaction in the ordinary facts of sense-perception. The second paragraph[2] has more claim to be considered as an independent proof, but Kant himself says that it is meant to elucidate what he has already said.[3] It should be regarded as, at the most, a supplementary statement of the original proof, intended to bring out points not made sufficiently clear.

Kant begins by explaining that he uses the German word '*Gemeinschaft*' in the sense of '*commercium*' (dynamical communion or interaction), and not in the sense of '*communio*' (mere togetherness in space); and he asserts that togetherness in space could not be empirically known apart from interaction.[4]

For confirmation of this assertion he appeals to the facts of sense-perception as revealed by empirical psychology.

---

[1] A 213–14 = B 260–1.   [2] A 214–15 = B 261–2.

[3] '*Zur Erläuterung kann folgendes dienen.*'

[4] When Professor Prichard says (*Kant's Theory of Knowledge*, p. 307) that 'the apprehension of a body in space in itself involves the apprehension that it exists together with all other bodies in space', he is (1) using the word 'apprehension' in a non-Kantian sense, for however loose may be Kant's use of 'apprehension', it is never taken, as here, to mean *a priori* knowledge of what is not directly present to the senses; (2) he is using the word 'body' as equivalent to 'substance' (which in strict parlance should be avoided); and (3) he is treating 'togetherness' in space as something quite general, whereas Kant is thinking of it as involving a definite position in space of one body relatively to other bodies. It is in the latter sense that Kant maintains we cannot have *empirical* knowledge of togetherness in space (or coexistence in time) apart from interaction.

In one of his long and complicated sentences he propounds a variety of theories whose meaning and interconnexion is not altogether clear.

(1) Only continuous '*influences*' in all parts of space can lead our senses from one body to another; (2) *light*, which plays between our eye and the heavenly bodies, causes a mediate interaction[1] between us and them, and thereby establishes their coexistence; (3) we cannot change our position empirically, or rather we cannot be empirically aware of our changes of position, unless *matter* everywhere makes perception of our position possible; and (4) it is only through their reciprocal influence (or interaction) that the parts of matter in different places can exhibit their coexistence,[2] and so exhibit (although only mediately) the coexistence[3] of the most remote objects.

All this is difficult. It has been suggested or implied by Kant that if substances did not interact, the space between them would be completely empty.[4] We are now given some hints as to what does fill space, and this appears to be identified (1) with continuous 'influences', (2) with light, and (3) with matter. A possible conclusion would seem to be that when space is filled with 'continuous influences', it is filled with 'matter in interaction', one example of which is light. This accords with the theory that 'what fills space' is matter.

[1] '*Gemeinschaft*', in view of the previous sentence, must be interpreted as equivalent to '*commercium*' or 'interaction'.

[2] '*Zugleichsein*' (translated by Kemp Smith as 'simultaneous existence').

[3] '*Koexistenz*' (translated by Kemp Smith as 'coexistence'). I presume that there is no difference in sense between '*Zugleichsein*' (the word usually used by Kant) and '*Koexistenz*' (which is only the Latin translation). The sentence is obscure; but I do not think Kant is suggesting that the parts of matter establish their 'simultaneous existence' by interaction and thereby establish their 'coexistence', as if these two things were different. Nor can I see what he does mean, unless he means that the parts of matter actually perceived establish their coexistence through interaction with one another and with our bodies, and thereby establish the coexistence of remote objects which we do not perceive, although only mediately through their interaction with the bodies we do perceive.

[4] See A 212 = B 259 and § 1, II, above.

Furthermore we have the doctrine (based on empirical evidence) that sense-perception involves interaction between our bodies and the bodies perceived,[1] and that remote bodies interact with our bodies *mediately* through their interaction with the intervening matter.[2] Hence sense-perception is possible only because all parts of matter (and therefore all substances) are in interaction.

These statements seem to me to be meant not as a proof, but as an illustration, or perhaps a confirmation, of the doctrine of interaction.

Kant goes on to maintain that without interaction every sense-perception of spatial objects would be broken off from every other, and the chain of ideas which constitutes experience would have to begin afresh with every new object.[3] It would in fact cease to be a chain; for every link in it would lack connexion with previous links, and so would fail to stand in time-relations at all.[4] He adds that he does not profess to refute the possibility of empty space by this doctrine, but only to show that it can be no object of experience.[5]

[1] This doctrine is here stated without the slightest element of ambiguity—especially in what is said about light and the eye—and I believe with Adickes that it is an essential part of the Critical Philosophy. Compare *Metaphysik*, p. 111 and also p. 77.

[2] We can say that the intervening space is filled with continuous influences, if the causal action of a body is transmitted from one part of matter to another until it affects our sense-organs. I take it that the ether would be regarded as matter on this view.

[3] I take this to rest on the view that if substances did not interact, they would be separated by an empty space which we could not perceive; compare A 212 = B 258–9.

[4] We must, I think, take this to mean objective time-relations. This would be obvious on Kant's theory, because apart from interaction we should be unable to distinguish objective coexistence from objective succession.

[5] Compare Chapter XXXVIII § 8. Kant always displays a proper caution in his attitude to the mechanical theory of 'atoms and the void'. All that he maintains is that it cannot be established by empirical evidence, but is a metaphysical assumption of a highly doubtful kind.

§ 3. *Interaction and the Unity of Apperception*

Kant's final 'elucidation'[1] of his position brings in the doctrine of apperception, upon which all the Critical proofs necessarily rest.[2]

All appearances, as contained in one possible experience, must be combined under the unity of apperception. This— the central doctrine of the Transcendental Deduction—is here expressed in an unusual form, for Kant says that all appearances must stand in communion of apperception.[3] This might perhaps mean that all appearances are parts of a whole which mutually exclude and determine one another, and so are subject to the pure category (as opposed to the schematised category) of communion. But it seems more likely to mean merely that they must possess that necessary synthetic unity which is implied in the unity of apperception and articulated in the whole scheme of categories.

Hitherto Kant has been speaking of all appearances (so far as they are combined by thought into objects). He now proceeds to deal with objects which are combined by thought in a special way—namely, as standing to one another in a relation of coexistence. When thought combines objects in this way (or, more simply, when we think of objects as coexisting), the objects must reciprocally or mutually determine[4] their

---

[1] A 214–15 = B 261–2.

[2] Similarly the unity of apperception is referred to at the close of the section dealing with the Second Analogy. See A 210 = B 256 and compare A 216 = B 263 and A 217 = B 264.

[3] The word used is '*Gemeinschaft*' in the sense of *communio*, which, as we have seen, does not involve dynamical connexion. A *communio* of apperception seems to mean only 'togetherness' in apperception, as *communio spatii* means 'togetherness' in space. The word '*Gemeinschaft*' might here refer to the *pure* category of communion, which is the concept (of the synthesis) of a whole whose parts mutually exclude and determine one another; see Chapter XXXIII § 4. But I think we shall be on safer ground, if we interpret it in a much more general sense.

[4] Here 'determine' can scarcely mean 'causally determine'; but it is difficult to see what it does mean, unless it means that they are mutually exclusive parts of a spatial whole and that their temporal position or date is determined, not by their relation to absolute time, but by their relation to one another. The same kind of difficulty was encountered in A 212 = B 259—see § 1, III, above.

position in one time, so as to constitute a whole. This is a particular kind of *subjective* communion,[1] in the sense that it exists for thought.

If this subjective communion (or the togetherness of appearances at one time as a whole for thought) is to rest on an objective ground, if in other words the appearances thought of as together in one time are to be regarded as coexistent objects in space[2] (and not merely as combined together in one time by an arbitrary act of the mind),[3] there is necessary a certain condition, which Kant goes on to state. *The sense-perception of one of the coexistent objects[4] must, as a ground, make possible the sense-perception of the others[5] and* vice versa. Only on this condition can we avoid attributing to the objects the succession which is always present in our sense-perceptions (considered, not as states of an object, but as elements in our successive apprehension); and only on this condition can we say that the objects coexist.

The whole argument turns on the 'condition' which I have put in italics, but unfortunately the interpretation of Kant's

[1] '*Gemeinschaft.*' *All* 'togetherness' for thought has been called communion, which as existing for thought is so far subjective. Here we are dealing with the *special* case where togetherness for thought is togetherness in one part of time. Kant does not mean by this merely that we *think* of them together at one time, but that we think of them as-being-together-at-one-time. He probably means also—although he does not say so—that we think of them as-being-together-in-one-space-at-one-time.

[2] Kant's own expression is 'If this subjective communion is to rest on an objective ground or be referred to phenomenal substances'. Here again he seems to be thinking of *substances* as coexisting, but by 'coexisting' he means 'being in a certain *state* during the same period or part of time.' We might say: '*If the objects thought of as together are to be regarded as coexisting substances*', provided we understand 'coexisting' in the sense I have explained.

[3] Such an act would be an act of imagination rather than of thought, for thought always involves assertion of an object; but this side of thought Kant has here so far ignored.

[4] Or coexisting substances in the sense suggested in the last note but one.

[5] The plural seems the most natural interpretation of '*der anderen*' here, but it may be singular, as Kemp Smith takes it. This certainly gives the simpler case.

statement is perhaps even more difficult than usual. I take what Kant calls the 'ground' to be equivalent to 'cause'. One sense-perception considered as an element in our apprehension can hardly be the cause of another, so we must assume that the sense-perceptions in question are to be regarded as states of an object. Even so there is still an element of uncertainty. If we take the simple case of two objects A and B with states a_1 a_2 a_3 a_4 . . . and β_1 β_2 β_3 β_4 . . ., does Kant mean that a_1 must be the partial cause of β_2, β_2 must be the partial cause of a_3, a_3 must be the partial cause of β_4, and so on? Or does he mean that the two simultaneous states a_1 and β_1 are related to one another partly as cause and partly as effect?[1]

The two interpretations may not in the end be so different as they look at first sight, but the second one seems to be the most natural way of taking Kant's words. In either case we have at every moment the reciprocal causality of coexistent substances;[2] and in either case we have to face great difficulties in the argument.

In the first case, while the objects are coexistent, the states which are causally connected are successive;[3] and the causality of the states is reciprocal only in the sense that β_2 is partly caused by a_1, and a_2 is partly caused by β_1. Even this could not be established on the basis of the Second Analogy; for the Second Analogy professes to prove only that the succession $a_1 \beta_2$ must be causally determined, not that a_1 must be the cause of β_2. We must have a new argument resting, not on succession, but on simultaneity, and unless we have such an argument, Kant's conclusion seems unjustifiable.

[1] The fact that a_1 and β_1 cannot be perceived simultaneously does not exclude this interpretation, since for Kant the states of an object are not only actual, but also possible, sense-perceptions.

[2] In the first case not only is β_2 the joint product of a_1 and β_1, but also a_2 is the joint product of β_1 and a_1: we are not confined to the states which we actually perceive, but are concerned also with the states which *ex hypothesi* we could have perceived. I am assuming that a substance 'acts' as a cause in virtue of its states.

[3] Even this is true only where the objects are changing, as in the case of the fire and the ice. When the objects are unchanging, there is no objective succession in the states.

This suggests that we must accept the second interpretation, which seems in any case to be the more natural. If so, the relation of reciprocal causality must hold, not only between coexistent substances, but also between simultaneous states of these substances. Our *actual* sense-perceptions are always in a succession, and even if we regard them as states of an object, they cannot be in a reciprocal relation of cause and effect. Kant must have in mind the *possible*, as well as the actual, sense-perceptions; and he appears to be saying that if we are to perceive two objects A and B as coexistent in space, we must presuppose that the simultaneous states a_1 and β_1 are in a relation of reciprocal causality, and so too with a_2 and β_2, and with a_3 and β_3. Only so can a reversible series of states, which we take up successively in apprehension,[1] be regarded as revealing coexistent objects.

What is the reason for Kant's assertion? We must assume that the simultaneous states cannot be perceived together,[2] and also that we cannot perceive an absolute time in reference to which each perceived state could be dated.[3] If so, the simultaneity of states can be *objectively* determined only if it is *necessarily* determined; or in other words we can claim to know that the states are simultaneous in the object only on the presupposition that they are necessarily simultaneous. This seems to be a particular case of Kant's more general principle that the temporal position of states relatively to one another can be objectively determined only if it is necessarily determined; but he appears to assume that because we are here concerned with necessary simultaneity (and not with necessary succession), the necessity must, so to speak, work equally in

---

[1] We take up, for example $a_1 \beta_2 a_3 \beta_4 \ldots$, but if the series is reversible we could equally take up $\beta_1 a_2 \beta_3 a_4 \ldots$. If so, it seems legitimate to hold that a_1 and β_1 are simultaneous. Compare reciprocal succession in Chapter XLVII § 3, V.

[2] Even if they could, there would still, I think, be a question whether the states were simultaneous in the objects.

[3] If this could be done, presumably we should be entitled to fill in the gaps, that is, to assume, on the ground of continuity, the existence and character of the states which we had not perceived.

both directions (and not in one direction only). At any rate, just as objective succession must be necessary succession, so objective simultaneity must be necessary simultaneity; and just as we are entitled to apply the schematised category of cause and effect where we find necessary succession, so, Kant appears to hold, we are entitled to apply the schematised category of interaction where we find necessary simultaneity. Without this presupposition the *empirical* relation of coexistence cannot be met with in experience.[1]

This argument, if correctly interpreted, is full of difficulty, and even its conclusion raises serious problems. It suggests that not only must coexistent *things* mutually determine the simultaneous states of one another, but that the simultaneous *states* must themselves mutually determine one another in the sense of being reciprocally cause and effect—a relation which many philosophers since Schopenhauer have maintained to be impossible. Clearly if there is interaction between simultaneous states, there is interaction between coexistent substances, as Kant immediately goes on to assert.[2] It is not so clear that interaction between coexistent substances implies a relation of interaction (or reciprocal causality) between their simultaneous states.

There is a further manifest difficulty in the conclusion. Even if we accepted this doctrine in the case of a fire melting

---

[1] A 214-15 = B 261. I take 'coexistence' here to be the coexistence of substances or things, which of course implies that they must have simultaneous states.

[2] A 214-15 = B 261. Kant speaks of a reciprocal influence or real *commercium* of substances. He adds that this *commercium* makes the appearances a *compositum reale*. A *compositum* is a whole which is possible only through its parts: it is opposed to a *totum*, where the parts are possible only in the whole (A 438 = B 466). This accords with the statement (A 218 n. = B 265 n.) that the unity of the world whole is a mere consequence of the tacitly assumed principle of inter-action. A *compositum reale* is opposed to a *compositum ideale*, such, for example, as space would be, if it were not, strictly speaking, a *totum*; see A 438 = B 466.

'*Compositio*' in B 201 n. is used in a different sense; for it concerns the synthesis of the homogeneous manifold only.

ice,[1] there seem to be other cases where it does not apply. When I look at the earth and then at the moon, I do not assume that the colour or brightness or shape or size which I see in the one is the cause of the colour or brightness or shape or size which I see in the other. It is not possible to regard every perceived state of a substance as causing and caused by all simultaneous states of another substance—at any rate if we are concerned with principal causes. The states with which Kant is concerned appear to be states of motion or of moving forces, states in virtue of which matter, and so substance, may be said to fill space. If so, the doctrine requires a more detailed exposition than it receives.

§ 4. *Interaction and Coexistence*

I do not think it can reasonably be doubted that the concept of interaction is the most fundamental concept of science. Scientific laws are not expressed in the form 'A is the cause of B', but in the form of equations;[2] and the world as known to science is not a series of causal successions parallel to, and independent of, one another, but is rather a *system* of functional relations between measurable quantities.[3] Kant's description of the concept of interaction in terms of 'substance' and 'cause' may be antiquated; but I imagine that it could be restated in more modern terms, or at least that the concept which must take its place will be regarded by the future historian of science as in the direct line of evolution from the concept described by Kant.

If we look at the question from the standpoint of Kant's own period, it seems clear enough that the isolated concepts

[1] Even this is perhaps a case of mediate interaction, if it takes time for the heat of the fire to reach the ice. Gravitation is presumably a case of immediate interaction.

[2] For example, the law of gravitation, of which Kant is thinking, is expressed in the equation

$$F = k \frac{m_1 m_2}{d^2}$$

[3] Compare Schlick, *University of California Publications*, Vol. 15, p. 111.

of substance and causation require to be combined into the concept of interaction between substances, and that by such combination we have a new and independent concept. Indeed had the argument not been so complicated, there would have been only one Principle of the Analogies—the Principle of Interaction—just as there is only one Principle of the Axioms and one Principle of the Anticipations.

A knowledge of eighteenth-century science would, I think, help to make clear much that seems to be obscure in Kant's exposition—notably the empirical examples which he gives at the conclusion of the argument in the first edition.[1] Lacking such knowledge, I am compelled to make my criticisms in a way that may be naïve. I can only hope that for this very reason they may be useful to those whose ignorance in these matters is as great as my own.

As we have seen, Kant generally speaks of interaction as taking place between coexistent substances; but he is concerned primarily with the substances of which we have empirical knowledge, substances whose accidents remain relatively constant so that they can be spoken of as 'things' (like the earth and the moon). Coexistent substances in this sense are said to be cordinated in such a way that each is simultaneously and reciprocally a cause in relation to the determinations or states of the other.[2] Such a description appears to be justified in Professor Prichard's example of the fire and the ice, or again in Kant's own example of the parts of a body which reciprocally attract and repel one another.[3] We know that for Kant substances are 'the first subject' of all causality,[4] and that 'action' is a sufficient empirical criterion of substantiality.[5] Every substance must contain in itself the 'causality' of certain determinations in the other substance, and at the same time the effects of the causality of that other.[6] The reciprocal causality of coexistent substances in respect of their determinations is clearly implied

---

[1] A 213 = B 260.   [2] See B 112.
[3] See B 112. It should be remembered that all parts of a body are themselves substances.   [4] A 205 = B 251.
[5] A 205 = B 250.   [6] A 212 = B 259.

in all such phrases as 'dynamical communion', 'interaction', '*commercium*', and 'reciprocal influence'. On this point I have no doubt at all.

Without enquiring closely into the nature of the causality exercised by substances we may, I think, say that a substance exercises causality in virtue of its accidents or states.[1] I presume that we have to discover empirically the state of a substance in virtue of which it exercises causality upon the state of another substance. This is always Kant's view in regard to particular applications of the principle of causality; and manifestly (if we are concerned with principal causes) we cannot take one state of a substance at random, and say that in virtue of this state the substance exercises causality upon all the states of other coexisting substances. It is not, for example, in virtue of its shape or colour that fire reduces the temperature of ice.[2]

If we take the simple case when two substances A and B interact in virtue of their states α and β, we may suggest that on Kant's view α_2 is caused by β_1 and α_1 jointly, and similarly β_2 is caused by α_1 and β_1 jointly.[3]

This appears to be a plausible interpretation of Kant's doctrine. Nevertheless the question arises whether he does not mean more than this. On this view it might be said that in the

[1] Kant, I think, is primarily concerned with the 'moving forces' in virtue of which matter fills space—particularly those of attraction and repulsion.

[2] I do not mean to deny that a substance may exercise causality in regard to all the states of coexisting substances—perhaps Kant holds that it does. But clearly there is, so to speak, a main line of causation. The heat of the fire causes the ice to melt, and thereby it may cause the ice to change its colour and shape; but although the colour and shape of the fire may be connected with its heat, the colour of the fire does not cause the ice to change its colour, nor does the shape of the fire cause the ice to change its shape; and still less does the colour of the fire cause the ice to change its shape or the shape of the fire cause the ice to change its colour. I imagine that for Kant all interaction of substances is due to moving forces, but the relation of these to other qualities of substance stands in need of elucidation.

[3] I need hardly say that I am taking α_1 and β_1 to be the simultaneous states of A and B which immediately precede the stages α_2 and β_2.

coexistent substances A and B the states which are simultaneous[1]
are not in a relation of cause and effect; and on the other hand
the states which are in a relation of cause and effect are not
simultaneous, but successive. Clearly at every instant the
coexistent substances are in a relation of interaction or reciprocal
causality; for at every instant each contains in itself a state
which is partly caused by the action of the other. But does
Kant mean also that the simultaneous *states* are themselves in a
relation of reciprocal causality so that each is at once the cause
and effect of the other?[2]

If Kant holds the latter doctrine, it must be because the
action of causality is continuous.[3] The time between the
causality of the cause and its immediate effect can be a
vanishing quantity, so that cause and effect can, in a sense, be
regarded as simultaneous.[4] For this view Kant's previous

[1] By 'simultaneous' I mean 'occurring at the same instant of time'.

[2] In symbols, can we say that a_2 is partly the effect of β_2, and β_2
partly the effect of a_2?   [3] A 208 = B 254.

[4] A 203 = B 248. Let us represent the interaction of two things A
and B thus:

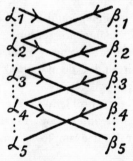

If we remember that the series $a_1 \, a_2 \, a_3 \, a_4 \, a_5 \ldots$ and the series
$\beta_1 \, \beta_2 \, \beta_3 \, \beta_4 \, \beta_5 \ldots$ are really continuous series, and if we remember
also that there is no passage of time between cause and effect, we may,
so to speak, close up the above diagram like a concertina, and in the
limiting case we seem to have something like this:

$$a_1 \longleftrightarrow \beta_1$$
$$a_2 \longleftrightarrow \beta_2$$
$$a_3 \longleftrightarrow \beta_3$$
$$a_4 \longleftrightarrow \beta_4$$
$$a_5 \longleftrightarrow \beta_5$$

discussion[1] has prepared us; but it must be remembered that although there is no interval or passage of time between cause and effect, the temporal relation or order still remains;[2] and it is difficult to reconcile this with the reciprocal causality of simultaneous states.[3] I am not prepared to say that it is impossible.

So far as I can see, the text of the Third Analogy is not conclusive on this point. There can be no doubt that Kant is primarily concerned with the reciprocal causality of coexistent substances, not with the reciprocal causality of simultaneous states. There is, I think, only one passage[4] which seems to point clearly to the latter view. Kant says that the perception of the one substance must as ground make possible the perception of the other, and *vice versa*. If we take 'perception', as I have done, to be equivalent to state of a substance, this appears to indicate that there is a relation of reciprocal causality between simultaneous states. But even here it is perhaps barely possible for him to mean only that a_1 is the ground of β_2, and β_2 the ground of a_3, although in that case it is difficult to see how this assertion could be justified.[5]

This problem, I imagine, could be settled with comparative ease in the light of eighteenth-century science and perhaps of Kant's own scientific writings.[6] I must confine myself to raising the question, and I do not think it should be really difficult to answer.

Connected with this problem is the difference between immediate and mediate interaction. Repulsion and attraction I imagine to be for Kant examples of immediate interaction,

[1] A 202–4 = B 247–9.   [2] A 203 = B 248.

[3] I do not think there is any difficulty about the reciprocal causality of coexistent substances.

[4] A 214 = B 261. It must be remembered that '*Erscheinung*' need not mean a perceived state, but may be a thing or substance. '*Wahrnehmung*' (sense-perception) might, I think, be used as equivalent to '*Erscheinung*' in this sense, but I find it difficult, or even impossible, to suppose that it is so used in this passage.

[5] Compare § 3 above.

[6] See especially for the third law of motion *M.A.d.N.* 3. *Hauptstück, Lehrsatz* 4. (IV 544 ff.).

and he may here suppose that there is reciprocal causality between simultaneous states of coexistent substances. In the case of mediate interaction there appears to be a lapse of time involved. He certainly regards light as producing a mediate communion or interaction between the heavenly bodies and the human eye;[1] and although this is a very special case, it would seem to imply that a period of time may be required for mediate interaction to take place.

In such a case, although the bodies which interact are coexistent, the determining state of the one body is not necessarily coexistent with the determined state of the other. The star may have ceased to shine before I see its light. Indeed it may be said that not even the bodies need coexist; for the star which I now see may have been broken up before I was born. If so, it is only the substances which coexist, and hence it may be thought that Kant's principle tells us nothing; for we know *a priori* that all substances coexist, since they are necessarily permanent. This criticism is not, I think, valid. Kant's principle tells us that a particular substance which had at one time the empirical characteristics of a star coexists with another substance, namely my body, in a form which, if we had sufficient knowledge, we could now describe. This remains true, even if the star has been broken up into several substances now distributed throughout space.

§ 5. *Kant's Proof of Interaction*

On the method of Kant's proof I need add little to what I have already said. The arguments in the first edition are by themselves insufficiently clear, and even the argument of the second edition leaves much to be desired. Nevertheless the

---

[1] I confess I do not understand what is the action of the human eye upon the heavenly bodies; but perhaps the following passage from Professor Broad (*Scientific Thought*, p. 172) gives some indication of what Kant means. 'When a beam of light from the sun strikes upon any surface on the earth it produces a pressure on that surface. If there be any reaction from the earth, it will be exerted primarily on the surface of the ether next to the earth, and will not be conveyed back to the sun in less time than light takes to travel between the two.'

method employed is the same as the method of the Second Analogy. Kant holds that (if it be granted that we experience objective coexistence) there is a presupposition of necessity in our sense-perceptions, and this necessity must belong to the states of the objects we perceive, provided we accept the Critical doctrine supposed to have been already established— that an object is made up of possible or actual sense-perceptions combined in a necessary synthetic unity. He is quite right in maintaining that such a proof, if it is possible at all, is possible only on Critical presuppositions. There is more danger of falling into incidental fallacies in the proof of interaction, because the concept of interaction involves greater complication than the concept of cause and effect; but the fundamental method employed would seem to be valid either in both cases or in neither. Although I feel much uncertainty as regards the details, the whole argument seems to me essentially Critical; and it is concerned, not with an alleged process by which we pass from the subjective to the objective, but with the conditions which are presupposed by our experience. I hope I have at least persuaded the reader that Kant is putting forward a novel argument with a definite meaning, and not merely deceiving himself with words.

On questions of detail I would add only two points. In the first place I do not think that Kant's argument must rest upon the doctrine that we cannot directly perceive coexisting states of bodies, but the fact that he seems to hold this view of perception is apt to arouse suspicion in his readers. Thus he does not even raise the question whether we cannot actually see the earth and the moon at the same time, as seems obvious, at least when the moon is rising or setting. In the second place Kant might have given to space a more prominent part in his argument without departing from his Critical method. He himself recognised, at any rate after the publication of the first edition, that it is space which makes interaction possible;[1] and if substance and causation are necessary to represent empirically the unity and successiveness of time, interaction

[1] See Erdmann, *Nachträge* LXXXVI.

would seem to be necessary to represent empirically the unity of space. If Kant had been living to-day, I think he would have held that interaction (which combines the concepts of substance and causality) is necessary to represent the unity of space-time.

The whole argument raises further questions which cannot be discussed here—notably the coexistence of minds or ideas and the unity of the world-whole. These questions belong to the Dialectic, and it need only be said at present (1) that since for Kant souls are not permanent substances, it looks as if our ideas must be regarded empirically as states of our bodies (which are substances) and their coexistence determined like that of any other states of substance;[1] and (2) that the unity of the world-whole is a consequence of the principle of interaction and not a presupposition of it.[2]

---

[1] This may be questioned, but it seems to me the inevitable outcome of Kant's doctrine.

[2] See A 218 n. = B 265 n., and compare A 215 = B 261-2.

BOOK XI

THE POSTULATES OF EMPIRICAL THOUGHT

CHAPTER XLIX

POSSIBILITY

§ 1. *The Principles of Possibility, Actuality, and Necessity*

Kant's account of the Postulates of Empirical Thought[1] is simpler and easier than the proofs of the Analogies. It does little more than set out in systematic form the presuppositions upon which the whole argument has hitherto proceeded. Hence it is called an 'explanation' or 'elucidation'[2] and not a 'proof'; and its business is to explain what is, in the Critical Philosophy, the meaning of the three categories of modality, namely, possibility, actuality, and necessity. Kant found it unnecessary to restate his explanation in the second edition, as he restated the proofs of the other Principles. He does, however, add a new section on the Refutation of Idealism, which will be reserved for separate consideration.[3]

The formulation of the three Postulates is as follows:

(1) *That which agrees with the formal conditions of experience (as regards intuitions and concepts) is possible.*[4]

(2) *That which is connected*[5] *with the material conditions of experience (sensation) is actual.*

(3) *That of which the connexion*[6] *with the actual is determined*

---

[1] A 218 = B 265 ff. Compare also Chapter XXXVI § 2.

[2] '*Erläuterung.*'   [3] See Chapter LI.

[4] We may put this more clearly by saying that what agrees with the formal conditions of experience, that is, *with the conditions of intuition (space and time) and with the conditions of thought (the unity of apperception and the categories)*, is possible.   [5] '*zusammenhängt.*'

[6] '*Zusammenhang.*' '*Zusammenhang*' here (and, as a verb, in the definition of actuality) is equivalent to '*Verknüpfung*', or '*nexus*', the technical term for '*connexion*'; see B 201–2 n. The word '*Verknüpfung*' is used in A 227 = B 279. The connexion spoken of is by means of the Analogies, and it seems to me a mistake to blame Kant, as Kemp Smith does (*Commentary*, p. 397), for defining actuality without reference to the Analogies. Compare the formulation in A 376: 'What is connected with a sense-perception in accordance with empirical laws is actual'. Empirical laws presuppose the Analogies.

according to universal conditions of experience is necessary (or exists necessarily).

These three statements are intended to be definitions of the possible, the actual, and the necessary, and we are entitled to convert them simply. They are concerned with *real* (and not with merely *logical*) possibility, actuality, and necessity. That is to say, they are concerned, as is indicated by the parenthesis in the Third Postulate, with possible, actual, and necessary *existence*, or with the possibility, actuality, and necessity, not of *thoughts*, but of *objects*.[1]

Hitherto we have been attempting to prove that if an object is to be an object of a spatio-temporal human experience, it must have in itself certain necessary characteristics or determinations; it must have extensive and intensive quantity, and be a substance (with changing accidents) in causal interaction with all other similar substances. Possibility, actuality, and necessity are not characteristics of objects in the same sense, and they are not contained in the concept of the object considered only in itself. Our concept of an object may be complete,[2] and yet we may still ask whether the object itself is only possible, or whether it is also actual; and if it is actual, we may ask whether it is also necessary. These questions, Kant believes, are concerned, not with the content of the object, but with its relation to our mind or with the way in which we cognise it.

---

[1] Compare *Metaphysik*, p. 28. Real possibility is agreement with the conditions of a possible experience. The connexion of a thing with experience is actuality. This connexion, so far as it can be known *a priori*, is necessity.

[2] Kant's discussion of definitions (in A 727 = B 755 ff.) suggests that completeness is never found in empirical concepts, but only in factitious and mathematical concepts. In his lectures on Logic inner completeness is attributed also to pure concepts of reason; *Log. Einl.* VIII (IX 62–3). Outer completeness (*Ausführlichkeit*) is, however, denied to these in A 728–9 = B 756–7; and if so, inner completeness should presumably be denied also. Outer (or extensive) completeness involves the clarity of the *coordinate* marks in a concept: inner (or intensive) completeness involves the clarity of the *subordinate* marks in a concept.

Just as Kant connected logical possibility, actuality, and necessity with understanding, judgement, and reason *in their logical use*;[1] so he here connects what we may call real or material possibility, actuality, and necessity[2] with understanding, judgement, and reason *in their empirical use*, that is, as applied to experience.[3] In his final summary[4] he expresses the same view without the use of these technical terms. The Postulates add to the concept of an object only the cognitive power in which it originates and has its seat. If the concept is merely in the understanding,[5] and agrees with[6] the *formal* conditions of experience, then its object is possible; if it is connected with sense-perception or sensation (that is, with the *matter* of the senses) and is determined through the senses by means of understanding,[7] then its object is actual; if it is determined through the connexion of sense-perceptions in

[1] See A 75 n. = B 100 n. See also A 130–1 = B 169 and A 304 = B 360–1 and compare Chapters IX § 2 and XXXIII § 5. The logical use is the general (or formal) use, studied by Formal Logic in abstraction from all differences in objects.

[2] That is, the possibility, actuality, and necessity of *objects*, not of *thoughts*.

[3] If an object is to be possible, it must be conceived by *understanding* in accordance with the formal conditions of experience; if it is to be actual, it must be asserted by the power of *judgement* on the basis of sense-perception; if it is to be necessary, it must be inferred by *reason* to be determined in accordance with the universal laws of experience, that is, in accordance with the Principles of the Understanding, and especially the Analogies.
It should be noted that the power of judgement (which subsumes an actual case under a concept) rests either on pure or on empirical intuition. Kant refers expressly in the present passage to the *empirical* power of judgement to show that we are concerned with empirical intuition or sense-perception.

[4] A 234 = B 286.

[5] Here taken in the narrow sense (as opposed to judgement and reason).

[6] Kant says 'is in *connexion* with' (*Verknüpfung*), but this is not the technical meaning of '*Verknüpfung*'.

[7] Here, I think, 'understanding' is that form of understanding (in the wider sense) which is called the power of judgement. The reference to understanding shows that for Kant existence is not to be found by sense apart from thought.

accordance with the categories,[1] then its object is necessary.[2] The content of the concept is the same in all these cases, but its relation to the mind is different.

It will be seen that Kant is explaining real possibility, actuality, and necessity by reference to experience. Possibility depends on the form of experience, actuality primarily on the matter of experience, and necessity on the combination of the two. His doctrine therefore differs expressly from any rationalist doctrine which maintains that by pure reason apart from experience we can know the possibility, the actuality, and even the necessity, of things.[3] In particular he is in these definitions restricting all the categories to a merely empirical use and excluding their transcendental use[4] by means of pure reason alone. The categories in their purely logical significance are, as we have so often seen, identical with the empty forms of judgement. If they are taken as concepts of an object in general, then they have 'sense and significance' only as concepts of an object of possible experience.[5] They do not give us

[1] This is the work of reason in its empirical use—I presume in seeking higher conditions for the conditioned (A 309 = B 365), although this work can never be completed. The 'concepts' of which Kant speaks are the categories.

[2] I feel some difficulty about the use of the word 'determined' in the statements about the actual and the necessary. A concept is determined, if it is related to given intuition, and intuition is determind, if it is brought under a concept. The first of these senses seems to be used as regards the actual; but as regards the necessary there must be, in addition to the determination of the concept, a determination of the object (or of its connexion with sense-perception) through the categories.

[3] Such possibility, actuality, and necessity may be called absolute, as opposed to the possibility, actuality, and necessity of Kant which is hypothetical and relative to experience; compare A 232 = B 285.

[4] See Chapters XI § 4 and LIV. If we can regard objects as possible, actual, and necessary only by reference to experience, this must apply to the objects thought by means of the categories.

[5] The categories of quantity are concerned, as we have seen in Chapter XXXIII § 5, with the synthesis of the form of intuition; the categories of quality are concerned with the synthesis of the matter of intuition; the categories of relation are concerned with the synthesis of the form and matter of intuition. We must not, however, think that there are three syntheses; for there is only one synthesis with dis-

absolute knowledge of things in-themselves; indeed as applied
to things-in-themselves they are empty.

The necessity for a discussion of the Postulates should
be manifest. Throughout the Principles an appeal has been
made to the possibility of experience, and so of objects of
experience. In the Analogies Kant has argued that the objective
or the actual, as opposed to the subjective or imaginary, must
be governed by necessity. Without some explanation of the
use of these terms, the argument would be incomplete. To
say that the Postulates are due merely to what Professor
Adickes calls Kant's '*Systematik*', and to what Professor Kemp
Smith calls Kant's 'architectonic', seems to me erroneous.[1]
Kant has shown what objects must be, if they are given to
intuition and if they exist in relation to one another in a common
space and time. He has still to show what relations they must
have to the mind which knows them.

§ 2. *The Interdependence of the Categories of Modality*

The categories of modality, like all other categories, necessarily apply to all objects of experience, so that every object
of experience is both possible, actual, and necessary. Possibility

tinguishable aspects. By supposing that there are three separate
syntheses, we take far too seriously abstractions which are necessary
only for purposes of analysis, and attribute to Kant all sorts of errors
and distortions which seem to me remote from his actual doctrine.

Perhaps it should be added that the synthesis with which a category
is concerned is always itself a formal synthesis. Whether the synthesis
deals with the form (that is, with the pure manifold) of intuition, or
whether it deals with the matter (that is, with the empirical manifold)
of intuition, or with both form and matter, the category is the concept
of the synthesis *in general* and ignores differences dependent on
differences in the given matter.

[1] Adickes in his commentary even asserts that the Postulates are
not Principles, because they do not make experience possible. The
Postulates, like other Principles, state conditions apart from which
experience is impossible; for the objects of experience must be possible,
actual, and necessary, not absolutely, but in relation to our minds.
Adickes' further objection, that men have experience without any
idea of the way in which the possible and necessary depend upon the
powers of the mind, shows a curious blindness to what Kant meant
by the *a priori* conditions of experience.

is no wider than actuality,[1] and actuality no wider than necessity. The category of necessity, like the third category in every class, combines in itself the other two categories: it combines, in short, possibility and actuality.[2]

The fact that the three categories of modality must apply to any and every object does not make it superfluous to distinguish these categories from one another; we might as well suggest that it is superfluous to distinguish any category from any other, since they must all apply (if they are to be categories at all) to any and every object. It may, however, be thought that the other categories apply to objects in virtue of distinguishable aspects in the objects, while this cannot be so in the case of the categories of modality, since they are concerned only with the different relations of the total object to the knowing mind.[3]

I do not think that this criticism is sound. We are no doubt considering the object in its relation to the mind; but Kant's whole point is surely that the object has different relations to the mind in virtue of different aspects in it which we have already discussed. Every object has a form imposed by the mind, and in virtue of that form the object is possible. Every object has a matter given to the mind and synthetised under that form; and in virtue of the matter so given and synthetised, the object is actual.[4] Finally every object is a combined whole of form and matter, which means that it is a substance whose accidents are causally determined; and in virtue of this determination the object is necessary.

---

[1] See A 231 = B 284.

[2] Compare B 111. I must confess that I still find obscure Kant's statement in this passage that necessity is simply existence which is given through possibility itself. When we infer the necessary existence of the effect from the cause, existence is given through the formal conditions of experience, but we must always start from what is actual.

[3] I think this is what Professor Kemp Smith must mean when he says (*Commentary*, p. 393) that 'one and the same definition adequately covers all three terms alike'.

[4] The matter need not be given directly, it may be inferred in virtue of known causal laws.

It is tempting to suggest[1] that the synthesis of quantity gives us the possibility of the object, the synthesis of quality its actuality, and the synthesis of relation its necessity. This has the great merit of simplicity; and it makes an object possible in virtue of its conformity to the nature of time and space, a doctrine not without a certain plausibility, Nevertheless the teaching of the Postulates is more complicated than this; for possibility is said to involve conformity with the formal conditions, not of intuition, but of experience in general; and these formal conditions (the objective form of experience in general) are said to contain all synthesis demanded for knowledge of objects.[2] This is a clear allusion to the categories, and confirms the definition of possibility in the First Postulate itself.

We must, I think, take Kant to mean that an object is possible so far as it conforms, not only to space and time, but also to the categories—that is, to all the formal conditions of experience. An object is actual so far as it is connected with the material conditions of experience, that is, with sensation. The fact that this 'connexion' must be in accordance with the categories, and in particular with the categories of relation, manifestly does not mean that the actuality of an object is the same thing as its possibility: possibility and actuality are still distinct from one another. It may, however, be maintained that there is no real difference between actuality and necessity; for when we say that an object is necessary, or exists necessarily, so far as its connexion with the actual is determined in accordance with the universal conditions of experience, we are saying no more than has already been said in our definition of the actual.

The reference to the universal conditions of experience (in distinction from the formal and material conditions) can hardly constitute the difference between actuality and necessity;

[1] I did so provisionally in Chapter XXXIII § 5. There is some support for this in A 180 = B 223, if what is called 'the synthesis of mere intuition (that is, of the form of appearance)' can be identified with the synthesis of pure intuition (which I have called above the synthesis of quantity).   [2] A 220 = B 267.

for these universal conditions appear to be only the formal
and material conditions taken together; and, as we have seen,
formal as well as material conditions are necessary to actuality.[1]
At the most the reference to universal conditions could indicate
only a difference of emphasis; when we consider an object
as actual, we emphasise the material conditions of experience,
and when we consider it as necessary we emphasise the combination of formal and material conditions. A difference of
emphasis is hardly enough to establish a distinction between
categories.

This criticism appears to me sound so far as it goes, but it
fails to notice the word 'determined'. An object possesses
actuality, if, for example, it is connected as a cause with what
is given as an effect. It does not, however, possess necessity,
except in so far as it is *determined* as the effect of a given cause.[2]
Kant's distinction is not stated too clearly, but it is there
none the less, and it is brought out in his discussion of the
Third Postulate.

The categories of modality (like those of quantity, quality,
and relation) are interdependent; but this is no reason why
we should regard them as indistinguishable.[3]

§ 3. *Thought and its Object*

If Kant had confined himself to elucidating the meaning
of the categories of modality, his exposition would have been
more simple. It would have been clear that every object must
be possible, actual, and necessary, and that the three categories
must apply to every object of experience. Kant, however,

[1] I think the reference to material *conditions* (not merely to matter)
itself indicates the presence of something else, namely form.

[2] Compare A 194 = B 239 and many other passages in the Second
Analogy.

[3] The difficult account of the schemata of modality (in A 144–5
= B 184) suggests that to know the possibility of a thing we must
know that it is at some time or other; to know its actuality we must
know that it is at a definite time; to know its necessity we must know
its relation to the whole of time (presumably by knowing the chain of
causes through which it is produced).

concerns himself also with a wider question—whether the categories of modality (and consequently all the categories) apply to objects beyond experience.

Even on Kant's view, as I have so often insisted, the pure categories have a *prima facie* claim to apply to objects beyond experience; for in themselves (as derived from the nature of understanding) they have no reference to sensuous intuition. On the ordinary rationalist view there is a still wider claim that by means of concepts we can know objects not given to sensuous experience. Such claims raise the whole question of the relation of thought to its objects. They also raise the question whether we are entitled to regard objects as possible in some sense other than that which Kant has ascribed to real possibility.

If the claim to know objects by means of concepts apart from sensuous intuition is maintained, then clearly such knowledge must be *a priori* knowledge. On Kant's view *a priori* knowledge can be justified only by reference to the forms or conditions of experience, and in particular by reference to the forms or conditions of sensuous intuition; but in connexion with the First Postulate he takes it upon himself to examine the main types of concept, and to consider whether by themselves they can give us knowledge of possible objects and so possess objective reality. This is a source of complication in his exposition.

These complications we shall discuss in due course. At present we must keep it clear in our own minds that for Kant, as I have said, possibility is no wider than actuality, and actuality is no wider than necessity. The latter contention seems to me to be established beyond a doubt by the doctrine of the Analogies, which alone is concerned with existence. It may be suggested that the former contention is more doubtful; for if we can think an object without knowing it—and Kant habitually makes this distinction—then it would seem that on his theory the sphere of possible objects must be wider than that of actual objects.

Such a suggestion would be erroneous: we cannot make

an object possible by mere thinking. I can think what I will, so long as I do not contradict myself; but in such a case although the thought is a (logically) possible thought, it does not follow that a corresponding object is (really) possible.[1] Such a thought or conception is a problematic judgement; and for Kant a problematic judgement is one in which affirmation or denial is taken as possible (optional):[2] it is accompanied by consciousness of the mere possibility of the judgement.[3] For the real possibility of the object (or the objective validity of the thought) more is required than consistent thinking.[4] The fact that we can think what we do not know does not extend the range of possible objects beyond that of actual objects.

It may be objected that a thinking or conceiving thus divorced from the affirmation of reality exists only by a kind of abstraction from our whole experience of the actual or the real. I do not see why Kant should deny this: it is his central doctrine that our concepts are empty apart from reference to the matter of intuition. Nevertheless in conception the matter given to sense can be combined in ways which we do not know to be possible, and we must still ask whether such a concept refers to a possible object. We can also entertain a concept without affirming its objective reality—this is involved in what is called 'supposing' and even in the making of hypotheses. Such supposing no doubt cannot occur independently of experience of the actual, but Kant nowhere asserts that it can.

Kant is surely right in saying that although we can conceive the existence of God and the immortality of the soul, we are not thereby entitled to assert straight away that God's existence is either possible or actual or necessary, and that the soul is possibly or actually or necessarily immortal. It may be held that these are not instances of genuine conceiving or thinking; but once we begin to distinguish genuine thinking from what

---

[1] B XXVI n.   [2] A 74 = B 100.

[3] *Log.* § 30 (IX 108–9). Compare also A 286–7 = B 343, where it is said that the concept of a noumenon (as the object of a non-sensuous intuition) is problematic, that is, is the idea of a thing of which we can neither say that it is possib'e nor that it is impossible.

[4] A 220 = B 268.

only seems to be thinking, we have to face a series of difficulties which, so far as I know, have never been satisfactorily solved. Whether Kant is using the most suitable terminology or not is a matter of minor importance. He is calling attention to a real problem, and I do not think we can put his doctrine out of court on the ground that if we know a thing to be possible, we know it to be actual and necessary.

§ 4. *The First Postulate*

The First Postulate insists that if *things* are to be possible, the *concept* of these things must agree with the formal conditions of an experience in general;[1] in other words, the concept must agree with the forms of intuition (space and time) and with the unity of apperception.

It should be noted that Kant is dealing with the possibility of *things*. Here the thing is said to be possible if its *concept* agrees with the formal conditions of experience, whereas it was implied in the original formula that the possible *thing* itself must agree with the formal conditions of experience. In this there is no contradiction; for if the concept of a thing agrees with the formal conditions of experience, the thing conceived must agree with the formal conditions of experience. When Kant attributes this agreement to the concept, he means that what is conceived (the content of the concept) must agree with the formal conditions of experience; but his language indicates that, apart from such agreement, what is conceived might be, not a thing, but a mere phantom of the mind.

Strictly speaking, the *thing* is possible, while the concept of a possible thing is said to have *objective reality* or (in the case of *a priori* concepts) transcendental truth.[2] Such is Kant's

---

[1] A 220 = B 267. Compare A 234 = B 286.

[2] A 220 = B 268 and A 221-2 = B 269. A concept has objective reality (or validity), if it refers to a possible object of experience. It has no objective reality, if it refers to a mere '*Hirngespinst*' or phantom of the mind. When Kant says that it has transcendental truth, he is thinking only of concepts whose objects are known *a priori* to be possible, as is manifest from the context. An empirical concept can have objective reality, but not transcendental truth: an *a priori* concept can have both, and if it has one, it has the other.

exact terminology, to which he adheres when he is being careful; but at times[1] he speaks of the possibility of a *concept*, implying that the concept of a possible object is itself a *possible concept*.

This more careless usage has a real disadvantage, because for Kant the possibility of a concept is mere logical possibility, and a concept is logically possible, if it is consistent with itself (whether its object is a possible object or not).[2] Nevertheless the usage is natural enough. It indicates no change of doctrine or confusion of thought; and the intelligent reader, if he were not examining Kant with great care, would probably fail to notice the difference in terminology, and would make the necessary adjustments unconsciously.[3]

§ 5. *Possibility in Relation to Different Types of Concept*

Kant recognises four types of concept.[4] There are empirical concepts, pure concepts,[5] factitious concepts, and mathematical

---

[1] E.g. in A 222 = B 269. In B XXVI n. Kant equates the real (as opposed to the logical) possibility of a concept with its objective validity.   [2] Compare B XXVI n.

[3] It is because of this carelessness of terminology that Professor Adickes in his edition charges Kant with inconsistencies which can be explained only by an application of the patchwork theory. The elaborate structure which he erects on this frail foundation—even Professor Kemp Smith (*Commentary*, p. 397) seems to have some mild qualms about it—is an admirable illustration of the fantastic lengths to which the patchwork theory has been carried.

Adickes' services to Kantian studies have been so great that one wishes to avoid harsh judgements about him of the type which he too often passed on other people. I think it can be said that he grew wiser as he grew older, though he certainly never lost the defects of his qualities. But one is sometimes tempted to say of his edition of the *Kritik* (and of his other early works) what he himself says about Simmel's Dissertation on the *Monadologia Physica* (in *Kant als Naturforscher*, p. 165 n.): 'He repeatedly charges Kant with obscurity, but the alleged obscurities have first of all been introduced by himself'.

[4] See A 727 = B 755 ff. and *Log.* §§ 3–5, and compare Chapter IX § 5.

[5] Pure concepts in the strictest sense are concepts (or categories) of the understanding—we may for the present purpose ignore the Ideas of Reason.

concepts.¹ It is necessary to consider Kant's theory of possibility in regard to all these types of concept. We must remember that for Kant to conceive an object is to hold together or synthetise different elements, and (since to conceive involves a consciousness, clear or obscure, that we are conceiving) a concept is always a concept, not only of the object, but also of the synthesis by which the different elements in the object are held together.²

I. With the possibility of objects of empirical concepts Kant is not really concerned.³ Empirical concepts are generalisations from experience, and we know that their objects are possible only because we know that they are actual.¹ As generalisations from experience, empirical concepts must inevitably conform to the formal conditions of the experience from which they are derived; but if we know that there are actual dogs in the world, we know that dogs are possible without enquiring into the relation between the concept of dog and the formal conditions of experience; and we cannot know that dogs are possible, except by knowing that they are actual.⁵

---

¹ Mathematical concepts are a kind of factitious concept, but their objects can be constructed *a priori* in pure intuition, and they are often regarded as pure concepts, although not as pure concepts of the understanding (in the strict sense).

² Compare A 220 = B 267. The synthesis thought in a non-factitious concept belongs to experience, either as borrowed from experience (empirical concepts) or as grounded on the form of experience (pure concepts). The form of experience is said to contain *every* synthesis necessary for knowing an object.

³ Nevertheless I take it, when we say that they are possible, we mean that they are possible in the sense explained by the First Postulate.

⁴ A 223 = B 270. Compare A 220 = B 267. Both of these passages show that Kant's concern is with the possibility of things known through *a priori* concepts.

⁵ Compare A 451 = B 479, where Kant asserts that if we did not know by experience that change is actual, we could never know *a priori* that it was possible.

It may be objected that we can know a dog to be possible in the sense of the First Postulate, because it is conceived as a substance and so on. Kant seems to me to deny this, and to be right in denying it. A dog, simply so far as it is a substance, must be a possible object, if a

What Kant is concerned with is the possibility of objects known independently of experience and therefore through *a priori* concepts; and his doctrine is that we cannot know such objects to be possible merely by an examination of the concepts. We must always consider whether the concept agrees with or expresses the formal conditions of experience.[1]

Under *a priori* concepts Kant seems here to include not only the categories (pure concepts in the strictest sense) and mathematical concepts (pure concepts in a looser sense), but also factitious concepts. At any rate he considers the problem of possibility in relation to all three.

II. As regards the categories, he points out that the mere possession of the concepts of substance, causality, and interaction does not by itself prove that there are possible things to which these concepts apply.[2] We know the objective reality or transcendental truth of such concepts, or in other words we know that their objects are possible, only because we know that they express *a priori* the necessary relations of sense-perceptions in every experience. We know this independently of experience (although not of course before experience); but we do not know it independently of all relation to the form of experience in general and to the synthetic unity in which alone objects can be empirically known.[3] That is to say, we know that if there is any experience at all, it must be experience of such objects; for if we grant that experience is always experience of objects which are in one time and space, and which must be conceived by one and the same mind, then we have proved (or so Kant believes) that the objects

substance is a possible object; but what we are concerned with is the possibility, not of substances in general, but of that special kind of substance which is known as a dog. Apart from experience of dogs (or of their causes or effects), we could never know that a dog was a possible object.

[1] A 223 = B 270-1. I have retained the original formula with the addition 'or expresses', since Kant regards the categories as *being* themselves formal and objective conditions of an experience in general. The categories may be said to express, as well as to agree with, such conditions.   [2] A 221 = B 268-9.   [3] A 222 = B 269.

must be permanent substances which possess changing accidents and interact causally with one another. Apart from
relation to the form of experience, that is, to time and space
and the unity of apperception, we could have no such knowledge. The same principle of course holds for the categories
of quantity and quality.[1]

III. As regards factitious concepts, there would seem to
be two main types—if we exclude mathematical concepts—
although Kant does not himself say so. All factitious concepts
are in a sense independent of experience; for the combination
of the elements thought in them is an arbitrary product of
the mind and is not found in experience itself. But in some
factitious concepts the elements combined are primarily
empirical, as when we talk of a ship's clock (Kant's own rather
surprising example[2]) or of chimaeras and centaurs. Kant seems
here to have in view mainly the factitious concepts which we make
by combining elements that are primarily *a priori*, and which
therefore have some show of being *a priori* concepts themselves.[3]

Once we have pure concepts such as substance, force,[4]
and interaction, we can use the stuff given to us in sense-
perception for the purpose of making new concepts; but the
objects so conceived are mere phantoms of the brain,[5] unless
the combination of their elements is found in actual experience.[6]
The examples given are the concept of a substance which is
permanent in space without filling space,[7] the concept of a

---

[1] Note also that we cannot know the objects thought in the categories
to be possible apart from intuition, or even apart from outer intuition;
see B 288 and B 291.　　　　　　　　　　　　　　　　　[2] A 729 = B 757.

[3] I do not mean to assert that this distinction could be philo-
sophically maintained, but only that it seems to be at the back of
Kant's mind. The same tendency is present in A 96. The examples
there given were 'spirit' and 'God'.

[4] This is connected with causality (as a 'predicable'). See
A 82 = B 108.　　　　　　　　　　　　　　　　[5] '*Hirngespinste*.'

[6] A 222 = B 269. Compare also A 729 = B 757: 'For if the concept
depends on empirical conditions (for example, a ship's clock), the
object and its *possibility* is not yet given through this arbitrary concept.'

[7] This was apparently something invented as intermediate between
matter and mind.

power[1] of foreseeing the future (and not merely predicting it by means of inference), and the concept of spiritual interaction (or some form of telepathy). Such concepts, in spite of the *a priori* character of their elements, cannot be shown, like the categories, to have possible objects on the ground that they express necessary conditions of experience. The possibility of objects of this kind must either be shown by the actual existence of these objects in experience or it cannot be shown at all. Kant believes that in these particular cases it cannot be shown at all, and the concepts are mere arbitrary combinations of thought with no claim to objective reality.[2]

We may sum up Kant's position with regard to factitious concepts by saying that (whatever be the character of the elements which are arbitrarily combined in them) they are to be treated as empirical concepts, and the possibility of their objects can be proved only by showing that such objects are experienced (directly or indirectly). Possibility in such cases is known only as an inference from actuality.

IV. The remaining case is the case of mathematical concepts, which are sometimes taken to be a special class of factitious concepts. They are arbitrary constructions of the mind and are independent of experience, but they have the special

---

[1] Kant calls it a 'ground-force' (*Grundkraft*), which is more than a mere 'power' though less than an 'action'.

[2] Kant adds, somewhat obscurely: 'As regards reality, it is obviously out of the question to think this *in concreto* without calling experience to our aid: for reality is connected only with sensation, the matter of experience, and does not concern the form of relations . . .' (A 223 = B 270). He may mean that the factitious concepts with which he has dealt are concerned with the form of relation—substances, powers, interactions. Factitious concepts which are more concrete in that they are concerned with reality or sensation—such as concepts of centaurs and chimaeras—need not be discussed; for it is obvious in their case that the mere possession of the concept does not show the thing to be possible in abstraction from actual experience. Or he may, and I think he does, mean that even in the case of the concepts discussed, since their possibility must be shown *a posteriori*, an appeal to reality is involved, and this must involve sensation and not a mere play of invented concepts.

characteristic that they can—in Kant's terminology—be constructed *a priori*, or in other words the intuition corresponding to them can be 'exhibited' *a priori*.[1] For this reason they are also described as a kind of pure concept.

There is some plausibility in the view that by simple inspection of a mathematical concept we can tell that its object is possible.[2] Even here, however, we must distinguish between the *logical* possibility of the concept, which (since it depends only on the absence of self-contradiction) can be known from the concept itself, and the *real* possibility of the object, which cannot be so known. Thus the concept of a figure enclosed by two straight lines is logically possible; for there is no logical contradiction between the concept of a figure and the concept of two straight lines and their combination.[3] But there is no corresponding object possible, for such a figure cannot be constructed in space.[4]

Even if we take a concept like that of triangle, we do not know that its object is possible merely from the fact that it can be constructed *a priori* in space. Such a construction gives us, not an object in the strict sense (for that must always have an empirical matter), but merely the form of an object.[5] Such a pseudo-object might be a mere product of the imagination, and we must have other grounds for saying *a priori* that objects such as triangles are possible objects of experience. Our real ground for asserting *a priori* the possibility of triangles is that space is a formal *a priori* condition of outer experience, and that the same figurative[6] synthesis whereby we construct a triangle *a priori* in imagination is therefore identical with the

---

[1] A 713 = B 741. Compare A 719 = B 747 and also *Log. Einl.* III and § 102 (IX 23 and 141). We can also say that their object can be 'exhibited', or 'constructed' *a priori* in intuition.

[2] A 223 = B 271.   [3] A 220 = B 268.

[4] On the supposition that space is Euclidean.

[5] A 223 = B 271. The same doctrine is expressed in B 147; compare A 156 = B 195.

[6] '*bildende.*' This is the *synthesis speciosa* (or figurative synthesis) opposed to the *synthesis intellectualis* of the concept or judgement in B 151.

synthesis exercised in the apprehension of appearances for the purpose of making, not a mathematical, but an empirical, concept of triangle.[1]

The same principle holds for the possibility of continuous quantities and indeed for quantities in general. The concepts of such quantities are known to have objective reality, not from the character of the concepts in themselves, but because they express the formal conditions of experience as found in time and space.

Kant is surely right in saying that if we take Euclidean space to be a necessary condition of human experience, we know *a priori* that triangles, squares, circles, and hyperboloids are possible objects of experience. This knowledge is independent of our having actually seen or touched figures of this kind. It rests only on our knowledge of space and our knowledge that space is a condition of experience.[2]

If there is any doubt on this matter, it must be based on the view that to know the possibility even of a mathematical figure, we must know, not only that it is compatible with the nature of space, but also that it is in accordance with the causal laws of experience. These laws might be such that nature never could produce hyperboloids (or approximations to them); and we know that it can do so only if we have actually experienced hyperboloids, or if we have experienced objects which we know to be connected with hyperboloids

---

[1] This is simply a statement of Kant's central doctrine that every empirical synthesis of apprehension (which combines the matter of intuition) is also an *a priori* synthesis of imagination (which combines the form of intuition). I think it would be more exact to say that the *a priori* synthesis is present in the empirical synthesis than to say that it is identical with it.

[2] If Euclidean space is not a necessary condition of experience, Kant's doctrine must be modified; but even so, if space-time is a necessary condition of experience, we can still say *a priori* that some concepts refer to possible objects of experience and others do not.

It may be objected that in this sense we can equally know *a priori* that chimaeras are possible objects. This is, however, true only if we take 'chimaera' to mean a body of a certain shape. It is not true, if we take 'chimaera' to mean a living organism.

either as effects or as causes. In such a case we should know
hyperboloids to be not only possible, but also actual and
even (in the last case) necessary.

There is, I think, something to be said for this view, and
it has the advantage of making the possible no wider than the
actual and necessary. Perhaps Kant would hold that if we
know a hyperboloid to be compatible with the nature of space,
we know that we could ourselves construct an actual hyperboloid, and therefore know that it is a possible object of experience.[1] The whole criticism, however, suggests that we should
concern ourselves with the possibility, not of pure mathematical
figures (which are only pseudo-objects), but of the imperfect
approximations to them in nature; and in that case the concepts
in question are empirical.[2]

Kant's doctrine is relatively simple and, I think, sound. He
is not offering us an elaborate analysis of the meaning of real
possibility, but only asking how far we can have *a priori* knowledge of the possibility of objects. He declares it futile to
imagine that because we can invent concepts which are not
self-contradictory, therefore objects corresponding to these concepts must be possible. We can say that a concept must have
possible objects only if the concept expresses the necessary
conditions of experience, either as a category or as a mathematical concept; in the case of all other concepts we can know
their objects to be possible only if we know them to be actual.
Since the categories have sense and significance only by reference to space and time, and since all mathematical concepts
depend on pure intuitions of space and time, our *a priori*
knowledge of the possibility of objects depends on the fact
that space and time are conditions of experience, and the
Leibnizian discussions in regard to possible worlds other than
the world we know are nothing but a waste of breath.

Time and space are separable from empirical intuition
only by an act of abstraction or elimination; and in a general
remark added in the second edition[3] Kant insists, not only

---

[1] The difficulty is that in that case the possible seems to be wider than
the actual.   [2] Compare A 239-40 = B 299.   [3] B 288 ff.

that we cannot comprehend the possibility of a thing by means of the mere category (apart from the reference to conditions of experience), but also that we require to have at hand an intuition, and indeed an outer intuition. I take this intuition to be empirical.[1] The reference to outer intuition is important for the Refutation of Idealism.

§ 6. *The Possibility of Experience*

I confess I should have liked Kant to explain also in this connexion how the phrase 'possible experience' is related to the present account of possibility. Can we say that experience (like an object) is possible because it agrees with the formal conditions of experience? Is the possibility ascribed to experience of the same nature as the possibility ascribed to objects?

It may be thought that the possibility of experience must be something different from the possibility ascribed to objects within experience. The subject is a difficult one, but I suggest that the close connexion between experience and its object makes it almost impossible to uphold this view of Kant's doctrine. We can know an experience to be possible only if it conforms to the formal conditions of experience which our argument professes to have established.

The difficulty of this is that it appears to involve us in a vicious circle. Are we to maintain that the categories must apply to objects because they express the conditions of a possible experience, and then to maintain that experience is possible because it (or its concept) is in conformity with the categories?

The argument would be a vicious circle, if Kant had merely asserted that as a matter of fact the categories are assumed in experience, and are therefore conditions of experience, and therefore experience is possible only through conformity to them. But this, as I have pointed out already,[2] is not his

[1] Compare A 156 = B 195, where the idea of space and time is said to be a mere schema which would have no meaning, unless the reproductive imagination called up objects of experience.

[2] Compare Chapter XXX § 5, and also Chapters XXXVI § 4 and XLV § 7.

argument at all. What Kant has maintained is that if we analyse experience into its elements, we can understand that it must involve both intuition and thought. We can understand that space and time are the necessary forms (or conditions) of intuition, not only because we can have no intuition apart from them, but also because we have *a priori* knowledge of their own nature when we eliminate the element of empirical intuition. We can also understand that the thought involved in experience must have unity (the unity of apperception), and that this unity must manifest itself in certain necessary forms (the forms of thought). Starting from these ultimate principles, he claims to have proved that the categories express the necessary conditions of experience and must apply to any and every object of experience.[1]

What Kant claims in the last resort is that experience is possible only if it is experience by one thinking mind of objects given to intuition in one time and space: all the rest of his doctrine is supposed to be derived from this. Such a view of experience, however supported by insight into the necessary character of space and time and discursive thinking, is taken to be an ultimate fact beyond which it is impossible for us to go.[2] To talk of other kinds of possible experience is empty and meaningless speculation. Other forms of intuition and thought cannot be conceived by us; and even if they could be conceived, they would not belong to our experience as the only kind of knowledge in which objects are given to us.[3] We have to do only with the synthesis by human thought and imagination of the matter given to us under the forms of space and time. The *a priori* knowledge which we possess has no claim, on Kant's view, to be knowledge of ultimate reality: it is all relative to the human experience we actually enjoy. By analysis of that experience we can discover certain conditions which have a kind of intelligible necessity in themselves and

---

[1] The pure categories are derived from the forms of thought, and their schemata are derived from the necessity of synthetising the given manifold in one space and time.

[2] B 145–6.　　　　　　　　　　[3] A 230 = B 283. Compare B 139.

in relation to experience in general. For this reason we regard them as conditions of experience, and we claim that we know experience to be possible if it conforms to these conditions. An experience which does not conform to these conditions we cannot conceive at all, and still less can we know it to be possible. From these ultimate conditions the categories are supposed to be derived; and it is not a vicious argument to assert that therefore the categories are objectively valid as expressing necessary conditions of a possible experience, and experience itself is possible only if it is in conformity with them.[1]

---

[1] By far the best discussion of Kant's use of the words 'possible', 'actual' and 'necessary' is to be found in *Kants Konzeption der Modalbegriffe* by Guido Schneeberger (Basel, 1952). This work is essential for an understanding of the *Postulates* and indeed of Kant's doctrine as a whole.

CHAPTER L

ACTUALITY AND NECESSITY

§ 1. *The Second Postulate*

The Second Postulate affirms that what is connected with the material conditions of experience (namely sensation) is actual. This means that for knowledge of the actuality[1] of things, we must have sense-perception, here explained to be sensation of which one is conscious.[2] To say this is not to say that we must have, or even that we must have had, an immediate sense-perception of the thing which we affirm to be actual. We can say that a thing is actual, if it is connected with any actual sense-perception in accordance with the Analogies. The back of the house which we do not see is as actual as the front of the house which we do see, and so are the unseen atoms of which it is composed. The example Kant himself gives[3] is a magnetic matter penetrating all bodies; and if modern science is right in asserting that protons and electrons are necessary to explain the phenomena perceived in the laboratory, then we may say that on Kant's principles such protons and electrons exist. They exist just as much as the houses and trees which we see, and they could be perceived if our senses were finer. The crudity of our senses is not to be taken as determining the form of a possible experience in general.[4]

[1] '*Wirklichkeit*.' 'Existence', it will be remembered, is the term used for the being in time of substances and their accidents, while 'reality' is the term used for the qualitative matter given in sensation. I do not think there is any essential difference between existence and actuality—Kant uses the two terms as equivalent even in the present passage—but reality, although necessary to existence, is not identical with it. There are degrees of reality, but there are no degrees of existence; for a thing either exists or does not exist.

[2] A 225 = B 272. Compare A 120, B 147, and B 160; also A 116, B 207, and A 374. Sensation must be 'taken up' into consciousness, or be 'apprehended', in order to be sense-perception.

[3] See A 226 = B 273, and compare A 492-3 = B 521.

[4] This accords with Kant's description of the possible, in which no reference is made to the limitations of our organs of sense.

Kant does not restrict existence to the present, and he believes that the cause exists just as much as the effect. Hence from the present existence of fossils we are entitled to affirm the past existence of animals now extinct. Whether Kant believes we can know existence in the future is perhaps more doubtful. He says that we can know things before perceiving them, and therefore we can know them comparatively *a priori*.[1] This may be compared with another statement[2] that if we undermine our house, we can know *a priori*, although not entirely *a priori*, that it will fall in. In the present passage, however, he may be speaking only about things at present existing which we have not yet perceived.

It must not be forgotten that this doctrine applies only to the world of appearances, and not to things-in-themselves, with reference to which 'existence' in time has no meaning. By sense-perception and thought we have before us a world of appearances spread out in infinite time and space and connected by the law of interaction. But this world is still only a world of appearances (actual and possible), as Kant is careful to remind us. With the clue of the Analogies we can pass from our actual sense-perception to the thing in the series of *possible* sense-perceptions.[3]

Kant's central contention is that unless we have a starting-point in sense-perception, we can say nothing about the existence of things. The concept of a thing contains absolutely no mark of its existence.[4] However complete the concept may be, however fully we may be able to think a thing with all its inner determinations, we can never justifiably pass from the concept to an affirmation of the existence of the thing conceived. We have seen that in some cases we can, by considering the conditions of experience, pass from the concept to the affirmation that the thing conceived is possible[5]; but nothing

---

[1] A 225 = B 273.   [2] B 2.
[3] A 226 = B 273. Compare also A 493 = B 521.
[4] A 225 = B 272.
[5] Even this we cannot do without intuition, and even outer intuition; see B 288 and B 291.

except sense-perception can entitle us to affirm its actual existence.

This doctrine is a preparation for Kant's attack on the Ontological Proof of God's existence.[1] Without prejudging this question, or considering the ultimate issues which it raises, we may say that at least as regards the existence of finite things Kant's position is fundamentally sound.

Kant is not asserting that existence belongs only to the matter in complete separation from the form of experience; and the suggestion that he is making such an assertion seems to me, in view of the references to the doctrine of the Analogies,[2] to be untenable. When Kant says that sense-perception is the only mark of actuality, we have no right to separate this statement from its context, and to suppose that for Kant sense-perception by itself, apart from thought, can give us knowledge of existence.[3] The most we can say is that this is a rather loose way of asserting that all our categories and all our concepts will never give us the mark of actuality which sense-perception alone can supply.[4] Kant's doctrine is not so easy that we need add unnecessarily to its difficulties.

---

[1] A 592 = B 620 ff.   [2] Compare p. 335 n. 6.

[3] Compare also A 234 = B 286, where the object is said to be actual, if it is connected with perception (sensation as matter of the senses), and *is thereby determined by means of the understanding*. Kant's account of the difference between dreams and waking experience also bears out the view that actuality or existence is known through a combination of sense-perception and thought: indeed to deny this is to give up the whole Critical doctrine. Compare B 233-4, A 201-2 = B 246-7, A 376, A 451 = B 479, A 492 = B 520-1, A 493 = B 521, and *Prol.* § 13 *Anmerk.* III (IV 290).

[4] Kemp Smith (*Commentary*, p. 398) also attributes to Kant the corresponding doctrine that there are 'mere concepts' which have no reference to the contingently given. This is based on Kant's statement that 'in the mere concept of a thing no mark of its existence can be found' (A 225 = B 272). Kant's statement is obviously true, if we can in any way (and surely we can) consider, or entertain, a concept without having knowledge that a corresponding object exists; and I cannot see any ground for taking it to involve a theory of the concept incompatible with the Critical, or indeed with any other, philosophical view. Still less can I see in it any reason for the assertion that Kant's thinking is 'perverted' by the influence of Leibnizian rationalism.

It should be sufficiently clear from what has been said, and indeed from the doctrine of Kant throughout the *Kritik*, that while the essential mark of the actual is a connexion with sense-perception, the *connexion* (which is a *necessary* connexion in accordance with the Analogies) is as essential to knowledge of the actual as is *sense-perception* itself.[1] Indeed Kant's very formula shows this; for he does not say that the actual is *either* what is given in sensation *or* what is connected with sensation. He says on the contrary that the actual is what is *connected*[2] with sensation. The merely given in sensation is of all things the most subjective, unless it is *connected* with a substance as one of its accidents; and what exists—in the technical sense—is not a mere sensation, but the substance of accidents connected with the sensation. The accidents are the ways in which the substance exists; and to recognise them as accidents of an existing substance is to recognise, however 'obscurely', that they are parts of a system which is causally determined throughout.

It follows that the actual is also the necessary. This does not excuse us from the obligation of distinguishing actuality from necessity, although the two are so closely bound up together that we can distinguish them only by abstraction. Furthermore we must remember that it is one thing to recognise that every object must be possible, actual, and necessary, and quite another thing to recognise the possibility, actuality, and necessity of any particular object. The general doctrine of the categories does not free us from the duty of looking for empirical evidence when we seek to apply the categories, and even the categories of modality, to particular objects.

[1] It may be objected that our knowledge of the actual is primarily by means of perception, and that when we know the actual in virtue of *connexion*, our knowledge is indirect. This is in a sense true; but even in direct perception we must connect what is given with a substance, if we are to be aware of an object; and we must (however 'obscurely') regard the given accidents as having a place in an ordered world, and therefore as determined by causation and interaction (although we need not know the actual cause empirically).

[2] This connexion, as I pointed out above, is connexion by means of the Analogies. Compare also A 374 and A 376.

Thus, although we know *a priori* that if an object exists, it must be necessary (in the sense of being causally determined), we do not understand the necessity of this particular object till we have discovered empirically the chain of causes by which this particular object is determined.

One more point must be added for the sake of completeness. Kant does not here distinguish logical from real actuality,[1] as he distinguishes logical possibility and necessity from real possibility and necessity. Logical actuality is a characteristic of assertoric judgements, and is identified by Kant with (logical) truth:[2] truth in this sense seems to involve (1) assertion (or reference to an object) and (2) agreement with the formal laws of understanding;[3] hence it might be described as a claim to truth rather than truth itself. For real actuality we require something more: we require that the object asserted should be connected with sense-perception in accordance with the Analogies. Although for Kant such real actuality or existence in time is impossible apart from human minds and human judgements, it is not made by mere thinking, and depends on sense as well as thought. This is the doctrine against which Caird, from his Hegelian standpoint, consistently protests;[4] but I think that modern philosophy as a whole

[1] Or formal from material actuality.

[2] See A 75–6 = B 101; compare *Log.* § 30 (IX 108) and *Einl.* II (IX 16 and 20). I take it this truth is logical truth, or the general form of truth, with which alone Formal Logic is concerned (see A 59 = B 84 and compare A 151–2 = B 191 and A 191 = B 236): what we may call material truth involves correspondence with a particular object; but Formal Logic ignores the differences between objects, and cannot tell us whether a proposition is true in the sense of corresponding with its object.

[3] This second point I take from A 59 = B 84, which seems to give a clearer statement of what is said obscurely in A 76 = B 101. Kant's illustration is taken from a hypothetical syllogism in which the antecedent (which is only problematic in the major premise) is assertoric in the minor. When it is assertoric, it is said to indicate that the proposition is bound up with the understanding in accordance with its laws. I confess that the precise meaning of this statement is not to me wholly clear: it is not repeated in the lectures on Logic.

[4] For example, see *The Critical Philosophy of Kant*, Vol. I, p. 596 (if I have understood it aright).

is on this subject more inclined to agree with Kant than with Hegel.[1]

§ 2. *The Third Postulate*

The Third Postulate[2] asserts that the necessary is that whose connexion with the actual is determined in accordance with the universal conditions of experience. These conditions are the Analogies. Actual things, that is, the bodies which constitute the physical world, are themselves actual only so far as they are connected through the Analogies with their appearances revealed to us in sense-perception, so that it is not to be thought that the actual can be known to us apart from the Analogies. Nevertheless we now take the actual for granted, and consider what is implied by our knowledge of necessity. We are concerned, not with the *logical* or *formal* necessity to be found in the connexion of concepts and judgements in accordance with the laws of thought,[3] but with the *real* or *material* necessity for the existence of objects in accordance with the Analogies.

We have seen that the actual existence of objects can never be known *a priori* by mere concepts apart from sense-perception, any more than it can be known by mere sense-perceptions apart from concepts, and in particular apart from the Analogies. The same is true of the necessary existence of objects. We cannot know such necessary existence merely from concepts. The knowledge that objects necessarily exist is dependent on their connexion with the actually perceived, a connexion which must be in accordance with the universal laws of experience.

The only kind of existence which we can know to be necessary in accordance with these laws is the existence of the *effects* of causes which are given to us and taken as actual. It may seem odd of Kant to assert only that given the cause we know the effect to be necessary, and not also that given the effect we know the cause to be necessary. I think Kant's reason

---

[1] Meyerson, for example, seems to accept the Kantian antithesis.

[2] A 226 = B 279 ff.   [3] Compare A 76 = B 101.

is that the cause makes the effect necessary, but not *vice versa*.[1] Although the cause is no doubt necessary (for everything actual is necessary), it is not necessary *quâ* cause, but only *quâ* effect of something else.[2]

Since substances, as permanent, cannot be the effect of anything, we can have no insight into the necessity for the existence of substances.[3] We can know only that their states must exist; and this we can know, in accordance with the empirical causal laws discovered by science, only from a knowledge of preceding states (given to us in sense-perception) which are the causes of their existence.

The criterion of necessity is therefore the causal law expressed in the Second Analogy,[4] and this is a law of experience and of experience alone. It applies only to the phenomenal world, and in the phenomenal world it applies only to the states of substance and not to the substances themselves. Real necessity is therefore not absolute, but hypothetical, necessity.[5] That is to say, we cannot by mere concepts, not even by the concept of 'God', know *a priori* that the object must exist; but by the

[1] We know that if the effect is actual, the cause is actual, but this does not enable us to understand the ground of the existence of the cause. The effect in relation to the cause is only a *causa cognoscendi*, while the cause in relation to the effect is a *causa essendi* or a *causa fiendi*.

[2] Compare the repeated assertion (found, for example, in A 194 = B 239) that the event (or effect), as the conditioned, gives a sure indication of *some* condition, but the condition *determines* the event. All this seems to me to imply that for Kant causation is more than uniform succession; for if it were mere uniform succession, the cause would be as necessary in relation to the effect as the effect in relation to the cause.

[3] We know *a priori* that substances must be *possible* (A 220–1 = B 268–9); for if there is to be experience of objects in one time and space, it must be an experience of the states of permanent substances. We may also be said to know *a priori* that all substances must be permanent. To say this is not to say that we know the grounds or causes why particular substances exist, and so why these particular substances are necessary: our knowledge of necessity is confined to their accidents.

[4] Kant might equally, or perhaps even better, have said the Third Analogy.   [5] A 228 = B 280. Compare *Metaphysik*, p. 27.

aid of experience we can say that, granted the cause is actual, the effect must exist. We can therefore affirm the necessary existence of objects by thought and without actual experience of these objects, but we can do so only if we have experience of their cause.

In this respect also Kant's doctrine would appear to be sound. I do not think he should be taken to mean that only when we are actually experiencing the cause can we say that the existence of the effect is necessary. On such a principle necessary existence would be confined to the future. I take the principle to be more general, and to mean that wherever we know a cause to be actual, whether that cause is present or past, there we can say that its effect is necessary. We can do so of course, not in virtue of our *a priori* knowledge of the general causal principle, but in virtue of the empirical causal laws discovered by science in accordance with that principle. Apart from such empirical laws, while we could know that the cause must have some effect, we could not know what its effect was.

§ 3. *Some Traditional Conceptions*

In his usual manner Kant adds some general observations after his main task is accomplished.

The first is only of historical interest. Of the four traditional principles (*in mundo non datur hiatus, non datur saltus, non datur casus, non datur fatum*)[1] Kant asserts the third to be a consequence of the Second Analogy, since the affirmation of the universal principle of causality is a denial of blind chance. The fourth, he declares, belongs to the Principles of Modality, since the doctrine of the Third Postulate—that the necessary is the conditionally or hypothetically necessary—is a denial of blind fate or unconditioned necessity. He hints further that the denial of discontinuity (*saltus*) is connected

---

[1] A 229 = B 282. '*Casus*' is, I think, equivalent to '*Glück*' and '*fatum*' to '*Schicksal*', which are said to be '*usurpierte Begriffe*' (pseudo-concepts) in A 84 = B 117. In A 74 = B 99 the word for '*casus*' is '*Zufall*'.

with the assertion of continuity in the Anticipations (although the proof of this was given in the Second Analogy[1]); and that the denial of the void (*hiatus* or *vacuum*) is connected with the account of quantity in the Axioms (although he himself discussed it in the Anticipations and in the Third Analogy[2]). I think he derives some pleasure from the affirmation that the question of empty space is a matter for 'ideal reason', which goes beyond the sphere of possible experience. He is always anxious to insist that the materialists who believe in atoms and the void are speaking, not as scientists, but as unconscious metaphysicians.[3]

We can afford to smile at Kant's preoccupation with phrases which have no longer a living part in our tradition, at his desire to fit these phrases into the framework of the categories, and at the ingenuity and plausibility which, to my mind at least, he displays in doing so. But the suggestion that his attempt is a grotesque example of pedantry seems to me much more grotesque than the attempt itself. We must look at Kant's work in the setting of a formalistic age, where he stands as a giant shaking off the chains which weighed men down. It is natural that he should adjust his doctrine to traditional conceptions; and it is obvious that if his discovery of the complete list of categories were sound, then all true traditional doctrines must fit into that list of categories and ought to be shown to do so. We can see to-day that he was mistaken; but we ought to see also that he was not unreasonable, and that what is regarded as mere pedantry is a proper attempt to work out his conclusions to their logical end.

[1] A 207 = B 253 ff.
[2] A 172 = B 214 ff. and A 214 = B 261. There is a certain plausibility in saying that discontinuity is primarily discontinuity in the qualitative matter of intuition (as treated in the Anticipations); and that the void is a question of the nature of space, which is the quantitative form of intuition dealt with in the Axioms.
[3] Compare A 173 = B 215.

§ 4. *Leibnizian Possibility*

When we turn to his remarks on Leibniz's doctrine of possibility, we are faced with matters of more importance.[1] The question is asked whether the field of the possible is wider than that of the actual, and the field of the actual wider than that of the necessary.[2]

Kant regards these as questions not for understanding but for reason, not for the Analytic but for the Dialectic. He takes them to be asking whether phenomena can fit only one system of experience[3] or whether they might fit into several different systems of experience. To such a question understanding can give no answer, since it is concerned only with the rules which govern the one experience that we have and the one world that we know. It has to do only with the synthesis of what is given, not with the other possible worlds of which this is alleged to be the best. We cannot conceive other forms of intuition or of thought; and if we could, such forms of intuition and thought would have no place in the human experience in which alone understanding plays its part.

Nevertheless Kant finds it impossible to refrain at this stage from some remarks about the Leibnizian doctrine. He points out that in any case the poverty of the conclusions reached, on the basis of a supposed wide realm of possibility extending beyond the world we know, is obvious enough in

---

[1] A 230 = B 282.

[2] Here again the charge is brought against Kant that he suddenly uses the word 'possible' in a different sense. But this question was perfectly familiar to the audience for which he was writing, and he has to discuss it in order to bring out the fact that it presupposes a false meaning of 'possibility'. I do not think his method of exposition here would offer any difficulty to contemporary readers. It certainly indicates no confusion on the part of Kant.

[3] It is very clear from what he says here and a little later that he regards the phenomenal world as one experience, not in the sense that it is all present to one all-embracing mind, but in the sense that it forms one system of actual and possible sense-perceptions of which my actual sense-perceptions are a necessary part. He calls it a '*series*' of appearances and identifies it with a single all-comprehensive experience in A 231–2 = B 284. Compare A 110.

itself. He suggests that because we can say 'All the actual is possible' and can convert this proposition into 'Some possible is actual', we therefore imagine that there must be many things possible which are not actual. Finally he turns to a more serious argument. It may seem that the possible must be wider than the actual, because something must be added to the possible if it is to become actual.

This, however, is precisely what Kant denies.[1] Actuality is not another quality added to things which are already possible. If anything were to be added to the possible, it would itself be impossible. What is added is not an additional quality in the object, but a relation to the knowing mind. A thing is possible, on Kant's doctrine, if it agrees with the possible conditions of experience. What can be added for my understanding[2] is connexion with some sense-perception;[3] but if any possible object has such a connexion, it is not only possible, but actual (whether I perceive it immediately or not).

On the basis of what is given to sense-perception I can, by means of understanding and with the aid of the Analogies, arrive at wider knowledge of the actual objects in the one phenomenal world or all-embracing system of human experience. On this basis of the given I have, however, no means of deciding whether my sense-perceptions could fit into a quite different phenomenal world and a quite different system of experience; and if I am to work without this basis of the given I have still less means of deciding such a question, for apart from given matter thinking is quite impossible.[4]

What is possible under conditions which are themselves

---

[1] A 231 = B 284.

[2] Kant says this is added '*zu meinem Verstande*'. Does this mean 'to my understanding' or 'for my understanding'?

[3] Kemp Smith (*Commentary*, p. 402) asserts that Kant is here giving 'the correct Critical definition of the possible by combining the two first postulates'. It would be odd indeed if this were so, but (as Kant himself points out) when the addition is made we are defining, not the possible, but the actual. What the passage does show—if it needed any showing—is that for Kant the actual is not the matter apart from the form of experience.   [4] Compare A 96.

only possible[1]—and this is the only sense of the possible which Kant recognises—is not possible absolutely or in all respects. We can ask and answer the question 'What is possible under conditions of possible experience?' If we ask whether the possibility of things extends beyond experience, we are asking a question about absolute possibility, which we have no possible means of answering. This question has been raised here only because of the common belief that the concept of absolute possibility is one of the concepts of the understanding.[2] The problem must at present be left in obscurity, since its discussion really belongs to the Dialectic.

§ 5. *The Meaning of the Word 'Postulate'*

Kant in conclusion explains why he uses the word 'postulate' for the Principles of Modality.

He does not use the word 'postulate', as was apparently done at the time, for propositions which are immediately certain or self-evident. He believes that such propositions, although they cannot be 'deduced' in the ordinary sense of 'inferred'—the Principles, as we have seen, are a matter for the power of *judgement*, and not for reason—can be 'deduced' in the Kantian sense, that is, 'justified' by showing their relation to possible experience. Merely to accept self-evidence at its face value is fundamentally opposed to the whole spirit of Criticism; Kant regards it as legitimate in science, but not in philosophy. Once we admit self-evidence as ultimate, we are faced with a whole host of audacious pretensions claiming such self-evidence; and nothing is more usual than for the deliverances of common sense or tradition (in themselves no guarantee of truth) to be mistaken for axioms, that is, for propositions which have a genuine measure of self-evidence.

---

[1] I think that by 'conditions which are themselves only possible Kant may mean 'conditions of possible experience'; only if conditions are conditions of possible experience can we show them to be really possible (or objectively valid); but the phrase is obscure. In A 374 space (the condition or form of outer intuition) is said to be the idea of a mere possibility of togetherness (*Beisammenseins*).

[2] A 232 = B 284–5.

All synthetic *a priori* propositions demand, if not a proof, at least a deduction or justification. In Kant's language we must answer the question *how they are possible*, before we can admit their claims to philosophical acceptance.[1]

What Kant has called the Postulates are, however, in a special position. Although, like the other Principles, they are synthetic, they add, as we have seen, nothing to the necessary characteristics of the object. What they add to the concept of the thing is not a necessary quality of the thing itself, but a necessary relation to the mind which knows it; or, in other words, they refer to the *action* of the mind by which the concept is produced.[2]

It is because of this reference to the mind's action that Kant chooses the word 'postulate' for the Principles of Modality. In mathematics a postulate is a *practical* proposition. It concerns only the synthesis by which we construct an object and produce the concept of an object. It tells us, for example, with a given line to describe a circle from a given point. Such a proposition cannot be proved, because the procedure which it enjoins is the very act through which we first of all produce the concept of a circle.[3]

In the same way the Postulates of Modality are concerned with the synthesis (or aspects of synthesis) through which alone the concepts of possibility, actuality, and necessity can arise; and they add nothing to the concept of the thing other than its relation to the mind which knows it.

We need not, I think, quarrel with Kant either about his terminology or about his reasons for it. It is true that his Postulates, like the mathematical postulates (if his account of the latter is correct), are concerned with the activities of

[1] Compare A 148–9 = B 188.

[2] A 234 = B 287. This action is the synthesis of the mind which imposes form or unity on the given matter and is necessary for knowledge of the object. It produces the concept in the sense that the concept is the principle at work in the synthesis, and to be conscious of the principle of the synthesis is to know the concept. Compare A 220 = B 267.

[3] The concept is produced through the act in the sense explained by the previous note.

the mind through which an object is constructed and a concept produced. This resemblance is not destroyed by the presence of differences in the two cases, differences which are obvious enough, since the mathematical postulate determines the character of the object through and through, whereas Kant's Postulates determine the inner character of the object not at all. Yet even this difference is by no means so profound as it appears; for the synthesis of form and matter, in whose different subjective aspects Kant finds the origin of possibility, actuality, and necessity, is also, when viewed from another angle, the synthesis which imposes the categories of quantity, quality, and relation upon the matter given to sense, and so determines through and through the character of 'an object in general'. The term 'postulate' in Kant's sense may be said —as he himself said both of the term 'anticipation'[1] and of the term 'analogy'[2]—to apply in some degree to all Principles of the Understanding, but to apply in a preeminent degree to one particular group of Principles, in this case to the Principles of Modality.

§ 6. *The Competence of Kant's Exposition*

Kant's exposition of the Postulates is, as I have already suggested, comparatively simple and straightforward. I do not say that it is elegantly written, or that it is well arranged, or that it is a model of exact and careful expression—such merits are not to be found in the later works of Kant. Again I admit that difficulties can be found in the doctrine and that these difficulties are real—it has not been my good fortune to discover any philosophical writing of which the same could not be said. But I do say that Kant's exposition can be understood by any intelligent reader of good will who has mastered the arguments for the preceding Principles and is prepared to assume— provisionally—that these Principles have been proved.

When I turn to the *Commentary* of Professor Kemp Smith,

[1] A 166–7 = B 208–9. Compare A 210 = B 256.
[2] A 180–1 = B 223–4.

I find here, as elsewhere, that on almost every page he applies to Kant's exposition words like 'ambiguous', 'one-sided', 'misleading', 'obscure', 'confused', 'perverted', and 'perverse'; that on his view the 'so-called' principles are not really principles at all—in spite of the admitted fact that they state characteristics which necessarily belong to every object of experience in its relation to the mind; and even that the 'complicated and hazardous' patchwork theory of Adickes receives at least a qualified approval. Such an estimate, the more striking because of the comparative clarity of the passage in question, seems to me, like so much of Mr. Kemp Smith's writing, to do less than justice to the ability of Kant: so far from helping the student, it places additional difficulties in his way. The impression which I get throughout—I do not know whether it is the impression which Mr. Kemp Smith intended to give—is that Kant was grossly incompetent; that he had a wholly imperfect grasp of what he was trying to say; and that the Critical Philosophy, which in the *Kritik* is partly embedded in a mass of non-Critical doctrine and partly not even expressed at all, is known in its full stature only to a few choice spirits of whom Kant certainly was not one. For such an attitude in a Hegelian like Caird—although Caird seems to me to do greater justice to the merits of the *Kritik*— some justification could be found; for a Hegelian is in the happy position of knowing that all other philosophies are imperfect attempts to express the philosophy of Hegel, and that Kant in particular only marks an important stage on the way towards the final goal. But Mr. Kemp Smith is no Hegelian; and his account of the philosophy which Kant was unsuccessfully trying to expound, for me at least, carries no conviction and awakens no response. The modern tendency to treat Kant with condescension seems to me based on no rational grounds; and, paradoxical though it may appear to the present age, I will venture to express the opinion—an opinion which grows ever firmer the more I study the *Kritik*—that Immanuel Kant had a far better understanding of the Critical Philosophy than any commentator who ever lived.

BOOK XII

TRANSCENDENTAL IDEALISM

CHAPTER LI

EMPIRICAL REALISM

§ 1. *Problems of the Critical Philosophy*

We have now—to borrow Kant's expression—explored and surveyed the land of pure understanding or of truth,[1] and I do not at present propose to embark with him upon the stormy sea of illusion. Nevertheless as we look, on his suggestion,[2] at the map of the area we have left, we cannot but be conscious that the character of certain regions is still regrettably vague, or at any rate that we have concentrated more upon the physical features than upon the spiritual life of the country. More simply, we have dealt in some detail with the objects of outer sense, but the study of inner sense and its objects has been comparatively slight. Kant himself was obviously conscious of this weakness, for in the second edition he attempts to deal more fully, although not fully enough, with the problem of inner sense and with the cognate problem of the relation between inner and outer sense.

These two problems, together with a third, namely the meaning of the distinction between phenomena and noumena, must be touched upon before our task is finished. All of them raise fundamental questions as to the nature of Kant's transcendental idealism and its combination with what he calls empirical realism. In the second edition the emphasis on empirical realism becomes much stronger, because his contemporaries tended, naturally enough, to assimilate his idealism to doctrines which they already knew, such as the idealism of Berkeley. In reply to such a tendency Kant is forced to insist that objects in space are for him as real as the succession of our ideas; they are not known by an uncertain inference from the succession of our ideas in inner sense; for apart from knowledge of bodies in space we could not be aware of the

---

[1] A 235 = B 294.   [2] A 236 = B 295.

succession of our ideas. This doctrine is set forth in the Refutation of Idealism, and before we examine inner sense itself, we must first examine the Refutation.[1]

§ 2. *Descartes and Berkeley*

The idealism which Kant wishes to refute is what he calls material idealism as opposed to his own formal or Critical idealism.[2] It might also be called empirical idealism[3] as opposed to transcendental idealism. This material or empirical idealism is of two types—the problematic idealism of Descartes and the dogmatic idealism of Berkeley. The former view regards the existence of bodies in space as doubtful and incapable of proof; it is essentially a kind of representative idealism which admits the certainty of self-knowledge, but accepts the existence of bodies only by a kind of faith. The latter view explicitly denies the existence of bodies, and asserts (according to Kant) that things in space are only fictions or products of imagination.[4]

As Kant is clearly not a believer in representative idealism, it was natural that his doctrine should be regarded as akin to Berkeley's. His anxiety to deny this perhaps explains a certain animus which he shows against that philosopher, whom he refers to as 'the good Berkeley',[5] while other thinkers are referred to as 'the illustrious' so and so.[6] It may be doubted whether Kant had a very exact knowledge of Berkeley's philosophy; for he appears to suggest that Berkeleyan idealism rests on the alleged impossibility of space and therefore of

[1] B 274 ff. The Refutation is a substitute for the Fourth Paralogism of the first edition, which, in dealing with the existence of bodies in space, laid itself open (by its insistence that we know the existent equally through outer and inner sense) to mistaken charges of subjective idealism. It is introduced into Kant's discussion of the Second Postulate, inasmuch as idealism is opposed to the doctrine of the Second Postulate—that on the basis of sense-perception our thought can know objects actually existing in space. [2] B 274.

[3] A 369, A 371. In B XXXIX n. it is called psychological idealism.

[4] '*Einbildungen.*' This assertion suggests that Kant's knowledge of Berkeley was very imperfect.

[5] See B 71. [6] E.g. '*der berühmte Locke*' in B 127.

things in space. Kant maintains that this is an inevitable result of taking space as a quality of things-in-themselves; to treat space in this way is to make it a non-entity or 'unthing',[1] whose contradictions infect all spatial things with unreality. He therefore holds that this type of idealism is refuted by the doctrine of the Transcendental Aesthetic, which showed that space is neither a thing-in-itself nor a quality of things-in-themselves, but only a form of intuition. Whether this is really relevant to a refutation of Berkeley, we need not here consider.[2]

For the view of Descartes he has a much greater respect. He believes that it is the inevitable consequence of transcendental realism, that is, of the view which starts by holding that our knowledge is of things-in-themselves which are independent of our senses;[3] for on such a theory we can never pass from our sensuous ideas to their supposed corresponding, but independent, objects. The great merit of Descartes's position is that it refuses to assert the existence of objects in space until adequate grounds have been shown for doing so. It is a scandal to philosophy that such a proof has not yet been given,[4] and this proof Kant now proposes to supply. He will show that the inner experience which Descartes regarded as indubitable is itself possible only under the presupposition of outer experience.

§ 3. *The Refutation of Idealism*

The theorem[5] which Kant seeks to prove is stated as follows:

The mere, but empirically determined, consciousness of my own existence proves the existence of objects in space outside me.

There are two points to be noted in regard to the meaning of this theorem. The consciousness of my own existence, since

---

[1] '*Unding.*' The concept of such an object is self-contradictory; see A 291 = B 348.

[2] The same type of argument is used against Berkeley in B 71.

[3] A 371.   [4] B XXXIX n.   [5] '*Lehrsatz.*'

it is said to be *empirically* determined, is not pure apperception, but involves consciousness of the succession of thoughts, ideas, feelings, desires, and volitions present to inner sense.[1] The existence of objects in space outside me can mean only phenomenal objects, and not things-in-themselves. The words 'outside me' are indeed ambiguous[2]—they may refer either to a thing-in-itself different from, and independent of, the knower, or they may refer to phenomenal things in space— but here there is no doubt that they refer to phenomenal things in space.[3]

I. Kant's argument starts from two premises: (1) that *I am aware of my own existence as determined in time*; and (2) that *all time-determination presupposes something permanent in sense-perception*. Of these premises the first is taken for granted by Descartes and by idealists generally;[4] the second we must assume to have been proved by the First and Third Analogies.

II. *Now this 'something permanent' cannot be an intuition in me.*[5] An intuition in me is simply one of the ideas which are grounds for determining my existence in time, one of the events in my changing mental history. If the succession of my ideas can be determined—as is implied by our second premise—only by reference to the permanent, it is obvious that the permanent cannot be one of the ideas whose place in the succession has to be determined.

Kant is assuming that in inner sense we have only a succession of ideas and nothing permanent in relation to which the

---

[1] Compare A 357–9 and B XL n.   [2] A 373.

[3] This is one of the few points on which there seems to be general agreement among modern commentators. Professor Prichard does indeed urge (*Kant's Theory of Knowledge*, p. 321) that the argument *implies* spatial objects to be things-in-themselves, but he recognises that Kant himself is unaware of this implication.

[4] It is taken for granted by Berkeley also. This doctrine could not be attributed to Hume, but I think that Kant's argument would apply equally to any view which holds, as Hume did, that we are aware of a succession of ideas in time.

[5] I follow the correction given by Kant in B XXXIX n.

succession can be determined. This doctrine he holds consistently—it is indeed at the very root of his argument in the Paralogisms. I think that the doctrine is true, but the grounds for holding it ought to have been stated.[1] We ought to be told whether the absence of the permanent from inner sense is only an empirical fact or whether it rests on *a priori* grounds. If Kant had rested his proof of substance on the nature of space, his position would have been stronger.

III. His conclusion is that *the sense-perception*[2] *of the permanent* (*which is necessary if we are to be aware of a succession*) *is possible only through a* thing *outside me in space, and not through the mere* idea *of a thing outside me.*[3] By a 'thing' Kant means a permanent phenomenal substance in space (*substantia phaenomenon*). Such a 'thing' is not to be regarded as one idea among other ideas and, like them, present in our mind at one time and absent at another. It is the permanent substratum in space to which we refer all the changing states perceived by us in succession, and as such it is a necessary condition of our experience of objects in one space and one time; but it is none the less phenomenal.

Whatever difficulty may be found here is certainly not new: it is simply the difficulty of the First Analogy; and this again is only a particular example of the general difficulty that for Kant an object—though it is not one idea among

---

[1] Such grounds as are stated by Kant are to be found in Note 2 (B 277–8). There he insists that all time-determination depends on motion in relation to the permanent in space (compare B 291); that the only permanent given to us in intuition is matter; that the permanence of matter is not known by mere generalisation, but is an *a priori* condition of time-determination; and that there is no permanent ego in inner sense known through intuition as matter is known through our intuitions of impenetrability.

[2] It should be noted that the permanent in sense-perception which was said in the premise to be 'presupposed' is here said to be 'perceived'. There are difficulties as to the sense in which the permanent is perceived. See Chapter XLII § 5.

[3] The same doctrine is stated in A 197 = B 242, where it is said that an idea cannot have objective significance merely by being related to another idea, the idea 'object'.

other ideas—is a combination of our ideas in a necessary synthetic unity. If we cannot accept this possibility, we must say with Mr. Prichard that Kant's argument really implies the existence of things-in-themselves; and we can then accept the argument (Mr. Prichard himself accepts it) only if we consider ourselves entitled to hold that the existence of permanent substances in space *as things-in-themselves* is a condition of our awareness of change. On Kant's view, however, the existence of permanent substances in space can never be proved unless these permanent substances are phenomenal substances dependent, like time and space, on the constitution of the human mind. Hence he is not departing in the slightest degree from his own doctrine; and we must, I think, recognise this, even if we hold, with Mr. Prichard, that his doctrine is untenable and that a permanent phenomenal substance (or a phenomenal object which can be distinguished from our ideas) is a contradiction in terms.

IV. The rest of the argument offers no difficulty. It follows at once that *the determination of my own existence in time* (or knowledge of the succession of my ideas) *is possible only through the existence of actual things*[1] *which I perceive in space.*

V. *My consciousness* (or my existence—for I exist as consciousness) *is essentially consciousness* (or existence) *in time,*[2] *and so knowledge of my existence necessarily involves the possibility of determining existence in time.*

VI. *Hence knowledge of my existence is necessarily bound up with the existence of permanent spatial things; or in other words knowledge of my own existence is at the same time an immediate*[3] *knowledge of the existence of permanent spatial things.*

[1] These actual things must here be permanent substances.

[2] Here again we may note a clear statement that for Kant knowing is not timeless or noumenal.

[3] I feel some difficulty as to the use of the word 'immediate'. See § 4 below.

§ 4. *Turning the Tables on Idealism*

Kant insists that the usual argument of idealism is here turned, with greater justification, against itself.[1] Problematic idealism rested its case on the certainty of immediate experience, and assumed that *the only immediate experience is inner experience*.[2] On this view our knowledge of things in space is inferential: it depends upon an inference from our ideas as supposed effects to bodies as their supposed causes. Such an inference from given effects to *determinate* causes is always uncertain, although we can know *a priori* that every effect must have *some* cause. In this particular case it is possible that we are ourselves unconsciously the cause of our ideas when we perceive,[3] just as we are consciously the cause of our ideas when we indulge in arbitrary imagination. Hence the existence of bodies in space is a matter, not of knowledge, but of faith.

Kant has turned the tables on this argument by proving (as he believes) that *outer experience is really immediate experience*, and that inner experience is possible only if we have immediate experience of bodies in space. This proof depends on the assumption that inner experience is more than pure apperception, more than the 'I think' which must accompany all our ideas of objects. The sense in which Kant believes that this 'I think'—here identified with 'I am'—immediately includes in itself the existence of a subject cannot be discussed here.[4] Knowledge of my existence in time requires more than pure apperception, more than the mere thought or concept that something or some subject exists. We must have intuition,

[1] Note 1, B 276.

[2] Inner experience is experience of the self and its states, these states being thoughts, feelings, and volitions.

[3] This possibility is recognised by Descartes himself, as is also the hypothesis of Berkeley—that God, and not bodies or matter, is the cause of our ideas; see Meditation III and Meditation VI.

[4] It involves consciousness, not of *how* I appear to myself or *how* I am in myself, but only *that* I am. This consciousness is conception and not intuition, a mere intellectual idea of the activity of a thinking subject. See B 278 and compare B 157 and B XL–XLI n. as well as the Paralogisms. Compare also Chapters LII and LIII.

and, indeed, inner intuition under the form of time, if we are to have determinate empirical knowledge of the existence of the subject in time.[1] In short, inner experience is empirical knowledge of the succession of my ideas or states in time, and we have proved that such knowledge is impossible apart from immediate experience of permanent objects in space.

Kant insists in a footnote that he has proved, and not merely presupposed, the immediate consciousness of the existence of spatial things. This proof holds whether we have insight into the possibility of this consciousness or not.[2] Kant's discussion of this possibility might suggest that he believes us to have such insight,[3] but this does not appear to be the case.[4]

I confess I always find difficulty in proofs that knowledge of some particular kind is immediate; for if the knowledge is immediate, what need, and indeed what possibility, is there of proving its immediacy? I confess also that I think Kant is

[1] Compare also B 135. In B XL n. we are told that if apperception were itself intellectual intuition, the argument would not hold.

[2] Compare A 171 = B 213, where 'insight' is said to fail us in many cases of *a priori* knowledge. Insight ('*einsehen*' or '*perspicere*') belongs to reason, not understanding, and we possess insight in regard to very few things. See *Log. Einl.* VIII (IX 65).

[3] B 276–7 n. The question as to the possibility of such immediate outer experience Kant identifies with the question whether we could have an inner sense and no outer sense, that is, whether objects of outer sense could be products of mere imagination. He answers that our imagination of objects of outer sense would be impossible, and that we could not 'exhibit' such objects imaginatively in intuition, unless we already had an outer sense. He even suggests that we must distinguish *immediately* the receptivity of outer sense from the spontaneity of imagination; for merely to imagine an outer sense would be to destroy the very power of intuition which we were trying to determine by means of imagination. I do not understand how the immediacy of this distinction is established by this obscure reason, nor how it can be reconciled with Kant's general doctrine. Compare § 6 below, and *Prol.* § 13 *Anmerk.* III (IV 290), where Kant deals with the cognate problem of the distinction between truth and dream.

[4] In B XLI n. we are told that it is as impossible to explain *how* the existence of a permanent spatial thing different from all my ideas is necessarily involved in the determination of my existence ('*in der Bestimmung meines eigenen Daseins notwendig mit eingeschlossen wird*'), as it is to explain *how* we think the permanent in time.

carried away by his zeal when he asserts, not only that inner
experience is impossible apart from outer, but also that it is
itself possible only mediately—does he intend to deny that
inner experience is as immediate as outer experience? If so,
he must, I think, be using 'immediate' as equivalent to 'self-
sufficient'. He does appear to hold that outer sense is possible
apart from inner and not *vice versa*, for he attributes outer
sense, but not inner, to animals;[1] but animal consciousness
(*Erlebnis*) is not strictly experience (*Erfahrung*). Experience
of bodies in space certainly involves thought and imagination;
and even although consciousness of thinking (or pure apperception) is not experience of our existence in time, I find it
hard to believe that pure apperception (which is a condition
of outer experience) can, on Kant's view, be found apart from
experience of our existence in time and of the succession of our
ideas. Furthermore experience of bodies in space is experience
of bodies moving; and since this is impossible apart from time,
inner experience would seem to be the condition of outer,
just as much as outer experience is the condition of inner,
unless we are to abandon the doctrine of the Aesthetic that time
is the immediate condition of inner appearances and the mediate
condition of outer appearances.[2]

I would suggest that (granted the validity of the argument
in the First Analogy) Kant has shown inner experience to be
conditioned by outer experience, but not that outer experience
can be independent of inner experience. The two types of
experience cannot be separated from each other; and although
an element of immediacy must be allowed to both in so far as
both involve direct intuition, neither can be regarded as immediate in the sense of being self-sufficient.

I would suggest also that Kant is right in saying that the
Refutation of Idealism does not add anything new to his
doctrine, but only to his method of proof.[3] He has already
proved that *all* awareness of change presupposes the existence

[1] See *Metaphysik*, p. 129.
[2] See A 34 = B 50. To abandon this doctrine would, I think, be
inconsistent with the doctrine of the Analogies.   [3] B XXXIX n.

of permanent substances in space. What he now adds is only that awareness of *subjective* change presupposes the existence of permanent substances in space. Furthermore he has always insisted that consciousness of the objective is inseparable from consciousness of the subjective and *vice versa*; and although consciousness of the subjective was, in the Transcendental Deduction, primarily a consciousness of the synthetic activity of the self rather than of its changing states, I do not think that these two aspects of self-consciousness can exist apart from one another, and I see no reason to believe that Kant ever thought they could.

§ 5. *Empirical Realism and Transcendental Idealism*

The strength of the expressions which Kant uses in his desire to distinguish his doctrine of transcendental idealism and empirical realism from problematic idealism must not mislead us into thinking that he is going back upon his doctrine that the world we know is a world which (although it is an appearance of things-in-themselves) is essentially relative to human minds. I do not think we need feel any difficulty when he says, with obvious truth, that the idea of something permanent is not the same as a permanent idea,[1] but may be very variable like all our other ideas (including the idea of matter).[2] We may feel more doubt when he asserts that this permanent must be an external thing which is different from all my ideas, but I think that on reflexion we shall see that this is only a particular application of the doctrine which Kant has always preached in regard to the nature of the object.[3]

---

[1] In B 412 Kant speaks as if we required 'a permanent intuition for knowledge of substance', but this seems to be a loose phrase for 'intuition of the permanent'. There are not the same objections to the phrase 'a permanent appearance' in A 364. In Chapter XLII § 5 I have discussed the difficulty of Kant's repeated statements that we not only presuppose, but also observe or perceive, the permanent.

[2] B XLI n.

[3] The object is indeed only a totality of ideas (possible and actual) —compare A 191 = B 236—but it possesses a necessary synthetic unity, and one condition (or manifestation) of this necessary synthetic

Consciousness of my own empirical existence is more than consciousness of an idea of my existence; it is consciousness, not of a present idea, but of that succession of thoughts, feelings, and volitions in time[1] which constitutes my existence as a thinking being; and I can determine or know such existence only in relation to a permanent spatial world. Hence Kant holds—and surely he is right—that consciousness of my existence is impossible apart from consciousness of a spatial world of substances which are permanent amid change; and such consciousness in turn is consciousness, not of a present idea, but of a world spread out in space and time. The fact that the self we know and the world we know are to be distinguished from our momentary idea of them does not mean that either the self or the world ceases to be phenomenal—Kant is still a transcendental idealist. But he is also an empirical realist; and he believes, not that we have ideas to which the world and the self correspond,[2] but that the phenomenal world and self are directly present to our minds through thought and sense. The fact that they are so present is compatible with (and indeed on Kant's theory inseparable from) the doctrine that they are determined by the forms of thought and intuition.

§ 6. *Sense and Imagination*

We must not suppose Kant's doctrine to involve the absurd consequence that every idea of spatial objects which bears the character of intuition involves the existence of these objects.[3] Such an idea, for example in dreams or in madness, may be the product of imagination. It is nevertheless possible only through the reproduction and combination of past perceptions of spatial objects; and what has been shown is that these

unity is that these ideas must be regarded as states or accidents of a permanent substance in space. We must also remember that the inner nature of the object is the thing-in-itself, but is to us unknown.

[1] Compare B XL n.

[2] Although Kant uses the word 'correspond' sometimes rather loosely, it is only the concept considered in abstraction from its object which corresponds to the object presented to us in intuition and thought.   [3] Note 3, B 278-9.

past perceptions were possible only through the existence of actual spatial objects. Kant's argument is quite general; it asserts only that inner experience in general presupposes outer experience in general. Whether a particular supposed experience is experience or mere imagination must be decided in accordance with the ordinary criteria, or in other words by means of the Analogies. These Analogies (and especially the Second Analogy) are the rules by which we distinguish experience in general (including experience of the self) from mere imagination.[1]

Kant appears to assume, and with justice, that we have usually no difficulty in distinguishing the products of our waking imagination from actual objects in space. The chief difficulty for sane men is to be found in the case of dreams. Kant's clearest statement in regard to them is to be found in the *Prolegomena*.[2] The difference between truth and dream does not lie in the character or constitution[3] of the ideas in the two cases, for the ideas are of the same character in both. We deny that dream-objects are real, because they do not conform to the rules necessary for determining an object, and because they cannot cohere with other objects in an experience which rests throughout upon causal law.

[1] B XLI n. Compare A 201–2 = B 246–7. In A 376 Kant applies the same principle to the 'illusion of sense' (*Betrug der Sinne*). The rule which he there gives is the Second Postulate—'What is connected with a sense-perception in accordance with empirical laws is actual'. The empirical laws in question are, however, primarily causal laws.

In *Prol*. § 13 *Anmerk*. III (IV 290–1) Kant again discusses illusions of sense, and maintains that strictly speaking illusion is due, not to the senses, but to the understanding which makes false judgements on the basis of given appearances.

[2] § 13 *Anmerk*. III (IV 290).   [3] '*Beschaffenheit*.'

CHAPTER LII

INNER SENSE AND SELF-KNOWLEDGE

§ 1. *The Paradox of Inner Sense*

After a period of comparatively easy going we must unfortunately turn to one of the most difficult aspects of the Critical Philosophy—the nature of inner sense. I have deliberately kept this topic to the end.[1] Kant's primary concern throughout the *Kritik* is with physical objects; and if we can first of all understand his account of our knowledge of the physical world, we may at least hope that we shall be in a better position to understand his account of self-knowledge. Nevertheless it cannot be too strongly insisted that the *Kritik* professes to give an account of all knowledge and all experience, not merely of the knowledge or experience of physical objects; and indeed that the account of time as the form of inner sense is an integral and essential part of the whole Critical Philosophy.

The full treatment of this question demands a detailed discussion of the Paralogisms, which is outside the scope of this book. Here we must be content to examine only what Kant calls the 'paradox' of inner sense, as it is expounded in the Transcendental Deduction of the second edition.[2] I feel far from confident that I have mastered this doctrine, and I am not sure whether my difficulties are due to my own incapacity in following Kant's complicated expressions, or whether they are partly due to a real obscurity in his thought; but at least it may be possible to bring out certain aspects of his teaching which are implicit in what we have already learned.

Kant takes the paradox to be that by inner sense we know ourselves, not as we are in ourselves, but only as we appear to ourselves. In view of his doctrine that time, like space, is only a form of our sensibility, this paradox may seem not to

[1] Inner sense has been discussed briefly in Chapters II § 3, IV § 4, and VII § 2. For the discussion of apperception see the Transcendental Deduction, especially Chapters XXI–XXXI.　　　　[2] B 152 ff.

be so very great. Kant himself has dismissed an analogous objection somewhat lightly—perhaps too lightly—in his first edition.[1] The special difficulty of his theory seems to be found in the reasons which lie behind it—namely that we can intuit ourselves only as we are affected internally. This appears self-contradictory; for it means that we stand to ourselves in a passive relation.[2] This difficulty may, I think, be put more clearly by saying that the self both affects and is affected by itself. Inner sense, since it is sense, must be passive—that is the differentia of sense. Yet to give us knowledge of the self, it must be affected by the self.[3] More precisely, inner sense, which is a passive capacity of the self, must be affected by apperception, which is an active power of the same self.[4]

For this reason Kant carefully distinguishes inner sense from apperception, although they are commonly identified.[5]

It does appear a trifle paradoxical that the self should have two powers of self-consciousness, one active and the other passive; and that it should have to act upon, or affect, its own passivity in order to produce a self-knowledge which in the end will be knowledge of the self only as it must appear, not as it really is.

Part of the difficulty lies, I think, in the fact that when Kant speaks of the self as 'affecting' inner sense, he is not using the word 'affects' in the same way as when he speaks of physical objects, or things-in-themselves, as affecting outer sense. The self affects itself through the transcendental synthesis of imagination, and this kind of affection is clearly necessary even for our knowledge of the external world. The difference

[1] A 36 = B 53 ff. Compare Chapter VIII § 9, and also B 155–6.
[2] B 153.   [3] B 156 n.
[4] I take this to be the implication of Kant's distinction between inner sense and the active faculty or power (*Vermögen*) of apperception. It is, I think, confirmed by the fact that he goes on to speak of understanding as determining inner sense. This of course takes place through the transcendental synthesis of imagination.
[5] Compare A 107 when what is commonly called inner sense is equated with empirical apperception. Compare also B 139–40.

between outer and inner sense appears to lie in this—that outer
sense might receive external impressions (though it could
never give us knowledge of an external world) apart from
the transcendental synthesis of imagination and the unity
of apperception; but apart from the transcendental synthesis
of imagination and the unity of apperception nothing could
be received by inner sense at all, and there could be no consciousness of the stream of our ideas under the form of time.
This seems to be implied by Kant's references to the consciousness of animals, who are said to have outer sense but not
inner, intuitions but not concepts.[1] Yet it may also be held
that outer sense is really in the same position as inner sense,
if we take Kant's view to be that in order to intuit any line
however short there must be a successive synthesis of the parts,
and consequently a transcendental synthesis which holds
together the past and the present.[2]

⌊In any case, if inner sense involves a direct awareness of my
ideas as succeeding one another in time, and if a transcendental
synthesis holding together the past and the present is necessary
for such awareness, then clearly the mind must 'affect' itself
by this transcendental synthesis, and only so can there be
inner sense at all.⌋ Such 'affection' does not supply a *matter*
to inner sense as the affection by objects (whether phenomenal
or transcendental) supplies matter to outer sense; for the ideas
of the outer senses are said to constitute the proper stuff
or matter of inner sense.[3] On the contrary, the affection of the
self by itself seems to be concerned rather with determining
inner sense as regards its *form*, which is time.

Once we have grasped this principle, the paradox of Kant's
doctrine will be diminished, and his account of self-knowledge
will approximate, in spite of real differences, to his account of
knowledge of physical objects. I take it for granted that however

[1] See *Metaphysik*, p. 129, and compare Chapter XVI § 13.
[2] This is the commonly accepted view, but I think that Kant
holds it only for experience or measurement, not for mere intuition.
Compare A 426 n. = B 454 n.
[3] B XXXIX n. and B 67. Compare Chapter IV § 4.

unsatisfactory the terms 'inner' and 'outer' may be, what Kant attempts to describe is really an element in our experience: we have a direct and immediate awareness, which must therefore be intuitive and not conceptual, of what is present to our minds at any moment;[1] and our *immediate* awareness is always awareness of the time at which a sensum or idea is given, not awareness of the time at which objects exist and change.[2] Such immediate awareness is called by Kant (whether appropriately or not) inner intuition, and is ascribed to inner sense, the form of which is time. Pure apperception, on the other hand, is consciousness of the necessary unity of our thought and of the necessary forms in which this unity is manifested. In abstraction this implies the necessary unity of some sort of intuition (intuition *in general*); for thought apart from intuition is empty. It does not imply any particular kind of intuition, and it has in itself no reference to time.[3]

§ 2. *Understanding, Imagination, and Inner Sense*

Understanding is said to determine inner sense.[4] 'Determine inner sense' seems to mean here 'hold together the manifold of inner sense in necessary synthetic unity'; for understanding performs this task in virtue of its *original*[5] power to combine the manifold of intuition, and to combine is to bring under an apperception,[6] which always implies necessary synthetic unity.

---

[1] See Chapter IV § 4.

[2] See Chapter VII § 2. An object may change as our sensa do (when we perceive an objective succession), but it may not; for we may perceive successively the coexistent states of the object. The time of the states of the object we must determine by thought, not by intuition; but the time of our own ideas is known as immediately as anything can be.   [3] Compare B 150–1.   [4] B 153.

[5] 'Original' in the sense of being wholly independent of anything else and particularly of intuition.

[6] Apperception appears to be the act here rather than the power; see Chapter XXI § 1. As a power apperception and understanding appear to be identical (though 'apperception' indicates, not only a power of thinking, but a power of thinking which is in some degree self-conscious). Apperception in B 154 is the source of all combination,

The question then arises, as usual, how understanding, as a power of thinking by means of concepts, can be said to combine the manifold of intuition. It is not itself a power of intuiting; nor, even if intuitions are given, can it take them up directly into itself (as a power of conceiving) and make them, as it were, its own intuitions.

If we consider the synthesis of understanding in complete abstraction from what is synthetised, all we are left with is the unity of the act of thought. Of this act understanding is said to be conscious even apart from sensibility, but this is only by abstraction; for without sense-data there could be no such thing as thought.[1] The unity of the act of thought, it may be added, manifests itself in the forms of judgment, which are the same whatever be the matter thought. The act of thought (with its necessary unity and its necessary forms), although having a nature in no way determined by sensibility,[2] is able to determine sensibility inwardly in regard to the manifold which may be given to understanding; but this determination is concerned with the manifold only so far as it is given in accordance with a form of intuition, namely time.[3] [The understanding can impose the principles of synthesis native to itself upon the pure manifold of time, and so upon all appearances to inner sense.[4]]

How can it do so? It can do so only through a transcendental synthesis of imagination which combines, as Kant has all along insisted, the pure manifold of time, and consequently

---

while in B 130 (and indeed in the present passage) all combination is ascribed to understanding.

The possibility of understanding is said to rest on apperception. I do not know whether this means more than that understanding is manifested only in acts of apperception. In A 97–8 the three subjective sources of knowledge are said to make understanding possible (as a power of knowing), but I am not sure whether this is relevant.

[1] Compare A 96 and A 86 = B 118.

[2] In the sense that it is always the same whatever be the nature of given intuitions—the differences in acts of thought are here irrelevant.

[3] Compare B 150 and A 99. Space may be involved as well—perhaps must be involved; see B 155.

[4] Compare A 76–7 = B 102 and A 79 = B 104–5.

the empirical manifold given in time, in accordance with the unity of apperception.[1] Indeed Kant speaks here as if the transcendental synthesis of imagination were the work of understanding at a lower level (or of understanding considered, not as a power of pure thinking, but as a power of *a priori* knowledge).

In this way the understanding can be said to exercise its activity on the passive or receptive self of which it is an active faculty; and thus the active faculty may be said to affect inner sense.

There is therefore a complete contrast between apperception and inner sense.

Apperception and its synthetic unity is the source of all combination.[2] As involving the forms of judgment it applies to a manifold *in general*; for whatever manifold may be given, if it is to be judged and known, it must be combined in accordance with the forms of judgment or the categories. And this means that the categories, as principles of synthesis involved in the very nature of understanding, are independent of all differences in sensuous intuition, and apply *a priori* to all objects *in general*.

Inner sense, on the other hand, if we eliminate the given impressions which are its matter, contains only the form of time, which is the form of all inner intuition, and so of all intuition without exception.[3] Such a form, however—and this is a doctrine stressed specially in the second edition[4]—contains in itself no combination of the manifold, and so contains no *determinate* intuition. This is obvious, if combination is due

---

[1] We must remember that conception is always consciousness of the general principle at work in a synthesis of imagination, and that the categories are ultimate principles of synthesis necessary to all conception and imposed upon imagination by understanding itself.

[2] I would again remind the reader that Kant is speaking of the ultimate principles of combination which condition empirical combination. We must always combine the given as accidents of a substance, for example, but it is a matter of empirical observation that the accidents of sugar are to be hard and white and sweet.

[3] Every intuition 'taken up' into consciousness is thereby an inner intuition (whatever else it may be).   [4] Compare B 160 n.

only to understanding working through the transcendental synthesis of imagination; but apart from such combination the form of time is a mere abstraction.

In order that time may be, not only a form of intuition, but also a pure and determinate intuition, there must be a determination or combination of the pure manifold through the transcendental synthesis of imagination (which Kant has called the *synthesis speciosa*[1] as opposed to the *synthesis intellectualis*). There must also be a consciousness of this determination (or of the principle of this determination), and such consciousness is a conceptual consciousness of the understanding. Indeed the ultimate principle of this determination is not merely one which the understanding finds in the transcendental synthesis of imagination, but one which it imposes *a priori* upon the transcendental synthesis of imagination.[2] Hence we are entitled to speak of the synthetic influence of the understanding upon inner sense.[3]

§ 3. *Illustrations of Kant's Doctrine*

Kant goes so far as to say that we *always* perceive this in ourselves.[4] Such an assertion is an overstatement; for our knowledge of the synthetic activities of the self may be what he calls 'obscure'.[5] It nevertheless serves to bring out sharply how far Kant was from regarding the transcendental synthesis as necessarily unconscious. His subsequent statement that the act of synthesis *successively* determines inner sense shows also how far he was from regarding the transcendental synthesis as timeless. There could be no more explicit contradiction of the fantastic and, in my opinion, baseless interpretation of Vaihinger so widely accepted at the present time.

Kant's illustrations are interesting, and they bear out the view that the matter of inner sense is derived from outer sense.

---

[1] See B 151.   [2] Compare Chapters XIV § 3 and XXXIV § 3.
[3] This is another way of saying that inner sense is affected by the synthetic activity of understanding.   [4] B 154.
[5] Compare A 103, A 117 n., and B 414-15 n.

We cannot think a line without drawing it in thought.[1] We cannot think a circle without describing it. We cannot represent the three dimensions of space save by setting three lines at right angles to one another from the same point. How little are these illustrations concerned with the unconscious, the timeless, or the noumenal! Here indeed we are concerned with the synthetic influence of understanding by means of mathematical concepts, though at least the category of quantity is necessarily involved. It may seem strange that the illustrations are concerned with the objects of outer sense, if we forget that the matter of inner sense is derived from outer sense; but Kant goes on to explain how the determination of outer sense is a determination of inner sense as well, and indeed how, in accordance with the doctrine of the second edition, the determination of inner sense must also be a determination of outer sense.

In order to think time—and here, as in the previous cases, the thinking is manifestly a knowing, and involves intuition as well as concepts—in order to think time we must draw a straight line (which has to serve as the spatial image of time).[2] Kant's main point, however, is that we must attend only to the act of synthesis whereby we determine inner sense successively (or successively combine the manifold in inner sense). In other words we must attend to the succession of our acts of combining the manifold and so determining inner sense.[3]

[1] Here thought is manifestly equivalent to imagination.

[2] Compare B 156. I suppose other spatial representations might be possible, but they would be less appropriate; for a straight line alone has one dimension. I am not so sure as Kant seems to be that we could not adequately represent time concretely by a tune; but if all change is relative to the permanent in space, his doctrine is not groundless.

[3] Kant says we must attend 'to the succession of this determination *in inner sense*' rather than 'of inner sense' (which we should expect). I suppose that the act of determination, so far as it is an act of adding a new manifold to what we already have, may be said to be *in inner sense*. Strictly speaking, I take it, it is the new manifold or the combined manifold which is present in inner sense through our act. For awareness of the act in the full sense, I should imagine that we require, not only inner sense, but also empirical as well as pure apperception

The act of combination or synthesis is here regarded as a synthesis of the manifold in space. It is again seen to be successive; for it is described, perhaps a little misleadingly, as 'motion'—motion as an act of the subject, not as the character of an object. The subject may be said to 'move' only in the sense that it successively describes a spatial figure in imagination: this is a pure act of successive synthesis of the manifold in outer intuition in general, an act of the productive imagination. When we regard this act in abstraction from the spatial elements involved, when we consider it, in short, only as determining inner sense in accordance with the form of time—then, and apparently then only, have we the concept of succession. This concept, it should be noted, is a concept of a mode of time[1]: it should be sharply distinguished from the concept of change, which is empirical.[2]

The concept of succession, on Kant's view, is the concept of a principle at work in the synthesis of imagination. In this it resembles other concepts; for in concepts we conceive a principle at work in the synthesis of imagination whereby an object is produced.[3] Kant is attempting, whether successfully or not, to connect our concept of time with that of space; and even the mere attempt was, I imagine, an advance on the accepted views of his own period. The subject is, however, full of difficulty. It is not altogether clear why for our concept of succession, and apparently even of time,[4] we must have in mind the synthesis of a spatial manifold in a straight line; for we must immediately consider the synthesis in abstraction from the spatial elements involved. Partly no doubt it is in order to have an image whereby we can indicate that time is of one dimension;[5] but is this due to more than the accidental prominence of

(consciousness of the special as well as the universal nature of our activity); unless indeed, which seems to me very unlikely, acts of imagination (as opposed to acts of thought) are themselves known through inner sense. Compare Chapter XXI § 3.

[1] See Chapter XXXIX § 3.
[2] B 3, A 171 = B 213, A 206–7 = B 252.
[3] The exceptions to this rule, if any, need not be here considered.
[4] B 156.   [5] Ibid.

sight in our experience? Partly perhaps it is that we may be able to understand the successiveness of time as against the non-successiveness of space.[1]

Furthermore the successiveness of our act of synthesis seems already to presuppose time. On the other hand, there is no time apart from the act of synthesis whereby past and present are held together before the mind. Hence Kant can speak of producing time itself in apprehension,[2] and can say that the ideas of a determinate time (or space) are *produced* through the synthesis or combination of a homogeneous manifold.[3] It is a little surprising that he here makes no reference to the synthesis of the pure manifold of time itself; but perhaps he thinks it unnecessary to do so, since in the preceding paragraph he has said that there is no determinate intuition of time apart from the transcendental synthesis of imagination.[4] The successive synthesis of the manifold of space in the imaginative construction of a straight line must also be a successive synthesis of the manifold of time in which the parts of the line are successively present to inner sense.[5] Otherwise we could not be aware of the line (as a determinate quantity).[6]

Kant may have this point in mind when he adds that understanding does not *find* in inner sense such a combination of the manifold,[7] but *produces* it, in that it *affects* that sense.

It must be remembered that in all apprehension of appearances in space and time there must be present a transcendental synthesis of the space and time in which these appearances

---

[1] This is suggested by the statement that we can be conscious of inner changes only against a permanent in space; see B 292.

[2] A 143 = B 182.

[3] B 202. Compare also A 210 = B 255.   [4] B 154.

[5] There is no question here of a synthesis of points or instants. The synthesis is continuous.

[6] Compare (in spite of differences) A 99–100, A 102, and A 103. The reader may also be referred again to the difference between a determinate, and an indeterminate, quantity (or quantum) in A 426 n. = B 454 n.

[7] It is perhaps possible that the combination of the manifold referred to is the combination of the manifold in space.

are. Nevertheless I should have liked to see here a few of the empirical illustrations which Kant so sternly denies himself.[1] It is, however, clear enough that—leaving aside the question of desires and volitions which are also present to inner sense— the appearances given to inner sense are the same as the appearances given to outer sense. All appearances, so far as we are conscious of them, or at least so far as we are conscious of them as present to our minds, are appearances to inner sense— even a line or a circle which we construct *a priori* in imagination. Understanding, through the imagination, affects inner sense by bringing these appearances successively before the mind, and by holding them together before the mind in one time.[2] This, I presume, is true, whether we are imagining objects like mathematical circles or are actually perceiving physical bodies.

I cannot think that Kant is nearly so confused or so obscure on this side of his doctrine as is commonly alleged. Many of the confusions attributed to him arise, as it seems to me, from reading into his words meanings which they cannot possibly have. And I believe that, however much his account requires expansion and modification, he is at least dealing with a very real problem, and that he is right in saying that all our ideas, whatever their origin, may be regarded as modifications of the mind and so as belonging to inner sense.[3] Kant always distinguishes our own mental history from the history of the world we know. Indeed we can regard our own mental history—and I think Kant does so regard it—as only a part of the history of the world which we know. But from another point of view we can regard the whole world known to us as a succession of appearances revealed to us in inner sense under the form of time.[4]

Nevertheless Kant's doctrine requires a much fuller working out than it has received. Our knowledge of time, like that of

---

[1] See A XVIII.   [2] Compare B 156 n.   [3] A 98–9.
[4] The effort to do this seems to me rather like the effort to see a picture (or the contents of a mirror) in one plane. When we do this we are not looking at anything different from what we were before.

space, is primarily intuitional and not conceptual.[1] We do not make time out of nothing either by understanding or by imagination. Time, like space and even like sensation, is something given, however much it may be given through the nature of our own sensibility. Our concept, as opposed to our intuition, of time is derived by abstraction as are empirical concepts, although like them it presupposes a synthesis in accordance with the categories. It does not, like the pure categories, have its origin in the understanding; and its content is a given manifold, although that manifold is pure and in this respect unlike the contents of empirical concepts. All this seems to me to suggest that Kant's theory must be supplemented by something like the modern doctrine of the specious present, though I do not think that that doctrine, even as expounded by the most able modern philosophers, is wholly immune from criticism.[2]

§ 4. *Inner Sense and the Phenomenal Self*

Having attempted to explain the way in which the mind is internally affected by itself Kant returns to the paradox that in this way we can know the mind only as it appears to itself, and not as it really is in itself.[3]

The problem is this. How can there be one and the same self or subject, if we distinguish the I which thinks[4] (apperception) from the I which intuits itself (inner sense)?[5] If I

[1] See Chapter V § 8.

[2] Compare my article in *Mind*, Vol. XXXVIII, N.S. No. 151.

[3] B 155.

[4] It seems to me unnecessary to change, as Vaihinger does, '*das Ich, der ich denke*' into '*das Ich, das denkt*'. This is the ordinary Kantian idiom; see B 407 and B 429. Other examples could be found in other works.

[5] Kant adds in parenthesis 'for I can think of another kind of intuition as at least possible'. Strictly speaking, we have on Kant's view no means of deciding whether another kind of intuition is possible, and it is at least doubtful whether we can even conceive another kind of intuition; compare A 230 = B 283. Setting aside this difficulty in terminology, I find it difficult to see the point of the observation, unless he means that the self which thinks might be identical with a self

am an intelligence and a *thinking* subject, how can I know myself as a *thought* object, so far as (in addition to being a thinking subject) I am given to myself in intuition?[1] And how can such knowledge be knowledge of myself only as I appear to myself in intuition, and not as I really am in myself for understanding?[2]

Kant answers that this question—and he appears to have in mind especially the last question—has no more and no less difficulty than the question how I can be an object to myself at all, and indeed an object of intuition and of inner perception.[3] That I can know myself only as I appear to myself in intuition, can, he claims, be shown clearly, provided only we accept the view that space is merely a pure form of appearances to outer sense. His argument rests primarily on the contention that time is on the same footing as space. This doctrine he develops in a sentence of very great length.

Time, he insists, while it is no object of outer intuition,[4] cannot be represented by us except under the image of a line, in so far as we produce it; for apart from this we could not know that time has only one dimension. Similarly, we can determine the periods, and even the moments, of our inner intuitions only in relation to changes in spatial objects. Consequently we must order or arrange the determinations of inner sense as appearances in time in precisely the same way that we order or arrange the determinations of outer sense as appearances in space. Now we have admitted that we know objects through the determinations of outer sense only so far as we are externally affected (presumably by things-in-them-

which intuited itself in some other way (for example, by intellectual intuition), and so would be different from a self which intuited itself sensuously under the form of time; compare B 68.

[1] I think Kant must mean this, though the language is obscure. I am here differing from Kemp Smith's translation.

[2] Understanding involves a kind of self-consciousness or apperception, but this (as Kant shows in the Paralogisms) does not give us determinate knowledge of the self except in so far as the form of our thinking receives a content from the intuitions of inner sense.

[3] Compare B 68.   [4] B 156; compare A 23 = B 37.

selves). We must also admit that we can know ourselves through
the determinations of inner sense only so far as we are internally affected by ourselves. And just as we can know objects,
not as they are in themselves, but only as they appear to us in
space, the form of our outer intuition; so we can know ourselves,
not as we are in ourselves, but only as we appear to ourselves
in time, the form of our inner intuition.

I have pointed out above[1] that there is a difference between
the two cases, since the affection by outer objects gives us the
matter of intuition, whereas the affection by ourselves does not
give us a new matter, but merely combines the given matter
under the form of time. This Kant himself seems to support
in a footnote;[2] for he mentions attention as an example of the
kind of affection or influence he has in mind. This would be
simple enough, if he had merely said that by attention we
bring new objects or appearances before the mind, and so add
to the content of inner sense, not indeed by giving something
new (as is done in sensation), but by bringing into consciousness what is already given in sensation. Kant himself gives a
much more complicated account of attention. In attention,
he suggests, the understanding always determines inner sense
to inner intuition. That is to say, in attention understanding,
through the transcendental synthesis of imagination, combines
a given matter under the form of time, and does so in accordance
with the categories of thought.[3] In so doing it gives rise to an
inner intuition;[4] and this intuition corresponds to the manifold
thought[5] in the synthesis of the understanding (or, as I should
prefer to say, corresponds, as regards its combination, to the
synthesis of the manifold of intuition *in general* which is
thought in the pure category of the understanding).[6]

I can hardly help thinking that Kant weakens the effect of
his illustration by describing it in such highly abstract and

---

[1] See § 1 above.   [2] B 156 n.

[3] Kant says 'according to the combination which it thinks'.

[4] Intuition here is a combination of form and matter.

[5] I have introduced the word 'thought'.

[6] It is perhaps possible for Kant to have in mind empirical concepts
as well as (or in place of) categories.

general terms; but I suppose that the allusion to an activity
with which the plain man is familiar may perhaps help him to
understand what is being talked about, even if he fails to understand what is being said about it.

§ 5. *Apperception and Self-Knowledge*

Kant has now shown that inner sense as affected by apperception gives us knowledge of the self, not as it is, but only
as it appears. He proceeds to show that apperception, taken
by itself, does not give us knowledge of the self either as it is
or as it appears.[1] In apperception we are conscious only of the
necessary synthetic unity of thought.[2] This consciousness
Kant describes—perhaps in reminiscence of Descartes—as a
consciousness *that* I am. It is not, however, consciousness
of *what* I am (either in myself or as an appearance). It is a
mere thinking and not an intuiting: it gives us no object.
For knowledge of the self as an object we require more than
the act of thought which brings the manifold of every possible
intuition (or of intuition *in general*) to the unity of apperception
—even although this act is in some ways transparent to itself or
self-conscious. We require a definite kind of intuition, intuition
given under an assignable form, such as time; and this must take
the place of the manifold of intuition *in general*, which is all
that we can combine in pure thought.

Hence my own existence as known through thinking is not
appearance, and still less is it illusion. We may be tempted to
imagine Kant means by this that consciousness of thought
presupposes the I as a thing-in-itself, just as an appearance
presupposes the thing-in-itself of which it is the appearance.[3]
I am inclined to believe he means that, by thinking, my own
existence is known only as an act of thinking,[4] or perhaps even

[1] B 157.
[2] I have simplified the statement here. What I am conscious of is
said to be myself in the transcendental synthesis of the manifold of
ideas *in general* (that is, in the intellectual synthesis, not the *synthesis
speciosa*).   [3] Compare B XXVII and A 251–2.
[4] He asserts in B 422 n. that 'I am' cannot be inferred, as Descartes
maintained, from the proposition 'I think', but it is identical with it.

that it is known only as a form of thought.[1] In any case my existence as known through thinking is completely indeterminate: in order to determine my existence I must know, not only that I think, but what I think, and this is impossible apart from inner sense.[2] 'The determination of my existence can happen only in conformity with the form of inner sense, according to the special way in which the manifold which I combine[3] is given in inner intuition.' I can know my own existence, not as a thinking subject in abstraction, but only as thinking this and that concretely in a temporal succession. If so, then (granting that time is a form of my sensibility) I can know my existence determinately only as I appear to myself in time, and not as I am in myself.

The self-consciousness of thought, considered in abstraction, is far from giving us knowledge of the self. It involves indeed thought of the categories; for the categories are the necessary forms of thought in which the unity of apperception is manifested. As Kant says, they constitute the thought of an object *in general*: they are indeed concepts of the combination of a manifold of intuition *in general* in one act of apperception, and it is this combination which constitutes the essential nature of an object *quâ* object. But in themselves the categories do not give us knowledge of any object. To know an object different from myself, I require more than the concept of an object *in general* (which I think in the categories): I require also an

[1] Compare B 133 and B 138. In B 423 n. 'existence' in this sense is said not to be a category: it is related, not, like the category, to an indeterminately given object, but only to an object of which we have a concept without yet knowing whether such an object is also 'posited' apart from the concept. A form of thought has no objective validity apart from the known possibility that there may be a corresponding intuition.

[2] I take it that for Kant we cannot, except by pure abstraction, be conscious of the nature of our thinking apart from what is thought; and there is no awareness of what is thought apart from inner sense.

[3] In pure thought I may be said to combine the manifold of intuition *in general*; but in order to determine my existence, a corresponding combination of the manifold *in time* must be given to inner sense through the transcendental synthesis of imagination.

outer spatial intuition to give content and determination to my concept. Similarly for knowledge of myself, besides self-consciousness or the mere thought of myself (as a subject thinking in accordance with the categories) I require an inner temporal intuition to give content and determination to the thought of myself. I exist indeed as intelligence, which is conscious only of its own power of synthesis (in accordance with the categories); but for the manifold that I must thereby combine in order to have self-knowledge I am subject to a limiting condition, namely, that the manifold must be given to inner sense under the form of time. Hence the combination or synthesis in question can be a combination of intuitions only if it is in accordance with relations in time which lie entirely outside the pure concepts of the understanding.[1] Such an intelligence can know itself only in relation to an intuition which is not intellectual (or which cannot be given through understanding itself). Consequently it can know itself only as it appears in intuitions given under the form of time. It cannot know itself as it is, nor as it would know itself if it were possessed of intellectual intuition.

[1] The text seems to be corrupt: I give the general sense.

CHAPTER LIII

SELF-KNOWLEDGE AND KNOWLEDGE OF OBJECTS

§ 1. *The Existence of Self*

We have now seen that self-knowledge is more than consciousness of the universal nature of thought. To know ourselves we must not only think and be conscious of thinking: our thought must, through the transcendental synthesis of imagination, 'affect' inner sense in respect of its form, which is time. In this way alone can our thinking receive a content, or manifold, without which there can be no determinate existence or knowledge of determinate existence. But such existence is existence in time, and therefore is phenomenal. Consequently we can know our existence determinately only as we appear to ourselves in time, and not as we are in ourselves.

Such is the essence of Kant's doctrine, but we have still to consider some of its further implications. These concern, not only the existence and knowledge of the self, but also the existence and knowledge of objects; for apart from objects the self could neither exist as a thinking being nor be aware of its own existence.

We must first of all examine the difficult footnote[1] in which Kant summarises his general doctrine in regard to the existence of the self.

The judgement 'I think' expresses the act whereby I determine my existence. Therefore in this judgement existence, Kant maintains, is given.[2] But such existence is indeterminate, and the way in which I am to determine it is not given; for the way in which I am to determine it is not merely a way in which I think, but a way in which I have to posit or arrange

---

[1] B 157–8 n.

[2] 'I think' expresses, it may be noted, the act whereby any existence is determined; but apparently it is only my existence that is given in the act. Is this because I can think without knowing?

in myself a manifold[1] belonging to my existence. This manifold
is not given to thought in abstraction, but to inner sense or
self-intuition; self-intuition presupposes time, as a form which
is given *a priori*; and this form is sensuous, not intellectual, a
form, not of the active thought which determines, but of the
passive sensibility which receives the manifold to be determined.

For knowledge of self (as for knowledge of anything else)
we require a *determining* activity of thought and a *determinable*
manifold. We have an intellectual conceptual consciousness of
the nature of our determining activity in abstraction from
what it determines, but we must not imagine that we have an
intellectual intuition of it. We should have such an intellectual
intuition only if all the manifold in the nature of the subject
were given by the mere activity of thought.[2] Kant even implies
here that intellectual intuition would give us not a mere consciousness of the general character of our activity—we have
that in any case—but the actual determining factor itself; and
it would give us this determining factor prior to the act of
determination,[3] just as time gives us the determinable manifold
prior to its actual reception.[4] The precise character of this
intellectual intuition is obscure, but Kant's main point is
clear enough: there is no such intellectual intuition in human
experience. That is to say, my consciousness of my thought
(or of my activity of determining) is purely conceptual; it is not
intellectual intuition; it gives us no manifold, and consequently
no determinate existence. By such conceptual consciousness of
my thought I cannot determine the existence of myself as a

[1] Kant is assuming that existence cannot be determined by mere
conception, but only through connexion with a manifold; compare
A 218 = B 266.　　　　　　　　　　　　　　[2] Compare B 68.
[3] I am not sure what Kant means by this, unless he means that it
would give us understanding in its real nature as a thing-in-itself
independently of its manifestation in successive acts of determination
or thought.
[4] I have added 'prior to its actual reception'. I take Kant to mean,
not that time gives us a pure manifold to be determined, but that
time, in virtue of containing a manifold of pure intuition, enables us
to know *a priori* (in its necessary temporal relations) the empirical
manifold of which time is the form.

spontaneously active being. I can determine my existence as a thinking being only by reference to a given manifold: I can, in short, determine my own existence only so far as my thought determines under the form of time a manifold given passively to sense. Hence my existence cannot be determined other than sensuously; and this means that it is determinable only as the existence of an appearance in time. The fact that I can call myself intelligence in virtue of my conceptual consciousness of my own activity does not mean that thereby I can determine my existence as it is in itself for understanding alone.

All this is complicated and difficult, as Kant puts it; but I am inclined to think he is trying to state something which is both simple and true. If we are to know the existence of the self we must pass beyond a mere conception of the formal nature of thought. The self is known to exist only as thinking something given to it in time; and we cannot have knowledge of our own existence apart from our knowledge of our existence as a succession of definite thoughts, with definite objects, in time. But if time is the form of our sensibility, it follows that we can know ourselves only as an appearance in time, not as a thing-in-itself.[1]

§ 2. *The Existence of the Object*

In all this we have little more than a restatement of what we have already learned. The determination of my own existence cannot take place by a mere thinking which is conscious only of the nature of thought: it must always have reference to a manifold given to inner sense under the form of time. But this manifold, although it is given as a manifold of *inner* sense in time because of the synthetic activity of the imagination, is not itself given through that activity. The activity of imagination merely takes up and combines in time what is given, according to Kant, from without.[2] The given which is thus taken up and combined is given, primarily at least, to outer sense under the

[1] Compare A 37 = B 54.

[2] This statement may require some modification in regard to emotions and desires.

form of space; and even the synthesis whereby it is combined in time as a modification of inner sense is also (or at any rate is accompanied by) a successive synthesis of the manifold in space.

Whether I am observing physical objects, or constructing mathematical figures in space, or determining the past history of the physical universe, or of the human race, with the aid of present evidence supplemented by causal law, I am always, not only successively synthetising a manifold in space, but also determining inner sense; for I am successively bringing a manifold before the mind, and I am immediately aware of the presence of this manifold to the mind.[1] Hence in being aware of physical objects and their changes I am also—from another point of view—aware of a succession of ideas in my mind, this succession of ideas being (as we have seen from the Analogies) by no means necessarily identical with the succession of changes in the objects which we know.[2] Kant also holds that we can make such a succession of ideas in inner sense intelligible only by representing time imaginatively as a line, and representing inner change through the drawing of a line: in fact we can make the successive existence of the self in different states imaginatively comprehensible only through outer intuition. The reason for this is that we can be aware of changes, and consequently of change in our ideas, only over against something permanent; and the permanent is given to us only in space.[3]

This permanent, as we have seen in the Refutation of Idealism,[4] cannot be an intuition in me. I can determine the change in my ideas, and consequently can determine my existence during the time in which these ideas succeed one another, only by reference to a permanent which is different from my ideas.[5]

There is an obvious objection to this theory. I am supposed

---

[1] Compare A 210 = B 255.

[2] The identity between the succession of our ideas and the succession of changes in the objects takes place only when we are directly observing an objective change.   [3] See B 292; compare Chapter LII § 4.

[4] Compare Chapter LI § 3, II.   [5] B XXXIX n.

to be immediately aware only of what is in me, namely, my idea of outer things. It must therefore remain uncertain whether there can be anything corresponding to my idea, and in particular whether there can be in space permanent substances which can be distinguished from my changing ideas. This objection Kant endeavours to meet.[1]

Through inner experience, he says, I am aware of more than my ideas. I am aware of my own existence in time, and consequently I am aware that my own existence can be determined in time—by which I take him to mean that my existence can be known to be, not merely at some time or other, but at a definite time.[2] Such determination of my existence in time is possible only in relation to something which, while it is bound up with my existence, is nevertheless external to myself. To be conscious of my existence in time is to be conscious of a relation to something which is external to myself; and only so is it experience and not invention, sense and not imagination. This implies that what is external to myself is inseparably bound up with inner sense.

As we have seen,[3] the words 'inner' and 'outer', 'internal' and 'external', are by no means clear in such a context. If we are speaking of an empirical or phenomenal object, to say that it is an outer or external object is to say only that it is in space. To say that it is an inner or internal object is to say that it is only in time or possesses only temporal relations.[4] The word 'outer' is, however, sometimes employed to indicate something which exists as a thing-in-itself and is different from us. Since such a thing-in-itself cannot be known at all, and still less can be known to be permanent, there can be no question of such a usage in the present context. Kant does indeed speak here of the permanent as 'external to myself'; but by this he appears to mean only that, as permanent, it must be different from the successive and transitory ideas in which it is temporarily

---

[1] B XL n.
[2] Compare A 145 = B 184 for the schema of actuality.
[3] Compare Chapter IV § 4.
[4] A 372–3. Compare for space Chapter VII § 1.

revealed: it is in short the permanent spatial substance to which we refer our changing ideas as states or accidents. Kant doubtless believes that the inner nature of such a substance is a thing-in-itself which is different from me and wholly independent of my knowing; but this inner nature is unknown to me, and I have no ground whatever for regarding it either as spatial or as permanent.

The phenomenal character of the permanent substance external to myself is shown, not only by the statement that it is inseparably bound up with inner sense, but also by the further implication that it is revealed to outer sense. Unfortunately what Kant says about outer sense in this connexion is obscure. He appears to be giving a further reason why what is external to myself is inseparably bound up with inner sense.[1] The reason is that what is external to myself is revealed to outer sense, and outer sense depends for its reality (presumably its objective reality or validity) upon the fact that it (as outer *sense* and not mere outer imagination) is a condition of inner experience.

This argument, which I have simplified and abbreviated, offers considerable difficulty in detail. Kant says that outer sense is—I should prefer to say 'involves'—in itself a relation of intuition to something actual outside me. He must, I think, mean that a spatial intuition is distinguished from a mere spatial image (such as we can invent in imagination) by the fact that it is regarded as a state, or accident, of a permanent substance in space.[2] In this way a spatial intuition given to outer sense has a reality, or an objective validity, which a mere image has not. In the Analogies Kant claims to have shown that spatial intuitions must be referred to permanent substances in space, if we are to have experience of objects in one time Here he asserts that spatial intuitions must be referred to permanent substances in space, and so must have objective reality, because this is a condition of the possibility of inner

---

[1] B XL n. As often in Kant, this appears both to be a conclusion from what precedes, and to receive support from what follows.

[2] The fact that it is also the appearance to us of a thing-in-itself is, I think, here irrelevant.

experience as an experience of change or succession in our ideas. In other words—if there is to be inner experience at all, outer sense must be genuine outer sense (not mere imagination): it must, that is to say, reveal to us permanent substances in space, and so possess reality or objective validity.

Whatever be the difficulties of Kant's argument in detail, his general position is clear. We can be aware of the succession of our ideas in inner sense only if we set this succession over against something permanent in space. Permanent spatial substances are presupposed as a condition of outer and inner experience alike. We therefore know *a priori* that there must be such permanent spatial substances; but their nature must be revealed empirically to outer sense, and even their permanence must, I think, find some confirmation in what is revealed empirically to outer sense.[1]

§ 3. *Reality of Inner and Outer Sense*

Kant adds some further considerations, which are comparatively simple.[2]

If the intellectual consciousness of my existence, in the thought 'I am' (or 'I think'), were an intellectual intuition by which my existence could be determined, consciousness of a relation to something external to myself would be unnecessary.[3] In human experience such intellectual consciousness, while independent of inner intuition, requires to be supplemented by inner intuition, and only so can my existence be determined. Inner intuition is sensuous (or passive) and subject to the form of time. The determination of my existence, and consequently inner experience itself, is therefore a determination in time; and since determination in time is impossible except by reference to something permanent over against myself, inner experience depends on the existence of such a permanent something or substance. Apart from the curious statement that because the permanent something is not in me, it must be in something

---

[1] Compare Chapter XLII § 5.   [2] B XL–XLI n.
[3] There would be no need to introduce inner sense and time and the permanent. Compare Chapter LII § 5.

outside me, all this adds nothing to what we are already supposed to know.

Kant's conclusion is that for the possibility of experience *in general* the reality of outer sense is necessarily bound up with the reality of inner sense. In other words, I can know that I exist determinately in time only if I know that there are permanent substances in space which are revealed to outer sense. Both of these kinds of knowledge—knowledge of the self as thinking and knowing (as well as feeling and willing) in time, and knowledge of physical objects existing permanently in space—are equally necessary to what we call experience. This seems to me to be true; and it is a refutation of what is ordinarily called idealism—the view that we have an immediate knowledge of our own ideas or our own states, but that our knowledge of spatial objects is at best inferential. It is not, however, a refutation of transcendental idealism, which holds that the existence of physical objects and the self is alike phenomenal and is only an appearance to finite minds of a deeper reality which lies beyond.

Two minor points are added. We have still to distinguish the images and illusions of imagination from genuine intuitions of objects (not only physical objects but also ourselves): this we do by means of the Analogies.[1] And we must not confuse our idea of something permanent in existence with a permanent idea. We have no permanent idea.[2] Our idea of the permanent and even of matter is liable to change; but it always refers to something permanent in space, whose existence is necessarily involved in the determination of my own existence. Inner and outer experience constitute only one experience; and there could be no inner experience unless it was at the same time also partly an outer experience, that is, an experience of permanent objects in space.

§ 4. *Ideality of Inner and Outer Sense*

The doctrine we have just examined may be described as Kant's empirical realism. It establishes what he calls the 'reality'

[1] Compare Chapter LI § 6.   [2] Compare B 292

of inner and outer sense.[1] The one experience which we have
consists of more than mere ideas: it reveals to us *both* a phenomenal self whose ideas succeed one another in time *and* a world
of permanent phenomenal substances in space. We must now
turn to that aspect of his doctrine which may be described as
transcendental idealism, the doctrine that the self and the
world so revealed are only phenomenal: we cannot penetrate
into their inner nature as they are in themselves. With this
doctrine and its grounds we are familiar; but we have still to
consider some additional arguments which he added in the
second edition in order to *confirm* the theory of the 'ideality'
alike of inner and of outer sense.[2]

If we set aside feelings of pleasure and pain and also the
will, and consider only knowledge, everything that belongs to
outer intuition is said to contain nothing but relations. These
relations are identified with extension (relations of place),
motion (or change of place), and moving forces (described
rather strangely as laws in accordance with which change of
place is determined). In this obviously more than mere intuition is involved. What Kant has in mind are the primary
qualities revealed by means of outer intuition, and it is these
primary qualities which he reduces to mere relations.

Although we know these relations, we do not know what it is
that is present in a place[3] or what (apart from change of place) is
really at work in the things as they are in themselves. Position,
motion, and force, in so far as they are bound up with space,
which is only a form of our sensibility, can reveal reality only
as it appears to us, not as it is in itself; but Kant reinforces
his established doctrine by the further contention that these
things are all relational, and through mere relations we cannot
know a thing as it is in itself. In order to do this we should
require to know what it is that is related: we should require
to know the inner character of the object itself.

If Kant's premises are correct, the conclusion seems to

[1] Compare B XLI n.   [2] B 66 ff.
[3] Strictly speaking, a thing-in-itself is not present in a place, though
it appears to us as present in a place.

follow. He may, I think, even be right in saying that if outer
sense gives us only relations (and not the inner nature of the
thing which appears in these relations), then it gives us only
the relation of the object to the subject; for this seems to mean
that it gives the object only as it appears to the subject, or as
it is in relation to the subject, not as it is in itself.

If this is true of outer sense, it must equally be true of inner
sense; for in the first place the ideas of outer sense constitute
the proper stuff of inner sense; and in the second place we
may assume that if outer sense gives us only relations which
are in some way spatial, inner sense will give us only temporal
relations, and the same general argument will apply.

The second contention Kant expresses in a very elaborate
form, and his reference to relations is not developed in the
same direct way as it is in regard to space. Instead it is used to
support the view that time is only a form of intuition, and
from this the required conclusion follows. But we must examine
the argument in more detail.

§ 5. *Time and Inner Sense*

According to Kant we 'posit' the ideas of outer sense in
time. I am not sure whether he means only we must take up
and combine these ideas successively and be aware of the succession in our minds, or whether he means also (as the word
'posit' suggests) that we must assign to these ideas a position
in what we take to be the development of the physical world.
In any case he insists that time is a prior condition of our
consciousness of spatial ideas in experience—though apparently
it is not so in a purely animal *Erlebnis*. As such a prior and
formal condition, time conditions the way in which we posit
spatial ideas in the mind;[1] and it contains in itself the relations
of succession, simultaneity, and permanence—the permanent
being what coexists with a succession.[2] These relations are

---

[1] B 67. The words 'in the mind' perhaps support the former
alternative mentioned above.

[2] The reference to the permanent (which is not in the mind) supports
the second alternative mentioned above.

identical with what he calls elsewhere the 'modes' of time.[1]

Instead of going straight on to assert that inner sense, as concerned only with temporal relations, cannot give us reality as it is in itself, Kant proceeds to (what I take to be) a description of time. That which as an idea can be prior to all activity of thinking any object[2] is intuition; and if it contains only relations, is the form of intuition.[3] The inseparability of such a form from the matter of which it is the form is shown by Kant's statement that this form represents nothing except in so far as something, presumably outer intuition, is posited in the mind.[4]

From this last assertion Kant makes an inference which is curiously expressed. This intuition or this form of intuition (which, I take it, can only be time) is nothing other than the way in which the mind is affected through its own activity, namely, through this positing of its idea,[5] and therefore through itself. He further describes this 'way' in which the mind is affected through itself as 'an inner sense in respect of the form of that sense'.[6] This seems an unnecessarily elaborate method of saying what we know already—that time is the form of inner sense.

---

[1] A 177 = B 219. Compare A 182–3 = B 225–6 and Chapter XXXIX § 3.

[2] Such priority need not be, and probably is not, temporal priority; but it is less objectionable to ascribe temporal priority to intuition than it is to ascribe temporal priority to thought (or to the form of intuition in relation to intuition itself). For Kant intuition is given independently of thought (A 90 = B 122).

[3] Compare B 160–1 n., where the form is said to contain only a manifold without unity. Incidentally this passage also suggests that if unity is necessary for intuition, then intuition cannot be given apart from thought. This would not imply that the manifold of intuition could not be given apart from thought. See also A 107.

[4] Compare A 452 n. = B 480 n.

[5] B 67–8. I should have expected 'ideas' in the plural.

[6] This seems to mean that the mind is affected passively from within, and that such affection is necessarily under the form of time: it necessarily produces a succession of ideas. A little later he says that the way in which the manifold is given in the mind apart from spontaneity must be called sensibility.

Kant's main point appears to be that inner sense, or at least time as the form of inner sense, can arise only because the mind is affected by the activity which posits ideas in the mind.[1] But if he is adding anything to what we have already learned, I must confess I do not know what it is. I am not even certain what he means by 'positing,' unless he means 'taking up' and 'combining'.

§ 6. *Inner Sense and the Phenomenal Self*

Kant insists that everything known through sense is so far always appearance.[2] The reason for this I take to be that sense is always conditioned by a form of sensibility. In any case, if we accept the premise, we must either deny inner sense, or else admit that the subject known through inner sense can only be the subject as an appearance or phenomenon—not the subject as it really is, and as it would be known to itself if it possessed an intellectual or active (as opposed to a sensuous or passive) intuition. Assuming that we do not possess an intellectual intuition, Kant insists that the only difficulty is to understand how a thinking subject can have an inner sensuous intuition of itself. This we cannot explain;[3] but it is simply a fact, and so is a difficulty common to every theory.

On Kant's view we admittedly possess an active intellectual consciousness of the self in apperception, which he identifies here with the simple idea 'I' (equivalent to 'I am' or 'I think'). If through this idea alone all the manifold in the subject were given by means of its own activitity, we should have an inner intellectual intuition, and nothing more would be required. In human beings, and indeed in all finite beings, determinate knowledge of the self (which always involves a manifold) requires, in addition to apperception, an inner perception of a manifold which is given in the subject independently of thought.[4] Such an inner perception must therefore be sensuous

---

[1] Compare A 210 = B 255.   [2] B 68.   [3] Compare B XLI n.
[4] This is, I think, already implied in the fact that the manifold is not given in thought.

and passive; or (in Kant's elaborate terminology) the way in which the manifold is given in the mind apart from spontaneity must (because the manifold is given apart from spontaneity) be called sensibility.

All this is common form and offers no difficulty. His method of stating his conclusion is not so simple. If the active intellectual faculty of self-consciousness (here manifestly including imagination as well as thought) is to seek out, that is, to apprehend or take up, what lies in the mind, it must so far *affect* the mind, and only in this way can it produce an intuition of itself. The form (or *a priori* condition) of this intuition, however, has its origin in the mind as passive, and it determines, in the idea of time, the way in which the manifold is together in the mind.[1] Hence the mind intuits itself, not as it would if it knew itself by an active intellectual intuition, but in accordance with the way in which the mind is affected by its own activity from within. In other words, the mind intuits itself, not as it is in itself, but only as it appears to itself.

Kant's conclusion is obvious enough on his premises; but the details of the way in which the mind affects itself, I am sorry to say, still elude me, though I have no doubt that he is trying to say something of real importance. The general direction of his thought is clear enough.

§ 7. *Appearance and Illusion*

We must guard against a possible misunderstanding of all this.[2] We have seen that by outer intuition we know spatial objects only as they affect the mind, and by inner intuition we know the self only as it affects the self. That is to say, since such affection is conditioned by space and time, which are only forms of our sensibility, we know objects, and we know the self, only as they appear, and not as they are in themselves.

---

[1] I think the *togetherness* of the manifold in the mind must be the result of the activity, not (like the manifold and the form of time) given in the mind as passive; but the kind of togetherness (as temporal) is conditioned by the fact that the nature of time depends on the passivity or sensibility of the mind.   [2] B 69.

This must not be taken to imply that objects and the self, as known, are alike illusions.[1] In appearances, as opposed to illusion or mere seeming, the objects are regarded as something really given; and this is true even of the characteristics which we attribute to them, but with this qualification—that in the relation of the given object to the knowing subject the characteristics in question depend (for their universal form) upon the kind of intuition possessed by the subject. That is to say, the characteristics of the object are transmuted in so far as they must be intuited by a subject, the forms of whose sensibility are space and time. For this reason we must distinguish the object as appearance from the same object as it is in itself.

There could hardly be a clearer statement of Kant's view that an appearance is not a mere product of our own mind taken as a reality; if it were, it would be an illusion.[2] An appearance is always the appearance of a thing wholly independent of our mind and existing in its own right. Even the spatial and temporal characteristics which it possesses are appearances of real characteristics of the thing as it is in itself. Because of the nature of our mind things must appear to us as spatial and temporal; but it is because of the character of the thing-in-itself that we see one object as round and another as square.[3] We do not know what this character is, but we cannot regard it as roundness or squareness, because we cannot regard it as spatial at all. Indeed we know the thing only as it appears to us, or as it is in relation to our minds;[4] and consequently we do not know whether we can rightly speak of it as 'existing' or possessing 'characteristics,' since for us these terms must imply a reference to time and space.

Hence Kant does not say that bodies merely *seem* to be outside us, or that the soul merely *seems* to be given in my self-consciousness. This would imply that a body and a soul might be a mere illusion, and not the appearance of an independent reality. For Kant such a doctrine is unthinkable. What he holds is this: that the spatial and temporal character of bodies and

[1] Compare B XL n. and A 396. [2] Compare A 395.
[3] Compare Chapter VI § 8. [4] Compare B 67 and B 70 n.

souls, the 'quality' of space and time in accordance with which, as a condition of their existence for me, I must posit the one and the other—this lies wholly in the nature of my intuition, and not in the thing as it is in itself. It would be my own fault, if out of that which ought to be reckoned as appearance, I made a mere illusion.

Such an error is not the result of recognising the ideality of space and time, and so of all our sensuous intuitions. On the contrary, this error arises from regarding space and time as characteristics of things-in-themselves—a doctrine producing so many absurdities and contradictions that the whole world of space and time becomes a mere illusion, as Kant imagined that it did in that philosophy of the 'good' Berkeley of which he appears to have had so little exact knowledge.

§ 8. *Difficulties of Inner Sense*

It will be observed that our examination of inner sense rests primarily on passages added in the second edition. This is partly due to the fact that in the first edition this problem was treated chiefly in the Paralogisms, which lie outside the scope of the present book. It is also partly due to the fact that in the second edition Kant was attempting to dispel misunderstandings of his theory, and felt obliged to articulate more fully his doctrine of inner sense and its relation to permanent substances in space. These two doctrines are closely bound up together. A fuller discussion of them is impossible without trenching upon the argument of the Dialectic. Here I can only register my opinion that both these doctrines are essential to the Critical Philosophy,[1] and that what is added in the second edition is not a correction, but a development, of what Kant has held all along.

When I say this, I have no wish to deny that Kant's whole theory is difficult, and in some of its details very difficult. But I find in it no trace of the contradictions and the muddle so commonly attributed to him by his critics. Kant suffers from

[1] I am glad to have at least the partial support of the Master of Balliol on this point; see Lindsay, *Kant*, p. 53.

the weakness common to all human thinking, especially where that thinking is not content to achieve clarity at the expense of being superficial. Some of the difficulty in his thought is due to the fact that he is dealing with a difficult problem, and I am far from suggesting that he has given a final solution. I think it is true to say that a fuller working out of his doctrine is urgently required. But the alleged muddle seems to me largely the invention of critics, who too often continue to repeat charges which rest on little or no evidence and sometimes on complete misunderstanding.

If we are to know our own thinking and thereby to determine our existence as thinking beings, it is not enough that we should conceive the necessary unity of thought or even the necessary forms of judgement in which that unity is manifested. The universal nature of our thinking, if we separate it from what we think, does not by itself give us grounds for describing the kind of existence which we as thinking beings possess: it is only by Paralogisms of Reason that we claim on this basis to be substances, immaterial, incorruptible, personal, and therefore spiritual.[1] We can determine the existence of our thought, and of ourselves as thinking beings, only as we have a direct awareness of what we think and know—a direct awareness that such and such is present to our minds. Such a direct awareness is inner sense, and what is present to our minds is thereby revealed to us under the form of time as a succession of ideas.

On Kant's view all our thinking involves, at least ultimately, an imaginative synthesis of a manifold passively received by sense.[2] So far as this thinking can claim to be knowing and to have an object which is more than its own creation, there must be a transcendental synthesis of the imagination which combines the given manifold in one space and time. This combination, on Kant's theory, must always be in accordance with the categories of the understanding; but the crucial con-

---

[1] Compare A 345 = B 403.
[2] Compare A 19 = B 33, A 51 = B 75, A 77–8 = B 103. We need not here consider the complications involved in highly abstract thinking such as Kant's own thinking in the *Kritik*.

tention for our present purpose is specially concerned with the
category of substance. If we are to know a world in one time
and space, our outer intuitions must be referred to permanent
spatial substances as their accidents. This we are doing at
every moment: Kant insists that our awareness of our own
thinking and knowing is always an awareness of ourselves as
thinking and knowing a permanent spatial world; and indeed
that it must be so; for if it were not so, we could not even be
aware of the succession of our own ideas. This is the precise contrary of an idealism which claims that we know only the succession of our own ideas and make doubtful inferences to a world
of bodies in space.

Taken thus, Kant's doctrine seems to me to be true. He is
also surely correct in saying that what is directly revealed to
us as before our minds and so as our idea is, and must be,
revealed successively in time (just as the objects which we
distinguish from ourselves are, and must be, revealed to us as
external to one another in space). We know immediately only
the time at which objects appear to us or are our ideas: the
time which we ascribe to them as objects we know, not immediately, but as a result of thought. I have immediate knowledge
of the fact that I am thinking about the Critical Philosophy now.
I can have no such immediate knowledge of the fact that the
Critical Philosophy was produced before I was born.[1]

If Kant is right in holding that because time is necessary
and universal, it is therefore only a form of our sensibility, his
conclusion immediately follows that the self (and indeed any
object) revealed to us as temporal cannot be revealed to us as
it is in itself.[2]

[1] The fact that when I watch a moving body, the motions take
place in the same time (at least approximately) as I perceive them is
no exception to this principle. It is only by thought I can know that
what I experience is an objective succession; for the succession of my
perceptions is equally compatible with objective coexistence.

[2] Or, more strictly, we cannot know that it is in itself as it is revealed
to us; but the possibility that time should be both a form of sensibility
and a character of things-in-themselves is not worth considering, when
there can be no grounds whatever known to us why this should be so.
Compare Chapter VIII § 8.

The most difficult part of Kant's doctrine is his account of the way in which the self is affected by itself from within. The self in its direct awareness of its own thinkings and knowings—it is not the place here to consider its feelings and volitions—must be passive, though it must also have, in the act of thinking itself, an active conceptual awareness, however obscure, of the necessary unity and form of thought. The manifold or content of our thought must be given to a mind which receives it passively and perceives it immediately: our awareness of what we think and know is not a creating of what we think and know. It is here that the complications begin; for the manifold must originally be given to outer sense. If the manifold is given to outer sense, does not this imply that we are aware of it? And if we are aware of it, are we not aware of it as before our minds? And if so, is it not given to inner sense as well?

On this point Kant gives us, so far as I know, no clear statement; but his account of animal *Erlebnis* (which cannot strictly be called experience) suggests that awareness of spatial intuitions is possible apart from inner sense. Such an awareness would be, I take it, momentary: it would not be awareness of a succession, and still less of an object distinct from the self. To be aware of a succession I must take up, run through, reproduce, and hold together, or in one word synthetise, the manifold. This synthesis must be also a synthesis of space and time, and it is so far a transcendental synthesis of imagination without which there could be for us no succession and no time, and perhaps (though this is more doubtful) no space.[1]

According to Kant, when the mind is affected by itself, inner sense is affected by this transcendental synthesis of imagination and so ultimately by the understanding; for the transcendental synthesis of imagination combines the manifold in accordance with the principles of synthesis involved in thinking itself.

The general direction of Kant's thought seems to me sound, and there is nothing arbitrary or unreal about his problem, but there are many difficulties. Time is not a product of the trans-

---

[1] There could certainly be no physical measurable space.

cendental synthesis, but is the form of inner sense. It originates, like space, in the nature of the mind, but of the mind as passive: in this respect it is given to thought and imagination, not created by them. Yet without the synthetic activity of thought and imagination, it could not have unity, and it could not be an intuition (or object of intuition). Furthermore, since the synthetic activity of thought and imagination is itself successive, it clearly presupposes time; and this is perhaps another reason why time must belong to inner sense. Kant will certainly not allow us on this ground to maintain that time must be something real.[1] If, on the other hand, we suggest that our synthetic activity is timeless, unconscious, and noumenal, we not only contradict Kant's express statements,[2] but we contradict ourselves; for we are claiming to describe in detail what we assert to be unknown and unknowable; and we are describing as timeless a synthesis which is intelligible to us only because it is, and must be, successive.[3]

Whatever be the difficulties in regard to time—and these are not peculiar to Kant—he is surely right both in maintaining that time, like space, must be given, and yet that we can be aware of it, and of succession in it, only by an act of synthesis which holds together the past and the present.[4] We can also, I think, understand how the synthetic activity of the mind working upon a given manifold, not only constructs the phenomenal world which we know (a world extended in space and lasting through time), but also gives to our inner sense that whole world as a succession of ideas in us; for all awareness of that world is also an immediate awareness of it as present to our own minds.

In this again there are difficulties of which Kant gives no detailed discussion. In knowing the world we are, so to speak,

[1] See Chapter VIII § 9.

[2] The mere fact that our thoughts are said to be objects of inner sense—compare A 342 = B 400 and A 357—shows how far Kant is from regarding our thinking as timeless or unconscious. Compare also B 154 and B 156. See Chapter XXXI §§ 4–6.   [3] Compare B 292.

[4] This certainly holds for any determinate measurable time, and I am inclined to think that it holds even for the specious present.

making our own mental history; and nothing that we know, or have known, is without its place in that history. Furthermore, since knowing is conscious, in knowing our world we are aware of our mental history. Nevertheless we can turn back and reflect upon our mental history, and treat it as only a part, and a very small part, of the world which we know. This is recognised by Kant, and is indeed regarded by him as an essential element in all experience; for he holds that all consciousness of the succession of our ideas, and still more all determination of the time at which our ideas occur,[1] is possible only in relation to a world of permanent substances, whose accidents change in an objective time which must be distinguished from the time in which we perceive them.

In the Analogies Kant has given an account of the principles in accordance with which we determine the time of objective events. He has omitted to give a similar account of the way in which we determine the time of our own thinkings and perceivings. No doubt he holds that there too the same principles are at work;[2] but in the absence of greater detail some critics have thought that the categories cannot apply to the self. This seems to me to be a mistake except in regard to the category of substance; and here, although the question is full of difficulty, I am inclined to think that from one point of view Kant must regard our thoughts as the accidents of our body; but this is a conclusion which, for whatever reason, he certainly fails to make explicit.[3]

The difficulties which we have to face may legitimately raise the question whether it is possible to think out Kant's system consistently. An attempt to solve these difficulties would demand a book to itself; and I must be content if I have made comparatively clear what his problem is. I should like to think that

[1] See B 156 and Chapter LII § 4.
[2] See Chapter LI § 6 and § 3 above.
[3] The best discussion of the application of the categories to the self is to be found in Ewing, *Kant's Treatment of Causality*, Chapter VI. This is perhaps the most valuable, as it is the most independent, part of a too much neglected book, which has the great merit of being clear even where (in my opinion) it is mistaken.

I have shown it to be a real problem, and that the difficulties in his doctrine are at least partly difficulties which arise from the very nature of human experience itself.

§ 9. *A Rough Analogy*

It is no part of the philosopher's task to substitute images or parables for thinking. Such images and parables are bound to be inadequate, and likely to be misleading. Nevertheless it may perhaps help the beginner, at least a little, if I develop very briefly the analogy of which I have already made use.[1]

I suggested[2] that Kant probably regarded reality as made up of monads. The mind of man is, however, not a windowless monad, but looks out through its windows at reality. We may consider the colour or distortions in the glass of these windows as imposing certain universal characteristics upon the objects we see; and this is parallel to the imposition of a spatial character on all objects by the nature of our sensibility.

We have now to add that for experience it is not enough that our windows should be affected from without: they must also be affected from within. There is, as it were, a film of steam continually forming on our windows; and it is only as we remove this film, now from one part and now from another, that we can see different parts of the outside reality. It is this internal action on our part which makes us see the outside reality as a succession; and it is also this internal action which enables us to see our own inner nature, and to regard the appearances of the outside world as, from one point of view, changes on the surface of the windows of our own mind.

We might perhaps also, and in some ways better, regard the windows of our mind as photographic plates. They must be acted upon from without, if anything is to be seen on them. But they must also be treated chemically from within; and this successive affection from within brings out successively the different results of the affection from without. This image

---

[1] See Chapter VIII §§ 3, 8, and 10.
[2] Chapter VIII § 10.

perhaps does more justice to Kant's use of the word 'affection'; but it fails to bring out what I believe to be the heart of Kant's doctrine—that what we are aware of in intuition is no mere effect of an outside reality, but is a direct appearance to us, through the medium of our own sensibility, of that very reality itself.

CHAPTER LIV

THE TRANSCENDENTAL USE OF CONCEPTS

§ 1. *Empirical Realism and Transcendental Idealism*

The philosophy of Kant is always to be conceived as empirical realism and transcendental idealism. These two main aspects of his doctrine are so closely inter-related that neither is intelligible apart from the other; but in the last three chapters we have considered primarily his empirical realism—the theory that we have direct knowledge both of a self which thinks and feels and wills in time and of permanent physical bodies which interact in space. These two kinds of knowledge constitute one single human experience. We must not imagine that our knowledge of bodies is merely inferential: if we had no direct knowledge of permanent physical substances in space, we could have no knowledge of our own successive mental states.

We have now to consider the other side of Kant's doctrine—his transcendental idealism. The self and the bodies which we know are in themselves realities which are not created by our knowing: Kant never doubts that they are what they are, whether we know them or not. On the other hand we do not, and we cannot, know them as they are in themselves. We know them only as they are in relation to us, or as they must appear to finite minds whose knowledge, or experience, is made up of two elements—thought and intuition. All objects known to us must be given to intuition under the forms of time and space, and must be thought by means of categories which spring from the nature of thought itself. Things as objects, or as known to us, have therefore a universal form[1] imposed upon them which has its origin in human sensibility and human understanding. Hence Kant's doctrine may be called *formal* idealism—the universal form of the objects we know is due to the human

---

[1] It is only the universal form which is imposed. All differences between objects are due to differences in the matter, and the matter is not imposed but given.

mind, and not to things. The self and the world as known to us is therefore only phenomenal: apart from human experience there would be no space and time, and no spatial and temporal world. What would remain would be the thing as it is in itself, but we have no reason to regard this as spatial or temporal, and consequently no reason to describe it as either changing or permanent.

The limitation of our knowledge to phenomena and our ignorance of the thing-in-itself is the one problem which has still to be discussed. This problem Kant claims[1] he has already solved in the course of the Analytic. All we require now is a summary statement of our solution, a bird's-eye view which may strengthen our conviction. We shall see that we can, and must, be content with our knowledge of the phenomenal world, since we have no means of other knowledge; and we shall understand more clearly the title under which we possess what knowledge we have.

To any one who has understood Kant's argument the present exposition, if we except the passage omitted in the second edition, is so easy that it hardly requires a commentary. The first part especially[2] is, as he says, little more than a summary of his previous argument; but he gives in it a clearer indication than he has yet given, at least in the first edition, of what he means by a pure category, and he also deals with the nature of the pure categories separately. In the second part,[3] although he is still working out the implications of his doctrine, he breaks what is to some extent new ground in his discussion of phenomena and noumena, although here also there is more preparation for this discussion in the second edition than there was in the first.

§ 2. *The Empirical Use of Concepts*

We have seen that the understanding derives from itself certain pure concepts or categories.[4] These are not, like

---

[1] A 236 = B 295 ff. [2] A 235-48 = B 294-305.
[3] A 248-60 = B 305-15. [4] A 236 = B 295.

empirical concepts, merely borrowed from experience by abstraction. Nevertheless they can be applied only in experience. That is to say, they are only of empirical use or application: they have as objects only what is given to intuition under the forms of space and time.

The universal application of the categories to all objects of experience is formulated in the Principles of the Understanding. These Principles, whether mathematical or dynamical, are said to contain, as it were, only the pure schema of possible experience. They state the general framework into which the given manifold must be fitted (or, less metaphorically, the principles of combination to which the manifold must conform), if experience is to be one. The unity of experience is that necessary synthetic unity which the understanding, from its own nature, contributes to the synthesis of imagination so far as that synthesis is determined by apperception and not by the given manifold.[1] The unity of thought, without which there could be no experience, demands that the given manifold, whatever it may be, must be combined by the transcendental synthesis of imagination in one space and time; and Kant claims to have proved that such a combination of the manifold in one space and time must be in conformity with the pure categories of the understanding. Hence appearances, as data for a possible experience, must possess the necessary synthetic unity which is thought in the categories and articulated in the Principles.

It may be suggested that all this is of comparatively little importance. No doubt these Principles express the rules by which understanding is actually guided. They are not only *a priori* truths themselves, but the source of all truth. Apart from them there can be no truth, that is, no correspondence between knowledge and its object, since apart from them there can be no object; in Kant's language they contain the ground of the possibility of experience (as the totality of all knowledge) in which objects can be given to us.[2] Yet when all is said

[1] Compare A 118. The synthesis of imagination as so determined is transcendental.   [2] A 237 = B 296.

and done, we have learnt no more than we actually presuppose and apply in our ordinary empirical thinking. Has it really been worth all the trouble we have taken?

Kant protests—apparently forgetting that the reader has followed him all this weary way—that no kind of inquisitiveness is more detrimental to the extension of human knowledge than that which[1] asks what is the use of an enquiry before we have undertaken the enquiry, and before we are in a position to understand that use, even if it were clearly explained. There is, however, one use of our transcendental enquiry which can be made intelligible, and even important, to the most reluctant student. An understanding which occupies itself only in ordinary empirical thinking, without reflecting on the sources of its knowledge, can get on very well in its own way; but it can never determine the limits of its own knowledge. It can never know what is inside and what is outside its own sphere. Consequently without the difficult enquiries we have made, it can never be sure of the soundness of its claim to possess knowledge; and it must expect to meet humiliating reproof when, as is inevitable, it steps beyond its own boundaries and wanders in error and illusion.

Hence the doctrine that the Principles of the Understanding, and indeed all concepts without exception, have only an empirical application is one which, when it is really known and understood, carries with it the most important consequences.

§ 3. The Transcendental Use of Concepts

Against the empirical use of concepts we must set their transcendental use.[2] In the empirical use the concept is applied only to appearances, that is, to objects of a possible human experience. In the transcendental use it is applied to things in general, that is, to things-in-themselves. These things-in-themselves may be described, in accordance with one of Kant's

---

[1] I differ here from Kemp Smith's translation.
[2] A 238–9 = B 297–8.   Compare   A 56 = B 81 and ¿ Chapter XI § 4.

own notes in his copy of the *Kritik*, as objects given to us in no intuition, and consequently not sensible objects.[1]

It is commonly held that Kant should have termed this use 'transcendent' rather than 'transcendental'. Such terminology would, however, be at variance with his own distinction between a 'transcendent' and a 'transcendental' use.[2] The point is of no great importance, and Kant may mean by a transcendental use merely one which transcends the limits of experience by accident or by lack of criticism, whereas a transcendent use is one which transcends the limits of experience by a kind of necessity. But it seems to me possible that by a transcendental use he means one in which, not only the origin of a concept, but its actual application, may be entirely *a priori*. Such an application is always illegitimate, and strictly speaking there is no transcendental use of concepts at all.

If a concept is to give us knowledge of objects, two things are necessary. First, the concept must have the logical form of a concept *in general*, and this Kant identifies with the form of thought. By this, I think, he means more than that the concept must not be self-contradictory. He means that it must possess universality; and this it can possess only as the predicate of a possible judgement.[3] To conceive is to judge, and if so every concept must have the form of thought.[4]

The important point, however, is the second one: we must be

---

[1] *Nachträge* CXVII.   [2] See A 296 = B 352.   [3] A 69 = B 94.

[4] Hence it must either be a category or presuppose the categories. This is the reason why all concepts are a source of necessity: see A 105–6 and compare B 142.

Kant also says that every concept must contain the logical function of making a concept out of some kind of data—data in general. The function (or form) here looks like the function of making concepts by analysis and abstraction: see A 68 = B 93, A 76 = B 102, A 78 = B 104. But we have seen that the same function which gives unity to different ideas (or objects) *in a judgement* by that act of analysis whereby concepts are made also gives unity to the bare synthesis of different ideas *in an intuition*: see A 79 = B 104. Hence every concept is the concept of a synthesis, and the categories are concepts of the universal synthesis which is present in, and presupposed by, all empirical synthesis and all empirical concepts.

able to show that there can be given an object to which the concept may be related. Apart from this the concept contains only the form of thought and nothing more. But for human beings an object can be given only to sensuous intuition.

We have indeed pure sensuous intuitions (of time and space) which are logically prior to given objects; but even they can have objective validity, or application to an object, only if the object is given to empirical intuition.[1]

It follows that all concepts, and consequently all Principles, however *a priori* they may be, must in the last resort be related to empirical intuition. Without this they have no objective validity, but are a mere play of imagination, or of understanding, with the ideas that belong to them respectively.[2]

A transcendental use of concepts, therefore, inasmuch as it affects to have no need of empirical intuition, is quite incapable of giving us knowledge of any object.

§ 4. *Mathematical Concepts*

This doctrine is illustrated by examples. Let us consider the case of mathematical concepts, taking them first of all 'in their pure intuitions'.[3] This phrase is difficult, unless Kant means that they have a secondary reference to empirical intuitions.[4]

Space has three dimensions: between two points there is only one straight line. Such are the principles, or axioms, on which

---

[1] Strictly speaking, I think it is the concepts of spatiality and temporality, rather than the intuitions of space and time, which have objects given to empirical intuition.

[2] The elements or marks in empirical factitious concepts are arbitrarily combined by imagination. In applying the categories to things-in-themselves, we have an arbitrary play, not of imagination, but of understanding.   [3] A 239 = B 298–9.

[4] The examples given seem to be what Kant calls axioms; compare A 163 = B 204 and A 31 = B 47. This may not have any particular significance, and I do not see that it can have any special connexion with the phrase 'in their pure intuitions'. It shows, however, clearly enough that Kant believes a combination of thought and intuition to be necessary, if we are to know space and time as objects. Compare Chapter V § 8 and also B 160 n. and A 107.

Euclidean geometry rests. Their object I take to be space as such, and according to Kant our idea of it is produced *a priori* in the mind. Yet although these principles are thus entirely *a priori*, they would have no significance—that is to say, we could not know that they referred to a possible object—unless we could exhibit their significance in appearances (or empirical objects).

Hence if we take a concept in abstraction from its object, and wish to make certain whether it is the concept of an object, we must make the concept sensuous;[1] that is, we must exhibit an object corresponding to it in intuition. Apart from this, a concept is without sense[2] or objective significance.

This requirement mathematics fulfils by the construction of a figure. Such a figure is constructed *a priori* in accordance with a concept; but it is nevertheless, whether constructed in imagination or on paper, an appearance present to the senses. In mathematical reasoning we attend only to the elements in it which are the necessary consequences of construction in accordance with the concept: its merely accidental features are, or at least ought to be, entirely ignored.[3]

§ 5. *The Categories*

Kant's main concern is with the categories. He turns naturally to the category of quantity,[4] the fundamental category of mathematics, and so makes a transition to categories in general.

The category of quantity finds its sense and significance in number, which is its schema. Number is employed in arithmetic,

[1] Compare A 51 = B 75.

[2] It seems to me quite clear that Kant is playing on the ambiguity of the word 'sense'.

[3] Compare A 713–14 = B 741–2. It is commonly said that in the first proposition of his first book Euclid failed to do so; for he assumed from looking at the diagram that two circles could intersect only in two points, and this requires to be proved. If this cannot be seen directly to follow, without proof, from the very nature of a circle as defined, then he made the mistake of mixing up empirical with *a priori* evidence. The fact that he made this mistake is taken by modern mathematical theorists to show that Euclidean geometry is empirical. This appears to me to be an error.   [4] A 240 = B 299.

and Kant seems to regard it as the basis of all mathematics.[1] Number in turn finds its sense and significance in the fingers, in the beads of the abacus, or in strokes and points written on paper.

In all this Kant is very insistent that however much a concept may be *a priori* (and however much the universal synthetic principles—that is, axioms—or the individual formulae[2] based upon it may be *a priori*), its use or application, and its reference to objects, can be sought, in the last resort, only in experience: indeed these *a priori* concepts are said to 'contain' the possibility of experience in the sense that they are concepts of its form or necessary conditions.[3]

The same principle applies to all the categories.[4] This is shown by the fact that we cannot give a *real* definition to any category (that is, a definition showing that it applies to a possible object) without a reference to its schema, and so to space and time as conditions of sensibility, or forms of appearances.[5] Consequently the categories must be limited to appearances. If we remove the reference to conditions of sensibility, the whole significance of the concept, that is, its reference to an object, disappears. We cannot give any example which would enable us to grasp what kind of thing could possibly be thought by such a concept.

In a passage omitted in the second edition, this contention is further elaborated.[6]

In his earlier discussion[7] Kant stated that although he had in mind definitions of the categories, he deliberately omitted them on the ground that they were not required for his limited purposes and might rouse doubt and opposition. He promised to articulate them later so far as was necessary, but not in the detail demanded by a complete *system* of pure reason, of which

---

[1] Compare its relation to spatial figures and temporal durations as described in A 724 = B 752.   [2] Compare A 165 = B 205–6.

[3] Compare Chapter XLIX § 5.   [4] A 240 = B 300.

[5] The phrase 'forms of appearances' suggests that Kant means space and time by 'conditions of sensibility'; but 'conditions of sensibility' might equally mean the transcendental schemata (see A 140 = B 179).   [6] A 241–2.   [7] A 82–3 = B 108–9.

his work is only an outline.[1] He now asserts that there was a deeper reason for his procedure.

The earlier discussion, strictly speaking, is concerned only with pure categories, though the names applied to them are, in some cases at least, the names of schematised categories. If we remove—as for pure categories we must remove—all reference to those conditions of sensibility which mark out the categories as concepts whose use is empirical, if in short we regard the categories as concepts of things in general and so as having a transcendental use,[2] what are we left with? Only the logical forms of judgement considered as *somehow* conditions of the possibility of things themselves.[3] But in such a case we have not the slightest idea of how they could apply to any object, and consequently we are unable to give any *real* definition of them.

It will be observed that for Kant—and we shall see this more clearly in the sequel—the pure categories, as having their origin in the understanding, are so far not restricted to sensible objects, but have a *prima facie* claim to apply to things-in-themselves. It will also be observed that there is no difficulty in saying what a pure category is. Kant himself has just done so, and he is about to explain the nature of the separate pure categories. The only reason why this is not regarded as a definition is that such a description cannot show that there is any possible object to which a pure category can apply. A little later[4] Kant adds as a further reason that the forms of judgement, and so the pure categories, cannot be defined without a circular definition; for the definition would itself be a judgement, and therefore would already contain these forms.[5] This does not prevent us from recognising that every pure category is a form of judgement considered as determining the combination of a manifold of intuition *in general*, and so as the concept of an object *in general*.[6] Kant would have made the *Kritik* much

---

[1] Compare A 13–14 = B 27–8.   [2] See A 238 = B 298.
[3] Compare Chapter XIV § 8.   [4] A 245.
[5] This suggests that all the forms of judgement are for Kant, as they ought to be, present in every judgement.   [6] Compare A 245–6.

easier to understand, if he had given this explanation at the beginning of the Analytic, instead of at the end. He himself does so, if not too clearly, in the second edition.[1]

Kant's discussion of the separate categories, both as pure and schematised, has already been examined and elaborated in my account of the transcendental schemata.[2] I need add no more here.[3]

§ 6. *Kant's Conclusion*

It follows that the use of the categories is always empirical, and never transcendental.[4] The Principles of Pure Understanding must apply only to objects of the senses, and never to things in general or things-in-themselves; for apart from the universal conditions of a possible sensuous, and indeed human,[5] experience, the categories have for us no reference to any object known to be possible.

Kant's conclusion is therefore that understanding can anticipate only the form of a possible experience in general. In so doing, it can never go beyond the limits of sensibility, within which alone can objects be given to us. We must give up the proud name of Ontology—a science which professes to give us *a priori* synthetic knowledge of things in general, and so of things-in-themselves. This supposed science must give place to a modest Analytic of the pure understanding.

Kant reinforces his conclusion by referring to the doctrine of the transcendental schema, a doctrine which lies at the root of all his arguments throughout this chapter.

Thinking, he says, is the act of relating a given intuition to an object.[6] This may seem to contradict his view that there is a kind of thinking which gives us no knowledge of an object

---

[1] B 128-9.   [2] See Chapter XXXIII.
[3] The passage omitted in the second edition (A 244-6) is repetitive, and is probably omitted for this reason.   [4] A 246 = B 303.
[5] The pure categories would apply to any finite experience which had a manifold given to it under forms of intuition other than time and space; but of such an experience we have no real conception.
[6] A 247 = B 304. Compare the definition of judgement in B 141.

but is merely problematic, the entertaining of a possible concept without enquiring whether its object is also possible. Even such thinking, however, has for him a vague reference to some sort of object—how otherwise could we ask whether its object is possible? It has even a vague reference to some sort of manifold of intuition *in general*—though we do not ask ourselves how such an intuition could be given. Indeed, as we shall see, it is this kind of problematic thinking which he has here primarily in view,[1] although his description is intended to cover all thinking, including problematic thinking.

This is borne out already by his statement that if the kind of intuition in question is in no way given,[2] then the object is merely transcendental: it is just an unknown something $= X$.[3] The concept entertained must be a concept of the understanding, since all other concepts have reference to some sort of intuition or combination of intuitions; and its use must be transcendental in the sense that the application of the concept so far makes no claim to rest on an intuition which could be described as given to sense.

At this stage Kant, rather loosely, identifies the transcendental use with 'the unity of the thought of a manifold of a possible intuition in general'.[4] He must, I think, mean that the concept in this transcendental use can 'contain' only the unity imposed by thought on a manifold of intuition in general.[5] This manifestly is no determinate object, and such thinking by itself

[1] Compare A 255 = B 310.
[2] He may mean 'if the form of this intuition is in no way given', but perhaps his statement is meant to be more general.
[3] Compare A 104 and A 109.
[4] I follow Kant's own obvious emendation (*Nachträge* CXXV). Kemp Smith translates the actual text thus: 'The concept of the understanding has only transcendental employment, namely, as the unity of the thought of a manifold in general'. I am not sure whether the 'as' can thus be understood without amending the German, but the general sense seems right. Incidentally the transcendental object itself might almost be defined in the same way; see A 105.
[5] If so, this accords with the doctrine of A 105 and A 109, and indicates the only way in which we can give any sort of definite meaning to the transcendental object.

gives us no knowledge. As Kant says, through a pure category (in abstraction from every condition of sensuous intuition—the only kind of intuition that is possible to us) no object is determined, and nothing is known.[1] All we have is the thought of an object in general expressed according to different forms of judgement.[2]

For the use of a concept—if it is to give us knowledge—we require more than conception or problematic thinking: we require also, as we have seen in connexion with the transcendental schemata,[3] a function of judgement (in the technical sense). Only so can an object be subsumed under the concept. For such judgement we must have at least the formal condition under which something can be given in intuition. The formal condition in question is the transcendental schema.

If we do not have this schema, which is the condition of judgement, all subsumption under the category is impossible; for there is simply nothing given which can be subsumed under the category. Hence the transcendental use of the category, which professes to have no reference to sense or conditions of sense, is in fact no use at all; or at any rate no use whereby anything can be known.[4] It applies to no determinate object, not even to the form (or schema) of an object which could be determined.[5]

Kant therefore sums up his position as follows. Apart from the formal conditions of sensibility—by which he might mean

[1] Here again I follow Kant's own emendation (*Nachträge* CXXVI)

[2] '*nach verschiedenen modis.*'

[3] A 132 = B 172 ff. There the power of judgement (*Urteilskraft*) is opposed to understanding and reason.

[4] Again I follow Kant's emendation (*Nachträge* CXXVII).

[5] Literally, 'it has no even merely (as regards its form) determinable object'. This is obscurely expressed, but I can hardly think Kant means 'it has not even a determinable object in the sense of a manifold of intuition which remains to be determined by being brought under a form (or schema)'. I think he must mean that it has not even a determinable object in the sense of a form (or schema) which could be determined by receiving under it a particular manifold of intuition. For Kant both the form and the matter, the concept and the intuition, are 'determinable' in relation to each other.

space and time,[1] but more probably means the transcendental schemata[2]—the pure categories have a merely transcendental significance:[3] they profess to apply to an object given to no sensuous intuition. They have no transcendental use. A transcendental use is in itself impossible; for in it all the conditions of using the categories in judgements disappear, namely the formal conditions[4] for subsuming an alleged object under the categories. Hence if we take the categories as pure categories alone, and not as schematised categories, they are not supposed to have an empirical use, and they cannot have a transcendental use. In short, they are of no use at all. That is to say, in abstraction from all sensibility they cannot be applied to any alleged object. They are merely the pure form[5] of the use of understanding (or the pure form of thought) in relation to objects in general; but through this pure form alone they cannot think (in the sense of 'determine') any object.

The whole of this elaborate discussion is little more than an expansion of Kant's doctrine of the transcendental schemata.[6]

---

[1] Compare A 138 = B 177.   [2] Compare A 140 = B 179.
[3] Yet Kant might equally have said they have no significance at all; see A 240 = B 299 and A 242.   [4] Here clearly the schemata.
[5] Perhaps it would be better to say 'concepts of the pure form'.
[6] See especially A 139–40 = B 178–9.

CHAPTER LV

NOUMENON AND TRANSCENDENTAL OBJECT

§ 1. *Phenomena and Noumena*

In their empirical use concepts are applied to sensible objects, which may be described as appearances, or, more technically, phenomena. In their transcendental use concepts are applied— or such at least is the intention—to things as they are in themselves and as they can be grasped by understanding without the aid of sense. Such objects are called 'noumena', that is, understandable or intelligible (and not sensible) objects. Thus the opposition between phenomena and noumena corresponds to the opposition between the empirical and the transcendental use of concepts.

We have now seen that there is no transcendental use of concepts. It is therefore natural enough to conclude that there are no such things as noumena, and even that there are no things-in-themselves. A doctrine of this kind is often read into Kant's discussion of phenomena and noumena:[1] it chimes in with certain idealistic predilections, and it has also been welcomed by minds of a more realistic tendency. To abolish the thing-in-itself may be to improve Kant's theory, though I do not feel so confident about this as I did when my ignorance was greater than it is to-day. What seems to me to be certain is that this improvement was never made by Kant himself. His discussion of phenomena and noumena is an attempt to show that things-in-themselves can never be known by human minds. This is a very different thing from an attempt to show that there are no things-in-themselves; and I doubt whether Kant even envisaged a hypothesis so revolutionary. Belief in the reality and independent existence of things-in-themselves seems to me to be the presupposition of his present discussion,

---

[1] I think this is roughly the view of Hermann Cohen and his followers, but I find traces of it almost everywhere.

as it is of the whole Critical Philosophy.[1] This is a complicated and controversial question which can be settled only by careful analysis. Unfortunately, for part of the discussion a new version is substituted in the second edition, and this means that we have to cover more or less the same ground twice over.

The rest of this chapter will be an examination of the argument peculiar to the first edition. This argument is difficult, mainly because it occupies itself with the distinction between the noumenon and the transcendental object. It repeats some of the complicated theories which we have already studied in the provisional exposition of the Transcendental Deduction. The reader who is anxious to grasp Kant's main doctrine without the study of unnecessary detail will be well advised to devote himself to the very much clearer account given in the second edition, an account which will be examined in Chapter LVI.

§ 2. *Alleged Knowledge of Noumena*

In the first edition[2] Kant begins by explaining the ground on which we may be tempted to claim that we have knowledge of noumena.

He defines phenomena very clearly: they are 'appearances so far as these are thought *as objects* in accordance with the unity of the categories'. If he had only used the word 'phenomenon' consistently for the appearance as an object (or for the phenomenal object), we should have been saved many difficulties of interpretation; for he habitually uses the word 'appearance' without making clear whether by that he means the whole object or only a partial and temporary aspect of it.

Appearance for Kant is always an appearance to sensuous intuition. We may suppose that there are things which are not appearances in this sense, but are mere objects of the understanding. Such objects, since they are not given to sense

---

[1] On this point compare Adickes, *Kant und das Ding an sich*. This work seems to me of great importance.   [2] A 248-9.

and cannot be given to discursive thinking,[1] would have to be given to some sort of active intellectual intuition. They would then be called 'noumena'[2] or 'intelligibilia'.

It might be thought that the doctrine of the Transcendental Aesthetic justifies a belief in the objective reality of such noumena. The doctrine of the Aesthetic limits appearances to sensible appearances given to us passively under the forms of our sensibility—space and time. Since it separates passive sensibility from active understanding, the understanding is manifestly in no way confined to sensible appearances; and this suggests the possibility of a distinction between phenomena and noumena, between a sensible and an intelligible world.

This implication was accepted by Kant himself in the Dissertation of 1770, though I am inclined to doubt whether even then he was so confident about it as he appeared to be. It was in any case a new possibility which had not been open to the followers of Leibniz. According to Leibniz the same object is known indistinctly by sense and distinctly by thought, the difference between sense and thought being only a difference between indistinctness and distinctness in our knowledge.[3] This means that the object as thought and the object as sensed differ only in the degree of distinctness with which they are known: there is no difference in kind. But if sense and understanding are two fundamentally different powers, and if objects may be given independently to these different powers, then there may be a distinction in kind between the object as sensed and the object as understood, between the phenomenon and the noumenon.

The possibility that an object which is not given to sense at all might be given to understanding[4] is not here discussed by Kant. He takes instead the case where the same object is

---

[1] Discursive thinking is always a thinking about something given to it from without, not given by the act of thinking itself.

[2] The word 'νοῦς' or 'νόησις' is used for the faculty whereby we have direct intellectual vision of reality without any help from the senses such as is present even in διάνοια; compare Plato, *Republic*, p. 511d.   [3] See Chapter XIX § 8.   [4] Compare B 306.

given independently to sense and understanding. If, as Kant has proved in the Aesthetic, the senses can represent something only *as it appears* under the human forms of time and space, the something which appears must be a thing-in-itself;[1] and if it is given to understanding, it must be an object of some kind of non-sensuous intuition—Kant assumes that conception (by which we merely think about given objects) cannot itself give us an object to think about.

Hence we seem to have established the possibility of a kind of knowledge in which there is no sensibility. This knowledge has by itself, apart from sensibility, an absolutely objective reality or validity: by it we know objects *as they are*, and not merely *as they appear*.

If we use our understanding empirically, if we apply our concepts only to appearances given under conditions of sensibility, we can know objects only as they appear. This follows at once from Kant's theory of space and time. But now we seem to have a whole new field of knowledge opening before us, a world of things-in-themselves which we can think by means of our pure categories[2] and in some sense apparently intuit, a far nobler object for the exercise of our pure understanding.

If this were really true, it would contradict everything that we have said before.

§ 3. *The Transcendental Object*

Kant discusses[3] this difficulty in the light of his previous account of the transcendental object.[4]

All our ideas are in fact referred by understanding to some object. Appearances, since they are ideas, are thus referred to a 'something'; that is, they are regarded as appearances of something; and this 'something' may be described as the transcendental object.[5] It is called transcendental, because it

---

[1] Compare B XXVI–XXVII.

[2] All other concepts contain an element derived from sense.

[3] A 250.   [4] A 104 ff.

[5] In a note Kant describes it as 'something as object of an intuition *in general*'; see *Nachträge* CXXXIV.

manifestly cannot be given to sense; for if it could, it would be only another appearance. Hence it must be known *a priori*, if at all.

Unfortunately, if our previous argument is correct, it is not, and it cannot be, known at all. Kant therefore proceeds to argue, exactly as he did in the Transcendental Deduction, that it can only be a correlate to the unity of apperception: it has to serve as, or to be identified with, that unity of the manifold whereby the understanding unites the manifold in the concept of an object.[1]

On this view the transcendental object, *so far as it is known*, must be identified with that necessary synthetic unity which is the only assignable and universal mark of objectivity, a unity which is itself imposed upon the manifold of intuition by the understanding.[2] As Kant says, the transcendental object in this sense cannot be separated from sensuous data—if it is, nothing is left over by which it can be thought. It is no object of knowledge in itself. I take this to mean it is not an object which we can know (by pure understanding) as it is in itself.

The double meaning of transcendental object is confusing, though we can understand how one meaning grows out of the other.[3] The passage affirms that we cannot know the transcendental object as a thing-in-itself. It might be interpreted as asserting that there is no transcendental object, and therefore by inference no thing-in-itself. I do not see that this interpretation is necessary, nor that if it were necessary in regard to the transcendental object, it would therefore hold of the thing as it is in itself.

Kant adds that the transcendental object is 'only the representation of appearances under the concept of an object *in general*, a concept which is determinable through the manifold of appearances'. I do not know what this means, unless the transcendental object is being identified with the act of thinking

---

[1] A 250.

[2] For this reason it would properly be called transcendental; see Chapter XXII § 2.

[3] Compare Chapter XXII § 2.

or the unity of apperception.[1] I do not think this is very intelligible in itself; but if this is the meaning, it can apply only to the transcendental object in its second sense. I should require very much more evidence before I could accept the view that Kant was here retracting his whole doctrine about things-in-themselves.

The doctrine of the transcendental object is then applied to the categories, which are concepts of an object in general, and consequently, at least in their pure form, concepts of something in general.[2] We think the object in general, or the transcendental object in its second sense, by means of the categories. This does not mean that by them we have knowledge of some special object given to the understanding by itself. The categories merely serve to determine the transcendental object —here apparently equated with the concept of something in general—through what is given in sensibility in order thereby to know appearances under concepts of objects.[3]

The ambiguity of so many of the terms makes the interpretation of this difficult. The general sense is that the pure categories give us no knowledge of things-in-themselves. Their only use is empirical. How they determine the transcendental object or its concept is not so clear; but by their reference to the transcendental schemata they supply a matter for the ultimate concept of something in general, and so enable us to apply this ultimate concept to an empirical manifold characterised by the transcendental schemata. In this way we can

[1] A 251. It would be much simpler to say that it is merely the universal form of an object and can be determined only by receiving an appropriate matter from sense. Kant later identifies it with the concept of something in general, which complicates matters. Perhaps this is what he means here—compare § 5 below—although if so, he has expressed himself loosely.

[2] It is not clear whether Kant intends to identify or to distinguish concepts of an object in general and concepts of something in general. Strictly speaking, an object in general should be an object of sense, though the concept of it is not always confined to this usage. 'Something in general' should be equivalent to 'a thing in general', and the concept of it should be wider in its application than the concept of an object in general.

[3] A 251. 'Concepts of objects' here may mean 'empirical concepts'.

know appearances through empirical concepts of objects, empirical concepts which presuppose the categories and the concept of the transcendental object itself.

This is a very elaborate way of describing phenomenal objects and explaining the use of the categories in relation to them.

§4. *Origin of the Belief in Noumena*

Kant endeavours to explain further why we refuse to be satisfied with phenomena and insist on adding noumena thought only by the pure understanding.[1]

The Transcendental Aesthetic has shown that since space and time are forms of our sensibility, we can by means of sensibility know things only as they appear to us, not as they are in themselves. This means that, so far as concerns sensibility, we are confined to knowledge of appearances only: it consequently implies a contrast with things-in-themselves. But even apart from this the concept of appearance itself implies some correlative which is not an appearance. An appearance is nothing in itself; it must be an appearance to something and an appearance of something.[2] The latter point is the one with which Kant is especially concerned. The very word 'appearance' implies a reference to 'something' in itself, that is, to an object independent of our sensibility.[3] The fact that the appearance itself (or our immediate idea of the object) is sensible does not affect this contention in the least.

From the limitation of our sensibility springs the concept of a noumenon. This concept Kant in the first edition treats

[1] A 251; he has already explained it in A 248–9. He says here that we are not satisfied with the 'substratum' of sensibility. This is a curious phrase for the transcendental object, yet I feel it hard to see what else he can mean. Appearances possessing the unity thought in the concept of the transcendental object are phenomena (or phenomenal objects).

[2] Compare B XXVI–XXVII. If the word 'appearance' is appropriately applied—a large question—this contention is true. And it seems impossible to believe that an appearance can be an appearance of an appearance, and so *ad infinitum*.

[3] This is what distinguishes an appearance from an illusion.

as negative:[1] it gives us no determinate knowledge of anything. This concept is merely the thought of something in general, and in this thought there is complete abstraction from any reference to the forms of sensuous intuition.[2] But if the noumenon is to be a genuine object distinct from phenomena, it is not enough that in the concept of it there should be abstraction from all the conditions[3] of sensuous intuition. I must have a positive ground for assuming a non-sensuous intuition to which such an object could be given. Otherwise my concept, though it may not be self-contradictory, will be empty—in the sense that I cannot know that it applies to a possible object.

Now we cannot prove that sensuous intuition is the only possible kind of intuition. But equally we cannot prove that there is any other kind of intuition. The fact that in thinking we can entertain a concept in abstraction from sensibility is quite inconclusive. It still remains an open question whether our concept is not the mere form of a concept, whether in abstraction from sensibility it can have any object, and indeed whether in such abstraction any possible intuition remains at all.[4]

So far as words are concerned, this question may be still open; but for Kant it is really closed. The concept of a noumenon is only the form of a concept, and we are quite unable, in abstraction from sensibility, to apply it to any object at all. This does not necessarily mean that Kant is entitled to assert, or that he wishes to assert, the unreality of noumena, and still less the unreality of things-in-themselves. It may mean only that we have no way of knowing them; and this is what I believe it does mean.

---

[1] In the second edition he distinguishes between positive and negative meanings of the word; see B 307.

[2] The concept of a thing in general or something in general stands to the concept of an object in general as the pure category stands to the schematised category; but unfortunately Kant does not always adhere consistently to this usage, and at times his statements are ambiguous.   [3] 'Conditions' are equivalent to 'forms'.

[4] The last point is added from Kant's own note; see *Nachträge* CXXXVII.

§ 5. *Kant's Conclusion in the First Edition*

The last section has been comparatively straightforward, but for the conclusion[1] we must turn again to the complications of the transcendental object.

The object to which I relate appearances is always the transcendental object. This Kant identifies with the thought, the wholly indeterminate thought, of something *in general*—I should prefer to say it is the content of that thought. It cannot be called the noumenon, by which we mean a thing known, by pure understanding, as it is in itself. In the case of the transcendental object we do not know what it is in itself.[2] Our only concept of it is the thought of the object of a sensuous intuition *in general*, an object which is therefore the same for all appearances.[3]

I cannot think the transcendental object[4] through the categories; for these apply only to phenomenal objects: they serve to bring empirical intuitions under the concept of an object *in general*. No doubt a pure, or rather a transcendental, use of the categories is logically possible; that is, it can be thought without contradiction; but it has no objective validity, for we cannot know that it has a possible object. More elaborately, we cannot know that it has reference to any non-sensuous intuition which could thereby acquire the unity

[1] A 253.

[2] This at least leaves it an open question whether the transcendental object (in the first sense) may not be a thing-in-itself.

[3] It is not clear in this statement whether Kant is thinking of the transcendental object in its first sense (as the unknown something to which any appearance must be referred) or in its second sense (as the unity of the manifold of any phenomenal object). I incline to think he means the latter. Compare A 109.

[4] Here clearly the transcendental object in its first sense. In the second sense the transcendental object is that necessary synthetic unity which is articulated in the categories, and is 'determined' by them through what is given in sensibility (see A 251). In this second sense we could, I imagine, be said to think the transcendental object through the categories; for it is through them that we think the necessary synthetic unity of the phenomenal object.

which characterises an object.[1] The category is a mere function (or form) of thought. Through it no object is given. The object which we think through the categories must be given as a manifold of intuition and combined by the transcendental synthesis of imagination in one time and space.

We must recognise that in the conclusions so stated there is a certain amount of ambiguity due to the intrusion of the transcendental object. As in the Transcendental Deduction, Kant first of all treats the transcendental object as the unknown 'something' to which we refer the manifold of appearances, and then reduces it, *so far as it can be known*, to the necessary synthetic unity of the appearances themselves. This seems to me to leave the question open whether we must still think that there is an unknown 'something', a thing-in-itself, a reality of which we know only the appearances to us. As I understand Kant, he has no intention whatever of giving up his belief in the unknown thing-in-itself or the noumenon in this negative sense. What he is anxious to assert is that by means of the pure categories we can have no *knowledge* of such a thing-in-itself, though even this he leaves as a logical possibility. If we take the noumenon in a positive sense, that is, as a reality intelligible by means of our pure categories alone, he certainly means to deny that we are justified in claiming to know any such reality. His position can be made clear only if we distinguish between a positive and a negative sense of the word 'noumenon', and this distinction is made explicit only in the second edition.

I need hardly add that Kant has no intention here, any more than in the Transcendental Deduction, of giving up his doctrine of the phenomenal object. The reduction of the transcendental object to the necessary synthetic unity of the manifold of appearances is in fact a way of insisting that the only objects we know are necessarily phenomenal.

There is a further source of difficulty in Kant's habit of identifying the concept with what is conceived, the thinking with

---

[1] At times Kant says roundly that our categories could apply only to sensuous or passive intuitions and not to intellectual or active intuitions; see B 145.

what is thought, the unity of thinking with the unity of the object, and so on. There was a time when I believed that this was due to mere carelessness and perhaps to confusion. I still find it puzzling, but I have an uneasy suspicion that if I understood Kant better, these difficulties might disappear.

CHAPTER LVI

PHENOMENA AND NOUMENA

§ 1. *Categories and Knowledge of Noumena*

The account given of the noumenon in the second edition is more brief, and also more clear, than that given in the first.

Kant begins with the categories.[1] These originate in the understanding, not (like the forms of time and space) in sensibility. Hence there seems no reason why they should be applied only to sensible objects: they have a *prima facie* claim to apply to objects other than those of sense.

This claim, however, is an illusion. The categories in themselves are mere forms of thought or of judgement. They contain no matter or manifold in themselves, and so cannot by themselves give us knowledge of any object. All that they contain is the logical power of uniting[2] *a priori* in one consciousness a manifold which must be given in intuition. If we consider them in abstraction from the only kind of intuition possible to us—namely, sensuous intuition under the forms of time and space—then they are empty: they have no meaning, in the sense that they refer to no assignable object. They have even less meaning than the pure forms of sense (time and space); for through these at least some sort of manifold, and so some sort of object, is given.[3] In the categories all we think is a way of combining the manifold, a way proper to understanding and involved in the very nature of thought itself. If we set

[1] B 305.

[2] Kant here seems to be thinking of the categories as acts (see A 57 = B 81) or as forms (or functions) of acts of the understanding (see A 69 = B 94). If we take them as concepts, what they 'contain' (or what is thought in them) is necessary synthetic unity in one of its aspects. This necessary synthetic unity is the unity of a manifold of intuition *in general*; but it remains an empty form till we consider it as the necessary synthetic unity of a manifold given under the form of time.

[3] The object given is only the form of an object; see B 147.

aside entirely the sensuous intuitions in which alone a manifold
can be given to us, then the mere way of combining by itself
has no *meaning*. We can still of course consider it as a form of
thought, but it tells us nothing about any object.

Hence, as has been said, the claim of the categories to apply
to objects not given to sense is an illusion. We must, however,
try to understand how this illusion arises.

The ordinary objects which we know may, as appearances
to us, be called phenomena (or sensible entities). This terminology implies a distinction between the objects as they
appear to us (or are intuited by us) and the objects as they are
in themselves with a character independent of our sensibility.[1]
For example, the table which we know appears to us as occupying space and lasting through time; but this is only because
space and time are the forms of our sensibility, and so we must
distinguish the character of the table as it appears to us from
its character, or inner nature, as it is in itself.

Consequently if we regard tables and similar objects as
phenomena, we are bound to set over against them the same
objects in their own character as they are in themselves,
although in this character we cannot intuit them; for we can
intuit them only as they appear under the forms of time and
space. We are also bound to suppose that there may be other
things which have their own character in themselves, even
although they are never intuited by us as phenomena at all.
These things as they are in themselves, whether they are
intuited by us as phenomena or not, we are obliged to regard
as objects which we think by mere understanding apart from
sense. We call these objects noumena (or intelligible entities).

The question then arises whether the pure categories may
not be applied to these noumena? Can the pure categories be
said to have meaning as applying to noumena, and can we
regard them as giving us knowledge of such noumena?[2]

---

[1] Compare B XXVII and A 251.

[2] B 306. Note that Kant does not even ask the question whether
we should give up our belief in these noumena. The only question is
whether we can know them.

§ 2. *The Positive and Negative Meaning of 'Noumenon'*

To answer these questions we must distinguish two different meanings of the word 'noumenon'.[1]

The understanding when it thinks of an object as a phenomenon in its relation to our senses, also thinks of an object as it is in itself apart from this relation. It supposes further—else how could it think of them?—that it must be able to make concepts of these objects as they are in themselves. The only concepts which the understanding can produce out of itself without the aid of sensibility are the pure categories. Hence it is only natural to believe that by means of these pure categories (if by no other concepts) we must be able to think objects as they are in themselves.

In this argument we are misled. We are confusing the quite *indeterminate* concept of a noumenon as a mere 'something in general' which is what it is independently of our senses—we are confusing this indeterminate concept of a noumenon with the *determinate* concept of a noumenon as an entity that admits of being known by understanding in a purely intellectual way.

Here then are clearly two different meanings of 'noumenon'. If by 'noumenon' we understand *a thing so far as it is not the object of our sensuous intuition*, this is a noumenon in the *negative* sense. Its concept is derived by making complete abstraction from our sensuous intuitions under the forms of time and space.[2] But if we understand by 'noumenon' *a thing so far as it is the object of a non-sensuous (or intellectual) intuition*, this is a noumenon in the *positive* sense. We are then not merely making abstraction from our own sensuous intuitions: we are supposing that there is another kind of intuition (an intellectual intuition through which the noumenon can be known), although we neither possess such an intuition nor have any insight into the possibility of such an intuition.

The concept of 'noumenon' in the negative sense is an

---

[1] B 306–7.
[2] Such abstraction gives us the pure concept of an object in general, or (better) the pure concept of a thing in general.

indeterminate concept: it gives us no knowledge, unless a manifold can be supplied for it.[1] The concept of 'noumenon' in the positive sense professes to be a *determinate* concept; but in the absence of an intellectual intuition it must fail to make good its claim.

§ 3. *Can We Know the Thing-in-Itself?*

We must now draw our conclusions from this distinction. Kant does so in a passage which is one of the most important, as it is one of the clearest, in the whole *Kritik*.[2] In it he shows beyond any reasonable doubt, not only that he holds the thing-in-itself to be unknowable, but also that he has not the remotest intention of giving up his belief in things-in-themselves. His incidental account of our knowledge of phenomena is also one of the most precise with which I am acquainted, and is in full accordance with the interpretation which I have attempted to give throughout.

The theory of sensibility as expounded in the *Kritik* is at the same time a doctrine of noumena in the negative sense. It implies that we must think of things as they are in themselves, not merely as they appear to us, or as they are in relation to our sensibility. Yet as we think of things in abstraction from our sensibility, we understand that in considering them thus we can make no use of the categories. The categories have meaning (or objects) only in relation to the unity of our intuitions in time and space; and they can determine this unity *a priori*, through universal concepts of combination, only because of the ideality of time and space.

This seems to me to indicate—what I have argued for consistently—that the transcendental synthesis of imagination can impose unity on objects in accordance with the pure categories only because time and space are at once pure intuitions and necessary forms of all appearances. And the categories, as we have demonstrated, can have objective validity only

---

[1] No manifold can be supplied for it, and it cannot become determinate without a manifold.   [2] B 307-9.

because all our intuitions, and all our objects, must be united in one time and one space.[1]

If this unity of all intuitions in time (and space) is lacking, as it must be *ex hypothesi* in the case of noumena, then the whole use of the categories, and their objective validity or meaning, entirely ceases. The very possibility[2] of things to which the categories might apply can never be comprehended[3] by us. We can never determine the possibility of a thing from the mere fact that the concept of it is not self-contradictory: we can do so only by showing that there is an intuition corresponding to the concept. If we wish to show that the categories apply to objects otherwise than as phenomena, we must base this on an intellectual intuition; and in that case the object would be a noumenon in the positive sense. Since such an intellectual intuition has no place in our cognitive powers, our use of the categories cannot go beyond objects of sensuous experience.

Nevertheless Kant does not doubt that corresponding to phenomena there are intelligible entities: every appearance is an appearance to us of a thing-in-itself. He does not even doubt that there may be intelligible entities which never appear to us in intuition at all.[4] All he asserts is that our categories cannot be applied to such entities; for our categories are mere forms of thought awaiting a manifold given in sensuous intuition. When we speak of a noumenon, we must interpret it only in the negative sense as a thing which is no object of our sensuous intuition.

We can see how this passage may be taken, by Hegelians and others, as showing that Kant *ought* to have given up a belief in things-in-themselves.[5] On that point I offer no opinion, beyond saying that if this is really so, Kant would have to

---

[1] This applies especially to the Analogies, but also to the other Principles.

[2] B 308. Compare also, as Kant himself suggests, B 288 ff.

[3] The word used is '*einsehen*', which is especially connected with reason.   [4] B 309.

[5] Fichte is perhaps to be regarded as the originator of this view.

re-write his entire philosophy. To assert that Kant *has* explicitly given up his belief in things-in-themselves seems to me a manifest contradiction of his express statements.

§ 4. *Thought and Intuition*

The rest of Kant's argument[1] is little more than an amplification of what has already been said; but it contains some points which are of interest in themselves, and others which are of interest because of the misunderstandings to which they have given rise. The main contention may be said to be the central contention of the Critical Philosophy—that although we must always distinguish thought and intuition, neither can give us knowledge of objects apart from the other.

Mere intuition by itself is blind.[2] The fact that there is an affection of sensibility in me—and even this could not be known as a fact without thought—does not constitute a reference of the idea so received to an object. To know that this appearance given to me is the appearance of an object, I must think, and think through the categories: I must, for example, regard this appearance as the state of a permanent substance; and it is only on this presupposition that I can apply empirical concepts of objects.

Mere thought by itself is empty. If I leave out all intuition, I am left only with the form of thought. Such a form of thought is simply a principle of synthesis, a way of combining some sort of manifold, and so a way of determining an object for the manifold of a possible intuition. The categories, as such principles of synthesis, contain, however, no reference to sensibility as the special way in which the manifold (and consequently the object) may be given. Elsewhere[3] Kant appears to suggest that the very nature of the categories implies that the manifold must be given passively and therefore to a sensuous intuition; but in any case the categories contain no

---

[1] A 253 = B 309 ff. It is to be noted that this passage occurs in both editions, and the passage peculiar to the first edition must be interpreted in the light of this.

[2] A 51 = B 75.   [3] See B 145 and compare B 149.

reference to time and space as the only forms of human sensibility. Therefore the categories, as concepts of objects in general, do have a *prima facie* claim to apply beyond the realm of sensuous intuition, or at least beyond the realm of human sensuous intuition. Nevertheless they do not give us determinate knowledge of any objects other than sensible phenomena; for we cannot assume that such objects would be given except by presupposing a non-sensuous or intellectual intuition; and this we are not entitled to do.[1]

§ 5. *The Concept of 'Noumenon' as a Limiting Concept*

Kant next proceeds to examine the concept of 'noumenon', and asserts that it is a limiting concept. This contention has often been misunderstood.

The concept of a noumenon (or of a thing as it is in itself and as it is known to be by pure understanding) is, in the first place, not self-contradictory; for there is no contradiction in assuming a non-sensuous intuition, as is done in this description of the concept. Secondly this concept coheres with the rest of our knowledge as setting a limit to other concepts, particularly the concept of sensibility: it is a concept of what is beyond sensibility. Thirdly we have no means of showing its objective reality or validity. On these grounds Kant calls it a problematic concept.[2]

The concept of a noumenon is more than this: it is also a necessary concept. It is necessary in order to limit the objective validity of our sensuous knowledge, that is, to prevent us from thinking that our sensuous intuitions give us knowledge of things as they are in themselves.

It is hard to see how Kant could have held this unless he believed in things-in-themselves, and unless he believed that we must think—though we can never know—things-in-themselves. Yet when all is said and done, we can, he insists, have no insight into the possibility of noumena. The area

---

[1] We are not even entitled to assume sensuous intuitions with forms other than time and space.   [2] A 254 = B 310.

outside the realm of appearances is empty—empty, he is careful to add, *for us*. Our understanding does extend *problematically* beyond the realm of appearances—how otherwise could it know the limits of that realm? But we have no intuition—we have not even any concept of an intuition—by which objects beyond the range of sensibility could be given to us. Hence our understanding cannot be used *assertorically* beyond the limit of sensuous appearances.

All this seems to me to mean that we must think there really are things-in-themselves beyond the realm of appearances (and even perhaps—though the thought is empty—that these things-in-themselves could be known only by an intelligence different from our own). All Kant is denying is that we can have any positive knowledge of such things-in-themselves. His whole thought seems to me utterly remote from the doctrine that the thing-in-itself is to be reduced to a mere concept of the mind.

Hence he concludes that the concept of a noumenon is a limiting concept.[1] Its use is only to limit the pretensions of sensibility, and is therefore negative, not positive. The concept, however, is far from arbitrary. It is bound up necessarily with the limitation of sensibility, although it can give us no positive knowledge of the inner nature of that which lies beyond sensibility. It is to me extraordinary that this passage should be used to show that Kant is consciously reducing the thing-in-itself to a mere concept. It should be noted that Kant does not assert the noumenon to be a limiting concept—he is sometimes quoted as saying this: he asserts only that the *concept* of a noumenon is a limiting concept (or the concept of a limit). To say this is to say only that it is a concept—an indeterminate concept no doubt—of what lies beyond the limits of our sensibility; for on Kant's theory that which limits must be different from that which it limits.[2] In the absence of a non-sensuous intuition we can never know what lies beyond the limits of our sensibility. But Kant does not doubt that something which is not an object of sensuous intuition does

[1] A 255 = B 310–11, '*Grenzbegriff*'.   [2] See A 515 = B 543.

lie beyond these limits—otherwise there would be no sense in talking about limits at all.[1]

§ 6. *Understanding not Limited by Sensibility*

In a further paragraph[2] Kant elaborates his doctrine without adding anything really new.

He insists that the division of objects into phenomena and noumena, and the distinction between a *mundus sensibilis* and a *mundus intelligibilis*, cannot be admitted *in the positive sense*. The latter phrase is added in the second edition; and, I suggest, it indicates that the distinction between noumenon in the positive, and noumenon in the negative, sense has been introduced mainly to guard against the interpretation that Kant is giving up the thing-in-itself instead of merely denying that we have knowledge in regard to it.

His further distinction between sensuous and intellectual concepts, and his insistence that the categories give us no knowledge unless we can indicate a possible intuition to which they can apply—all this calls for no comment.[3] The same applies to his contention that the concept of a noumenon as a problematic concept[4] is, not only admissible, but inevitable: nevertheless we must not interpret the concept positively, or suppose that thereby our understanding acquires a determinate object known by means of pure thought. An understanding which knew reality in this way, not discursively by categories

---

[1] I think some commentators have been misled by the modern associations of a 'limiting concept'. Kant does not mean by it the concept of something to which we can get closer and closer approximations. He does not mean to imply by it—as has been suggested, for example, by the Master of Balliol, *Kant*, p. 284—that we can come to know reality more and more as it· is. He means to imply, on the contrary, that we can never come to know reality as it is.

[2] A 255 = B 311.

[3] Except perhaps the qualification that the intellectual concepts (or categories) can be valid, and must be valid, of objects of empirical intuition: Kant's language might suggest that this is not so. When he says that we cannot determine any object for intellectual concepts, he must mean 'so long as they remain purely intellectual' (that is, unschematised).   [4] See A 254 = B 310.

which await an intuition given to sense, but intuitively in a non-sensuous intuition, is for us itself a problem: we have no means of showing that such an understanding is possible.

By the concept of a noumenon our understanding acquires an extension that is purely negative: it is not limited by sensibility, but rather limits sensibility; for it must think that beyond sensibility and beyond appearances there is the thing as it is in itself, which it calls a noumenon in distinction from phenomena. But it also immediately sets limits to itself; for it recognises that it cannot know these things-in-themselves by any of its categories. It can only think them under the name of an unknown something.

In all this there is no denial of the thing-in-itself. There is only an insistence that while we must think things-in-themselves, and thereby recognise the limits of our experience, we must never delude ourselves into the belief that we can know these things-in-themselves by pure understanding.

§ 7. *The Union of Understanding and Sensibility*

The distinction between the sensible and the intelligible world is not to be identified with the distinction between the world as known by observational astronomy and the world as known by theoretical (or mathematical) astronomy.[1] We can of course apply understanding and reason to appearances; but the phrase 'an intelligible world' should be confined to a world known by understanding alone. To ask whether we know such an intelligible world is to ask whether there is a transcendental, as well as an empirical, use of understanding; and this question we have answered in the negative.[2]

Therefore if we say that the senses represent objects *as they appear*, while understanding represents them *as they are*, we must use the latter phrase only in the empirical sense. To know things as they are is simply to know them as objects of experience—that is, as appearances bound together in one system in accordance with the categories. We cannot know

---

[1] A 256–7 = B 312–13.   [2] A 257 = B 313.

them as they may be apart from their relation to possible experience, and so we cannot know them as objects of mere understanding apart from sense. We cannot even know whether such a knowledge is possible—at least, Kant adds, if it is to stand under our human categories.

The last phrase may suggest speculations always at the back of Kant's mind, but never regarded as more than speculations. A finite understanding must receive a given manifold from without, and must combine it in accordance with the categories which originate in itself—how then can it possibly know reality as it is in itself? Surely this is the prerogative of an infinite mind which would have no reality beyond itself. Such an infinite mind might perhaps know all reality in its own intellectual, and yet intuitive, activity. In such knowledge our categories could have no place, but we have certainly no means of knowing that such a divine knowledge is possible.

If we confine ourselves to experience which we know to be possible, we must say that for us understanding and sensibility can determine objects only in *conjunction*.[1] If we separate them, we may indeed have intuitions without concepts, or concepts without intuitions, but neither of these by itself can give us a determinate object. The Analytic ends as it began.[2] The fundamental distinction and the necessary co-operation of sense and understanding, intuition and thought, in all our knowledge—this is the central and all-important doctrine of the *Kritik*.

§ 8. *The Limits of Knowledge*

If we are still unconvinced by this doctrine and reluctant to give up the transcendental use of the categories, Kant asks us to try the experiment of making synthetic judgements by means of the categories alone.[3] We may be able to make analytic judgements by means of the categories alone, but in that case we are only making explicit what is thought in the category: we do not show that the category applies to an object, and it may be merely a principle of synthesis involved in the nature

---

[1] A 258 = B 314.   [2] A 51 = B 75.   [3] A 258 = B 314.

of thought. If we try to make synthetic judgements—if, for example, starting merely from the concept of substance and accident, we say that everything which exists, exists as substance or accident—how can we justify our assertion? Such a judgement professes to apply to things-in-themselves as objects known by pure understanding. Where then is the third thing, or the necessary intuition,[1] which alone can carry us beyond our concept? We can never prove such a proposition except by appealing to something other than our original concept. This third thing can only be possible experience; but if we appeal to possible experience with its necessary forms, we thereby renounce our claim to make *a priori* judgements free from all reference to sense.

We have therefore no principles[2] by which we can apply the concept of a merely intelligible object, if we regard that concept as positive[3] and as a source of possible knowledge; for we cannot think of any way in which such objects could be given. We must treat the concept as problematical or negative. It then leaves open a place for such intelligible objects;[4] but it serves only, like an empty space, to limit the empirical Principles of the Understanding. We can say that the Principles of the Understanding (such as the law of causality), together with the sciences based on them, can be applied only to the phenomenal world. We must not delude ourselves into the supposition that this negative and necessary limitation is at the same time positive knowledge of a world beyond.

In Kant's whole discussion of phenomena and noumena I can see no suggestion that he gave up for a moment his belief in things-in-themselves. The passages in regard to the transcendental object might indeed with a certain plausibility be interpreted in this sense; but I do not believe that either here

---

[1] Compare *Nachträge* CXXXIX.

[2] 'Everything which exists, exists as substance or accident' would be such a principle, if it could be established.

[3] Compare *Nachträge* CXL.

[4] It is absolutely vital to Kant's philosophy that such a place should be *left open*.

or in the Transcendental Deduction such an interpretation is necessary, nor do I believe that it could express the intention of Kant's thought. These passages are in any case withdrawn in the second edition, perhaps because they are susceptible of this interpretation. There can at least be no reasonable doubt that in the second edition Kant's position in this matter is perfectly clear. Nor can there be any reasonable doubt that without the presupposition of things-in-themselves—whether we regard it as justified or not—the whole of the Critical Philosophy falls to pieces.

EPILOGUE

As I look back on the long and difficult road that we have traversed, I feel compelled to ask whether it has been worth while. For myself at least I must answer emphatically, Yes. I think I can now see Kant's theory as a whole, and even as a comparatively simple whole, so far as a theory which deals with the most ultimate questions possible to the human mind can ever be called simple. I think I can see also that the intricacy of his exposition is not due to incompetence, but mainly to the complications of his subject; and I have found not rarely that my own first simplifications of his argument were erroneous, and that his more intricate statement was the only one that was correct. His exposition would have been clearer, if it had been better arranged; and there are passages, unfortunately too often crucial passages, where there is unnecessary obscurity due presumably to excessive haste. Nevertheless on the whole Kant seems to me both to have a consistent philosophy and to have expressed it as it ought to be expressed. I have convinced at least myself that the prevalent charges of pedantry, formalism, incoherence, and confusion are wide of the mark: so far as they are true at all, they deal only with the surface of things; and they are bound to be set aside, in their present exaggerated form, as soon as men can acquire that internal understanding apart from which no great philosophy can be intelligible.

Such an internal understanding it is the business of every commentator, within the limits of his own capacity, to acquire and to communicate. In my belief this can be done only by a patient study of the details, by an attempt to follow the intricate workings of an author's mind, provided always we remember that there is a whole which we seek to know and in the light of which all the details are to be interpreted. This at any rate is the method which I have tried to follow. I could, I think, have written an easier, and certainly a shorter, book, had I attempted only to set forth my own views of Kant's philosophy. For such books there is certainly an urgent need, and at times I have felt the desire to try my hand at writing one of them. But, at the best, works of this kind do not enable the student to check the statements which they make; and no book, however good, can be a substitute for the direct understanding of Kant himself.

My hope is that by the method I have chosen the student may be helped in the reading of the *Kritik* itself and may be enabled thereby to form his own judgements. In no other way can Kant be restored to his real position in the history of philosophy, a position which, in my opinion, is generally misjudged at the present time. This seems to me particularly important when the modern idealisms to which he gave rise appear to have worked themselves out, at least for the moment, and when thinkers everywhere are approaching the same problems from a different point of view. I believe that the attitude of Kant is much nearer to the modern attitude than was that of his immediate successors; and I believe that a real, as opposed to a superficial, knowledge of the *Kritik* may help to save modern philosophy from unnecessary errors and to keep it in the path of progress.

The edifice which we have studied in detail is little more than the portico of that extraordinary structure which is called the Critical Philosophy. Nevertheless I believe that if we have mastered the principles of its architecture, we have already acquired the necessary clue for the understanding and appreciation of the whole. No philosopher is truly great whose work does not cover the whole range of human experience; and by this negative test at least Kant's *prima facie* claim to greatness cannot be questioned. I believe myself that Kant stands out among the greatest thinkers by all the tests which can reasonably be applied to men who share the common weaknesses of humanity. If I can persuade others to acquire, by patient study of the *Kritik*, some of that respect and admiration for Kant which has grown upon me the more I have examined his work, I shall feel that my long and at times depressing labours have not failed to find an appropriate reward.

GENERAL INDEX

abgeleitet, I 118 n. 2, 512 n. 1.
abstraction, I 200, 200 n. 6, 267; *see also* comparison.
————— different kinds of, I 124–6.
accident, *see* substance.
accurate, I 266 n. 4.
acquaintance, I 334, 334 n. 9.
act, and function, I 413.
—— identity of, *see* function, identity of.
actio mutua, I 297 n. 4, II 294 n. 2.
action, II 215, 215 n. 3, 216, 282, 325.
activity, causal, *see* substance.
————— ————— continuity of, II 287.
actual, *see* possible.
————— the, and the necessary, II 360.
actuality, II 57, 228 n. 4; *see also* existence.
————— and necessity, II 341; *see also* necessity; possibility.
————— logical and real, II 361.
————— no wider than necessity, II 340, 343.
————— pure category of, II 58.
————— schematised category of, II 59.
————— sense-perception the mark of, II 359.
————— transcendental schema of, II 59.
Adam, I 15, 159 n. 1.
Adickes, I 38, 40 n. 3, 41, 41 n. 1, 42 n. 1, 53 n. 2, 61 n. 2, 66 n. 4,
       70 n. 2, 237 n. 4, 301 n. 2, 308 n. 1 and n. 2, 320 n. 2,
       373 n. 2, 378 n. 3, 421, 421 n. 2, 424 n. 3, 426 n. 6,
       429 n. 2, 486 n. 1, 490 n. 4, 492 n. 7, 520 n. 6, II 60 n. 3,
       66 n. 2, 165 n. 7, 224 n. 2, 287 n. 1, 318 n. 1, 339,
       339 n. 1, 346 n. 3, 371, 440 n. 1.
Aesthetic, the Transcendental, I 52, 73, 93, 98, II 93, 96 n. 1, 445.
————— doctrine of the, II 121–4, 441.
————— principles of the, II 97.
affection, by ourselves, II 400.
————— by outer objects, II 400.
————— double, I 520 n. 6; *see also* causality, double.
————— of the self from within, II 421.
affects, meaning of, II 388.
affinity, I 366, 367, 369, 480 n. 6; *see also* appearances.
————— and association of ideas, I 448, 480.
————— and object, I 445.
————— association by, I 366, 367 n. 2.
————— transcendental, I 367–71, 395, 481–4.
————— transcendental and empirical, I 446–9.

experience, process to, II 271-3.
———— unity of, I 427-9.
———— universal conditions of, II 336, 341-2.
experiences, of different individual men, I 428.
exposition, II 194 n. 1.
———— Kant's method of, I 348, 382, 488 n. 4; the competence of, II 370-1, 463.
———— metaphysical, I 108; *see also* space and time.
———— transcendental, I 108, 108 n. 4; *see also* space and time.
extension, II 412.
extension, *see* denotation.
extent, I 225, 228, 240.

Fähigkeit, I 94 n. 4, 345 n. 4.
fate, I 197 n. 2, 315.
fatum, I 197 n. 2, II 364.
force, II 215 n. 3, 282.
forces, moving, II 135 n. 3, 137, 138 n. 3, 149, 212, 324, 326 n. 1, 412; *see also* repulsion and attraction.
form, and condition, I 103, 103 n. 4, 137.
—— and matter, I 97, 137-43.
—— empirical, I 140, 142 n. 3.
—— intellectual, I 497.
freedom, I 66, 74.
function, I 250, 281, 413; *see also* mind.
———— and act, I 413.
———— and power, I 419.
———— definition of, I 247.
———— identity of, and identity of act, I 440.
———— meaning of, I 245-8, 434-8.
functions, *see* synthesis.
———— of unity, I 246, 247, 248.

Galileo, I 75.
Garve, I 45 n. 4.
Gegenstand, I 193 n. 1.
Gegenwirkung, II 295 n. 2.
Gemeinschaft, I 297 n. 3, II 55 n. 3, 294 n. 1, 316, 319 n. 3.
Gemüt, I 95 n. 4.
genau, I 266 n. 4.
general, and universal, I 77.
geometries, modern, I 160-3.
geometry, I 126, 319-20; and arithmetic, II 131.
———— axioms of, II 124-5; *see also* axioms.
———— Euclidean, I 159, 161.
———— pure, I 106, 127.

intuition, permanent, II 384 n. 1.
————— pure, I 103–6.
————— pure, in two senses, I 105.
————— pure, and the categories, I 262; and form of intuition, I 104, 109; and pure concepts, I 338–40.
intuitions, blind, I 96, 98.
————— in general, I 526 n. 1.
————— intellectual, I 249, 527, 530.
————— pure, I 110.
————— space and time not concepts but, I 114–15.
————— unconscious, I 458.
investigation, psychological or physiological, I 200.
irreversibility, II 246; see also sense-perceptions.
'I think', I 463, 518–20.
————— the idea, I 510.

Jachmann, I 349 n. 1.
Joseph, I 204.
judgement, I 251–6, 548, II 337; see also imagination; judgements.
————— acts of understanding can be reduced to, I 251.
————— analysis in all, I 219, 283.
————— analysis and synthesis in, I 265, 269.
————— analytic, I 201, 549 n. 1.
————— apodeictic, I 202 n. 3.
————— a priori synthesis in all, I 516.
————— definition of, I 206, 220, 522.
————— form of, I 288.
————— form of, one ultimate, I 207; see also apperception.
————— forms of, I 204–6, 209, 246, 248–9, 294, 435; see also categories; judgement, moments of.
————— forms of, and the categories, I 259, 260, 293–7, 299, 341, 475, 524.
————— forms of, as moments, I 211, 294.
————— forms of, classification of, I 204.
————— forms of, common to all judgements, I 215.
————— forms of, table of the, I 204, 568.
————— forms of, universal and necessary, I 206–8.
————— functions of, I 246.
————— hypothetical form of, II 223.
————— infinite, I 205, 208 n. 2, 212 n. 2.
————— metaphysical, I 89.
————— moments of, I 211, 294.
————— moments and forms of, I 208.
————— power of, II 21.
————— problematic, I 202 n. 3, II 344.
————— singular, I 205, 208 n. 2.
————— synthesis in every, I 220, 509.

judgement, synthetic, different kinds of, II 84–6.
———— two aspects of, I 280, 287.
———— unity in, I 281–3.
Judgement, the Transcendental Doctrine of, I 236, II 21–4.
judgements, analytic, I 84–6, 189 n. 8, 214, 300 n. 5, II 84.
———— analytic, principle of, II 83–4.
———— analytic, truth of, I 214, 214 n. 3, II 84.
———— analytic and synthetic, I 81, 82–4, 220, 300–2, 508, II 460.
———— analytic and synthetic, analogy between, I 301.
———— copulative, I 204.
———— of physical science, I 89.
———— logical forms in all possible, I 213.
———— mathematical, I 87, 89, II 91.
———— matter of, I 206.
———— metaphysical, I 89.
———— modality of, I 205.
———— problematic, assertoric, and apodeictic, II 57.
———— quality of, II 51.
———— simple and complex, I 204.
———— synthetic, I 86–7, II 86, 461.
———— synthetic *a posteriori*, I 88, II 85, 94–5.
———— synthetic *a priori*, I 81–2, 87, II 91.
———— synthetic, different kinds of, II 84–6.
———— synthetic, form of, I 213–15.
———— synthetic, principle of all, II 94–6.
———— synthesis in all, I 509.
judging, *see* conceiving.

Kantliteratur, I 18.
Kemp Smith, I 19.
———— *Commentary*, I 37 n. 1, 38, 43 n. 1, 49 n. 2, 75 n. 3, 201
n. 4, 213 n. 5, 216 n. 2, 217 n. 5, 250 n. 6, 300 n. 4,
305 n. 4, 307 n. 1, 323 n. 4, 329–30, 332–3, 339 n. 5,
345 n. 2, 346 n. 6, 382, 397 n. 1, 413 n. 1, 421–5,
421 n. 7, 423 n. 1 and n. 2, 424 n. 3, 425 n. 4
and n. 5, 490 n. 2 and n. 3, 516 n. 2, 529 n. 2,
573 n. 2, 583 n. 1, II 21 n. 4, 24 n. 5, 25 n. 2,
66 n. 2, 69 n. 2, 165 n. 7, 182 n. 4, 224 n. 2, 282
n. 6, 289 n. 2, 294 n. 5, 301 n. 4, 335 n. 6, 339,
340 n. 3, 346 n. 3, 359 n. 3, 367 n. 3, 370–1.
———— *Translation*, I 147 n. 2, 195 n. 6, 339 n. 5, 371 n. 3,
378 n. 2, n. 3, and n. 5, 391 n. 1, 418 n. 4, 444 n. 4,
458 n. 5, 462 n. 3, 463 n. 2, 492 n. 7, 495 n. 2,
512 n. 1, 528 n. 6, 531 n. 5, 534 n. 2, 537 n. 1,
540 n. 1, II 24 n. 5, 36 n. 3, 50 n. 3, 60 n. 3, 84 n. 4,
86 n. 6, 87 n. 2, 90 n. 5, 91 n. 1 and n. 3, 92 n. 4,
115 n. 4, 163 n. 4, 166 n. 5, 169 n. 3, 178 n. 5,

play, of ideas, I 434, II 245, 263.
polytomy, I 306.
posit, meaning of, II 413.
posited, II 54 n. 2, 228, 252 n. 4.
position, *see* shape.
———— absolute, II 228 n. 4.
———— temporal, II 255.
possibility, II 57, 345.
———— absolute, II 368.
———— actuality, and necessity, II 57.
———— actuality, and necessity, absolute, II 338 n. 3; real, II 338;
      real and logical, II 336, 344; real or material, II 337.
———— actuality, and necessity, the Principles of, II 335–9.
———— and actuality, II 341, 350; *see also* necessity.
———— and intuition, II 354.
———— and outer intuition, II 354.
———— Leibnizian, II 366–8.
———— logical and real, I 66, II 344, 346, 351.
———— no wider than actuality, II 339–40, 343, 366–7.
———— pure category of, II 58.
———— real, II 95 n. 1, 336 n. 1, 353.
———— schematised category of, II 59.
———— transcendental schema of, II 59.
possible, the, and the actual, II 366–7.
Postulate, the First, II 345–6.
———— the meaning of the word, II 368–70.
———— the Second, II 357–62.
———— the Third, II 362–4.
postulates, mathematical, II 369–70.
power, I 94; *see also* function.
powers, I 345, 345 n. 4.
predicables, the, I 307–8.
predicates, universal, I 257.
prediction, II 283.
present, the specious, I 366, II 398.
Price, I 584 n. 1, II 150 n. 2, 151 n. 3, 175 n. 4, 205 n. 4, 279 n. 1.
Prichard, I 17, 77 n. 2, 80 n. 1, 177, 177 n. 2, 213 n. 5, 277 n. 1, 200
      n. 3, 337 n. 2, 405 n. 1, 500 n. 7, 565 n. 2, 581 n. 1,
      582 n. 1, II 34 n. 4, 136 n. 3, 214 n. 2, 217 n. 2, 225,
      234 n. 2, 240 n. 1, 241 n. 5, 242 n. 3, 249 n. 5, 266 n. 2,
      268 n. 1, 272 n. 1, 296, 298 n. 2, 299 n. 1, 300, 306,
      316 n. 4, 325, 378 n. 3, 380.
principle, different kinds of, II 97–8.
———— empirical, a contradiction in terms, II 97.
———— Kant's ultimate, an analytic proposition, I 518.
principles, synthetic, discursive, I 218.
Principles, I 226, 234, 493–4.
———— Analytic of, I 236, II 24.

INDEX OF ANNOTATED PASSAGES

The left-hand references in each column (e.g. A 4 = B 8) indicate the page where the passage annotated occurs in the first and second editions of the Kritik. *The right-hand references (e.g. I 81) indicate the volume and page where the annotation is to be found in the present commentary.*

GEORGE ALLEN & UNWIN LTD

Head office:
40 Museum Street, London, W.C.1
Telephone: 01-405 8577

Sales, Distribution and Accounts Departments
Park Lane, Hemel Hempstead, Herts.
Telephone: 0442 3244

Athens: 7 Stadiou Street
Auckland: P.O. Box 36013, Northcote Central, N.4
Barbados: P.O. Box 222, Bridgetown
Beirut: Deeb Building, Jeanne d'Arc Street
Bombay: 103/5 Fort Street, Bombay 1
Calcutta: 285J Bepin Behari Ganguli Street, Calcutta 12
Cape Town: 68 Shortmarket Street
Delhi: 1/18D Asaf Ali Road, New Delhi 1
Hong Kong: 105 Wing on Mansion, 26 Hankow Road, Kowloon
Ibadan: P.O. Box 62
Karachi: Karachi Chambers, McLeod Road
Madras: 2/18 Mount Road, Madras 6
Mexico: Villalongin 32, Mexico 5, D.F.
Nairobi: P.O. Box 30583
Pakistan: Alico Building, 18 Motijheel, Dacca 2
Philippines: P.O. Box 157, Quezon City, D-502
Rio de Janeiro: Caixa Postal 2537-Zc-00
Singapore: 36c Prinsep Street, Singapore 7
Sydney, N.S.W.: Bradbury House, 55 York Street
Tokyo: C.P.O. Box 1728, Tokyo 100-91
Toronto: 81 Curlew Drive, Don Mills

THE MODERN PREDICAMENT
H. J. PATON

Demy 8vo.

Professor Paton's Gifford Lectures, delivered in St. Andrews in 1950 and 1951, are not directed primarily to professional philosophers: they are intended for all thoughtful men who are affected by modern discontents. Free from the paraphernalia of footnotes and appendices, and written without the austerity of continual qualifications, they attempt to discuss, as simply and dispassioately as possible, the predicament of men, and especially religious men, living in an age of scientific scepticism and in a world wholly different from that in which religion had its birth and growth. Undeterred by vetoes from positivists and Barthians, Professor Paton analyses the character of religion, its manifold aberrations, the intellectual impediments to belief, and the varying responses to these impediments. After considering the claims made for religious and mystical experiences by such writers as Otto, Poulain, and Martin Buber—a Lutheran, a Catholic, and a Jew—he scrutinizes the traditional metaphysical and moral arguments for God's existence and their relation to religious experience itself as well as to scientific knowledge.

The central problem is to see how far it may be possible to combine the divergent points of view of religion and science; and if the problem is not "solved", its examination will at least help both the devout and the irreligious to understand their opponents' case and to assess the modern situation in which each man has to form his own philosophy of life.

A LAYMAN'S QUEST
SIR MALCOLM KNOX

Demy 8vo.

This book is a revised and enlarged version of Gifford Lectures delivered in Aberdeen. It begins by arguing that to have a religion is reasonable, but then asks: What religion? How much of orthodox Christianity is it reasonable to believe? The author thinks that an approach to answering this question must be through studying the course of New Testament criticism and considering recent theological developments which have laid less emphasis on historical facts and more on the proclamation of a Gospel.

GEORGE ALLEN & UNWIN LTD